Dance Pedagogy

Dance Pedagogy is a comprehensive resource designed for dance students and teaching artists to develop skills and strategies in the multifaceted practice of teaching dance.

This invaluable resource features essential components and considerations necessary for the dance teacher in any setting, including the private and community sector, university setting, and professional venues. Five distinct units provide insight into the paradigm, learning process, class environment factors, planning, and delivery of the dance class in a broad context through the use of examples within the dance forms of ballet, jazz, modern, tap, and hip-hop. Readers intently explore cognitive and motor learning, strategies for developing curricula and lesson plans, and methods of delivering material to students. Basic principles of anatomy, understanding student behavior and participation, the importance of diversity, equity, inclusion and accessibility (IDEA), music concepts for the dancer, injury prevention, and classroom management are included to provide a well-rounded approach to the many challenges faced in the classroom.

Dance Pedagogy provides the most holistic approach available in the art of teaching dance and is a core textbook for academic courses related to Dance Teaching Methods as well as an invaluable handbook for practicing dance teachers.

Amanda Clark is Professor and Dance Program Coordinator at Western Kentucky University, USA, and co-author of *Dance Appreciation* (Routledge, 2020).

Dance Pedagogy

Amanda Clark

LONDON AND NEW YORK

Designed cover image: © Photo by Jeffrey Smith/Western Kentucky University

First published 2024
by Routledge
4 Park Square, Milton Park, Abingdon, Oxon OX14 4RN

and by Routledge
605 Third Avenue, New York, NY 10158

Routledge is an imprint of the Taylor & Francis Group, an informa business

© 2024 Amanda Clark

The right of Amanda Clark to be identified as author of this work has been asserted in accordance with sections 77 and 78 of the Copyright, Designs and Patents Act 1988.

All rights reserved. No part of this book may be reprinted or reproduced or utilised in any form or by any electronic, mechanical, or other means, now known or hereafter invented, including photocopying and recording, or in any information storage or retrieval system, without permission in writing from the publishers.

Trademark notice: Product or corporate names may be trademarks or registered trademarks, and are used only for identification and explanation without intent to infringe.

British Library Cataloguing-in-Publication Data
A catalogue record for this book is available from the British Library

Library of Congress Cataloging-in-Publication Data
Names: Clark, Amanda (Writer on dance) author.
Title: Dance pedagogy / Amanda Clark.
Description: Abingdon, Oxon ; New York, NY : Routledge, 2024. |
    Includes bibliographical references and index.
Identifiers: LCCN 2023056970 (print) | LCCN 2023056971 (ebook) |
    ISBN 9781032286020 (hardback) | ISBN 9781032286013 (paperback) |
    ISBN 9781003297611 (ebook)
Subjects: LCSH: Dance—Study and teaching.
Classification: LCC GV1589 .C55 2024 (print) | LCC GV1589 (ebook) |
    DDC 792.807—dc23/eng/20240131
LC record available at https://lccn.loc.gov/2023056970
LC ebook record available at https://lccn.loc.gov/2023056971

ISBN: 978-1-032-28602-0 (hbk)
ISBN: 978-1-032-28601-3 (pbk)
ISBN: 978-1-003-29761-1 (ebk)

DOI: 10.4324/b22952

Typeset in Berling and Futura
by Apex CoVantage, LLC

Contents

Contributor	*xii*
Acknowledgments	*xiii*
Introduction	1

Unit 1: Exploration of Dance Pedagogy   5

1   The Development of Dance Education   7

Historical Context of Dance Education   8
   Early Efforts in Dance Education   8
   Shifting Paradigm within Higher Education   12
   Education Legislation and Emerging Standards   14
   National Organizational Support   15
Benefits of Dance   17
   Physical   18
   Emotional   18
   Behavioral   18
   Cognitive   18
   Social   19
   Therapeutic   19
Chapter Summary   21
Practical Applications   21

2   Roles in the Classroom   24

The Path of a Dance Teacher   25
Role of a Dance Teacher   26
   Types and Styles of Dance Teachers   28
   Characteristics of Effective Dance Teachers   30
The Teaching Philosophy Statement   33

The Role of a Student 34
Chapter Summary 36
Practical Applications 36

3   Fundamentals of Human Anatomy   38

Anatomical Terminology 39
  Mapping the Body 40
  Planes of the Body 41
  Directions of Movement 41
Systems of Movement 44
  Muscular System 44
  Skeletal System 46
  Joints 46
Structures of Anatomy 47
  Torso and Spine 47
  Hips 50
  Knees 52
  Ankles and Feet 53
  Shoulders, Arms, and Wrists 55
Chapter Summary 56
Practical Applications 56

Unit 2: Motor and Cognitive Learning Processes   59

4   Motor Control and Development   61

Motor Control 63
  Sensory Systems 64
Understanding Postural Control within Dance Training 69
Motor Control and Organization 70
  Open-Loop Systems 70
  Closed-Loop Systems 71
Motor Development 74
  Theories of Motor Development 74
  Motor Milestones 78
The Adolescent Dancer and Growth Spurts 81
Chapter Summary 81
Practical Applications 82

5   The Learning Process   85

Forms of Learning 86
The Basics of Motor Learning 87

Contents **vii**

Learning Is a Process 87
Practice and Experience 88
Transfer of Learning 88
Indicators of Learning 89
Learning Is Permanent 91
Understanding Memory 91
Theories of Motor Learning 93
Adams' Closed-Loop Theory 94
Schmidt's Schema Theory 94
Constraints-Led Approach 96
Learning Styles 97
The VARK Method 97
Gardner's Theory of Multiple Intelligences 98
Stages of Motor Learning 99
Fitts and Posner's Three-Stage Theory 100
Gentile's Two-Stage Theory 102
Characteristics of Learning 104
Chapter Summary 104
Practical Applications 104

Unit 3: Factors That Affect the Learning Environment **107**

6 Motivation 109

Categories of Motivation 110
Intrinsic Motivation 110
Extrinsic Motivation 111
Theories of Motivation 114
Maslow's Hierarchy of Needs 114
Self-Determination Theory 116
Goal Orientation Theory 117
Concept of Flow 118
Self-Esteem, Self-Efficacy, and Arousal 118
Role of the Dance Teacher 121
Keller's ARCS-V Model 121
The Six C's 122
Chapter Summary 127
Practical Applications 127

7 Understanding the Student Population 131

The Holistic Teacher 132
Age Effect 133

viii Contents

Sociocultural Considerations 137
  Family and Peer Influence 137
  Socioeconomic Status 139
  Cultural Considerations 139
Avoiding Stereotypes and Bias 142
Chapter Summary 144
Practical Applications 144

8   Inclusion, Diversity, Equity, and Accessibility   147

Culturally Relevant Teaching 147
  Implementation 148
IDEA 149
  Inclusion 149
  Diversity 150
  Equity 152
  Accessibility 153
Chapter Summary 154
Practical Applications 154

Unit 4: Class Content and Preparation   **157**

9   Curriculum Development and Lesson Planning   159

Basics of Planning 160
  Benefits of Planning 160
  Amount of Planning 161
  Goals and Objectives 162
  Bloom's Taxonomy 163
  SMART Planning 164
Creating a Curriculum 165
Devising Lesson Plans 169
  *Establishing Class Learning Goals
    and Objectives 169*
  Consideration of Class Structure 170
  Selection of Class Material 173
Chapter Summary 175
Practical Applications 176

10   Music Concepts for Dancers   178

Fundamental Music Terminology 179
  Music Organization 180

Rhythm 184
Dynamics 184
Form and Structure 185
Compositional Techniques 187
Working with an Accompanist 188
Selecting Music 190
Music Licensing 193
Chapter Summary 194
Practical Applications 195

11 Injury Prevention 197

Knowledge 198
Physical 198
Nutrition 199
Mental Health 202
Professional Consultation 204
Environment 205
Space 205
Culture 206
Movement Practices 207
Class Structure and Design 207
Periodization 207
Cross-Training 208
Chapter Summary 208
Practical Applications 209

12 Classroom Management 211

Formulating Guidelines and Policies 212
Classroom Etiquette 213
Classroom Procedures 214
Classroom Attire 215
Attendance Policy 216
Cultivating the Learning Environment 217
Preparing the Studio Space 217
Welcoming Students 218
Beginning the Class 218
Communication and Interaction 219
Disruptions and Discipline 221
Ending the Class 223
Chapter Summary 223
Practical Applications 223

x Contents

Unit 5: Presentation   **225**

13   Instructional Strategies   227

Presenting Material   *229*
   Visual Presentation   *229*
   Verbal Instruction   *233*
   Guided Discovery   *234*
Delivery in Parts   *237*
Attentional Focus   *238*
Use of Imagery   *241*
Cueing   *242*
   Visual Cues   *242*
   Tactile Cues   *244*
   Verbal Cues   *245*
Pacing   *246*
Building Blocks of Effective Teaching   *247*
Chapter Summary   *248*
Practical Applications   *248*

14   Practice Methods   251

Whole and Part Practice   *252*
   Whole Practice   *252*
   Part Practice   *252*
   Whole versus Part: Which to Choose?   *255*
Methods of Practice   *256*
Amount of Practice   *257*
Teaching and Practice Tools   *258*
   Mirrors   *258*
   Ballet Barre   *259*
   Miscellaneous Props   *259*
   Mental Practice   *259*
   Somatics   *260*
   Improvisation   *260*
Chapter Summary   *260*
Practical Applications   *261*

15   Feedback and Assessment   263

Augmented Feedback   *264*
   Forms of Augmented Feedback   *266*

Providing Feedback   271
Assessment and Evaluation   273
Chapter Summary   276
Practical Applications   277

Glossary   *279*
Index   *291*

Contributor

Pecina, Sara, MFA, is the director of dance and lecturer at Berry College. She received her MFA in Dance from the University of Oklahoma and a BA in Dance from Western Kentucky University. She is the co-author of *Dance Appreciation* (Routledge, 2020). Her teaching certifications include the American Tap Dance Foundation Tap Teacher Training Levels 1 and 2, Giordano Technique Teacher Certification Basic Level, Mark Morris Dance Group's Dance for PD® (Parkinson's Disease), and Balanced Body Pilates Mat 1 and 2. Sara has presented her research at the National Dance Education Organization National Conference and at the Dance Studies Association Annual Conference in Malta.

Acknowledgments

First and foremost, I want to acknowledge my mother and first dance teacher, Becky Seamster, the woman who has guided, mentored, and supported me throughout my dance journey. She has taught me to love and appreciate dance as an art form, inspiring me to work my hardest and be the best human I can be in the process. I also must acknowledge the many dance teachers from whom I have studied. I would specifically like to recognize Jo Rowan, Lyn Cramer, Jeremy Lindberg, Barbara Duffy, Margaret Morrison, Susan Hebach, Robert Reed, Steven Boyd, and Kenneth Green. Whether it was a single class experience or many classes over long periods of time, each teacher I have encountered has influenced my understanding of dance and my path as a dance educator. Additionally, I would like to thank the countless colleagues that have challenged my perspectives, shared methodologies, and motivated my pursuit of becoming an effective dance teacher. Perhaps none, though, have challenged me more than the great number of students I have taught over the years. Each student, in their own way, has brought me joy as they have encouraged me to fully embrace my role as a dance teacher. Additionally, I extend a sincere thank you to Grace Becker for her ceaseless research assistance and support throughout this writing process, along with Sara Pecina for her shared inspiration, insight, and editing assistance. Finally, I must thank my husband and daughter, Dean and Jasmine, for their never-ending love and support.

Introduction

Many young dancers participate in dance training with the hopes of one day becoming a professional dancer. They dream of the energy they will feel flowing through their bodies as they entertain a variety of audiences while performing exciting choreography in impressive venues. For many young students, this dream will become a reality. For a larger number of students, their years of dancing evolve into a hobby they once enjoyed as they journey on to chosen careers and time spent in other activities. Regardless of the path ultimately pursued by a dance student, there is one person they will recall as an influence within their life: the dance teacher.

Teaching dance can be described as an art, a science, or a profession. Instructing others in the art of dance is a joy that takes great skill, knowledge, practice, and reflection. One does not become an effective dance teacher overnight. Rather, they invest in years of study and personal engagement in the art form, extensive experience in the classroom, and meaningful personal assessment. Effective dance teachers share a sincere desire to connect to, inspire, and motivate others in both dance and life. They wish to transform the way others may think and move, share their appreciation for the art form, and develop dance artists. To students, the dance teacher may function in a myriad of roles ranging from movement guide to life mentor. The effective dance teacher often shares with their students not only dance technique and artistry but general life lessons along with individual encouragement and support. Thus, the role of teaching dance should be approached with respect and a sense of responsibility.

Teaching dance can be, and often is, an extremely rewarding experience. Dance teachers may find few moments in life more satisfying than when a student finally attains a challenging skill, makes a thoughtful connection in class, or displays powerful artistry on the stage. Whether instructing younger or older students, novice or advanced, teaching this art form allows one to embrace creativity and joy of movement throughout their adult lives. This profession, however, is not without occasional frustration. The dance teacher may face students resistant to learning, challenging parents, or motivational or creative ruts. Week after week, year after year, time is spent honing the skills and talents of others, sometimes with minimal recognition or thanks, unaware of the impact that they have made. Students come and go, yet the teacher remains in the studio ever striving to inspire and educate those standing before them. Persistence, patience, curiosity, concern, and passion drive the teacher forward as they continue to learn and grow alongside their students.

This book is intended to provide a comprehensive study of the art and science of teaching dance to students of all ages. The following chapters include a breadth of topics

DOI: 10.4324/b22952-1

and information designed to introduce the reader to the many facets inherent within the dance learning environment and challenge the reader to incorporate this knowledge into their own teaching. The reader may find some chapters to be a helpful reminder of considerations and strategies, while other chapters may offer new information and approaches. Examples are offered throughout the text to clarify the information and methods discussed. These examples are primarily rooted in the dance forms of ballet, jazz, tap, modern, and hip-hop dance yet are designed to help the reader create connections to various dance forms as appropriate to their needs.

This textbook is divided into five sections. Unit 1 explores the introductory topics related to teaching dance. Topics include the path of dance from creative movement and physical education to a viable discipline within educational systems. The plethora of benefits dance training can provide extend beyond the physical and are advantageous for the dance teacher to recognize. Additionally, basic human anatomy – including fundamental terminology and concepts – is shared and related specifically to dance training. The combination of these topics reminds the reader of the value and respect that accompanies the role of dance teacher. Part artist, athlete, scientist, and educator, the dance teacher serves many functions in and outside of the classroom. Understanding the path that dance education has taken over the past century helps dance educators, within academia or the private sector, advocate for dance education and create even more opportunities within the field of dance pedagogy that can be embraced by students of all ages and levels and in all dance learning environments. Awareness and understanding of fundamental human anatomy deepen the teacher's knowledge of dancing bodies and assist the teacher in creating a safe and injury-free environment.

Unit 2 provides the reader with information regarding motor and cognitive learning within dance training. Theories of motor behavior – specifically motor control and development – along with motor learning are explored along with their implications within the dance technique class. Chapters explore inquiries such as how the body develops, how one learns, and how the two areas intersect within dance training. Awareness and understanding of these aspects enable the dance teacher to construct appropriate lesson plans and better equip them to assist students of different ages and skill levels in the development of technique and artistry.

Unit 3 identifies and details factors, such as motivation, that affect the learning environment. There can be many variables that influence the dance teacher's lesson preparation and interaction with students. Elements such as student age, family dynamics, and sociocultural considerations are discussed, offering context to help the dance teacher understand potential student participation and behavior. Emphasis is given to the practice of holistic teaching, a teaching approach that provides many benefits within the dance learning environment. Finally, the roles of inclusion, diversity, equity, and accessibility are identified, and their importance within the learning environment is encouraged.

The final two units of the textbook shift from a study of factors that affect motor learning to the preparation and instruction of the dance class. Unit 4 dives into dance class content and preparation. Subject matter within this section of chapters includes the development of curricula and lesson plans, relationship between music and dance, importance of injury prevention, and methods for classroom management. The reader is equipped with key elements to consider, thus increasing their teaching effectiveness. Finally, Unit 5 prepares the reader to share their dance knowledge and deliver lesson plans within the classroom. Chapters highlight instructional and practice strategies, feedback, and assessment methods.

The ideas contained within this book demonstrate a synthesis of published findings gathered from research psychologists and documented measures taken by dance teachers, both of which have proven effective in the progression of student learning. There are many variables that influence the learning environment. Each dance form and setting incorporate distinct components and aspects that intricately affect teaching strategies. The personality, philosophy, and past experiences of the dance teacher directly influence their teaching style and approach within the classroom. Most importantly, though, every student is an individual with unique needs, backgrounds, and goals. The information within this book contains theories and strategies that may or may not prove effective with each student. It is the author's hope that novice teachers are introduced to and discover the interesting and unique facets inherent within teaching the art of dance, while experienced teachers are reminded of or uncover new considerations within dance instruction and garner inspiration in their ongoing efforts.

UNIT 1

Exploration of Dance Pedagogy

CHAPTER 1

The Development of Dance Education

> ## Box 1.1 Chapter Objectives
>
> After reading this chapter, you will be able to:
>
> - Describe in brief the early development of dance within higher education
> - Understand the importance of national agency in the evolution and continued support of dance education
> - Explain, articulate, defend, and advocate for dance and dance education by understanding its path to become a viable discipline within education and its many benefits in developing engaged, healthy citizens

> ## Box 1.2 Chapter Vocabulary
>
> dance as education
> dance education
> dance training

Throughout the 20th and 21st centuries, opportunities in dance training and education have expanded immensely in the United States. Training in dance has broadened from the recreational and studio settings to academia, incorporating additional educational approaches from those focused strictly on the acquisition of technical skill.

The terms dance training and dance education have distinct definitions. **Dance training** involves the acquisition of specific physical, technical, and practical skills. Dancers train their bodies and minds to perform movement with proper technique and style. **Dance education** includes information, theoretical concepts, and the application of that knowledge in a broad, general sense. Dancers study a range of dance-related topics – such as dance history and choreography – that shape their work as dance artists. One can become technically proficient by training in dance, but enhanced knowledge is power. Dance education provides a multifaceted intellectual approach to the dance experience. Within a school setting (elementary, secondary, and tertiary), dance education can include, but is certainly not

DOI: 10.4324/b22952-3

limited to, an understanding of the rich history of dance and the social context in which it evolved (Dance History courses), awareness and comprehension of human anatomy and kinesiology, specifically in regard to dance technique (Dance Anatomy and Kinesiology courses), rhythmical analysis (Music for Dance courses), and the creation of movement (Improvisation and Choreography courses). Furthermore, dance education fosters awareness of dance from a cultural and global perspective (Dance in Culture or Global Dance Forms courses). Yet, dance education need not be limited to the academic setting.

Dance teachers in any setting have an opportunity to not only train students in the technique and artistry of dance but to also provide an education in the art form. Students develop appreciation for dance when they can connect movement to the dance's history, understand the why and how of the movement that happens, and participate in the creative process. The more a teacher can share about the art form, the more the teacher can foster respect and passion for the art of dance. In turn, the more education that a teacher has, the more they will then have to offer to their students.

An additional term to consider is **dance as education**. Here, dance is not itself the subject matter, but rather the vehicle through which learning can occur. Conceptual skills, educational skills, and life skills can be acquired through the medium, or use of, movement and dance-based activities. Dance can serve as a tool for learning math concepts or history lessons. It can help teach problem-solving skills and teamwork. Utilizing dance within an academic classroom can also improve social and emotional skills within students. The opportunities and benefits are limitless.

Dance education has been heavily influenced by the inclusion of dance as an area of study within higher education in the United States. The incorporation of dance within academia raised awareness of dance as an art form and as one worthy of advanced study. As dance scholarship emerged, advocacy efforts increased, federal policy and support were generated, educational standards were established, and the field of dance expanded its reach into other disciplines of study. This chapter highlights significant events within the history of dance in education against the backdrop of higher education in the United States. The benefits of studying dance are also explored. The development of dance education directly impacts today's dance teachers. The journey of dance as a discipline of study along with dance's far-reaching benefits influence the role of dance training and education and help the dance teacher make informed decisions regarding lesson content and delivery. Additionally, teachers become equipped to explain, articulate, defend, and advocate for dance and dance education.

HISTORICAL CONTEXT OF DANCE EDUCATION

Early Efforts in Dance Education

Since the 17th century, immigrants of all kinds have migrated to America, carrying with them their academic ideals. By the 19th century, North American universities adopted the German emphasis of discipline-based specialization along with the idea of "the freedom of the learner."[1] This view maintained that the learner could have choice in what they studied, which helped to create a path for dance to enter the college setting.

American society underwent social and economic changes during the 19th century. In a reflection of an industrial society, the university became the path to secure a vocation. As the number of American public universities increased in the late 1800s, programs sought enrollment from a limited pool of candidates across the nation by expanding their curricula and elective offerings. One such area that emerged was physical education. Physical education promoted overall physical health and emotional and social well-being of the individual, which were important ideals within society. Additionally, Dalcroze Eurhythmics and the American Delsarte Movement also contributed to society's rising fascination with the human body. (See Box 1.3.)

Box 1.3 Rhythmical Training and Dance Education

Emile Jacques-Dalcroze, a Swiss music educator, developed a systematic method of utilizing rhythmic exercises to aid in the understanding of music. This technique in rhythmical training, known as Eurhythmics, connects motor movements and rhythm as a means to enhance musical understanding. This method promotes the body's kinesthetic response that occurs through the connection of whole-body movement and musical-based exercises. Conceptualized as a training method for musicians, Eurhythmics helps to develop the student's inner ear and neuromuscular sense of musicality, enabling students "to hear, feel, and express music with their whole being."[2] A student's "sense of rhythm and measure could be developed by movements of the body in time to music; that 'there is an intimate relation between rhythm in sound and rhythm in the body.'"[3]

In the late 1800s, French music and drama teacher Francoise Delsarte developed his system of utilizing gesture, posture, and movement to promote and enhance individual expression within learners. The Delsarte System focused on codified rhythmic gestures and dramatic poses that corresponded to emotion. His method was brought to the United States in the late 1800s by Steele MacKaye and was adopted by actors, physical education teachers, and others interested in mobility. The American Delsarte System "helped develop an appreciation for personal communication skills, relaxation, emotional expression, body awareness, and 'balance'."[4]

Eurhythmics and the Delsarte System specifically connect movement of the body and rhythmic concepts. Today, dance educators often incorporate musical training or rhythmical analysis as part of the dance student's training. Effective dancers embody rhythmic understanding and musical nuances as they convey meaning, emotions, and social and abstract forms of expression through movement.

By the end of the 19th century, the American education system had begun to incorporate physical education into its curriculum with movement forms derivative of military activities, German- and Swiss-based forms of gymnastics, and general calisthenics. As a result, special teacher training programs were established within colleges to prepare individuals to instruct the newly implemented physical education curriculum within public and private schools. The development of teacher programs in physical education helped pave the way to incorporate dance within higher education. Other factors occurring in the early years of the 20th century, such as social and economic growth, progressive education, women's education and suffrage, and diverging practices in the performing arts, propelled society's curiosity of the body and the emergence of dance within physical education programs.[5]

Box 1.4 Implementation of Dance Education in Ancient Civilizations

The American education system is far from the first civilization to include dance in an educational setting. Citizens of ancient Greece held annual festivals that included dancing. Though these performances were first done by amateurs, it later became a profession, and boys who went to school would learn to dance as part of their education. The Roman Empire adapted many practices of the peoples around them, including having private dance classes and dance schools.

Additionally, dance has played a major role in societies around the globe for all known time. Records as early as 3000 BCE show dance as a part of the early civilization that developed along the Nile River in present-day Egypt. Civilizations in present-day India, Japan, the Philippines, and elsewhere had ritual or political dance practices and trained future performers in an educational setting. Dance has long been a form of human communication taught in a variety of settings.

Gertrude Colby

In 1913, Gertrude Colby was invited to introduce a creative dance program at the Speyer School, a division of Teachers College of Columbia University in New York City.[6] Her physical education program was intended for children, with a focus on movement that was to be natural and free, allowing for self-expression. Colby's program, which was the first curriculum for dance within higher education, was ultimately enhanced and deepened and then implemented within the Teachers College in 1918 under the title of "Natural Dancing" as a teacher-training program.[7] Teachers throughout the nation enrolled in the program, carrying this training back to their schools and educating a new generation of students.

Margaret H'Doubler

In 1926, Margaret H'Doubler, an assistant instructor of women's physical education at the University of Wisconsin, proposed a specialized major in dance, which was immediately accepted and implemented into the Bachelor of Arts program in women's physical education at the university.[8] This marked the first undergraduate major in dance within higher education and brought greater recognition to dance within academia. It is interesting to note that H'Doubler was interested in not just the aesthetics of dance but also the "scientific knowledge of bodily movement."[9] H'Doubler had studied in New York with Bird Larson, a pupil of Gertrude Colby. Larson "believed that movement has its origins in control of the torso and paid particular attention to techniques for gaining better control of the body."[10] Her method for movement was labeled "Natural Rhythmic Expression," as she moved away from the storytelling and interpretative aspect of movement and focused rather on these three elements: "natural body movement, designed body movement, and controlled movement with music to express an idea."[11]

Serving as a foundation for dance pedagogy, this method can be traced within the teaching of H'Doubler and many other educators that soon followed. H'Doubler's teaching included learning about the body and the various actions and processes behind movement. She included a deeper level of intellect and theory within her dance instruction that extended beyond physical activity, creative movement, and expression. She believed that her approach in teaching educational dance provided substance to the art form beyond the movement itself. Little did she realize this was the beginning of a developing field in dance studies and an important component in the education of the effective dance teacher.

It is fascinating to note the power that H'Doubler found in the study of kinesiology, specifically in motor control and its relationship to training dancers and educating fellow and future dance teachers. In his article "Moving in Harmony with the Body: The Teaching

FIGURE 1.1 Margaret H'Doubler lectures alongside an anatomical skeleton to dance students while visiting the Mills College Dance Department between the years 1973 and 1975.

Source: Photo by James E. Graham.

Legacy of Margaret H'Doubler, 1916–1926," Thomas K. Hagood notes that "H'Doubler was the first American dance educator to intellectually appreciate the role of the kinesthetic sense in the teaching of dance."[12] It was this component of H'Doubler's work as a teacher that enhanced her ability "to develop the student's cognitive understanding of the nature of subjective sensation, the inherent rhythmic structure of movement, and the mechanical parameters of motor response."[13] Her connection to and awareness of how the body moved and functioned led to a greater awareness of the connection between rhythmical understanding and human movement.

The Bennington Experience

Throughout the 1920s and 1930s, three categories of dance were prevalent within American culture in distinct spheres. Dance entertainment presented in the form of authentic jazz and tap dance appeared in clubs and ballrooms, on Vaudeville and Broadway stages, and later in "talking pictures." Concert ballet and modern dancers performed ballets and concert dance choreography on professional stages throughout the country. Finally, physical education teachers taught creative movement/dance under a host of names within schools and college settings. This division was soon challenged as individuals from two of those three worlds of dance collided.

Bennington College, located in Bennington, Vermont, opened during the early years of the Great Depression. In 1934, a summer dance program was established at the college, under the direction of Martha Hill and administrative director Mary Josephine Shelly.[14] By bringing professional modern dancers and concert dance into the college setting, this program ultimately converged the professional and academic facets of dance and shifted the focus of dance in higher education.

The **Bennington Experience**, as it became known, lasted each summer until 1942, uniting hundreds of dance educators and professionals together in both concert and class settings. It was here that physical education dance teachers became exposed to professional modern dance artists and choreography. Coursework moved beyond dance technique and rhythmic studies and exercises. Dance pedagogical theories, composition, production, and criticism were discussed and taught. Dance educators began to question the role of dance in higher education. Was dance training within the collegiate programs for the non-professional a form of self-expression and physical well-being? Or, was dance training in the college setting to develop the professional dance artist? Or, could college dance programs be both?

Following the last summer dance session at Bennington College in 1942, Hill reinvented the program at Connecticut College in 1948. This program continued, evolving into the American Dance Festival, and later relocated to Duke University in Durham, North Carolina, in 1978.[15] The American Dance Festival (ADF) continues today as a five-week dance festival for professional and pre-professional dancers and choreographers worldwide. ADF now encompasses a range of dance forms and styles extending beyond a purely modern dance focus.

Shifting Paradigm within Higher Education

From the conception of dance within higher education through the 1960s, dance programs consistently faced an identity crisis of sorts. Housed within physical education units, dance programs fought for independence, autonomy, and even clarity in their goal and purpose. As arts advocacy organizations emerged and public funding and policy took hold in the mid-20th century, so did scholarship and research in dance. It was during this period that professional ballet companies along with modern dance companies became well established within the United States. By the 1970s, jazz dance had evolved into a concert dance form, and tap dance was enjoying a renaissance of its own and entering the concert dance world.

In 1972, Title IX was passed by the federal government, therefore mandating equal opportunity. As a result, men's and women's physical education programs were merged. This meant the women's programs, which included dance, were then contained within the larger athletic-based men's programs, and dance began to organically shift from physical education to fine arts–based departments. During this period, the university's focus also transitioned to developing professional-oriented skills with the creation and implementation of degrees such as the Bachelor of Fine Arts and the Master of Fine Arts. Degrees and coursework began highlighting dance performance and choreography as less focus was given to preparing the dance teacher.[16]

The presence of dance within the university made great strides through the end of the 20th century and into the 21st century. The number of universities that include dance programs and dance degrees has increased tremendously since the original program at the University of Wisconsin back in 1926. The advancements made within the higher education setting positively influence those teaching within K–12 systems and the private sector as well as the various national advocacy agencies and organizations supporting the field of dance and dance education.

Box 1.5 Continued Challenges for Dance in Higher Education

While the presence of dance in academia has steadily strengthened, there are still challenges that institutions, faculty, staff, and students face today. Given the path that led to the establishment of dance in the university system, a majority of institutions only offer ballet and modern dance technique or movement courses and focus their theory courses solely on these forms. There is a lack of diversity of dance genres being offered at the college and post-graduate levels. With the increase of jazz dance being presented on the Broadway stage and in commercial settings and the resurgence of tap dance performance, both occurring in the latter half of the 20th century, jazz and tap dance have slowly become more present in higher education since the 1990s.

Additionally, since its start in the 1970s, hip-hop dance has been mostly neglected by university scholars and programs. It was not until the 2010s that a few schools began including this form in their curricula. All three – jazz, tap, and hip-hop – are historically and originally black and Latinx dance forms. As higher education confronts their history of institutionalized racism, dance programs are reevaluating their course offerings and curricula to more accurately represent American dance forms on campus.

Inclusion, diversity, equity, and access are not the only challenges dance programs are facing but are perhaps the most prominent. The considerations by the teacher of inclusion, diversity, equity, and accessibility in the classroom are discussed in depth in Chapter 8.

Education Legislation and Emerging Standards

Dance education, in general, has received increased attention due in large part to legislation, public policy, and public funding. The original 1964 Elementary and Secondary Education Act (ESEA) was designed to address problems of educational equity, particularly for high-poverty students. This legislation proved beneficial to the arts in that it established alliances between education and the arts. One year after the ESEA was enacted, Congress founded the National Endowment for the Arts and the National Endowment for the Humanities, generating funds for research and development within arts education.

In 1994, President Clinton signed into legislation the Goals 2000: Educate America Act, which was an effort to replace President Johnson's Elementary and Secondary Education Act (ESEA). Goals 2000 identified dance as an individual art discipline on equal footing to other core subjects such as math, science, and language arts. Goals 2000 recognized the educational value of dance and movement and aligned dance with arts education standards. As a result of this legislation, the National Standards for Arts Education were developed in 1994. This detailed physical and conceptual standards in dance, as well as in each of the other arts. Although voluntary, these achievement standards were for state K–12 programs to assess students in grades four, eight, and 12. The National Standards for Arts Education were revised in 2014 and are now referred to as the National Core Arts Standards. These standards offer a conceptual framework of artistic literacy, with focus on creating, performing, responding, and connecting, and the standards serve as a guide or blueprint in the instruction and assessment of discipline-specific skills and concepts. Their aim is to foster success for both the educator and the student.

Congress once again revised ESEA from Goals 2000 to the No Child Left Behind Act (NCLB) in 2001 under the direction of President George W. Bush. This effort attempted to improve performance within elementary and secondary schools, holding schools accountable for student learning and helping to provide supplemental educational opportunities for eligible children. NCLB required schools to hire qualified teachers. In regard to dance, a "qualified teacher" was then dependent upon whether or not dance was taught within the fine arts unit or the physical education (PE) program of the school. If dance was within the PE program, then a PE coach could be considered a "qualified teacher." However, this did not always mean that the PE coach had the appropriate dance training or background. The NCLB Act pushed states to pause and consider specifically what dance education would be within their state. Now that legislation had designated dance as an art form equal to other art and core disciplines, states needed to decide if they wanted dance classes in school settings to be taught by a PE coach and focus on health and fitness or maintained in arts programs by a dance specialist and emphasize the creative and performance process.

The ESEA has been reauthorized most recently when the Every Student Succeeds Act (ESSA) was passed. The ESSA was approved in 2015 and enacted in 2017. It moved learning and performance accountability from the federal government to the individual states, meaning that each state may determine what standards they will apply and how they will assess students. States may choose to follow the National Core Arts Standards, a version of them, or create their own criteria, thus choosing to incorporate the arts to the degree to which they see fit for their state and funding purposes.

At the turn of the 21st century, research was conducted and collected by numerous individuals from not only the academic field but also from the political, non-profit, and corporate communities. As employers considered those entering the workforce, it was noted that the focus had shifted from hiring workers well-versed in literacy and numbers to those who also had skills in problem-solving, critical thinking, and teamwork. The Partnership for 21st Century Learning (P21) was established as a national organization in 2001 and developed the framework for the skills that have been incorporated into various educational organizations and disciplines. Its framework served as a guide for the development of the national Common Core Standards in 2010 with focus on what is referred to as the 4 C's – collaboration, communication, creativity, and critical thinking – and problem-solving. The 21st Century Skills continue to be considered as states continuously adapt their standards and education policies. The "21st Century Skills Map: The Arts" defines each skill and learning outcome and offers examples of application utilizing dance, theatre, music, and visual arts (including media arts). The Skills Map demonstrates to readers how the arts can be a vehicle for learning and developing these 21st Century Skills within students and can serve as a helpful resource, specifically for K–12 dance educators.[17]

National Organizational Support

During the mid-20th century, national organizations and publications developed in support of the advancement of dance as an educational and artistic discipline. The American Physical Education Association (APEA) was already established at the time that dance entered the academic setting. In 1931, members organized a National Section on Dancing within the APEA, which evolved into a Dance Division in 1961. This organization became the American Alliance of Health, Physical Education, Recreation, and Dance in 1974 yet is now known as Shape America. In 1948, the Halprin-Lathrop Studio published the first issue of *Impulse* following a summer intensive dance course held in San Francisco. Between the years 1948 and 1970, the periodical *Impulse* provided the dance community with a dedicated dance publication that allowed individuals and academics to address and debate specific issues regarding dance and dance education topics. The journal and its editorial direction "contributed to the maturation of dance related writing, helping to establish the intellectual bedrock upon which would stand a new generation of dance 'scholars,' a term rarely used in connection with dance education."[18] This publication furthered the field of dance education through its dissemination of information and advocacy for dance and dance education.

Due in part to the momentum that *Impulse* offered, dance advocacy gained momentum throughout the latter half of the 20th century. Several professional dance associations formed and continue to offer a variety of tools and resources to the dancer, dance educator, and dance community. These organizations include but are not limited to the following:

- American Dance Guild (ADG, 1956)
- Congress on Research in Dance (CORD, 1969)
- American Dance Therapy Association (ADTA, 1966)
- American College Dance Association (ACDA, 1971)
- Dance Critics Association (DCA, 1973)
- Society of Dance History Scholars (SDHS, 1978)
- CORD and SDHS merge to become Dance Studies Association (DSA, 2017)
- National Association of Schools of Dance (NASD, 1981)
- Dance/USA (1982)
- National Dance Education Organization (NDEO, 1998)

National Association of Schools of Dance

The National Association of Schools of Dance (NASD) was founded in 1981 and is the accrediting agency for educational programs in dance as recognized by the United States Department of Education. Today, the membership body includes both public and private institutions of higher education along with non-degree granting professional training programs, such as the Martha Graham School of Contemporary Dance, Inc. The organization currently maintains a membership of approximately 82 schools, and as a governing body, NASD ensures that its members uphold the curricular and procedural standards that have been established by the association.[19]

The founding of NASD was a milestone in the history of dance within higher education. The agency provides curricular, facility, and resource standards for accredited academic and professional programs. It ensures that quality is maintained within programs and provides an additional voice for educators in dialogue with administrators. NASD's continued efforts not only support and maintain the field of dance education but propel it forward.

National Dance Education Organization

The **National Dance Education Organization** (NDEO) was established in 1998 in Washington D.C., with the goal of supporting and furthering dance education. NDEO is an autonomous, non-profit, membership organization that publishes two dance education journals – *Journal of Dance Education* and *Dance Education in Practice* – and hosts a number of yearly conferences uniting dance educators to further develop the field and supports states in their pursuit of dance certifications. NDEO offers an Online Professional Development Institute wherein dance educators of all levels can further their own education. The organization has produced standards in dance education that serve as guides for both students and teachers of all levels. Finally, NDEO supports a National Honors Society for Dance Arts (NHSDA) at the secondary and collegiate levels. NHSDA recognizes and celebrates artistic merit and exceptional leadership and scholarship in dance students. NDEO is a recognized leader in the field of dance education, advocating for public policy, developing programs, and assisting dance educators within K–12, higher education, and the private sector.

NDEO was responsible for the development of the dance standards known as the National Standards of Arts Education in 1994. This document was the "first national document to identify and describe dance as a creative art form in education."[20] Along with federal policy, the standards legitimized dance as a discipline, aligned dance education with the other arts and core subjects within academic curricula, and supported sequential learning by competent dance educators. Following the NCLB Act, NDEO contributed to the states' research in dance certification and standards.

> Over the course of ten years, the NDEO . . . was required to provide expertise and documentation to state departments of education that provided evidence of teacher and student standards, opportunity-to-learn standards (standards regarding facilities, scheduling, safety, and curriculum), certification, and teacher preparation.[21]

In 2014, a working group of NDEO members contributed to the development of the National Core Art Standards, released in that year. NDEO continues to provide a network for dance educators and dancers, both novice and skilled. The tools, resources, forums,

The Development of Dance Education **17**

publications, and conferences offered by the organization are essential to dance education's continued support and advancement.

Box 1.6 Lack of Standardized Training

The Western theatrical genres of dance (ballet, modern, tap, jazz, and hip-hop) lack a standardized system for training teachers, although many professional dance schools and companies have devised their own certificate or certification programs. Private dance studios are not regulated by a national accrediting body or standard. While membership organizations such as NASD and NDEO exist to support dance education and promote standards, private dance studios, and even professional schools and institutions of higher education, are not required to seek membership in or thus abide by the teaching standards set forth by the organizations. Teachers do not have to be certified or receive dance degrees or certificates in order to open a dance studio or teach at a private dance studio. One is not required to gain specialized training in dance or dance education to begin instructing others in dance, nor is there a standard on how the dance curriculum within a studio or school is to be established. This lack of standardization creates a discrepancy specifically within early dance training. What one student may learn at one studio can be quite different both in scope and format from what another individual may learn at a different studio. With the lack of standardized systems for dance education across all avenues of dance training, teachers must be internally motivated and take their own initiative to train and invest in the study of dance pedagogy.

Many dance companies and organizations offer training certificates and certifications as an option for dance educators. While these do not replace a teaching license or certification within the educational system, they are attractive options to dance teachers and instructors. Dance teachers pursue certifications to further their intellect and ability as educators and instructors. Having a certificate may also demonstrate to students that the instructor has received additional training in a specific area and thus is a way for the instructor to earn recognition among their students and become more marketable as a teacher.

Because these types of programs often occur in as little as one day to a week or two, many educators find them manageable to attend. Such programs are typically offered from beginning to advanced levels and concentrate on specific genres, styles, methodologies, age ranges, levels, or aspects of teaching. The dance teacher should do their research in selecting the appropriate teaching workshop/certificate program to attend. The highest-quality programs include a significant level of hours of study in a focused genre with qualified and reputable educators, provided manuals and resources, and follow-up opportunities with the program coordinators/leaders.

BENEFITS OF DANCE

It is important for individuals to establish a healthy lifestyle and maintain an adequate level of physical fitness. It has been proven that a lifetime void of activity yields "greater percentages of body fat; poor cardiac conditioning, reduction in muscle mass; less body strength, endurance, and balance; consequently, these physiological limitations subject older adults to less than optimal quality of life."[22] Although many may not realize it, dance is a form of physical activity that leads to similar benefits as jogging, biking, or swimming. Yet, it can also offer an individual much more.

Engaging in dance has many positive benefits, which is why many parents enroll their children in dance lessons or why older individuals choose to join a class within their community. These benefits range from physical to cognitive to social and can have a lasting impact on the individual. The following section highlights six areas in which students can experience positive outcomes from their dance experience that extend beyond the acquisition of skill.

Physical

Dance training can help students develop basic motor skills and is uniquely tied to motor development and performance. Engaging in dance helps individuals to strengthen weight-bearing bones, increase range of motion, and improve muscle tone. Overall, strength and flexibility are enhanced. Through learning and practicing dance movement, students develop motor control and balance as they discover body awareness. Posture improves, along with coordination and agility. Stamina and muscular endurance will advance, and overall cardiovascular health is optimized.

Emotional

Dance is an expressive art form and naturally invites expressive thought from the dancer. Students are encouraged to express their personalities, feelings, and moods or a specific character or role in class and performance. Through the discipline of the dance form, the dance teacher can help a student to feel empowered and strong when they might otherwise not feel this way outside of the dance classroom. Students' self-confidence, self-efficacy, and self-esteem can increase. In dance training, a connection is made to the student's affective domain, which relates to the feelings, attitudes, and emotions embodied within the student. The student is able to discover joy in movement, appreciation for the art, and assurance and poise within themselves.

Behavioral

Engaging in dance training can offer a positive effect on the student's behavior. Through regular class participation and activity, the student's overall composure and level of focus can improve. Children become better at following directions, understanding classroom etiquette, and demonstrating respect for others, the teacher, and themselves. The art of dance instills discipline within students while allowing them to explore movement and creation.

Cognitive

Dance education ignites intellectual development at each level of training. Dance activity encourages new connections within the nervous system, increasing efficiency in movement. According to Dr. Patricia T. Alpert, "It also increases the temporal and prefrontal brain activity responsible for the improvement of memory, the ability to multitask and plan as well as improves attention."[23] As students learn dance skills, concepts, and choreography, they practice problem-solving through the motor, spatial, and dynamic choices they make. Dancers use judgment in navigating space, partner work, musicality, etc. They must remain focused in class, practice, and performance, a skill that is learned not automatically. Students are also encouraged to develop their creativity within the dance setting. The teacher fosters creativity within students through class activities and dance improvisation.

Social

Humans are social beings. The dance setting encourages interaction with others. Students learn social skills as they take turns with, partner, support, and encourage classmates. Students develop social awareness of, acceptance for, and sensitivity to others through engaging in the art of dance. They learn to rely on others within choreography and partner work. Dance helps empower individuals to communicate respectfully and effectively with others. Ability to cooperate, collaborate, and work with others are healthy skills that students gain through dance training.

Therapeutic

Engaging in dance can provide a healing effect for a variety of ailments that individuals may face. Dance can be movement therapy and promotes physical and emotional well-being. Movement serves as a medium to help individuals dealing with an array of issues that may range from eating disorders to stress to certain conditions such as Parkinson's disease. Dance can reduce feelings of isolation, body tension, chronic pain, and anxiety.

Additionally, individuals experience many emotions. The growing and developing child will experience a range of emotions, on a daily basis. Dance allows an individual to connect to their emotions and provides an outlet for the release of emotions. In this way, dance can serve as a therapeutic release for emotions, tension, stress, nervousness, fear, shyness, etc. Dance serves as a coping mechanism for many individuals who turn to the dance studio as a source of comfort stability, and community.

TABLE 1.1 A summarization of the benefits of dance.

Benefits of Dance

	Encourages motor control and development
	• Improves
	• Posture
	• Balance
	• Coordination
Physical	• Enhances body awareness
	Enhances strength and flexibility
	• Strengthens weight-bearing bones
	• Increases range of motion and agility
	• Improves muscle tone, strength, and endurance
	Improves cardiovascular health

(Continued)

TABLE 1.1 Continued

Benefits of Dance

Emotional	**Invites** • Expressive thought • Personal expression • Feelings of empowerment • Inner strength **Improves** • Self-confidence • Self-efficacy • Self-esteem **Develops** • Joy in movement • Assurance • Poise
Behavioral	**Develops personal behaviors, including** • Respect for others and oneself • Discipline • Focus • Ability to follow directions
Cognitive	**Enhances intellectual development** • Memory • Capacity for attention • Ability to multitask • Ability to plan **Develops** • Problem-solving skills • Critical thinking skills • Creativity
Social	**Encourages healthy interaction with others** • Cooperation, achieving individual goals • Collaboration, achieving shared goals • Supporting and encouraging others

Therapeutic	**Promotes physical and emotional well-being**
	• Helps to reduce feelings of
	  • Isolation
	  • Body tension
	  • Chronic pain
	  • Anxiety
	• Outlet for the release of
	  • Emotions
	  • Tension
	  • Stress
	  • Nervousness
	  • Fear
	  • Shyness

CHAPTER SUMMARY

Whether one teaches in the private sector, elementary, secondary, or tertiary education – or within another avenue – an awareness of the path that dance education has taken in the United States and the policy-making and national organizations that have guided its evolution help the dance teacher to articulate and defend their teaching methodology and benefits of learning. Understanding where dance education has been in our country can help us as dance educators to recognize the challenges that lie ahead and the ways in which we can contribute to keeping the art form of dance a part of the education system within the United States. Dance can offer an individual many rewards that lie beyond the physical capacity of movement and fitness, including enhanced cognitive abilities, increased self-confidence, self-efficacy and self-esteem, improved focus and discipline, willingness toward cooperation and collaboration, and reduced stress and tension.

PRACTICAL APPLICATIONS

1   Explain the difference between dance training, dance education, and dance as education.

2   Why is awareness of the evolution of dance education helpful knowledge for a dance teacher?

3   How did Margaret H'Doubler's research influence the direction of dance pedagogy?

4   What was a significant result from the work of the Bennington Experience?

5   What event within the 20th century do you believe had the greatest impact on the advancement of dance education? In what ways?

6   Conduct online research of the National Core Arts Standards for Dance. How could you utilize these standards within the dance classroom? Provide specific examples.

7   Identify the six areas in which dance can benefit an individual and provide specific examples of each. Can you think of additional examples not included in the text? How has dance positively influenced or enhanced your life?

NOTES

1   Thomas K. Hagood, *A History of Dance in American Higher Education: Dance and the American University* (Lewiston, NY: E. Mellen Press, 2000), 27.

2   Virginia Hoge Mead, "More Than Mere Movement: Dalcrose Eurythmics," *Music Educators Journal* 82, no. 4 (1996): 39.

3   Lucy Duncan Hall, "Dalcroze Eurythmics," *Francis W. Parker School Studies in Education* 6 (1920): 141.

4   Hagood, *A History of Dance*, 39–40.

5   Thomas K. Hagood, "Dance in American Colleges and Universities," in *The Dance Experience: Insights into History, Cultures and Creativity*. 3rd ed., eds. by Myron Howard Nadel and Marc Raymond Strauss (Princeton, NJ: Princeton Book Company, 2014), 81.

6   Hagood, "Dance in American Colleges and Universities," 81.

7 Hagood, "Dance in American Colleges and Universities," 83.

8 Hagood, "Dance in American Colleges and Universities," 83–86.

9 Curtis L. Carter, "The State of Dance in Education: Past and Present," *Theory Into Practice* 23, no. 4 (1984): 294.

10 Thomas K. Hagood, "Moving in Harmony with the Body: The Teaching Legacy of Margaret H'Doubler, 1916–1926," *Dance Research Journal* 32, no. 2 (2000): 35.

11 Hagood, "Dance in American Colleges and Universities," 35.

12 Hagood, "Dance in American Colleges and Universities," 38–39.

13 Hagood, "Dance in American Colleges and Universities," 39.

14 Hagood, "Dance in American Colleges and Universities," 87–88.

15 Hagood, "Dance in American Colleges and Universities," 91.

16 Hagood, "Dance in American Colleges and Universities," 92–93.

17 Colleen & Ebert Dean, et al., "21st Century Skills Map: The Arts," (2010), www.researchgate.net/publication/279372818_21st_Century_Skills_Map_The_Arts.

18 Hagood, A History of Dance, 175.

19 "National Association of Schools of Dance," Accessed April 2020, https://nasd.arts-accredit.org/.

20 Jane M. Bonbright, "Dance Education 1999: Status, Challenges, and Recommendations," *Arts Education Policy Review* 101, no. 1 (1999): 34.

21 Jane Bonbright and Susan McGreevy-Nichols, "National Dance Education Organization: Building a Future for Dance Education in the Arts," *Arts Education Policy Review* 113, no. 4 (2012): 2.

22 Patricia T. Alpert, "The Health Benefits of Dance," *Home health Care Management & Practice* 23, no. 2 (2011): 155.

23 Alpert, "The Health Benefits of Dance," 155–156.

BIBLIOGRAPHY

Agresta-Stratton, Abigail F., and Lynn Monson. "Dance and Physical Education: An Unartful Alliance." *Dance Education in Practice* 4, no. 3 (2018): 4–10.

Alpert, Patricia T. "The Health Benefits of Dance." *Home Health Care Management & Practice* 23, no. 2 (2011): 155–157.

Bonbright, Jane M. "Dance Education 1999: Status, Challenges, and Recommendations." *Arts Education Policy Review* 101, no. 1 (1999): 33–39.

Bonbright, Jane M., and Susan McGreevy-Nichols. "National Dance Education Organization: Building a Future for Dance Education in the Arts." *Arts Education Policy Review* 113, no. 4 (2012): 147–151.

Carter, Curtis L. "The State of Dance in Education: Past and Present." *Theory Into Practice* 23, no. 4 (1984): 293–99. https://doi.org/10.1080/00405848409543129.

Clark, Amanda, and Sara Pecina. *Dance Appreciation*. London: Routledge, Taylor & Francis Group, 2021.

Dean, Colleen & Ebert, et al. "21st Century Skills Map: The Arts." (2010) www.researchgate.net/publication/279372818_21st_Century_Skills_Map_The_Arts.

Frederiksen, Jo A.G. "Pedagogical Practices in Dance Education Addressing Motor, Aesthetic, Social, Emotional and Cognitive Development For Pre-Kindergarten through Post-Secondary Students," n.d. https://www.lausd.org/cms/lib/CA01000043/Centricity/Domain/218/Best%20Pedagogical%20Practices%20in%20Dance%20Education.pdf.

Gingrasso, Susan. "Practical Resources for Dance Educators! Considering the Health and Well-Being of Our Young Dancers." *Dance Education in Practice* 6, no. 2 (2020): 24–28.

Hagood, Thomas K. *A History of Dance in American Higher Education: Dance and the American University*. Lewiston, NY: E. Mellen Press, 2000.

Hagood, Thomas K. "Moving in Harmony with the Body: The Teaching Legacy of Margaret H'Doubler, 1916–1926." *Dance Research Journal* 32, no. 2 (2000): 32. https://doi.org/10.2307/1477980.

Hall, Lucy Duncan. "Dalcroze Eurythmics." *Francis W. Parker School Studies in Education* 6 (1920): 141–150.

Koff, Susan R. Dance Education: A Redefinition. London: Methuen Drama, 2021.

Kraus, Richard G., Sarah C. Hilsendager, and Brenda Dixon. *History of the Dance in Art and Education*. Englewood Cliffs, NJ: Prentice Hall, 1991.

Mead, Virginia Hoge. "More Than Mere Movement: Dalcrose Eurythmics." *Music Educators Journal* 82, no. 4 (1996): 38–41.

Nadel, Myron Howard, and Marc Strauss. *The Dance Experience: Insights into History, Culture, and Creativity*. Hightstown, NJ: Princeton Book Co., 2014.

Risner, Doug. "Dance Education Matters: Rebuilding Postsecondary Dance Education for Twenty-First Century Relevance and Resonance." *Journal of Dance Education* 10, no. 4 (2010): 95–110. https://doi.org/10.1080/15290824.2010.529761.

Warburton, Edward C. "Beyond Steps: The Need for Pedagogical Knowledge in Dance." *Journal of Dance Education* 8, no. 1 (2008): 7–12. https://doi.org/10.1080/15290824.2008.10387353.

CHAPTER 2

Roles in the Classroom

Box 2.1 Chapter Objectives

After reading this chapter, you will be able to:

- Identify the various roles the dance educator encompasses beyond the teaching of dance technique
- Articulate characteristics that contribute to the effectiveness of a dance teacher
- Understand the benefit of a personal teaching philosophy and how to formulate a statement
- Recognize the student's responsibilities within the dance classroom

Box 2.2 Chapter Vocabulary

personal teaching style
teaching philosophy statement

We choose to teach not just for our love of dance but also our fascination with the artistic movement of the human body, our interest in others, and our desire to further the art form. We have a connection to and sincere investment in the field of dance and wish to instill within others a love and joy for movement, self-confidence, and a mode for self-expression. As a teacher, we connect to students on a personal level, imparting more than theories in technique, but also lessons in life. Discipline, hard work, respect, professionalism, and teamwork are all learned within the dance class, as well as problem-solving, identity, and creativity. Dance teachers become a guide, a mentor, and an advisor to their students. We teach, facilitate, and nurture students, yet also receive a fair share of eye rolls and back talk from adolescent dancers and, at times, an earful of feedback from concerned parents. But what is it that propels a young teacher forward to the day they find themselves a mature and experienced, still-dedicated teacher, imparting wisdom to generations of students?

DOI: 10.4324/b22952-4

THE PATH OF A DANCE TEACHER

The path of a dance educator may be defined early in one's dance journey, teaching may be a career that is discovered along the way, or individuals may find themselves sporadically stepping into the studio as a dance teacher. Regardless of whether one decides to pursue teaching early or late in their dance training, competency as a dancer is a must. Individuals who wish to become dance teachers must gain advanced knowledge in the skill and technique of dance and acquire knowledge and understanding of at least one genre of dance, although, as the field of dance continues to evolve and becomes more immersive and collaborative, familiarity with and/or expertise in multiple dance forms is proving increasingly beneficial. An individual trained to a high level in a variety of techniques, forms, and/or theoretical fields of dance will find a greater range of employment opportunities than the individual that is singularly trained. This range of knowledge will also benefit the educator in their teaching style and instruction ability.

Whether skilled in several forms or a single form, the individual must be highly competent in that dance genre. The efficient dance teacher must have advanced knowledge and understanding of technique and the ability to clearly articulate and convey that information to students. Awareness of and proficiency in proper technique, distinct understanding of correct body mechanics, knowledge of the historical context and cultural significance of the dance form, and clear communication skills can often prove more effective in teaching than an individual who has a prowess in technique and artistry yet cannot explain to a young dancer how to successfully execute a common movement such as a turn or a jump. There are often factors that may prevent a dance educator from demonstrating superb technique themself, such as injury or physical limitations, but that does not necessarily restrict them from possessing the advanced knowledge and comprehension and the ability to effectively convey the technique to students.

FIGURE 2.1 A dance teacher instructs young dancers.
Source: Photo by Jeffrey Smith/Western Kentucky University.

This idea harkens to the ongoing tension between trained educators who often acquire certifications and/or degrees in dance and those educators with professional performance experience. Which experience better qualifies an individual to be an effective dance educator? We often hear the saying "Those who can, do; those who can't, teach." Perhaps it should read "Those who can teach, should teach; those who can't teach, shouldn't teach." It is a teacher that can create or break a dancer or an individual. It is the teacher who becomes not just the revealer and educator of dance steps and technique but also a guide, a mentor, a facilitator, and an advisor. There are many professional dancers that possess advanced understanding of dance technique, have first-hand experience of onstage performance, and have many professional contacts; however, they find themselves without the disposition to teach or the ability to articulate and break down the mechanics of a movement.

Once trained, a dance teacher must have the desire to teach and work with others. Learners come in all "shapes and sizes," meaning each student possesses unique characteristics. Students studying dance may be preschool aged, senior citizens, able-bodied, differently abled, joyful, stubborn, naturally talented, uncoordinated, recreational, preprofessional, and so on. Not all dance teachers will work with every type of learner listed here; however, many teachers in the private sector or in K–12 settings may. Upon deciding to enter the teaching profession, it is necessary to determine what type of dance teacher you want to be. Ask yourself what group of learners you enjoy working with the most. Which age group do you feel you connect with best? Do you have the patience it takes to work with younger dancers, or less-experienced dancers? Or do you prefer to work with older, professional students who have a greater depth of knowledge and learned ability? Understanding your personality and teaching preference will guide the decisions you make in your own training and the certifications you pursue as you prepare for your path in dance education.

ROLE OF A DANCE TEACHER

The primary role of the dance educator is to teach technique and artistry to their students while passing on the tradition of the dance form. In considering this role, we can quickly divide this into many smaller tasks. First and foremost, the dance teacher must be able to clearly transmit or convey dance movement and technique to the learner. To do this, the teacher must first possess knowledge of how the body works, more specifically, a sufficient comprehension of motor control and development and kinesiology. The teacher must also understand the factors that affect cognitive and motor learning within various learners so that their teaching style and methods can be adapted for the acquisition of skills to occur. Next, the dance teacher must recognize the best way(s) to prepare a curriculum appropriate to the earlier considerations as well as a singular lesson plan. Additionally, it is important for the teacher to employ instructional tools when delivering the lesson plan in a manner that will engage the class as a whole as well as individuals with differing personalities, learning styles, and sometimes skill levels. Finally, the dancer teacher must be prepared to assess student work and provide feedback in an appropriate manner.

TABLE 2.1 Summary of the aspects necessary to effectively teach dance technique and artistry.

To Effectively Teach Technique and Artistry, the Dance Teacher Should . . .

- Fully understand the dance genre they are teaching (including technique, history, and stylisti context)

- Possess knowledge of the human body, including motor and cognitive development

- Understand how learning occurs and create safe and conducive learning environments

- Devise appropriate curriculum and lesson plans

- Effectively present information to learners

- Provide appropriate feedback

- Continually assess the teaching process and continue to engage their own learning

Dance educators must also instill artistry within their students. The majority of children begin dance lessons for the excitement of performing onstage. Yet, artistry is a skill that is developed and honed through years of practice, coaching, and experience. The ability to dance the steps is enhanced when the students are also able to perform and express. Teaching students how to execute movement with nuance, musicality, energy, and artistry, and providing students with opportunity to sharpen these skills and put them into practice, is paramount. To enhance students' understanding of performance styles and qualities and help them make sense of distinctions within the art form, dance teachers must also share the history of the dance form in which they are teaching. Students develop a deeper appreciation of dance when the teacher makes connections to the dance's history. Understanding the dance form's history, its milestones, and influential figures past and present will help learners to better appreciate and understand the dance as they engage with the movement both in class and on stage. It is the job of the dance educator to not only share the tradition of the movement but also the history of the dance.

The role of a dance educator extends beyond that of teacher of dance technique. Many dance teachers work with students for extended periods of time, and through that tutelage, they become more than just a teacher but also a mentor and a guide. Students often look to their dance teacher as a friend, additional parental figure, or confidant. The teacher might be a disciplinarian or an employer. Many dance teachers find themselves also playing the role of costume designer, lighting designer, sound editor, and program designer when preparing for studio recitals, school showcases, or concerts. Most dance teachers are also choreographers and rehearsal directors. Those that own dance studios find themselves as office manager, janitor, event planner, record keeper, accountant, maintenance repairer, and mediator between students and/or parents. Many dance teachers are also workshop organizers, social media coordinators, and photographers/videographers.

Despite the various responsibilities of a dance teacher, it is also important to remember that the learning never ceases. Even for the dance educator, training never ends; the pursuit of knowledge never stops. Dance teachers must continue to practice technique and condition their bodies. They must find workshops and classes to attend to stay abreast of current styles and trends and pedagogical methods. Most importantly, dance teachers continually learn each time they step into the classroom. They discover new ways to communicate with students; they uncover something novel about dance technique; they realize something unknown about a student or themselves. The dance teacher must remain open to the learning experience in the same way that the learner is encouraged each time they walk into the dance studio.

Regardless of the specific role(s) one takes on as a dance educator, the most important priority that remains is the student. At the end of the day, it is the students and their acquisition of skill, attainment of goals, and personal accomplishments within (and sometimes outside of) the dance studio that drives the dance teacher. The teacher should be mindful that students are always observing them, and therefore they should strive to be positive role models at all times. It is important for the teacher to leave personal problems at the door and instead steer their attention to their students. Teachers will find themselves assessing students' needs each day and perhaps adjusting the lesson plan to accommodate students' energy, mood, or focus levels. Attention should be given to each student, treating each as an individual and working to meet their specific needs. The following chapters detail theories, methods, tools, and resources for developing and delivering effective lesson plans. Yet, it can become easy for the instructor to lose sight of what truly matters in the classroom. By remaining focused on the students, the teacher can devise the best strategy for instruction.

Types and Styles of Dance Teachers

Dance teachers are found within the private sector, primary and secondary schools, higher education, recreational centers, and professional schools. Some educators may be specialized in a certain technique or area of dance; others may be general practitioners where they teach in a range of genres and areas. A teaching artist is one whose primary career may not be rooted in teaching, but rather performance; however, they engage in workshop and guest classes offering a focused glimpse of their style over a short span of time. Teachers within the private sector may be specialized in a particular dance form or genre; however, many find themselves teaching multiple genres of dance to a wide range of ages and levels. The dance setting within the private sector is often geared toward students ranging from primary ages through early adulthood and beyond and offers dance training as an extracurricular activity, hobby, or pre-professional focus. K–12 programs may include dance within their core curriculum. Individuals teaching dance within these programs must be certified in the state they teach. These dance educators most likely teach a mix of dance technique and theory courses within the academic framework. Educators within collegiate dance programs are generally specialized in specific dance forms with knowledge in other areas of dance and are teaching degree-specific students and/or non-dance majors within the university setting. Individuals teaching in higher education are typically required to have either a terminal degree (Master of Fine Arts) in dance or a related field and/or significant professional experience as determined by the specifications of the job.

Teaching styles may vary with the category in which the dance teacher is employed. Some examples can include the authoritarian, collaborative, physical, or anatomy-based teacher. Perhaps you have found yourself in a dance class in which the authoritative teacher has dictated every aspect of the class. For some groups of students, this creates clear order, structure, and progression within the learning atmosphere. Other students appreciate and connect to a collaborative teacher who allows them freedom and input into the structure and content of a class. The physical teacher will demonstrate a significant amount of the class, consistently showing students how to execute or perform a movement, which can be helpful for the visual learner. Connecting specific muscles to movement and explaining how the body works to complete an action is the hallmark of the anatomy-based teacher. Many, if not most, dance teachers demonstrate a combination of these styles. Can you think of other teaching styles that you have witnessed?

Your personal teaching style is dictated by your personality, beliefs, and values and is manifested in your behavior. It can be influenced by your past training, teachers, and experiences as well as the students that are presently in front of you. One's **personal teaching style** is not the same thing as the instructional teaching method that one employs within the classroom. Instructional delivery methods are discussed in Chapter 13. The manner in which you speak to students, the rhetoric you use, and the body language you convey are examples of the philosophy and personal characteristics you hold as an educator, and they shape your teaching style. This approach is then coupled with the instructional method you choose to employ for the lesson plan of a specific class.

One's teaching style must be fluid and adaptable to the distinct class. As discussed in Chapter 5, there are a variety of learning styles and approaches students may utilize within the learning process. Individuals learn in different ways, and a single dance class is often comprised of students that each acquire information in distinct ways. A singular teaching style will not prove effective in communicating with or connecting to all types of learners. To effectively teach each student, the educator must adapt their teaching style to meet the needs of the individual learner as appropriate. A teaching style that is overly friendly and rarely disciplines may find difficulty in gaining cooperation from a hyperactive six-year-old who needs a firm voice and constant guidance. The teaching style that explains which specific muscles need to be engaged or relaxed to complete certain movements or achieve a particular aesthetic will connect with the analytical learner who thrives on understanding how the body works, yet this teaching style may frustrate a visual learner who simply wants to see the movement in action.

A dance educator will also need to adjust their teaching style to meet the needs of the overall population of the dance class they are teaching. For example, one's teaching style will change when working with young children versus college-aged students, recreational high-schoolers versus pre-professional middle-school-aged dancers, or even when teaching adults with Parkinson's disease. Dance teachers within the private sector will find that their teaching styles must rotate and vary most frequently as they often work with the widest range of ages and levels. However, it is important for every teacher to gauge their students upon entry into the classroom to be sensitive and flexible to their learners' needs on a class-to-class and day-to-day basis.

FIGURE 2.2 A ballet teacher instructs dancers in a center exercise.
Source: Photo by Clinton Lewis/Western Kentucky University.

Characteristics of Effective Dance Teachers

Every educator is unique, with their own set of values, ideals, behaviors, and personality traits. Teaching is a craft that develops with experience, tenacity, and a degree of natural instinct. While some may debate whether teachers are born or made, there are certain distinguishable characteristics that highly effective dance teachers often have in common. The following list is not exhaustive, but rather serves to highlight those characteristics that prove most beneficial among effective dance educators.

- **Competent in advanced knowledge and skill of dance technique** – For a teacher to properly train and educate a learner in a dance technique, they must be competent in that dance form, possessing advanced knowledge and technical skill in the genre. Familiarity and/or competency in more than one dance form can be beneficial within one's personal teaching and employment opportunities. The dance teacher who has not had proper training themself risks causing physical injury to their students and creating poor training and movement habits within their students.
- **Understanding of anatomy and kinesiology as it pertains to dance** – It is important for dance teachers to possess knowledge of the body's skeletal and muscular systems as well as the physiological processes of the body in relationship to movement execution. The better that an individual understands kinesthetic principles, including motor control and development, the more effective the individual can become in teaching students the acquisition of skills and helping prevent injuries in students.
- **Interested in others** – Students will engage most with a teacher who demonstrates a sincere interest in them. An effective teacher takes care to learn about their students

and has a desire to help others succeed. Seeking to understand what motivates a student and how they learn best will enable the teacher to best communicate with students and assist them in reaching their movement and artistic goals. Further, showing compassion can help a dance teacher to accurately access a student's emotional, as well as physical, needs.

- **Competent in basic music theory** – Dance teachers must have an understanding of basic music theory. In turn, this allows the teacher to then provide a clear rhythmical education for students and enhance the presentation of movement within the learning environment. A teacher's developed sense of music phrasing and musicality helps students relate the movement to the music in a nuanced manner and promote their own artistry and connection to the music. Additionally, music literacy aids in communication with accompanists and making choreographic decisions.
- **Communication skills** – In any teaching position, the ability to clearly articulate and convey the material is highly important. An effective dance educator must be able to communicate movement skills and theories to learners in a variety of manners and modes. It often takes practice for a dance teacher to learn how to teach dance vocabulary. Physically executing a dance step is very different from verbally breaking down the movement and guiding a learner through the steps necessary to complete the movement themself. This takes experience and a variety of approaches.

Truly teaching a student requires great skill in communication. The effective dance teacher must not only convey information but demonstrate the ability to listen to and receive information from students and parents of all communication styles and approaches. The teacher should adequately listen to student questions and discoveries, interpret student body language, and respond appropriately.

- **Creative** – Dancers are naturally creative individuals. Dance teachers are no different. The dance educator must constantly find innovative ways to devise lesson plans to keep learners engaged, to deliver material so as to connect with all learning styles, and to offer feedback in a manner that will inspire students to continue their efforts. Dance teachers should possess a visionary spirit that motivates them to conceive movement patterns and sequences that will meet learning objectives and encourage artistry. It takes ingenuity at times to communicate difficult technical theories to young minds; at other times, a teacher may find themselves constructing imaginative games designed to guide children through basic motor skills.
- **Resourceful** – Dance teachers must demonstrate resourcefulness. They need to quickly realize when a method or approach is not working with students and have the ability to shift their efforts in a new direction. When presented with a problem in the classroom, the dance teacher readily finds a solution, such as using different language to articulate the "how-to" of a movement, assessing conflict among dancers, or troubleshooting spatial issues within choreography or the environment. Additionally, the dance teacher utilizes available equipment (Hula-Hoops, rhythm sticks, ballet *barres*, technology, etc.) as appropriate to aid students in the learning of established objectives.
- **Patient** – Regardless of the discipline, teaching takes a tremendous amount of patience. The learning process can be arduous for students and teachers alike. The acquisition of skill, especially movement skill, does not come easily for some, nor does

it occur overnight. The dance teacher will interact with a wide variety of personality types among students and teachers. They must be patient with their students in the classroom and demonstrate tolerance as well as care in the manner in which feedback is delivered and in communication with parents.

- **Passion for the art form and for teaching** – Above all, the dance educator must have excitement, energy, and a great love for the art of dance and teaching. To dedicate one's time to training others, one must have a commitment to the discipline. The dance teacher will engage with dance not just in the classroom but outside of the studio as they plan lessons, curricula, and other business or production-related materials. Teaching is an investment, and without fascination of and zeal for the art form, the dance teacher can easily find themselves facing burnout. To truly instill an appreciation for dance within students, the teacher themself must demonstrate pure joy in the art.

There are, of course, many other characteristics that one can list to describe incredible and capable teachers. For instance, having a sense of humor, demonstrating honesty, and presenting empathy to gender and cultural differences helps build rapport, trust, and respect with students and creates a positive learning environment. Perhaps you find that you resonate with many of the earlier characteristics. Some traits are not fully realized until time is spent leading a classroom full of students through movement experiences. As mentioned earlier, teaching is a learning experience. Yet, it is also a process. Just as students develop and evolve as they learn, mature, and gain experiences, so does the teacher. One step that can help an individual better discover their teaching values and potentially shape their teaching characteristics is creating a teaching philosophy statement.

Box 2.3 Career Longevity

A professional dancer continues to train and participate in dance classes while maintaining a performance career in order to sustain a high level of technique. The dancer also attends regular class to keep the body strong and conditioned to prevent injury and in an effort to lengthen the amount of time which their bodies may continue to meet the demands of the art form. Similarly, dance teachers must also find ways to condition their bodies through regular dance class or supplemental exercise programs.

As the human body ages, a natural decrease in bone and muscle mass occurs. However, proper diet and regular exercise can be a deterrent to this process and promote bone growth and overall strength. It is important for the dance teacher to engage in supplemental modes of exercise. This can help the teacher to maintain a strong body. Just as a dancer is prone to injury, the teacher is also at risk of the same injuries, specifically since the teacher will find themselves not as warm as the students when executing movements and will typically perform movements repeatedly, and often on one side of the body, during the teaching process. Dance teachers should properly warm up their bodies prior to classroom demonstration, alternate the side on which they demonstrate in class so as not to overwork or favor a particular working/supporting side, and take time to stretch and cool-down after teaching long periods.

THE TEACHING PHILOSOPHY STATEMENT

A **teaching philosophy statement** offers insight into the personal values and beliefs that one holds as an educator. This self-reflective statement serves as a guide to one's teaching. It not only offers readers an understanding of the type of teacher that one is but also delineates the standards and ideals that one strives to uphold within their classroom. A teaching philosophy is helpful to an educator as it both guides and grounds the individual within their teaching principles. It reminds the teacher of *who* they are as a teacher and *why* they teach, along with their personal guidelines for *how* they will teach. As an inexperienced teacher is starting out in their career, a teaching philosophy can provide stability, continuity, and long-term guidance, helping them to remain focused on their teaching goals. Ultimately, the teaching philosophy serves as a personal mission statement for one's teaching, clarifying for the educator *why* they are doing *what* they are doing.

A teaching philosophy is beneficial for anyone that is teaching; however, those teaching within higher education are often required to have a personal statement of teaching for job applications, promotions, etc. A philosophy statement will and should evolve throughout one's career. Most likely, this statement will be short and narrow in scope when starting out. For the novice teacher, the statement may include expectations of oneself. Yet, as the teaching career evolves, the statement should also evolve and mature, including details and examples, pinpointing and affirming one's beliefs and values of teaching, and better clarifying one's approach within teaching. For example, questions to consider can include why do you teach, what do you teach, who do you teach, how do you teach, and how do you measure your effectiveness?

A statement of teaching philosophy is traditionally one to two pages in length. This narrative statement is written in first person, present tense. Beyond this, there are no set rules, formulas, or format. The only "rule" is that the statement coherently discusses who the author is as a teacher. A teaching philosophy statement should be unique to the individual, although there are some basic elements, listed subsequently, that can be considered when devising such a statement.

- **Identify your personal values as a teacher.** What is important to you when teaching? Describe your personal teaching style. How do you approach your lesson plans and/or conduct your classroom?
- **Identify the goals you set for your students.** What do you want students to take away from your classes? How do you approach setting goals for your students?
- **Share assumptions you have about teaching and learning.** What do you believe the dynamic should be between teachers and students in the classroom? What views do you have about the learning process? What does the learning process look like from your perspective? How do you facilitate learning? What methods and approaches do you utilize?
- **Offer your process for assessing teaching effectiveness.** How do you determine when you have succeeded as a teacher? How do you self-reflect and/or pivot?
- **Detail the difference(s) you want to make as an educator.** Why do you teach? What is the change that extends from your classroom?
- **Consider diversity, equity, and inclusion initiatives.** How is your teaching inclusive of all individuals? (While this area is important to include within your teaching philosophy, job applications may ask for an entirely separate diversity, equity, and inclusion statement.)

A statement of teaching philosophy is individual to the teacher who has created it. It should not reflect the teaching style or beliefs of someone else, but rather be unique to you. When devising your statement, the inclusion of metaphors is helpful, but do not over embellish with superfluous language that you would not normally use. This can be a distraction and creates a false representation of you as an individual. Allow your statement to encompass the essence of you and what you as an educator believe and practice, but refrain from including statements and phrases of what you think others want to hear. Of course, you want to make it memorable, but do not overdo it. Allow your statement to be a true reflection of who you are as a dance teacher.

THE ROLE OF A STUDENT

We have discussed in detail the role of the teacher within the dance class. But what about the role of the student? What influence does the student have within the learning atmosphere? What responsibilities lie with the student in acquiring skill and artistry or any of the other benefits of dance detailed in Chapter 1?

You may have heard the saying "You can lead a horse to water, but you cannot make them drink." The same is true for a student in the learning environment. A teacher can provide all of the tools, material, and encouragement required for a student to learn, yet unless the student desires and is ready to learn and puts forth their own effort, they will not gain the necessary skill or improve their ability. For skill acquisition to occur, students must be active participants in the learning process. Following is a list of qualities that the teacher expects the student to bring to the dance classroom. While it is not exhaustive, it does offer a starting point which a teacher can use in dialogue with students.

- **Willingness to learn** – Students should come to class with a desire to learn. Those who are invested in the process and willing to explore and engage in movement activities will reap the most benefits. Teachers should encourage regular attendance among students and discover ways to motivate and encourage student engagement.
- **Open-mindedness** – Students should be receptive to new perspectives and ideas and welcome feedback. Students who are closed off to any of these will find difficulty in acquiring skill and improving in their technique.
- **Mutual respect** – It is expected that students will trust the knowledge and expertise of their educator and treat them with respect. Students should be considerate of not only the instructor but also other students or accompanists within the classroom. Teachers should instill within students a respect for the art of dance as they also foster students' respect for their own work and bodies.
- **Curiosity** – Students should be curious. An engaged student will be inquisitive and interested in exploring movement and discovering new ways to express ideas with the body.
- **Effort** – Teachers expect that students will engage and work hard in class. Without the application of practice, within and outside of class, skill acquisition cannot occur.
- **Communication** – Students need to listen to their instructor and demonstrate professionalism and respect; however, they should feel empowered to appropriately communicate with their teachers. When something does not feel right or make sense, the student should be able to articulate their needs or convey questions or concerns.

FIGURE 2.3 Older students engage in a tap dance class.
Source: Photo by Clinton Lewis/Western Kentucky University.

The dance educator should model the desired qualities and behaviors they wish to see in their students. Children especially are continually observing the actions of peers and leaders around them. The teacher who demonstrates the classroom etiquette, including the attire and conduct that they expect students to produce, will notice these attitudes reciprocated among their students.

Box 2.4 Conditioning for the Student

Chapter 1 delineated the many benefits of dance, including the physical advantages. While dance can positively contribute to the physical development of an individual, the dance class alone does not provide ample opportunity to fully condition one's body for all the physical and technical demands of dance technique and performance. As a dancer advances in level, they will find supplemental body conditioning beyond the dance class to be paramount to their success in acquiring advanced technical competency and performance ability, specifically if they wish to pursue dance to a professional level.

The dance teacher should encourage students to work on flexibility and strength training outside of class and provide students with options to do so. This might include teaching conditioning exercises within the regular dance class that students can then continue to work on at home, offering a stand-alone dance conditioning class, sharing information about other fitness programs – such as Pilates or yoga – that students could join, or establishing weekly conditioning challenges for the class. It is important that the teacher informs students as to why body conditioning is important and how the various exercises and programs benefit their bodies and their dancing so that they understand the connection, are motivated to engage in various conditioning, and have a goal in mind. The teacher should never approach body conditioning as a weight loss method with children but rather a strength-gaining opportunity that can improve their mind-body connection and ultimately enhance their movement capabilities. It is also important to note that overstretching solely for the purpose of enhanced movement tricks can also cause physical harm to students. Chapter 11 provides detailed information regarding injury prevention.

CHAPTER SUMMARY

Teaching dance is both an innate and developed skill. It is a profession for which not all dancers may be suited, yet those who choose this path will discover a career full of joy and rewards as well as challenges. Whether instructing within the private sector, the educational system, or a professional setting, the primary role of the dance educator is to teach technique and artistry to their students while passing on the tradition of the dance form. Regardless of the setting, teaching styles may vary. Some examples include the authoritarian, collaborative, physical, or anatomy-based teacher. While dance teachers may have a range of personalities, there are certain distinguishable characteristics that highly effective dance teachers often have in common, such as competency in advanced knowledge and skill of dance technique, understanding of anatomy and kinesiology as it pertains to dance, musical awareness, patience, and passion for the art of dance and teaching. Constructing a teaching philosophy statement can help an individual connect to the type and style of teacher they are or wish to be. This self-reflective statement reminds the teacher of *who* they are as a teacher, *why* they teach, along with their personal guidelines for *how* they will teach. Understanding the role of the student within the dance class setting can provide the teacher greater opportunity to educate, interact with, and inspire a generation of learners.

PRACTICAL APPLICATIONS

1   Do you want to be a dance teacher? Why or why not?

2   What do you believe to be the most challenging aspect of teaching dance? Why?

3   Reflect on a dance teacher that you have had in the past or are currently studying with today. How would you describe their teaching style? What personal characteristics do they possess that contribute to their success or ineffectiveness in the classroom?

4   How do you describe an effective dance teacher? What do you think are the most important characteristics of an effective dance teacher? Why?

5   What do you think your strength(s) as a teacher will be? What do you think your weakness(es) will be? What steps can you take to further develop your strength(s) and improve upon your weakness(es)?

6 Why is it important for you to have a personal teaching philosophy? How do you fore-see your teaching philosophy changing over the next, 10, 20, 30 years?

7 What do you believe to be the most important quality in a dance student? Why?

BIBLIOGRAPHY

Ambrosio, Nora. *The Excellent Instructor and the Teaching of Dance Technique*. Dubuque, IA: Kendall Hunt Publishing Company, 2018.

Chapnick, Adam. "How to Write a Philosophy of Teaching and Learning Statement." *Magna Publication: Faculty Focus* (2009): 4–5. https://promoteach.net.technion.ac.il/files/2017/01/Philosophy-of-Teaching-Statements.pdf, accessed June 2022.

Clark, Amanda, and Sara Pecina. *Dance Appreciation*. London: Routledge, Taylor & Francis Group, 2021.

Haywood, Kathleen, and Nancy Getchell. *Life Span Motor Development*. 5th ed. Champaign, IL: Human Kinetics, 2009.

Kassing, Gayle, and Danielle M. Jay. *Dance Teaching Methods and Curriculum Design*. 2nd ed. Champaign, IL: Human Kinetics, 2021.

Ramani, P.N. "Writing a Teaching Philosophy: Why, What and How." *Magna Publication: Faculty Focus* (2009): 17–19. https://promoteach.net.technion.ac.il/files/2017/01/Philosophy-of-Teaching-Statements.pdf, accessed June 2022.

Schlaich, Joan, and Betty DuPont. *The Art of Teaching Dance Technique*. Reston, VA: National Dance Association, an Association of the American Alliance for Health, Physical Education, Recreation & Dance, 1996.

Willis, Cheryl M. *Dance Education Tips from the Trenches*. Champaign, IL: Human Kinetics, 2004.

CHAPTER 3

Fundamentals of Human Anatomy

Sara Pecina

Box 3.1 Chapter Objectives

After reading this chapter, you will be able to:

- Describe anatomical structures and movements using the basic terminology of anatomy and kinesiology
- Articulate how the muscular and skeletal systems work together to create movement
- Recognize the major bones, ligaments, and tendons involved in various movements and understand the ways in which they work together to articulate the joints

Box 3.2 Chapter Vocabulary

abduction
adduction
agonist
antagonist
cartilage
concentric contraction
depression
dorsiflexion
eccentric contraction
elevation
eversion
extension
external rotation
flexion
hyperextension
hypermobility

DOI: 10.4324/b22952-5

internal rotation
inversion
isometric contraction
ligament
plantar flexion
scoliosis
stabilizer
synergist
tendon

The human body and all of its anatomical components are the dancer's instrument. Just as a trumpet player must have an understanding of how their trumpet produces and manipulates sound in order to make music, a dancer should have knowledge of the science behind how their body moves. Likewise, a trumpet instructor should have a deeper understanding of the mechanics of the instrument in order to educate and guide the student, and a dance teacher must have enhanced knowledge of the musculoskeletal system and its movements in order to train dancers in technique, create and set choreography on dancers, and prevent injuries in their students.

Throughout the course of their training, it is common for advanced dance students to become interested in or fascinated by the mechanics of the human body. The responsibility of the dance teacher is to be able to answer, adequately seek answers, or properly guide students to another source for answers to questions relating to the science behind movement. Because of this subject's importance, many institutions that offer degrees or certifications in dance include a separate Anatomy and Kinesiology for Dance course in their curricula. For the aspiring or current dance teacher who has not had the opportunity to take such a course, basic anatomy and musculoskeletal function are discussed in this chapter, as well as examples of how they relate to alignment or movement in dance. Since this book focuses on dance and motor control and development, this anatomy chapter focuses on external body movement with bones, joints, and muscles as the foundation of this discussion, rather than systems such as the respiratory or cardiovascular system or organs in the body. The nervous and sensory systems are discussed in Chapter 4, and injury prevention is discussed in Chapter 11. This information will help facilitate discussion of material in later chapters and between students and teachers.

ANATOMICAL TERMINOLOGY

In order to discuss the human body, one must first understand anatomical terminology as it relates to navigating structures, planes of the body, and directions of movement. This terminology is predominantly rooted in Latin and Greek and used universally across

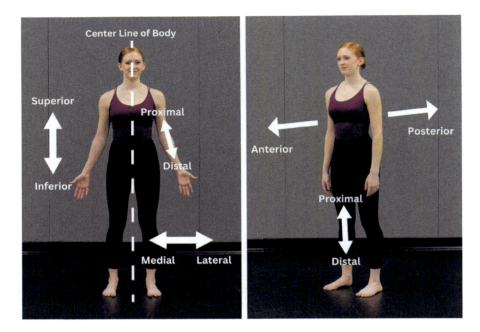

FIGURE 3.1 Diagram of the various terminology to map the body.
Source: Photo by Clinton Lewis/Western Kentucky University.

sciences and disciplines. These terms are based on the anatomical neutral position, in which the body is standing upright, feet flat, toes pointed forward, arms hanging by the sides, and palms turned to the front. (See Figure 3.1).

Mapping the Body

There are multiple ways to identify location in the human body. These organizational terms describe anatomical structures in relation to other structures in the body (e.g., the fifth metatarsal is lateral of the first metatarsal) as well as specific landmarks on one structure (e.g., the anterior superior iliac crest of the pelvis). Each term has a counterpart describing the opposite direction, so the words are learned in pairs. This vocabulary is foundational for anyone attempting to learn about body mechanics; it can also be useful in describing the location of pain to dance teachers or doctors.

When using the description **anterior**, it means that the structure is towards the front of the body, while **posterior** describes a structure to the back side of the body. Based on the anatomical neutral position, the toes are anterior to the heels, or the sternum (chest bone) is anterior to the spine. In ballet training, a common alignment issue is the anterior or posterior tilt of the pelvis. A typical imagery tool used for the pelvis is to imagine it as a bowl full of water. If the pelvis is in an anterior tilt, the bowl would be spilling water towards the front of the body. Dance teachers generally refer to this as arching the lower back as this position releases the lower abdominals and emphasizes the curve of the lumbar spine.

In contrast, a posterior pelvic tilt would cause water to spill out towards the back of the body, which dance teachers commonly refer to as "tucking." Meanwhile, in jazz classes, dance teachers utilize both the anterior and posterior pelvic tilts in isolations as a means to train dancers to articulate the body; through isolating the pelvis, jazz dancers create nuanced stylings in their movement.

When discussing lateral and medial, one must picture an imaginary line that splits the body in half with the right and left sides divided equally. The **medial** direction is towards this centerline of the body; the **lateral** direction is away from the centerline. For instance, in the anatomical neutral position, the clavicle, or "collarbone," is lateral of the sternum. Superior and inferior refer to positions above or below each other. When described as **superior**, the point is above; when described as **inferior** the point is below. The shoulder joint is superior to the hip joint, and the ankles are inferior to the knees.

Proximal and distal reference the distance from the trunk of the body or a major joint. A point in a **proximal** location is closer to the trunk or joint in question, which means that a point in a **distal** location is further away from the trunk or joint. When considering the trunk, the shoulder is proximal while the wrist is distal. If discussing points in reference to a major joint, for example the hip, the femoral head is proximal while the shaft of the femur is distal. The last two terms relate to the distance from the surface of the skin. Deep refers to a point farther away from the surface of the skin, and superficial is a point closer to the surface. The humerus bone in the upper arm is deep compared to the bicep muscles.

Though these ten terms are not frequently used verbatim in the dance classroom, they equip the reader to learn more about the structures of the body and understand research in dance science. The knowledge of these terms and their meanings helps deepen the dance students' cognitive and intellectual experience in dance through physical understanding and kinesthetic awareness of the movements in which they are training. This language also provides common ground for communication among teachers, students, and medical professionals if an injury does occur.

Planes of the Body

When discussing movement, there are three planes of the body to consider. The **sagittal plane** divides the right and left sides of the body in half symmetrically; *arabesque* and tap dance trenches happen in the sagittal plane. The **frontal plane** divides the front and back of the body in half. Movements like cartwheels and lateral Ts occur in the frontal plane. The **transverse plane** divides the top and bottom of the body in half; spiral actions take place in the transverse plane. Most dance movements involve more than one plane. A deeper understanding of the ways the body moves in space aids the dance teacher in explaining and correcting movement with students. (See Figures 3.2 and 3.3.)

Directions of Movement

Dance relies on the directions of movement being used. Anatomically, there are a limited number of directions each joint can move, each of which have a term to describe it. Later in this chapter, we will look at the specific structures of the major joints and muscles

42 Exploration of Dance Pedagogy

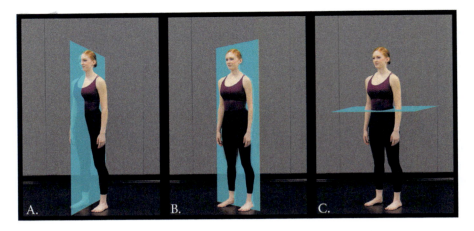

FIGURE 3.2 Diagram of the planes intersecting the body: A. sagittal plane/B. frontal plane/C. transverse plane.

Source: Photo by Clinton Lewis/Western Kentucky University

FIGURE 3.3 Diagram of dance movement within the anatomical planes.

Source: Photos by Jeffrey Smith/Western Kentucky University

involved in dance. Here, we explore the variety of types of movements in the body. Similar to the mapping terminology, each term has an opposite that describes the inverse movement. This language also helps instructors evaluate what is happening during a variety of movements and how to assess mistakes being made by students.

Perhaps the most commonly known directions of movement are flexion and extension. **Flexion** describes the bending or folding of a joint that produces an angle between the two bones forming said joint; **extension** is straightening or stretching of a joint, often causing the two bones of the joint to come into a straight line. When lifting the leg to a *retiré* position, flexion occurs at both the hip and the knee moving into position, and extension happens in these joints while returning the foot to the floor. Furthermore, **plantar flexion** is

Fundamentals of Human Anatomy   43

the action of pointing the foot, as the bottom or sole of the foot is the plantar surface. The opposition is **dorsiflexion** or flexing the foot, since the top of the foot is the dorsal surface. **Abduction** is movement away from the midline of the body, and conversely, **adduction** is movement towards the center of the body. Both abduction and adduction happen in the sagittal plane; a *battement* to second is considered abduction on the way up and adduction on the way down.

Rotation occurs when a bone can rotate on the center axis of the joint. Lateral or **external rotation** moves part of the body outward, for instance, the turnout used to create first position in ballet. Medial or **internal rotation** moves part of the body inward, which occurs when moving the palm of the hand from the anatomical neutral position to facing the leg. Inversion and eversion of the foot occurs at the ankle joint and moves in the frontal plane. **Inversion** turns the sole of the foot, or plantar surface, towards the midline of the body. In dance, this is commonly referred to as sickling the foot. **Eversion** is the opposite effect in which the sole of the foot turns away from the midline of the body. In ballet, dancers often use eversion to "wing" their foot in the *arabesque* position. Tap dancers use both positions in the flash step called a wing; the foot inverts during the ascent and everts during the descent to achieve the necessary sounds. Lastly, the scapulae and jawbone are able to elevate and depress. When the shoulders are raised upwards towards the ears, they are in **elevation**. In opposition, when the shoulders are pressed down towards the waistline, they are in **depression**. Table 3.1 summarizes the various directions of movement.

The body is able to move in a multitude of fascinating ways. Dance artists become experts in this movement through rigorous training of the body and dance technique in any form. An analytical understanding of the mechanics of the body strengthens the dancer's connection to their instrument and increases the dance teacher's comprehension of the movement that they are teaching.

TABLE 3.1 Depiction of various directions of movement of the body and their opposites.

Directions of Movement

Term	Movement	Opposite Term	Opposite Movement
Flexion	bending of a joint	**Extension**	straightening of a joint
Plantar flexion	pointing the foot	**Dorsiflexion**	flexing the foot
Abduction	movement away from the midline of the body	**Adduction**	movement towards the midline of the body
External rotation	rotation away from the midline of the body	**Internal rotation**	rotation towards the midline of the body
Inversion	turning the sole of the foot towards the midline of the body	**Eversion**	turning the sole of the foot away from the midline of the body
Elevation	upward movement	**Depression**	downward movement

SYSTEMS OF MOVEMENT

When considering external movement, there are three main systems to study. The muscles move the bones which are connected at joints. In other words, in order to understand how the body moves, there must be knowledge of the structure and actions of muscles upon the skeletal system and how joints are built to facilitate specific types of movement. Other systems to examine include the nervous and sensory systems; both of these are discussed in Chapter 4.

Muscular System

Muscles are responsible for all movement in the body; they are meaty structures that can be made of three different types of fiber. The muscle type that controls bodily movement is the skeletal muscles, which are made of striated fibers. This type of muscle is moved voluntarily; it is controlled by the brain and nervous system and includes the muscles responsible for limb movement, facial expressions, and respiration. Skeletal muscle is composed of bundles of fiber wrapped in connective tissue that runs lengthwise along the muscle belly. Each muscle has both an origin and insertion point on a bone or bones. These attachments are made by **tendons**, which are made of fibrous connective tissues and are extremely strong and not very elastic, or stretchy.

When a muscle contracts, the brain sends a message to the muscle stimulating the nerves, and a chemical reaction occurs that causes the muscle fibers to shorten, usually pulling both ends of the muscle towards the middle.[1] These contractions serve the different purposes of producing movement, stabilizing, or braking. Each purpose utilizes a different type of contraction. The most commonly understood is the **concentric contraction**, when the muscle fibers shorten to produce movement, such as the hamstrings on the posterior side of the femur contracting when bending the leg in a *passé*. An **isometric contraction** helps ligaments stabilize a structure; the muscle fibers neither straighten or lengthen. Isometric contractions occur around the ankle joint when balancing in any position. During an **eccentric contraction**, the muscle works against gravity to provide a stopping action; most of the muscle is lengthening while some elements contract to control the descent of the limb or body part, such as the various arm and chest muscles when lowering the body during a push-up.

Multiple muscles work together to complete a single movement. When skeletal muscles work together, they fall into one of four categories. A muscle working as an **agonist** is using concentric contractions to produce movement. There are both primary and secondary agonists for each movement; the primary muscles in an action are the most productive in creating the movement, while secondary muscles assist. The **antagonist** is located opposite of the agonist and either relaxes and lengthens to allow the movement to happen or contract to aid in the movement. A muscle working as a **stabilizer** holds a joint firm to allow other movement to happen. For instance, when a dance teacher reminds a student to focus on their supporting leg, they are reminding the dancer to pay attention to the isometric contractions provided by the stabilizers. **Synergists** work with the other muscles to either promote or neutralize movement and can define the way the movement is executed.

All of these details come heavily into play for every dance movement. The muscles work together as a kind of symphony controlled by the dancing artist to create movement in space. For example, during a simple *battement* tilt, we see each type of contraction category at work. While the leg is elevating, the quadriceps work as agonists performing concentric contractions

HOW DO MUSCLES WORK

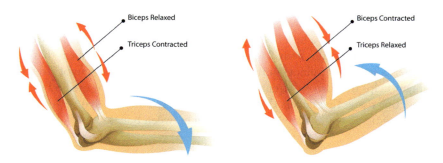

FIGURE 3.4 In this image, we see the movement of extension of the elbow completed with the triceps working as the agonists and biceps as the antagonists on the left. The opposite is true for the image on the right. Here, the elbow is in flexion, with the biceps working as agonists, while the triceps work as antagonists.

Source: Photo by grayjay/Shutterstock.com.

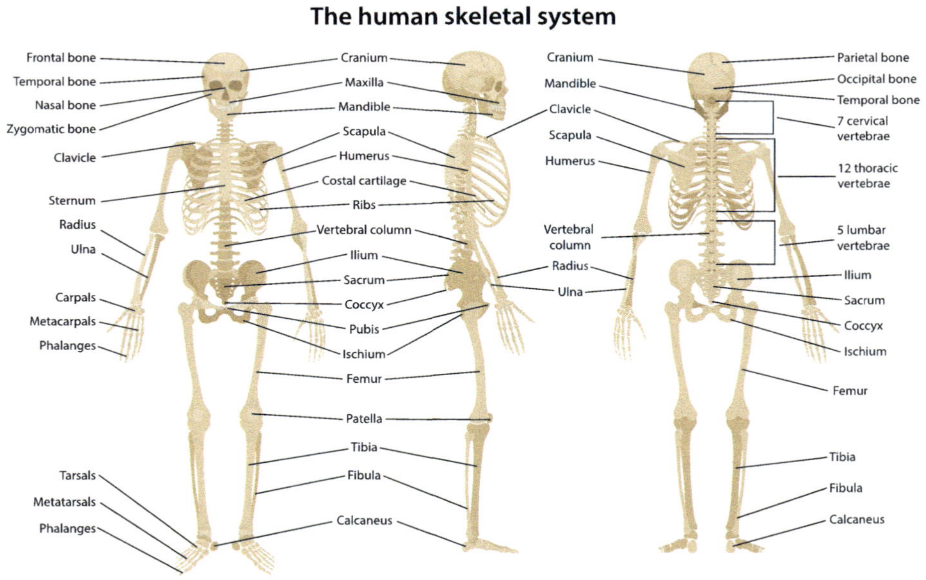

FIGURE 3.5 An anatomical image of the human skeleton.
Source: Photo by Olga Bolbot/Shutterstock.com.

to produce movement of the leg, and the hamstrings work as antagonists and lengthen to allow the movement to happen. The muscles of the standing leg use isometric contractions to work as a stabilizer, while smaller muscles within the hip function as synergists to aid in the action. As the leg descends from the height of the *battement* tilt, the same muscles that lifted the leg will use eccentric contractions to prevent the leg from simply falling.

Skeletal System

The skeletal structure of the body is shaped by 206 bones and also includes the cartilage and ligaments in the body. These structures support the body, protect organs, and serve as levers for the muscles to be able to move the body. Bones are living structures that are stable and hard but contain a bit of elasticity. There are long bones, short bones, and flat bones located throughout the body. **Ligaments** are bundles of strong fibers that connect bones to other bones; they cannot contract like muscles do, and most cannot stretch at all. Each ligament helps to passively strengthen and stabilize the joints of the body. **Cartilage** is the connective tissue that covers the articulating surfaces of bones. It serves to protect underlying bone tissue while allowing some sliding between bones.

Joints

A joint is where two bones meet; they allow movement between these bones. Different types of joints have varying degrees of mobility depending on their structure. This structure likewise determines how stable individual joints are. Most major dance movements are performed in synovial joints, which have a free movement range. In a synovial joint, the ends of bones are covered by cartilage and lubricated by synovial fluid. There are many types of joints in the body, which will be discussed more in depth in the structures section of this chapter.

Box 3.3 Hypermobility and Hyperextension

Hypermobility and hyperextension are similar to each other but also distinct. Both create an unusually large range of motion in a joint. Either could be present in just one or in multiple joints. **Hypermobility** stems from loose connective tissues in a joint or joints; in essence the joint is less stable because the tissues connecting the bones are weaker or abnormally loose. This extra flexibility can be inherited through an abnormality of the connective tissue, or attained through hard work and proper stretching in which the connective tissues are gradually stretched. **Hyperextension** allows a joint to straighten past the neutral or 180-degree range. This is caused by the shapes of one or multiple bones located in that joint. The head of a bone may be shallower, and/or the divot of the opposing bone may be deeper than average.

Often the dance aesthetic favors hypermobile joints. Ballet and modern dance exaggerate long lines created by the limbs. In these dance forms, hypermobility or hyperextension particularly of the hips, knees, ankles, and feet are desired to create extreme lines in various positions. Some hip-hop or break dancers utilize this increased flexibility to exaggerate the angles of the body or perform more extreme poses or freezes. Social and promotional media regularly feature photos of dancers in positions accentuating maximal bending of the joints; thus dancers learn to aspire to move the same way. Though the world of dance may nurture and promote these extreme uses of the joints, dance teachers and students must be wary of how they are utilized. Hypermobility and hyperextension both put dancers at greater risk of injury, decrease the effectiveness of proprioception, and cause the body to take longer to heal after an injury occurs.

Any dancer with hypermobility and/or hyperextension must be trained how to safely use this flexibility in their joints. In order to compensate for weaker or overstretched connective tissues, strength training in the surrounding muscles should be emphasized to help protect the joint. Dancers with hyperextension must work to develop the proprioception of the true neutral 180-degree angle, which to them will feel bent. However, this is crucial as hyperextension should never be used on a limb that is weight bearing, including the supporting leg during an extension or the weight bearing arm/s during floorwork. Teachers must be observant of students who are hypermobile and/or hyperextended and safely guide these dancers in movement. If proper precaution and training take place, injury can be avoided.

STRUCTURES OF ANATOMY

To truly understand the movements occurring at joints, one must have knowledge of the individual parts at play and how they interact. Each joint is composed of unique structures often with complicated mechanisms. Individual joint types, bones, ligaments, muscles, and tendons work together to create movement. An instructor should be equipped with a basic knowledge of kinesiology to better understand the movement that they teach, foster safe practice in their studio, and enhance communication with students. The details explored in this section are not comprehensive for each joint; instead we look at the most prominent structures involved in dance movement.

Torso and Spine

The torso is also known as the trunk of the body. This is where the limbs, or arms and legs, join the rest of the body and the major internal organs – excluding the brain – are housed. The main bony structures in the torso are the spine, rib cage, and pelvis. The pelvis will be examined in depth in the discussion of the hips; here we will focus on the spine and rib cage.

Bones and Joints of the Torso and Spine

The spine is made up of 33 strong bones called vertebrae and is capable of moving multiple directions including bending forward (flexion), backwards (extension), and sideways, as well as rotating (spiraling). Some vertebrae are also connected by ligaments or muscles and tendons to the skull, shoulders, rib cage, pelvis, and legs, making the spine central to the entire skeletal system. In addition to providing movement, the spine stabilizes the torso, protects the spinal cord (a part of the central nervous system), and absorbs shock, for instance when landing a jump. In between each vertebra, there is a gelatinous disc surrounded by strong fibers. These discs cushion the vertebrae between each other, equally distribute weight through the vertebral column, and aid in shock absorption for all types of movement.

The spine is divided into five segments. The most superior is the cervical spine, made up of seven vertebrae. The cervical spine carries the head, which is the heaviest part of the body. The first vertebra (C1) is roughly directly posterior of the nose. Included in the cervical spine are two unique vertebrae called the atlas (C1) and the axis (C2); these two vertebrae are shaped differently than the others and give the head its large range of motion for rotation, such as when spotting a turn.

The second segment is the thoracic spine, which consists of 12 vertebrae (T1 through T12). Each of these vertebrae connect to one of the 12 ribs that form the rib cage. The rib cage primarily protects vital organs and blood vessels, but it does allow some movement. The first ten ribs connect either directly or indirectly with the sternum, or chest bone, located centrally on the anterior side of the torso. This is the bone which dancers lift to the sky during a high release. The last two ribs are described as floating because they are only attached to vertebrae, not the sternum.

Below the thoracic spine is the lumbar spine, comprised of five vertebrae (L1 through L5). Since this section bears the weight of the first two, these are the largest vertebrae. The lumbar spine does not have much mobility as its roles are primarily weight bearing and stability. The last two segments of the spine are each fused. The sacrum is located in the posterior section of the pelvis and made up of five fused vertebrae. The most inferior section is the coccyx formed by four fused vertebrae.

Each segment of the spine features a natural curve to facilitate movement and aid in shock absorption. These curves are one of two types; **lordosis** curves towards the front of the body, and **kyphosis** curves towards the back of the body. Sequentially, the curves of the spine are cervical lordosis, thoracic kyphosis, lumbar lordosis, and sacral kyphosis. An exaggerated curve in any of the segments is a type of disorder that can limit mobility and cause injury. Additionally, **scoliosis** is the unnatural curvature of the spine to the right or left, creating an 'S' shape in an x-ray when viewed anteriorly or posteriorly. The primary curve can occur at a variety of segments in the spine, and this location determines what other limbs or parts of the body will be most affected. Some cases of scoliosis can be corrected while others cannot. It is imperative for a dance teacher to understand the limitations scoliosis places on the student's mobility, flexibility, and partner work and to not push harder than the spine is able to handle.

Muscles of the Torso and Spine

Within the spine, there are over 100 joints involving more than 200 muscles.[2] The erector spinae are small interwoven muscles that connect a vertebra to the adjacent vertebrae or skip over the adjacent vertebrae to connect to the next. These muscles run along the entire length of the spine and primarily assist in extension and lateral flexion of the spine. Deeper and larger muscles connect vertebrae to various other structures to stabilize the spine. Finally, a variety of muscles connect the spine to key bony landmarks of the limbs to aid in movement.

Dancers are constantly reminded to "use" or engage their core. While many only think of the abdominals with this cue, the core actually consists of the abdominals, back extensors, pelvic floor, and diaphragm; this creates the three-dimensional core. The abdominals are a complex, multilayer system of muscles that run in various directions. This group of muscles is mainly involved in flexion and rotation of the torso and stabilization.

VERTEBRAL COLUMN

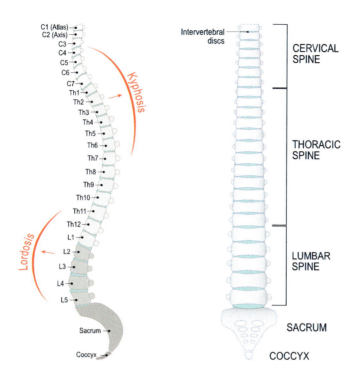

FIGURE 3.6 The human spinal column. The first image is a lateral view from the left showing each of the five sections (cervical, thoracic, lumbar, sacral, and coccygeal) and labeling the two types of curves. The second image is a posterior view of the spinal column.

Source: Photo by Designua/Shutterstock.com.

The rectus abdominis originates at the sternum and ribs and inserts at the pubic bone, running longitudinally down the front of the body on either side of the midline. It is divided vertically (by the linea alba) and horizontally by tendinous fibers, thus creating the look of the coveted "six-pack." This muscle is mainly responsible for flexing the spine and aiding in stabilizing and aligning the pelvis.

The external and internal obliques run in more or less opposing diagonals. The external obliques originate at ribs five through 12 and insert at the linea alba and pubic bone, while the internal obliques originate at the pelvis and insert at the cartilage connecting ribs eight through 12 to the sternum. Together, these muscles rotate and flex the torso. Lastly, the transverse abdominis is the deepest of these muscles. Its fibers run horizontally around the torso, acting like a belt or corset with the main purpose of stabilization.

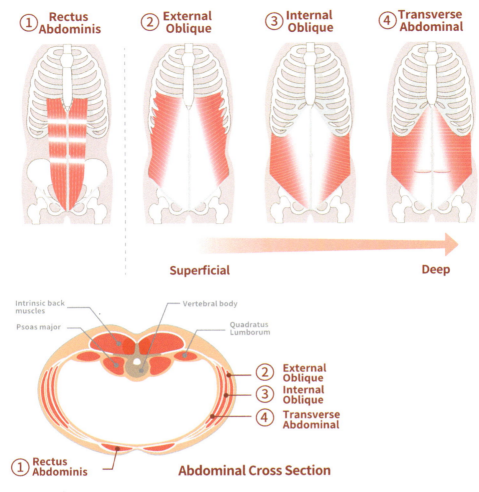

FIGURE 3.7 Diagram of the core muscles labeled from anterior and superior views.
Source: Photo by suma2020/Shutterstock.com.

Hips

The structures surrounding the hips are used for stabilization and movement of the legs and torso. Dance commonly pushes artists to extreme use of their hips. In general, the hips are a relatively stable joint; however, the frequency of and drastic range of motion that a dancer's hips sustain can cause injury. For example, labral tears are common in dancers and could require surgery. Teachers must know how to correctly articulate the hip to avoid this type of injury in their students.

Bones and Joints of the Hips

The hip joint is a ball and socket joint made up of the pelvis and femur, or upper leg bone. A ball and socket joint consists of one bone with a rounded head, in this case the femur, inserting into a socket-like pocket – in the hip known as the acetabulum – of another bone, here the pelvis. The acetabulum is covered by the labrum, which is fibrous cartilage, to stabilize the joint. Individuals are built slightly differently; some people have a relatively shallow socket in their hip, allowing for greater range of motion, while others may have a deeper pocket that can restrict movement. One reason ballet dancers utilize turnout, or external rotation of the hips, is that the way the femur head is rotated in the hip socket allows for a greater range of motion when lifting the leg. This joint is connected with three strong ligaments between the femur and pelvis; this structure is commonly referred to as the "Y" ligament as it creates a y-shape. The hip joint is able to flex, extend, abduct, adduct, and externally and internally rotate. Additionally, the pelvis is capable of tilting as a unit on the horizontal axis (tuck or arch), sagittal axis (lifting the left or right side), and vertical axis (twisting right or left).

The pelvis is the second heaviest part of the body. This large bone structure helps to stabilize the body as it articulates with the spine and the femur, which is the strongest and longest bone of the body. Dancers use the pelvis to analyze alignment or add accents and stylization to movement. The pelvis is made up of the ilium, ischium, and pubic bones, one of each on each the right and left side of the body, fused together. The sacrum of the spine sits between the two pubic bones.

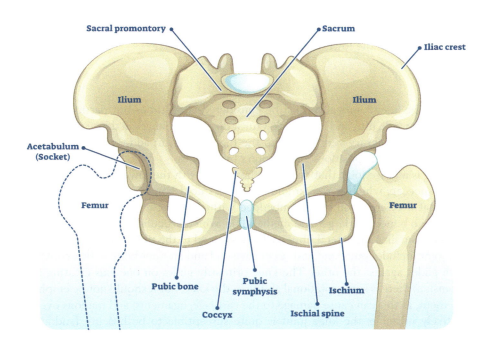

FIGURE 3.8 Anterior view of the hip joint.

Source: Photo by VectorMine/Shutterstock.com.

52 Exploration of Dance Pedagogy

Dance teachers often refer to the "bony part of the front of the hip," which in actuality is the anterior superior iliac spine (ASIS). This landmark is often utilized to observe whether or not the pelvis is level. A cue for young dancers is often to imagine headlights on the ASIS on each side and point them directly to the front in order to keep their hips square. When working in a seated position, teachers commonly refer to the sit bones that can be felt on the ground; anatomically these are the ischial tuberosities, a bony protuberance on the ischium on each side of the pelvis.

Muscles of the Hips

The muscles of the core and the upper leg all intersect at the hip joint, making it a power-house for stability and movement. Since the previous section discussed the trunk, we will focus on the muscles that articulate the femur in the pelvis. The main muscle groups moving this joint are the glutes, quadriceps, and hamstrings. The glutes are primarily located on the posterior of the pelvis and are a very strong muscle group. The gluteus maximus originates along the ilium and inserts on the femur; the gluteus medius is smaller and aids the gluteus maximus. The glutes are agonists in the extension of the hip. A group of small muscles deeper than the glutes, known as the "deep six," are primarily responsible for externally rotating the hip.

The quadriceps are named as such because this is a group of four muscles. Only one, the rectus femoris, is attached to the pelvis; this is an agonist in flexing the hip. Among the muscles aiding in this movement are the sartorius and psoas major. The psoas major is a unique muscle that originates on the lumbar spine, travels through the pelvis, and attaches to the femur. The hamstrings consist of three muscles – including the biceps femoris – which aid in extending the hip, such as in an *arabesque*. These muscles originate on the pelvis and insert into the lower leg.

Knees

Function of the knee joints also must be considered at all times but particularly during jumps, partner work, lifts, and floorwork. Quick direction changes in dance make the knee joint susceptible to injury very similar to the football player; additionally, dancers regularly use more extreme positions and flexion of the knees.

The knee is a hinge joint that connects the femur with the lower leg and includes the patella or kneecap, which is a sesamoid bone. Sesamoid bones are different from other bones in that they are small bones embedded within a muscle or tendon. The lower leg consists of two bones: the larger and medial tibia, which articulates with the femur at the knee, and the smaller and lateral fibula, which is joined to the tibia with connective tissue. A hinge joint includes one bone with a concave end and another bone with a convex end, and each glides against the other. The knee primarily glides on one axis creating flexion and extension; there is some rotational ability in the knee, but it should not be emphasized in movement, as this can cause damage to the cartilage, ligaments, and tendons over time.

Relatively unstable, the knee joint is quite susceptible to both acute (sudden) and overuse injuries in dance. The cruciate ligaments are so named because they cross each other at the joint; these are the most important ligaments in the knee. The anterior and posterior cruciate ligaments are towards the center of the joint, connecting the femur to the tibia, and help stabilize the knee when in flexion. A common injury heard of in many athletic activities is the tearing of the anterior cruciate ligament (or ACL) in the knee. The quadriceps work to extend the knee, and the hamstrings flex the knee. All originate on either the pelvis or femur and insert into the tibia or fibula.

The third bone that articulates at this joint is the patella. The posterior side of the patella glides along a groove at the front of the femur. The tendon of the quadriceps femoris inserts at the superior end of the patella, and the inferior end is connected to the tibia by the patellar ligament. This bone helps to protect the muscle in which it is embedded when the knee is in flexion, and provides leverage for knee extension. Weight should never be born directly on the patella in any type of floorwork or partner work; likewise, a partner should never use the back of the knee to grab, hold, or lift the other dancer.

Ankles and Feet

The ankles and feet endure a tremendous amount of stress in every dance form, with a majority of dance injuries occurring in the lower leg. The joints in the ankles and feet are often pushed to the extreme – for example in *pointe* work – while bearing the weight of the entire body. Additionally, for aesthetic, percussive, or stylistic reasons, the shoes worn by dancers lack cushion and support for the demands of the movement. The ankles are involved in nearly every movement, and the feet provide the foundation for the entire body. For these reasons, it is paramount for the dance teacher to understand the structures of which we demand so much in order to properly and safely train their students.

Bones and Joints of the Ankles and Feet

The ankle joint connects the lower leg to the base of the foot. This is a highly mobile joint that is able to plantar flex, dorsiflex, invert, and evert while remaining relatively stable. The malleoli, the protruding bones in the ankle, are actually the bases of the tibia and fibula. Specifically in the upper ankle joint, the tibia and fibula are joined to the talus. The lower ankle joint consists of four bones of the foot including the calcaneus, or heel.

A number of ligaments support the ankle joint. The three most well-known are in the upper ankle joint extending from the lateral malleolus of the fibula to the talus and calcaneus. The anterior talofibular ligament goes from the lateral malleolus forward to the talus. In opposition, the posterior talofibular ligament begins at the lateral malleolus and goes backward to the talus. Lastly, the calcaneofibular ligament connects the lateral malleolus to the lateral side of the calcaneus. It is interesting to note that the anterior talofibular ligament and calcaneofibular ligaments are the most commonly sprained, as these are the most susceptible to being overstretched when landing incorrectly from a jump or lift.

The bones of the foot can be considered in three sections. The hindfoot, or tarsus, is the posterior and ankle joint section and made up of the talus, calcaneus, cuboid, navicular, and three cuneiform bones. The midfoot has five metatarsals that are tubular in shape. The metatarsal on the medial side of the foot is the first metatarsal, and these are labeled sequentially to the lateral or fifth metatarsal. Lastly, the toes are each composed of three phalanges, except for the big toe, which only has two. An intricate system of ligaments weaves its way through the foot, providing both stability and mobility.

ANKLE JOINT

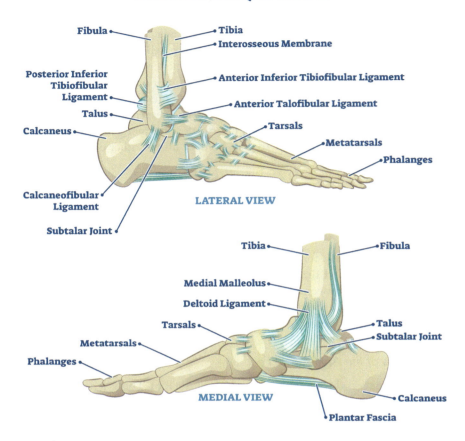

FIGURE 3.9 Labeled diagram of ankle and foot bones and ligaments in lateral (top image) and medial (bottom image) views.

Source: Photo by VectorMine/Shutterstock.com.

Muscles of the Ankles and Feet

A plethora of muscles are at work in the joints of the ankles and feet. The calf muscle, located on the posterior side of the lower leg, includes two muscles. The gastrocnemius is the large meaty muscle with which most people are familiar. This muscle originates on the posterior of the femur and inserts at the calcaneus. The soleus is a smaller and deeper muscle that originates on both bones of the lower leg and meets with the gastrocnemius at its calcaneus insertion. The Achilles tendon is the site of unification for these muscles; both of which work together in plantarflexion of the foot. It is important to stretch both of these muscles after a lot of jumping, *relevé* work, or *pointe* work. The standard calf stretch with the back leg straight targets the gastrocnemius, while bending the back leg stretches the soleus more.

Though not often discussed in class, the flexor hallucis longus plays a very important role in dance. This muscle travels from its origin on the posterior two-thirds of the fibula down the lateral side of the lower leg, through the posterior of the ankle joint to insert on the plantar side of the distal phalanx of the first toe. This muscle aids in plantarflexion, the action of pushing the big toe off the ground during jumps, and supporting the medial arch of the midfoot. It is common for dancers to develop tendinitis in this muscle. Additionally, 12 intrinsic muscles in the foot aid in its movement.[3] These muscles are what lengthen the toes. They also provide support for the foot overall.

Shoulders, Arms, and Wrists

The shoulders, arms, and wrists are sometimes undervalued in dance. Not only do the arms add aesthetic and stylistic refinement in movement but they also endure a heavy load in all partnering and floorwork. Training dancers to regularly work on strengthening the muscles in these joints is important. Outside of their previously listed purposes, the arms also work to help balance and stabilize the body in various positions and turns while providing power and momentum for movement.

Bones and Joints of the Shoulders, Arms, and Wrists

Working from proximal to distal joints, the shoulders connect the upper arm to the torso. The scapula, which is triangular, connects to the clavicle and humerus. The clavicle, or collarbone, articulates with the sternum and scapula. This is the bone that protrudes on either side of the top of the torso, often adding to the dance aesthetic. When a dance teacher instructs a student to "open" the chest, they are referring to engaging the posterior side of the shoulder joints to expand the space between the clavicles. The sternoclavicular joint is capable of flexion, extension, elevation, depression, and some rotation. These movements are generally secondary to the motion of the scapula.

In addition to the clavicle, the scapula articulates with the humerus, or upper arm bone, in the glenoid cavity. While the anterior surface of the scapula glides along the ribs (where it produces elevation and depression), there is also a ball and socket joint where the humerus connects to the scapula. This joint is quite shallower than the hip joint, thus is more susceptible to injury. It is capable of flexion, extension, abduction, adduction, and rotation.

The elbow is a hinge joint that joins the humerus to the radius and ulna, or lower arm bones. As a hinge joint, the elbow is capable of flexion and extension; the elbow also allows more rotation than the knee. The radius and ulna then connect at the wrist to the carpal bones. These eight small carpal bones form the base of the hand. These connect to the five metacarpals (similar to the metatarsals), which then join the phalanges of the fingers. The wrist joint is capable of flexion, extension, abduction, and adduction.

Muscles of the Shoulders, Arms, and Wrists

The shoulder, elbow, and wrist each have unique muscles to facilitate their movement. The most prominent muscle attached to the clavicle is the sternocleidomastoid. This is the muscle that, for example, protrudes along the neck as a ballet dancer uses their *épaulment*.

This muscle originates from the manubrium (the superior portion of the sternum), and the clavicle then inserts at the mandible, or jawbone. The sternocleidomastoid articulates the neck in various directions.

In the scapula's articulation with the humerus, four deep muscles are involved. These muscles form what is called the rotator cuff. The muscles connect the scapula to the humerus and provide stability while aiding in the shoulder's ability to abduct and rotate. Additionally, the trapezius originates on the cervical and thoracic spine and inserts on the clavicle and scapula. This muscle aids in elevation, depression, and adduction of the shoulder. The serratus anterior muscles originate from the first ten ribs and insert on the scapula. These fan-shaped muscles help in abduction and rotation of the shoulder and stabilize the scapula during forceful motions like push-ups.

The primary muscles that influence flexion and extension of the elbows are relatively well-known. Biceps brachii has two muscle bellies from different origins on the scapula that both insert at the radius. Their main role is in the flexion of the elbow. As the name indicates, triceps brachii has three muscle bellies, with two originating from the humerus and one from the scapula, and all insert at the ulna via the same tendon. The triceps' main function is to extend the elbow. Similar to the ankle and foot, the wrist and hand have larger muscles that cross the wrist joint, aiding in movement of the wrist, as well as small intrinsic muscles of the hand that stabilize the joints and produce movement of the fingers.

CHAPTER SUMMARY

Though it may be overlooked, an understanding of anatomical terminology, systems, and structures is crucial for a dance teacher. The terminology aids in communication with students and medical professionals, while equipping the individual to further their anatomical knowledge. Intelligence of the systems that are involved in movement and how they interact with one another informs the teacher of the mechanics behind the dance form they are teaching. This brings a deeper understanding of the movement. Finally, knowing what bones, ligaments, and muscles are at play in major joints provides the teacher with the information necessary to better articulate the movement that is happening to students while creating a safe learning environment that avoids injury.

PRACTICAL APPLICATIONS

1   Why is it important and helpful for a dance teacher to understand anatomical terminology?

2   Select one of your favorite dance movements. Using the terminology and kinesiology information earlier, describe

   a   in which plane the movement occurs;

   b   the joints involved in the movement and the anatomical direction in which they are moving;

   c   the structures of those joints that influence the movement; and

d which muscles work as agonists, antagonists, stabilizers, and synergists and what types of contractions are occurring in various muscles during each stage of the movement.

3 With a partner, try to get them to complete a dance movement using only the anatomical description (e.g., flex one hip anteriorly at a 90-degree angle, then flex that knee at a 45-degree angle, finally plantarflex the foot; to create a parallel *passé*).

4 How does the information in this chapter make you think about movement differently?

5 How can you as a teacher use the information about various structures of the joints to create a safer learning environment for your students?

NOTES

1 Jacqui Green Haas, *Dance Anatomy* (Champagne, IL: Human Kinetics, 2010), 4.
2 Liane Simmel, *Dance Medicine in Practice* (London: Routledge, 2009), 25.
3 Haas, *Dance Anatomy*, 148.

BIBLIOGRAPHY

Biel, Andrew. *Trail Guide to the Body*. 5th ed. Boulder, CO: Books of Discovery, 2014.
Calais-Germain, Blandine. *Anatomy of Movement*. Seattle, WA: Eastland Press, 2014.
Grieg, Valerie. *Inside Ballet Technique*. Hightstown, NJ: Princeton Book Company, 1994.
Haas, Jacqui Green. *Dance Anatomy*. Champagne, IL: Human Kinetics, 2010.
Howse, Justin, and Moira McCormack. *Anatomy Dance Technique and Injury Prevention*. London: Bloomsbury, 2009.
Simmel, Liane. *Dance Medicine in Practice*. London: Routledge, 2009.

UNIT 2

Motor and Cognitive Learning Processes

CHAPTER 4

Motor Control and Development

Box 4.1 Chapter Objectives

After reading this chapter, you will be able to:

- Understand the role of the sensory system in motor development and control
- Distinguish between the ways in which motor control is organized and coordinated
- Articulate the difference between two theories of motor development: the information-processing theory and the dynamic systems approach
- Recognize the fundamental motor milestones that emerge within young children and the ways in which these influence dance training

Box 4.2 Chapter Vocabulary

ability
alignment
auditory system
body awareness
central nervous system
closed-loop system
constraint
degrees of freedom problem
dynamic systems approach
general motor program
information-processing theory
long-term memory
motor behavior
motor control
motor development
motor learning
motor milestones

DOI: 10.4324/b22952-7

open-loop system
perception
posture
postural control
proprioception
rate limiter
short-term memory
skill
somatosensory system
visual system
working memory

In his book *Child Development and Learning Through Dance*, author James Humphrey writes, "Motor skill is judged according to the degree of proficiency with which a given bodily movement is performed. This is to say that a skill is a scientific way of moving the body and/or its segments so as to expend a minimum amount of energy while achieving maximum results."[1] A dance student strives to execute dance proficiently with minimal energy expenditure. A dance teacher who possesses not only an awareness of the anatomical structure of the body but also a clear understanding of kinesiology and motor learning and development can better aid students in the acquisition of movement skill and technique. Children develop tremendously from the time they are old enough to begin some form of dance or movement lessons, typically around age 4 or 5 years, through adolescence, and into adulthood. The physical, cognitive, and emotional changes they incur influence their motor abilities and learning process in a myriad of ways. The young child moves and learns differently than the teenage student who has movement capacities distinct from the senior learner. The more a dance educator is aware of and understands this developmental process, along with the physical capacities and limitations of the student, the better the teacher can prepare the curriculum, deliver the material, assist the learner in achieving movement and performance goals, and ensure the safety of each student. This chapter explores the relationship between motor control and development and their implications within the dance technique class.

Let us first distinguish between a few helpful terms. **Motor behavior** is an umbrella term for the various branches of study that encompass human movement, including motor control, motor development, and motor learning. The dance teacher considers a student's motor behavior in the way the student controls their body in action, develops their movement abilities, and learns the dance form.

Motor control examines the role of the nervous system in relationship to the joints and muscles producing coordinated movement. This field looks at the neural and physical components of human movement, with attention to how the body responds to sensory information and feedback from the environment. **Motor development** describes the changes in movement capacity and ability throughout the stages of one's life. Development is progressive; abilities build upon one another. Developmental outcomes result from efforts made by the individual but also interactions between the individual and the environment. Motor development is both a *process* (an individual continues to develop throughout one's life) and a *product* (an individual produces movement ability).[2] **Motor learning** is the change in skill and ability that occurs, not due to the individual's development but through the experience of movement or engagement in practice. Cognitive and physical aspects intertwine and become observable by the teacher. These changes are not directly measurable; however, one can begin to see the results of learning over time through the learner's continued and improved performance. Once motor learning has occurred, the learned results are relatively permanent.

It is also valuable to clarify a few terms before proceeding. **Ability** implies the genetic and predetermined characteristics that influence movement performance. An individual's dance ability is influenced by their biological, physiological, and environmental factors – such as training opportunities or instructor feedback. Each dance student possesses an innate level of ability. **Skill** is the proficiency level one demonstrates when executing movement. A student both experiences and practices movement to develop their skill. Through dance training, the teacher helps the student recognize their abilities and develop their skill.

Motor skill and movement skill can be interchangeable terms. Psychologists and researchers primarily use the term motor skill, which encompasses the neural and physical mechanisms behind an action, while dance teachers and students refer to movement skill. The dance teacher considers the motor aspect of dance-specific movement yet will also emphasize the elimination of any erroneous or superfluous action and the inclusion of certain aesthetics during execution. Within this text, motor skill is used to refer to the physical mechanics of an action, such as flexion of the hip joint, or basic locomotor actions, such as running and jumping. Movement skill is used to reference dance specific actions, such as *pirouette*, split leap, or shuffle.

MOTOR CONTROL

Individuals are constantly developing cognitively and physically throughout their lifespan. The human body will evolve and continue to go through physical changes that influence an individual's ability to learn and execute motor skills. For an individual to move the body at all, they must demonstrate a level of motor control, which then impacts motor development. This capacity for control of the muscles influences the dance student's ability to learn and develop movement skill. It is helpful for the dance educator to understand the systems at play in developing postural control and balance as it will enable the educator to train students more efficiently in meeting the demands of movement and choreography.

An individual learns postural control as an infant, and this ability is strengthened as they develop into adulthood. **Postural control** is the act of achieving, maintaining, or regaining a coordinated, upright position that does not place strain on the body during movement. Posture is distinct from alignment. **Posture** is the basic position in which the body is held when standing or in movement. **Alignment** focuses on the specific organization of the body in regard to gravity and the aesthetics of the dance movement. Proper body alignment is emphasized within dance technique to facilitate the movement, enhance the dance aesthetic, and perhaps most importantly, to ensure safety for the dancer while executing dance steps. It is important to note that proper alignment may look very different in each dance form. For example, ballet dancers emphasize a vertical alignment of the

FIGURE 4.1 Image depicts dancers posed in distinct genres of dance: classical ballet, tap dance, and commercial jazz dance. Together, the images represent the various ways in which alignment can be considered within dance movement.

Source: Photo by Clinton Lewis/Western Kentucky University.

torso; tap dancers generally bend at the hips, allowing the torso to shift or tip forward. In the Cunningham modern dance technique, the torso is often taken off the body line's central axis. Correct body alignment reduces the risk of injury while dancing. Before correct alignment can be achieved, an individual must have the muscular strength and sensory awareness to control posture and coordinate balance efforts.

As children or beginners of any age first learn a dance form, postural control and balance play an important role in the motor learning process. The body must first be able to maintain balance before coordinating itself to execute new motor skills and patterns. Without this ability, even basic locomotor movements such as running and hopping would be impossible for an individual to complete. Postural control is first developed in the head and neck and then progresses downward through the body; progression is in a head-to-tail sequence.[3]

The first sensory mapping of posture emerges in the brain and is integrated into the body as the sensory system generates the appropriate neural and muscular synapses downward into the individual's trunk. The infant gains control of the head, then learns independent sitting followed by crawling and standing. From here, the sensory information is further organized and related to the motor actions of a variety of body positions and movement. Just as individuals rely on sensory systems to aid in the development of basic motor functions, so do dancers. Let us take a closer look at these sensory systems to better understand how they aid in motor control and development.

Sensory Systems

One of the first levels in which we begin to analyze information is within the sensory systems. The sensory systems uncover information not only about our environment but also the body's position within it. The body then relies on this information to plan and execute movement successfully and efficiently. The body utilizes several sensory systems, for example the visual, auditory, and olfactory systems, and each receives and transmits sensory information to the brain through receptors and sensory neurons. Receptors – located in places such as the eye, inner ear, layers of the skin, joints, and muscles – monitor internal and external sensory information which inform us about our body and its position in space. The receptors take this information and convert it into a form that the central nervous system can understand and process so that we can then create and initiate a plan for movement.

It is important for the dance teacher to understand the relationship between the sensory systems and the **central nervous system** (CNS), which consists of the brain and spinal cord. When both systems function as they are supposed to, the brain can interpret sensory signals and formulate a plan for appropriate motor responses. Our interpretations of what we see, hear, or feel heavily influence our movements. Balance and control are specifically impacted by the brain's ability to integrate sensory feedback. If one area is limited in growth or restricted in capability, movement can be hindered or altered. A dance teacher plans movement classes and instructional approaches based on not only the physical abilities but also the cognitive and perceptual capabilities of students.

Visual System

The **visual system** is often referred to as the "queen of the senses."[4] Vision encompasses not only seeing but also perception, or processing what has been seen. This sensory system incorporates, but is not limited to, the eyes and the visual cortex located in the brain. The eyes act as receptors, receiving and transmitting visual information; the visual cortex processes and interprets the information. The visual sense is utilized greatly within the learning and performance atmospheres. This sense allows students to see the physical demonstrations executed by the teacher when learning movement. Vision assists with balance, serving as a child's primary aid in maintaining balance.[5] Students will often rely on mirrors to look at themselves for visual cues in finding correct alignment, placement, and body positions. The dancer uses vision to see where other dancers are in space in relation to them and to maintain timing or movement sequencing with groups of dancers. They use vision to avoid obstacles as they navigate space and pathways while moving. The use of the visual sense prepares the motor system prior to the execution of some movement. For example, vision helps the dancer to judge distances (in preparation for partner work, when changing formations, or locomoting through space) or landings (from jumps, leaps, or partner work) so that the movement can be done safely. Vision also allows the dancer to anticipate or monitor their timing by seeing the movement of the dancers in tandem with them.

Auditory System

The **auditory system** transmits sound to the brain so that it can be identified and processed. This system not only interprets how we hear sounds but also separates sounds within the environment. The ears serve as the receptors, transmitting the sensory information to the temporal lobes within the brain for processing.

Hearing and listening are extremely important and unique skills that dancers must develop. Dance educators most often teach through verbal instruction. Students must continually learn from listening to instruction and feedback from their teacher. As we will learn in Chapter 5, some students will learn best from listening to verbal instruction or hearing the terminology and/or sung rhythm of the movement to be performed. There may be times that the student cannot see the visual demonstration and must then rely on the verbal instruction for understanding. Some forms of dance are more percussive than others and make greater use of the auditory system both in learning and in performance. Tap dance, Irish step dancing, or flamenco are examples of auditory genres of dance. Students make continual use of their auditory system within tap dance and flamenco classes as they must listen to and replicate sounds and rhythms made with the feet.

Most dance forms are typically practiced with and performed to musical accompaniment; therefore, musical awareness must be developed within the dance student. In dance, the temporal relationship between movement and sound accompaniment becomes essential. The dancer must hear the music and match the tempo of the movement to that of the music. Auditory cues from sound accompaniment can help the dancer learn movement patterns or choreographic phrasing, along with recognize stylistic or dynamic needs for the movement. Of course, not all dance is performed with music or sound accompaniment. Even when dancing without musical accompaniment, the dancer may listen for the sound cues made by the moving body, that is, the brushing or stamping of the feet on the ground, the slapping of the hands upon the thighs or hips, or the inhale or exhale of breath during movement. These sounds can provide temporal cues and even execution cues. For example, a loud landing from a *grand jeté* in a ballet class can indicate that the dancer is not using the proper control and technique as they execute the movement. Finally, auditory sounds from the environment can offer the dancer spatial information. During performance, the dancer may listen for the sound of other dancers when visual contact cannot be made.

FIGURE 4.2 Older students tune into the auditory sense during a tap dance class.
Source: Photo by Jeffrey Smith/Western Kentucky University.

Somatosensory System

The **somatosensory system** is part of the sensory system that is a neural network responsible for transmitting information about the perception of touch, temperature, motion, and pain. The vestibular apparatus is also included within the somatosensory system and provides information to the brain about one's sense of balance, head position, and spatial orientation. Receptors located in the inner ear serve as the connection to the brain. It is the vestibular system that often contributes to the dizzy feeling one feels during turning motions.

Cutaneous receptors within the skin respond to sensations of touch and pressure, whereas proprioceptors offer an individual immediate information about what the body is doing. As we dance, receptors located within muscles, tendons, joints, ligaments, and fascia inform the brain about the position of each body part in relation to one another and of the body's general orientation in space, especially when we cannot use our visual sense. **Proprioception** is the ability of the body to sense movement, action, and location. Proprioception also assists an individual in developing body awareness. Dancers must form a heightened sense of **body awareness**, the ability to locate and know where the body is in space along with how to move it efficiently.

It is important for the dance teacher to understand the somatosensory system and incorporate opportunities for the student to enhance their proprioception skills. As individuals learn how to attune themselves to the somatosensory system, proprioceptors enable individuals to better control and coordinate movement. Use of proprioception can enhance one's aesthetic line and quality of movement, improve body alignment, coordination, and control, generate efficient energy use, further develop perception and memory skills, and prevent injury. When vision is absent, proprioception can provide the dancer with information about the body line they are making or bring attention to errors in technique that might be occurring. The dance teacher can also use cutaneous and proprioceptive cues to facilitate movement and encourage understanding during class. Students can benefit from feedback that uses proprioceptive cues. For example, a dance teacher can lightly tap the small of the dancer's back, to remind the dancer to engage their abdominals and lengthen their spine. Or the teacher might encourage students to "imagine as much space as possible between the shoulders and the ears," while the arms are held in a ballet first position to help them depress the shoulders and demonstrate improved alignment. Utilizing these cutaneous or imagery cues help the student connect to their kinesthetic sense. The proprioception-based cue can alert the body to uncover proper dance technique when the visual or auditory cue may have been unsuccessful.

Perception

The sensory system relies on our cognitive ability to process the information that the brain receives. **Perception** is the way in which we comprehend and interpret sensory information. How we perceive information will influence the choice that we make regarding our resulting movement outcome. If we perceive the stove to be hot when we touch it, we immediately pull our hand back. If a dancer looks in the mirror and sees that the working hip is lifted during a *retiré* balance, they will adjust the placement of the hips. Consider the way in which a dance teacher most often teaches dance movement. They will often offer phrases such as *"watch* me demonstrate," *"listen* to my tap sounds," or *"feel* the stretch through the back of your knee." Teachers are asking students to engage their senses as they teach and guide students through technique and movement patterns. As students develop their perceptual skills, their movement abilities can also improve.

The way in which we move is influenced by our ability to process sensory information. The sensory systems provide individuals with information before, during, and after action is executed. They help to guide individuals in planning movement responses as well as modifying movement plans. They also help individuals learn and relearn movement skills. It is important that a singular sensory system is not relied upon when one learns or when one teaches. The dance educator should help students discover their ability to engage all their sensory modalities during the learning and performing process. Additionally, some individuals may lack the ability to see or hear, in which case the teacher must heavily rely on the other senses to communicate information and facilitate the students' learning process. Understanding the role of the sensory systems in producing movement helps the dance educator as they choose which instructional devices and methods to employ.

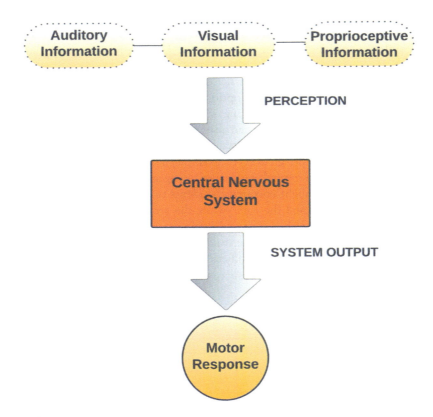

FIGURE 4.3 Diagram of the basic process of the central nervous system (CNS).

UNDERSTANDING POSTURAL CONTROL WITHIN DANCE TRAINING

Just as children achieve motor skills at general age markers (motor milestones), postural control also emerges and regresses along a guiding timeline. Teachers will notice that young dancers, age 3 to adolescence, will experience immense changes in postural control and that those students under the age of 12 will often rely most on their sense of vision for balance.[6] Around ages 4 to 6, a child will demonstrate varying outcomes in balance efforts, ranging from fairly stable to erratic, as their nervous systems experiment with a variety of methods and strategies during movement. These begin to even out near the age of 7 as their central nervous system matures.[7] From age 7 to 12, control and balance will be similar to the reactions of an adult, albeit slower in response time. Boys will develop slower than girls, and growth spurts may complicate control issues. Because balance tasks require the focus of the CNS, teachers should be mindful of cognitive loading. Overloading a student with cognitive information can have adverse reactions on a student's ability to demonstrate control and balance. Students will struggle to remain focused on the task at hand and efficiently execute movement when they are given too much information or too many cues to consider while executing a skill.

The dance teacher can help develop a student's sensory system in various ways. Incorporating action that will challenge or disrupt the system will force the individual to find new ways to navigate balance. For example, the teacher could ask the student to close their eyes while balancing in a given position or executing a simple movement. This removes the visual sense and forces the student to rely on their proprioception to balance. Dance improvisation is also an excellent tool to employ within the dance class setting to engage students and to assist in motor learning in a diverse modality. During improvisation, dancers are forced to navigate the challenges set forth by unplanned movement. When students execute planned movement, they know what to expect because they know what they are doing. Improvisation presents unexpected movement situations to which the student must spontaneously respond. These situations test the student's balance, disrupt the habits the student would normally employ, and invite the motor system to establish new responses. Improvisation presents unexpected movement situations, such as new interactions between dancers and sometimes unwelcome spatial conflicts that the student must quickly respond to with balance and control. The student's abilities in motor control will further develop as they navigate through these unplanned movement interactions.

With this information and understanding, the dance teacher can better align the content of lesson plans with the development of the students. With young primary dancers – those under the age of 5 – creative play can be an excellent tool in engaging imaginations and exploring physical capabilities and sensibilities. Dance vocabulary can then be introduced in an elementary manner, with a shift toward dance training and technique occurring around the age of 7 or 8 years when the sensory systems involved with posture and balance are integrated and more fully developed. Once the student reaches age 10 to 12, skill acquisition should be the primary focus.

MOTOR CONTROL AND ORGANIZATION

Control mechanisms, found throughout the central nervous system, are responsible for organizing and coordinating motor action. The CNS is organized into three levels, often considered as a hierarchy of motor control. Each level focuses on different elements of movement organization. In the bottom or lowest level of the system lies the spinal cord where automatic reflexes occur. The middle or second level consists of the brain stem which controls eye-and-head movement. The cerebral cortex is found at the highest or third level of the hierarchy. It is here that complex sequences of movement are coordinated, and a plan is sent forward to the muscles of the body. Motor control is established through two different processes referred to as open-loop and closed-loop systems. These systems are unique in the way they account for feedback during the execution of movement.

Open-Loop Systems

In the **open-loop system**, a movement goal is provided to the brain which then sends a plan for action to the muscles. The brain, considered the executive level, receives input which might be a visual demonstration by the dance teacher, verbal instructions, or another form of reference modeling the movement that is to be produced. The brain prepares a plan for this movement and sends it forward to the muscles, or effector level, of the body's motor system so that the desired movement, or outcome, may be produced. (See Figure 4.4.) Additionally, the open-loop system does not consider feedback, but rather relies solely on the brain to provide the plan for movement. Once the plan is initiated, it cannot be modified or altered within this system. Movement executed in an open-loop system allows no time for a response to stimuli. Here, the brain is in control of the movement as all decisions regarding movement output are made at the executive level.

An example of movement executed in an open-loop system is a center leap, or leap in second position, in jazz dance. A dancer performing this movement cannot change how the leap will be executed once it is initiated. If an instructor calls out a correction, or the dancer realizes an error mid-leap, the motor plan cannot be modified. Most fast and ballistic-type movements follow this operating system. A ballistic movement encompasses muscle contractions at high velocity and accelerations. An example is the repetitive pulse of a deep bend in a classical second position of the feet and legs, a leap or jump, or the quick kick of a leg or throw of an arm.

FIGURE 4.4 Diagram of the open-loop system of motor control.

FIGURE 4.5 A jazz dancer executes a leap in second.
Source: Photo by Jeffrey Smith/Western Kentucky University.

Closed-Loop Systems

Unlike the open-loop system, the **closed-loop system** takes into consideration external feedback. This system relies on both sensory information and feedback to create a plan for movement. (See Figure 4.6.) Movement executed in a closed-loop system is generally slower and self-paced, allowing time for external stimuli to be processed and become part of the response. During execution, sensory and external information can be considered, and modifications to the motor plan can be made. Movement can be refined. A *developpé* tilt would be an example of a closed-loop movement as the dancer would have an opportunity to incorporate feedback and adjust the body's position during the execution of the extension. Within the closed-loop system, internal and external feedback is perceived, and the information is sent back to the executive level for further processing during the loop, thus starting the processing cycle over again. Another example can be observed as a dancer maintains an elbow, or forearm, freeze in breakdancing. The dancer may self-cue or receive feedback from the dance instructor to then activate the appropriate muscles or alter the movement response during the balance skill.

72 Motor and Cognitive Learning Processes

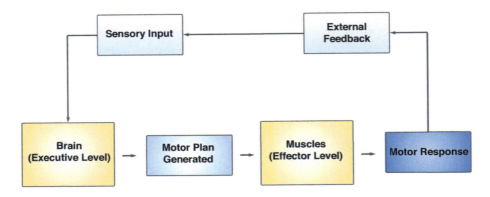

FIGURE 4.6 Diagram of the closed-loop system of motor control.

FIGURE 4.7 A dancer executes an elbow freeze.
Source: Photo by Jeffrey Smith/Western Kentucky University.

Box 4.3 Closed and Open Skills

Motor skills can be classified into categories, also called open and closed, based on the environment in which they are performed. These are separate from the open-loop and closed-loop systems of processing discussed in the text. Open skills are those that must be adaptable due to the variety of environments in which they may be performed. Consider a step hop, or *passé sauté*, in a contemporary class. This jump may be done traveling straight across the floor with power, speed, and command of the space, or it may be executed in place and exaggerated in tempo. The bottom leg could be tucked. The dancer could complete a partial or full turn in the air during the jump or add any choice of arm positions. Closed skills are performed in stable environments, and the goal of the performer is consistency in execution. An example in dance is a series of *fouetté* turns. The dancer practices this skill continuously until execution is consistent. Performance is not contingent upon other dancers or changing stage space.[8]

The concept of skill classification may be confusing among dancers who seem to perform a mix of closed and open skills all in one movement phrase. The classification of open and closed skills can be considered as a spectrum with the two opposing classes at either end.[9] Dance choreography tends to be at the closed end of the skills classification spectrum, although individual movement skills may be open. Dancers practice for consistency, despite changing environments, although they should always be prepared for the unexpected.

General Motor Programs

Once a movement has been learned, the movement idea and approach are stored within the memory of the individual. As movement is programmed within the brain, it can then be more readily produced when called upon. The development of generalized motor programs occurs throughout the learning process and allows for the execution of an action plan without the need for sensory information or feedback.

A **general motor program** is a grouping of commands stored in the memory that inform the musculature to execute a given movement or pattern of movements. Humans create general motor programs for the basic locomotor skills discussed later in this chapter. It explains how, once learned, one can initiate a walking pattern yet focus on another task without dedicating any, or very little attention, to the act of walking. It also explains how individuals learn a movement skill or pattern and can then execute variations of that skill or pattern fairly easily. Motor programs represent a motor learning theory that individuals can initiate a movement plan and then continue the action while focusing their attention elsewhere until they choose to stop the program. For instance, a tap dancer can repeat a double time step through several phrases of music while holding a separate conversation. General motor programs are explored in greater depth in Chapter 5.

MOTOR DEVELOPMENT

The field of motor development dates back to the end of the 19th century. Over the years, theories have emerged and evolved, shaping how researchers and educators understand motor development and skill acquisition. The following section explores two theories of motor development. The first theory – the information-processing theory – is an early theory within the field and supports the belief that the nervous system is chiefly in control of developing motor skills. A contrasting theory – the dynamic-systems approach – is then presented and offers a context for dance teachers as they comprehend and provide for the students' development of movement skill.

Theories of Motor Development

Information-Processing Theory

In the 1970s, the **information-processing theory** emerged and increased in popularity among physical educators.[10] This theory places the brain, which can be thought of as a computer, as the primary component of the processing system. Information provided externally or through the senses enters the brain where it is processed, and the resulting outcome is then coordinated movement (see Figure 4.8). This approach maintains that as individuals learn, they identify the material or stimulus through sensory modalities and retrieve relevant information from their long-term memory along with recall strategies that worked or did not work in past movement attempts. The brain then determines how the body will respond and prepares a motor response plan for the muscles to enact. For example, in a contact improvisation class, the dancer must lift their partner. The brain processes the information necessary to the skill, considers past success and failures, and

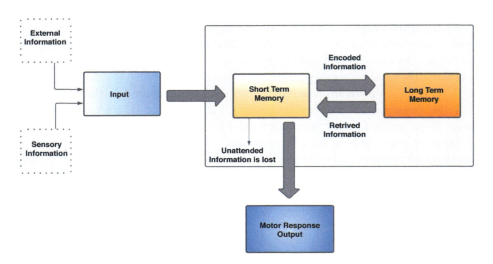

FIGURE 4.8 Diagram of the memory function with the information-processing theory of motor development.

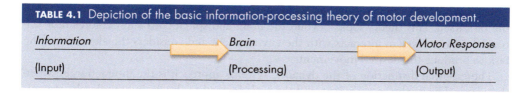

TABLE 4.1 Depiction of the basic information-processing theory of motor development.

prepares a plan to execute the action. The brain then tells the body to use a deeper *plié* in the preparation for the lift and to lean farther with the torso during weight sharing with the partner to avoid losing balance.

Central to the information-processing system is the individual's memory. When a dancer recalls a previous experience to assist a current movement attempt, they are accessing their memory to retrieve specific and relevant information. One's memory can also indirectly influence movement attempts. Dancers often subconsciously reproduce action that has been stored in their memory. An advanced dancer can execute a basic jazz square without focusing on the steps because the movement has been committed to their memory.

There are three types of memory to consider. **Short-term memory** is the system in which small amounts of information are stored for brief periods of time. This storage area is fragile as it has a limited capacity and a short duration of time in which information can be retained. Researchers find that an individual maintains approximately seven items of information at a time within short-term memory.[11] **Working memory** is an area within short-term memory where mental processing can be performed. This is the area of memory where environmental and sensory information is integrated with information retrieved from **long-term memory**. Individuals select response strategies and create action plans within working memory. Once a movement is learned, it is moved to the large storage capacity of long-term memory. These types of memory are detailed further in Chapter 5.

The early theory of information-processing influenced the development of later motor research, yet this theory does have limitations. It does not take into account how a learner's behavior can also affect movement.[12] This theory fails to include how emotions, or the environment, could impact one's motor development. Fatigue, stress, nervousness, or an overly heated studio could affect a student's ability to execute a movement skill. The information-processing perspective does remind the dance teacher of the importance of the cognitive aspect in motor development. Central to this approach is the development of an individual's perceptual motor skills. In learning situations, an individual must be able to perceive the desired action or movement goal, and therefore an interaction between the mental process of perception and the motor process of action must occur. This theory helps teachers recognize one way in which students may process movement concepts and technique.

Dynamic Systems Approach

A more current and widely accepted theory of motor control and development is the dynamic systems approach. This theory was developed by researchers in the early 1980s. The **dynamic systems approach** considers not only the individual's physical body and neuromuscular system but also factors in input from the surrounding environment and the task itself. This theory looks beyond the brain and spinal cord and explores how the central nervous system interacts with the environment and considers the elements of the task to produce the desired movement.

The essential distinction of the dynamic systems approach is the interaction between the *physical body*, the *environment*, and the *task*. Instead of the brain completely controlling the outcome of the movement, the body self-organizes or adapts its movement pattern structure in response to the synergy between the body, environment, and task. Each element contributes to the production of action. (See Figure 4.9.)

Within this approach is the idea of positive and negative aspects that influence the outcome or ability of the individual to produce the desired result. When considering the components of the physical body, we look at the anatomical structure and physical facility of the student, their physiological factors, the development of their CNS, and their

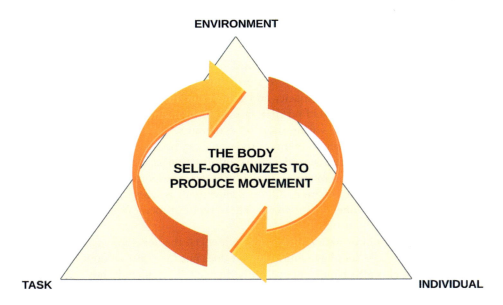

FIGURE 4.9 Diagram of the dynamic systems approach. The constraints of the environment, task, and physical body interact to influence motor development.

FIGURE 4.10 Diagram of the rate limiters that affect motor development.

individual physical and cognitive developmental levels. Environmental elements might be the instructional cues and feedback provided by the teacher, which could include motivating encouragement or verbal cues, as well as sensory feedback such as room temperature, ambient sounds, or visual distractions from within the environment. Familiarity with the components of the task or inherent challenges also affects the student's motor development.

Task aspects include the demands of the movement or movement sequence as well as what is known as the **degrees of freedom problem**. At each joint within the human body, there are multiple directions in which movement could be directed. For instance, the arm could be flexed or extended, abducted or adducted, or externally or internally rotated. One could move the ankle in plantarflexion, dorsiflexion, inversion, or eversion. A basic roll of the ankle or reach out to the side with the arm could be executed in a number of ways. The body will first do the most efficient, albeit often far from the desired aesthetic, method of execution. This explains why *port de bras* performed by novice ballet dancers are often choppy, rigid, and awkward when they are first learning the movement. It takes time and repetition for a more refined and artistic motion and movement pattern to be integrated into the neural and muscular systems.

The aesthetics of dance often complicate this problem within movement as the most efficient method of movement for the dancer may not be the preferred aesthetic within the art form, thus complicating matters for the moving body. Consider the landing of a jump. To help absorb the shock of landing a jump, an individual's hips should bend, and the torso should come forward. A basketball player might land a jump shot with a fall to the ground as they release into the downward gravitational pull and attempt to cushion their joints as they land. However, most dance forms require the dancer to remain in a vertical alignment when landing a jump. For the dancer, the degrees of freedom problem encompasses the myriad of anatomical possibilities for a given movement along with the demands of what is being asked by the body both physically and aesthetically. As the dancer develops physically and cognitively and practices the movement, the dancer's movement will become more fluid and smoother as they "solve" the degrees of freedom problem for a movement.

The dynamic systems approach considers the concept of constraints in the production of movement. **Constraints**, an aspect that deters or hinders movement, can come from three places: within the individual, from the task at hand, and from the environment. The individual can restrict movement through their lack of desire and motivation to execute the skill. Individual constraints could also be one's physical characteristics, such as height, weight, body structure, or anatomy, that either facilitate or hinder movement. **Rate limiters** are a type of individual constraint that slows or hinders the emergence of a motor skill. The systems and components within the body do not all mature at the same pace. Some develop slowly, while others may advance more quickly. This, in turn, will affect the rate at which an individual can acquire a motor skill. For example, leg strength can be a rate limiter for a child learning to hop.

It is interesting to note that rate limiters are not exclusive to physical characteristics. They need not be in the form of muscular or skeletal examples only. Aspects of the sensory system and even motivation and attention can serve as rate limiters within an individual during the motor development and control processes. An individual's inability to focus could restrict their progress in learning a movement skill. The educator should note that rate limiters also work in the reverse. As an individual ages, movement function will deteriorate and be adversely affected by rate limiters. For example, the functionality of the somatosensory system decreases in older adults, making it harder to balance or work without support. While the senior adult may comprehend the mechanics of the movement, their ability to balance and coordinate their muscular system may prohibit their learning and attainment of a movement skill.

Task constraints are those aspects that extend from the movement itself. The nature of the movement, or the goal of the exercise, impose a restraint in the process for how one coordinates, controls, and executes movement. A flash step in tap dance is a prime example of a task constraint. A dancer attempting to progress beyond a traditional wing step (three sounds) and learn a five-beat wing will struggle to execute the additional sounds of the feet while maintaining the extra "hang time" in the air. If a prop or piece of equipment is included in choreography, then this too adds a hindrance by creating a physical obstacle that must be considered. Finally, environmental constraints are those that are external to the individual. These could be the type of flooring, items located within the dance space, temperature, weather, or lighting. Regardless of the type, constraints affect how the body processes the action required to execute a desired movement. As a dance educator, it is beneficial to recognize the various constraints that may work against a student as they learn a new skill. This knowledge becomes especially important when preparing curriculum and lesson plans (discussed in Chapter 9) and in offering feedback (discussed in Chapter 15) to students.

Motor Milestones

As children grow and develop, they progress through **motor milestones**, or specific stages of development. Through each stage, a child acquires fundamental motor skills that enable them to advance to more complex movement behavior. These milestones can be considered as benchmarks in one's motor development, as they are motor progressions that typically occur amongst all children; however, variations in timing may exist among individual children.

From birth to the age of 2 years, children advance through several motor milestones including crawling, sitting, pulling to stand, independent stance, walking, and running. It is during even these early milestones that we notice that motor development is not linear. All children will experience phases of progress, regression, and advancement in the acquisition of motor skills. Just as children struggle to attain the typical motor milestones, and will do so in a nonlinear fashion, dance skills and technique will also be achieved in a similar mode. It is important that the dance teacher recognizes that the dance student may experience periods of regression during the acquisition of skill, and this is a normal part of the motor development and learning process.

There are four rate limiters that can affect the emergence of motor milestones within a child. These pertain to the brain, CNS, muscular strength and endurance, and balance. A child must have developed the ability to process information and sensory feedback, and their CNS must have the capability to organize the body structure and systems to produce the desired movement.[13] The body must develop the strength, endurance, and balance control to complete locomotor movement.

> **Box 4.4 Establishing Appropriate Building Blocks within Motor and Movement Skills**
>
> Children typically acquire the motor skill of running by age 2. This is an important developmental step for dancers as it provides a foundation for elevation movement. Running will be the first motor skill children learn that has an elevation component. If the child develops poor habits early on, such as inefficient patterns or mechanics within their running ability, dance movement could be affected down the road. This knowledge serves as a reminder to the dance educator of the importance of teaching and establishing proper technique within movement skills. It is important for students to learn the correct body mechanics and muscular patterning within motor and movement skills to prevent bad habits from forming and ensure physical safety. Remember, the initial motor skills learned as well as the basic movement skills and patterns will serve as the building blocks for future dance vocabulary and more complex skills and combinations.

Fundamental Locomotor Movement Development

Between the ages of approximately 2 and 7 years, individuals develop abilities in several traveling motor skills that then serve as foundational actions for a host of movements that are used in or enhanced through dance. The motor skills listed in the following text are often the first traveling steps explored in a creative dance/movement class. The dance teacher should be mindful of how children gain ability in these areas so that the teacher can set realistic goals and expectations for the student and approach lesson plans effectively.

The dance teacher should note that young children will acquire symmetrical traveling steps before executing asymmetrical movement. A symmetrical traveling step is one that is repeated in motion, gait structure, and/or rhythmic pattern on both feet. For example, children will develop the ability to execute skills such as walking, running, and jumping before the asymmetrical skills of galloping or skipping. Girls tend to produce the ability to execute locomotion skills before boys; however, boys can be encouraged to, for example, jump or hop higher or farther as a means of encouragement despite their coordination deficits.[14] It is important for the dance teacher to incorporate a range of locomotor experiences within the dance class. This will offer students the opportunity to improve balance and control and develop necessary strength.

Jumping

Children as young as 2 years of age may demonstrate a basic version of jumping, a symmetrical motor skill where one pushes off and lands on the ground with both feet. Early forms of jumping in children are awkward, shallow, and focus on the vertical aspects before a horizontal jump is achieved. Children may initially execute a small step before elevation to assist in generating power and momentum for the jump, thus creating an asymmetrical takeoff. As the child's ability improves, both the takeoff and the landing become symmetrical, and the child will incorporate a deeper bend before the jump and full extension of the legs during elevation.

The muscle force within the legs is the primary rate limiter for jumps. Until the legs are strong, children cannot work against gravity to propel their body into the air. It is important for the dance teacher to realize not to overdo jumps within the class since muscle strength is a constraint, and the muscles will fatigue easily as a result. It is also helpful to note that children will discover the ability to coordinate the action of their lower limbs before they are able to coordinate the arms or control the placement of their upper body during the jump.

Galloping

Galloping is an asymmetrical movement that can be performed traveling in various directions. When galloping forward, the movement requires a step forward with one foot, followed by an elevation as the back foot chases the front foot, landing back foot first. The gallop can be compared to the *chassé* in dance. The same foot will stay in front throughout the gallop. This traveling step could also be done moving sideways rather than forward. When initially learning this skill, children will lead with their dominant leg. It is helpful for teachers to allow young children to choose their lead leg when first learning to gallop. This allows the student to learn the mechanics of the movement and develop motor control, along with confidence, before encouraging the student to execute the step with the non-dominant leg leading. The main rate limiter for galloping is coordination. Galloping requires a shift in timing as well as differing muscular force than either walking or running motor patterns, which can make this skill challenging for young learners.

Hopping

Unlike jumping, children do not begin hopping until around 3 1/2 years of age. Hopping is an elevation movement where one pushes off from the ground on one foot and lands on the same foot. The main rate limiter is the balance mechanisms that will control the landing on a small base of support along with the strength to thrust the body into the air from one foot and execute a series of hops. As with jumping, the overall use of the body and the technique of the working leg improves in time and as control and the musculature develop. Initially, the dominant leg will be preferred by children. Children may struggle with the innate challenges of hopping, and asking young learners to use specific arm placement may overwhelm them.

Skipping

Skipping consists of a step followed by a hop that is continuously repeated and is the last of the locomotor movements to emerge, typically between 4 to 7 years of age. Here again, the dominant leg will take the lead, and children will often first execute a step hop with the dominant leg followed by a scurry of steps led by the non-dominant leg. Coordination between the arms and legs develops slowly, and movement will appear disjointed at first. The neuromuscular system is the rate limiter and must be able to coordinate the limbs as they perform asymmetrical tasks. The proficient skipper will demonstrate the oppositional swing of the arm, use of each leg, a lower knee lift, and fluidity in overall execution. Dance teachers should be careful not to force this skill on children too early in their development or dance experience.

THE ADOLESCENT DANCER AND GROWTH SPURTS

Adolescents undergo many physical and cognitive changes. This stage of development affects many of the systems within the body. Individuals will experience growth spurts typically between the ages of 11 and 14 years, and these can last anywhere from 18 to 24 months.[15] It is not uncommon for girls to experience growth spurts and puberty earlier than boys. During growth spurts, bone growth will occur before muscle development, which means there is a span of time where the muscles are actually shorter than the longer bones. As a result, a deficit will occur in strength and flexibility. The individual will become susceptible to injury, specifically in the areas where the muscle tendons attach to the bone. Additionally, the nervous system will struggle to keep up with bone growth, resulting in weakened coordination and balance.

Growth spurts can have adverse effects on skill acquisition. Technique may regress during this time. Good alignment can be harder for young dancers to establish and maintain. Dancers can become easily fatigued. They may demonstrate lower leg extensions due to the longer limbs, decrease in flexibility, and weaker muscles. Turns and balances can be hindered as equilibrium and coordination are disturbed. This stage can be increasingly difficult for female dancers who are also encountering menarche, breast development, and changes in their overall body proportion. These changes in females compound the issues earlier.

Additionally, the brain is still maturing into the teen years and early adulthood. This, in turn, affects cognition and the acquisition of motor skills. Areas of the brain responsible for tasks such as integrating sensory information, organization and planning, impulse control, and reasoning are continuing to develop and advance. The adolescent dancer may find that some skills that were once easy are now challenging. The difficulty in acquiring or maintaining skills can have an adverse effect on the dancer's psyche, leaving them with a decrease in self-esteem or confidence or a weakened body image. The dance teacher should remind dancers that they are experiencing a normal developmental stage and that their struggle is only temporary.

These milestones and age ranges are benchmarks and approximations; dance teachers should be mindful that not all students learn skills or physically mature at the same rate. The theories that have been contributed over the years by researchers and scientists help the dance educator to understand the progressive nature of basic motor movement. By keeping an eye on these milestones and growth developments with their students, dance teachers can plan more effective and cohesive classes and curricula.

CHAPTER SUMMARY

Motor behavior is an umbrella term for a branch of study that explores motor control, motor development, and motor learning. The dance teacher considers a student's motor behavior in the way the student controls their body movements, develops within their movement abilities, and learns the dance form. This chapter specifically explores motor development and control.

For a student to acquire skill in dancing and improve in technique, they must be able to control their muscles and movement. The three sensory systems – visual, auditory, and somatosensory – play a key role in developing motor control and balance within the dance student. The brain gathers information through the sensory systems and then helps the muscles and joints to coordinate the necessary movement. Motor control is established through two different processes referred to as open-loop and closed-loop systems. These systems are contrasted in the way they integrate feedback during movement planning and execution. As the dance teacher helps a student develop their motor control, the educator should strive to develop all the senses during dance training activities and provide instruction through both open-loop and closed-loop processes.

The information-processing theory and the dynamic systems approach, two theories of motor development, offer contrasting perspectives for dance teachers to better comprehend and assimilate the ways in which students develop movement ability and skill. As an individual grows and matures, they develop through motor milestones, which are influenced by rate limiters. The effective dance teacher recognizes how children progress through these milestones and how their movement development is affected by rate limiters and growth spurts, which enable realistic goals and expectations for the student to be established.

PRACTICAL APPLICATIONS

1 Describe how a student will use each of the three sensory systems detailed in the text within the dance classroom.

2 Compose a movement exercise or activity to enhance the students' connection to a specific sensory system.

3 Why is it important for the dance teacher to understand how a child develops balance and motor control?

4 Explain the difference between open-loop and closed-loop systems.

5 Describe the difference between the information-processing approach and the dynamic systems approach.

6 Compose an exercise to help a 4-year-old improve jumping abilities.

7 Compose an exercise to prepare a 5-year-old

   a   to improve skipping abilities and
   b   to challenge the five-year-old who has already mastered skipping.

NOTES

1 James Harry Humphrey, *Child Development and Learning through Dance* (New York: AMS Press, 1987), 99.
2 Donna Krasnow and Virginia Wilmerding, *Motor Learning and Control for Dance: Principles and Practices for Performers and Teachers* (Champaign, IL: Human Kinetics, 2015), 2.
3 Krasnow and Wilmerding, Motor Learning and Control for Dance, 34.

4 Richard A. Magill, *Motor Learning: Concepts and Applications* (Boston: McGraw-Hill, 2007), 71.
5 Debra J. Rose and Robert W. Christina, *A Multilevel Approach to the Study of Motor Control and Learning* (San Francisco, CA: Benjamin Cummings, 2008), 127.
6 Krasnow and Wilmerding, *Motor Learning and Control for Dance*, 34.
7 Krasnow and Wilmerding, *Motor Learning and Control for Dance*, 37.
8 Krasnow and Wilmerding, *Motor Learning and Control for Dance*, 174.
9 Rose and Christina, *A Multilevel Approach to the Study of Motor Control and Learning*, 183.
10 Krasnow and Wilmerding, *Motor Learning and Control for Dance*, 16.
11 Pamela S. Haibach-Beach, Greg Reid and Douglas Holden Collier, *Motor Learning and Development*, 2nd ed. (Champaign, IL: Human Kinetics, 2018), 43.
12 Krasnow and Wilmerding, *Motor Learning and Control for Dance*, 17.
13 Krasnow and Wilmerding, *Motor Learning and Control for Dance*, 46.
14 Krasnow and Wilmerding, *Motor Learning and Control for Dance*, 50, 59.
15 Kathryn Daniels, "The Challenges of the Adolescent Dancer," *International Association of Dance Medicine and Science*, Accessed August 2023, 2, https://iadms.org/research-publications/resources-paper/.

BIBLIOGRAPHY

Akito, Miura, Shinya Fujii, Yuji Yamamoto, and Kazutoshi Kudo. "Motor Control of Rhythmic Dance from a Dynamical Systems Perspective." *Journal of Dance Medicine & Science* 19, no. 1 (2015): 11–21. https://doi.org/10.12678/1089–313X.19.1.11.
Batson, Glenna. "Update on Proprioception: Considerations for Dance Education." *Journal of Dance Medicine & Science* 13, no. 2 (2009): 35–41.
Beckmann, Jürgen, Peter Gröpel, and Felix Ehrlenspiel. "Preventing Motor Skill Failure Through Hemisphere-Specific Priming: Cases From Choking Under Pressure." *Journal of Experimental Psychology: General* 142, no. 3 (2013): 679–691.
Daniels, Kathryn. "The Challenges of the Adolescent Dancer." *International Association of Dance Medicine and Science.* https://iadms.org/research-publications/resources-paper/, accessed August 2023.
Gingrasso, Susan. "Practical Resources for Dance Educators! Considering the Health and Well-Being of Our Young Dancers." *Dance Education in Practice* 6, no. 2 (2020): 24–28.
Haibach-Beach, Pamela S., Greg Reid, and Douglas Holden Collier. *Motor Learning and Development.* 2nd ed. Champaign, IL: Human Kinetics, 2018.
Haywood, Kathleen, and Nancy Getchell. *Life Span Motor Development.* 5th ed. Champaign, IL: Human Kinetics, 2009.
Henley, Matthew. "Sensation, Perception, and Choice in the Dance Classroom." *Journal of Dance Education* 14, no. 3 (2014): 95–100.
Humphrey, James Harry. *Child Development and Learning through Dance.* New York: AMS Press, 1987.
Krasnow, Donna, and Virginia Wilmerding. *Motor Learning and Control for Dance: Principles and Practices for Performers and Teachers.* Champaign, IL: Human Kinetics, 2015.
Magill, Richard A. *Motor Learning: Concepts and Applications.* Boston: McGraw-Hill, 2007.

Masaki, Hiroaki, Yuya Maruo, Alexandria Meyer, and Greg Hajcak. "Neural Correlates of Choking Under Pressure: Athletes High in Sports Anxiety Monitor Errors More When Performance Is Being Evaluated." *Developmental Neuropsychology* 42, no. 2 (2017): 104–112.

Oudejans, Raôul R.D., Wilma Kuijpers, Chris C. Kooijman, and Frank C. Bakker. "Thoughts and Attention of Athletes Under Pressure: Skill-Focus or Performance Worries?" *Anxiety, Stress, and Coping* 24, no. 1 (2011): 59–73.

Richardson, Megan, Marijeanne Liederbach, and Emily Sandow. "Functional Criteria for Assessing Pointe-Readiness." *Journal of Dance Medicine & Science* 14, no. 3 (2010): 82–88.

Rose, Debra J., and Robert W. Christina. *A Multilevel Approach to the Study of Motor Control and Learning.* San Francisco, CA: Benjamin Cummings, 2008.

Schmidt, Richard A., and Timothy Donald Lee. *Motor Control and Learning: A Behavioral Emphasis.* Champaign, IL: Human Kinetics, 1999.

Sigmundsson, Hermundur, Leif Trana, Remco Polman, and Monika Haga. "What is Trained Develops! Theoretical Perspective on Skill Learning." *Sports* 5, no. 2, (2017): 38. https://doi.org/10.3390/sports5020038.

Wulf, Gabriele. *Attention and Motor Skill Learning.* Champaign, IL: Human Kinetics, 2007.

Wyon, Matthew A., and Yiannis Koutedakis. "Muscular Fatigue: Considerations for Dance." *Journal of Dance Medicine & Science* 17, no. 2 (2013): 63–69.

CHAPTER 5

The Learning Process

Box 5.1 Chapter Objectives

After reading this chapter, you will be able to:

- Define motor learning
- Identify three theories of motor learning: Adam's closed-loop theory, Schmidt's schema theory, and the constraints-led approach
- Recognize the benefit of the dance teacher's consideration of student learning styles
- Explain the stages of motor learning as theorized by Fitts and Posner and Gentile
- Recognize characteristics that emerge during various stages of learning

Box 5.2 Chapter Vocabulary

associative stage
autonomous stage
bilateral transfer
cognitive stage
explicit learning
implicit learning
invariant feature
learning style
motor learning
negative transfer
nonregulatory condition
parameter
positive transfer
regulatory condition
schema
transfer of learning
zero transfer

DOI: 10.4324/b22952-8

Dance movement requires a voluntary action of muscles to produce a coordinated goal. Developing skill in dance movement implies that the student has attained a level of motor control and learning in a specific area. For students to acquire skill in dance, they must be active participants within the learning process. Each student learns in similar yet distinct modes. Some students require more time to mentally grasp material, while others may need additional time to embody the movement. Some learners will catch on quickly but have difficulty in retaining terminology from class to class. Each movement requires subtle yet distinctly different systematic motor and cognitive approaches within the body. Students may not be able to learn certain skills, such as a ballistic-type leap, in the same manner they grasp a deep hinge. It is important for the teacher to understand the motor learning process as well as the varying ways in which students may learn movement skills and concepts. Without this discernment, it will be difficult if not impossible for the teacher to effectively do their job, which is to help a student learn. Through understanding of the motor learning process, the dance teacher can better approach the dance curriculum and training environment. In turn, they can effectively help students progress from a novice to advanced level in technique and artistry.

FORMS OF LEARNING

Students experience different forms of cognitive learning within the dance class setting. They can acquire information without awareness or intention of learning, or they can learn through conscious and voluntary effort. These two primary forms of learning are referred to as implicit and explicit learning.

Implicit learning occurs without the student's conscious effort. As the student copies the dance teacher's visual demonstration, the movement becomes embodied within the student. Consider the call and response teaching pattern that is often utilized in a tap dance class. The teacher will execute a step or pattern, and the students must immediately replicate the movement in response without verbal instruction. The dancers are not given time to pause and think about how to do the step or emphasize aspects of the movement; they simply move. This instructional pattern is repeated many times until the dancers begin to implicitly learn the step or action being presented. Basic locomotor patterns, such as walking and running, are implicitly learned as a child.

Conversely, **explicit learning**, also referred to as declarative learning, is the result of the knowledge that is gained through focus and attention during the learning process. Explicit learning is not a form of motor learning, but instead refers to the cognitive functions that occur during motor learning.[1] Recognition of dance terminology, recalling the sequence of movement, and knowledge of dance facts and historical events are the results of explicit learning. In these learning situations, the student is using the visual or auditory sense to absorb and comprehend information. The learned information is then "expressed in declarative sentences."[2] For example, when asked by the instructor to identify the terminology for a movement, the student verbally responds with the correct term. Or a student may state, "I hear and understand the rhythm of the movement pattern." In both instances, the student had to consciously pay attention to visual or verbal instructions to learn the information.

Dancers will use both implicit and explicit learning within the dance class, although teachers will find that some students tend to lean toward one form of learning over the other. Some students will go with the flow and dive into attempting and practicing the movement at the dance teacher's prompt. They do not require explicit directions, but instead are comfortable modeling the movement of the teacher or other dancers. Other students will immediately have several questions and require a breakdown of the mechanics, structure, or timing of the movement in order to begin their attempts. The teacher must realize that both forms of learning are necessary and helpful to the healthy progression of the dance student.

THE BASICS OF MOTOR LEARNING

Motor learning is the change in ability that occurs through the experience of movement or engagement in practice. It is an internal process that requires practice, feedback, and knowledge of results, each of which are discussed in detail in later chapters. Leading motor behavior researcher Dr. Richard Schmidt identifies four characteristics specific to motor learning.[3] Learning is a process, requires practice or experience, results are relatively permanent, and outcomes cannot be directly observed but are inferred.

Learning Is a Process

Figure 5.1 reminds us that learning is a process. It does not happen in a vacuum, meaning it does not occur separate from other influences. A series of actions or events occur that direct a student to a new mental or physical state of being. Learning happens in stages (explored in depth in later sections). When a student first learns movement, they tend to focus on certain aspects of the skill. As their abilities improve, they begin to focus on the finer details and elements of the movement. The teacher and student may notice that, at times, plateaus in performance can arise. It is important to recognize that these are performance plateaus, not learning plateaus. Learning has not ceased during these periods of stagnation in skill improvement. Performance plateaus can be the result of a student's reduced motivation or limited ability to focus and pay attention to the task at hand. Extreme or abnormal amounts of fatigue could also interfere with students' performance. Dance educators should be mindful that performance plateaus are normal, and they do not mean that learning cannot continue. Do not dismiss the plateau, but rather work with the student to discover the reason for the pause in improvement.

Additionally, the teacher and student could be applying a faulty performance measure, known as the ceiling effect. In this instance, the definition of a successful performance is restricted, and scores cannot extend beyond a certain point of the metric used. For example, if a teacher is assessing the number of correctly executed axel turns out of a total of ten executions, peak performance would be capped at ten executions. Essentially, improvement is limited. Perhaps the dancer's motor learning can be further enhanced to incorporate an entire practice session of accurately executed axel turns. Performance measurements also do not account for the cognitive learning that transpires.

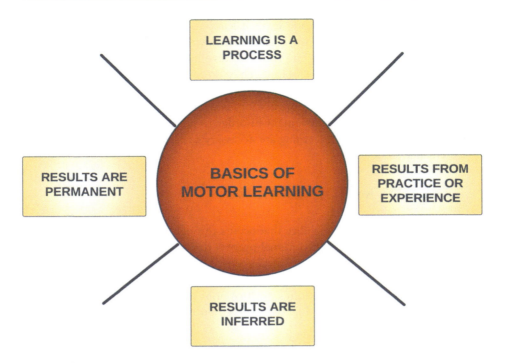

FIGURE 5.1 Depiction of the basic aspects of motor learning.

Practice and Experience

Motor learning occurs through practice and experience. The teacher introduces vocabulary and movement ideas and provides opportunity for the students to practice skills and apply concepts. It is through classroom and performative experiences that students engage in motor learning. Some students will require significant or extended periods of instruction and experience before learning can be observed by the teacher. Practice as a component of the dance class setting is discussed in detail in Chapter 14.

Transfer of Learning

Within any learning environment, educators consider how learning in one area can be applied within another area. This is the foundation on which curricula are developed. **Transfer of learning** occurs when one learned experience influences an individual's ability to learn or perform a new skill. For instance, the dance teacher will teach a young child a basic step hop pattern (a skip). Once this skill is learned, the motor pattern can be later transferred to an *arabesque sauté*. Transfer of learning is the generalization of a skill. The transfer is typically small and dependent upon the similarity between the two movement tasks that are being associated to one another.

Positive transfer occurs when a movement experience aids or facilitates the learning of a new movement skill. The effectiveness of this will depend on the similarities between the movements. These could be in the basic mechanics or patterning of the movement or in the concept and approach of the movement. A simple *assemblé* and a *jeté* are two different movements in ballet; however, they both begin from the same position and push off of one leg. Positive transfer is especially helpful for the novice dancer who is just beginning to learn various movements as opposed to the advanced dancer whose focus is on the nuances of movement. When a movement experience hinders or interferes with the learning of a new movement skill, it is called **negative transfer**. Some dancers who have significant experience in one form of dance may find it more difficult to then learn an entirely contrasting form of dance. For example, a dancer accustomed to always pointing their ankle and toes in ballet may find it difficult to relax the ankle and foot in tap dance. **Zero transfer** occurs when a movement experience has no effect on the learning of a new movement skill. Movement skills that can be more readily learned with one limb after it has been learned with the opposite limb is **bilateral transfer**. This is observed in the dance class as students are often more readily able to execute movement on the "second" side of an exercise.

The more movement experience a student has, the more likely the student will demonstrate evidence of transfer of learning. This explains the desire by many professional companies for versatility in training among their dancers. Dancers with diverse training backgrounds are then more prepared for a range of choreographic demands. Movement skills can be complex. When there is an element of transfer between skills, the dance teacher can make use of that to aid in the students' comprehension of the new movement skill and help their retention of the new movement. The teacher should be mindful that initial attempts are approached correctly so to avoid negative transfer in future skills. The attention of the students should be directed to the element that can be transferred, such as a specific movement, action, or rhythm. The teacher should strive to include a variety of examples when teaching. This will help the students understand how the skill can be applicable in many contexts.

Indicators of Learning

As indicated in Figure 5.1, we cannot observe learning; rather, we infer that it has occurred. It is important for the teacher to distinguish between performing and learning. When considering an individual's performance, the teacher observes and studies the student's behavior and movement characteristics and actions. Learning, however, is not directly observable. Rather, it is inferred based upon an individual's performance and change in state over a period of time. There are, however, some movement characteristics that help indicate when motor learning has occurred. These can include rate of improvement, consistency, movement efficiency, attention, and adaptability.

- **Rate of improvement** – The dance teacher monitors a student's performance over a period of time. The improvement rate decreases as the students progress through the learning stages (discussed later in this chapter). Beginning level dancers will improve by leaps and bounds, yet as they become advanced dancers, their improvement rate will slow. Although advanced dancers demonstrate a decrease in improvement rate, their learning is quite rich and will be sustained, unlike beginners who may struggle to retain information.

- **Consistency** – Is the student able to sustain a high level of performance over time? If so, it could be an indicator that motor learning has occurred; however, it is important that this is not the only measure used to assess learning. A student may have adapted a bad habit that they are consistently executing. The student's sustained ability may have execution errors in which case accurate learning has not taken place. The teacher should ensure that students are not consistently performing weakened or inefficient versions of a movement or skill.
- **Movement efficiency** – Once a student learns a skill, they will require less energy to execute the skill. Beginning dancers will exert more energy when first learning movement skills and struggle with the degrees of freedom problem (discussed in Chapter 4) and find difficulty in executing coordinated movement. Students will overuse certain muscles and often engage extra muscles unnecessarily during movement execution. As the learning process continues, dancers learn to be efficient with their use of muscle activation as well as their use of energy. Through the process of learning, students begin to understand and can apply appropriate technique to the movement, reducing the amount of effort applied in performance. Dancers learn to be efficient with their use of muscle activation and their use of energy.
- **Attention** – Similarly, the amount of attention the student must use to complete a movement will decrease once learning has occurred. The novice dancer will have trouble focusing on only the important or necessary aspect when learning movement. The experienced dancer can turn their attention to the relevant elements of a task. This dancer will also be able to perform movements with less conscious thought than the beginner.
- **Adaptability** – With learning comes the ability to alter muscles or movement as needed to match the environment. Once a student has learned a skill, they can adapt the movement as needed and embrace new approaches to movement. For example, dancers who have learned choreography can adjust accordingly to spatial conflicts when performing on a stage that may require movement to be done smaller or larger or in different directions. The dancers are still able to successfully perform the choreography despite the challenges that may arise mid-performance. Adaptability also relates to transfer of learning.

The dancer teacher should note that none of these measures can be used alone to assess learning. Rather, they are used in combination to assist the teacher and the student to determine if learning has occurred and the student is able to retain and transfer skills and knowledge. Learning takes time; it is not an instantaneous process. It requires the student's consistent application of effort, practice, and patience from both the teacher and student.

Box 5.3 Choking Under Pressure

Elite athletes should be in an advanced stage of learning where movement execution is essentially automatic in many ways. Here, these athletes can normally perform a movement without focus, but when under extreme pressure, their movement pattern may be disrupted, causing them to "choke," or demonstrate a severe decline in ability. This event is not limited to professional athletes; anyone who has demonstrated proficiency in a skill can find themselves unable to perform when under pressure. While this may be the result of anxiety, researchers have identified two theories that could also cause individuals to choke.

Distraction theories suggest that the individual shifts their attention from information pertinent to the movement to irrelevant thoughts related to the movement. They have distracted their attention from the fundamental aspects of the movement needed to proficiently perform the movement. Self-focus theories claim that individuals, in a sense, become hyper attentive to the sequential steps of the movement or in controlling the execution of those steps. This internal focus interferes with the normal processes of the body mechanics and impairs performance.

The dance teacher may see both of these theories at play within the dance class setting. The distraction theory can explain the student's sudden lack of balance when the instructor walks by or makes eye contact with the student. A student's inability to complete a riff combination in tap dance or a *fouetté* turn in ballet could be the result of their overfocusing on each individual sound or action of the movement. The dance teacher can help students with positive reinforcement and reminders of what the student can or should focus on during execution.

Learning Is Permanent

Once learning occurs, the results are relatively permanent. We cannot unlearn that which we have learned, although we may momentarily "forget" aspects of a learned skill, or our abilities may diminish over time. How often has a song played, and you immediately begin singing the lyrics? This is an example of having learned the material, and as a result it continues to remain stored in your memory. When learning transpires, proficiency is maintained over extended lengths of time with or without practice. The dance teacher may ask, "Does the student's ability to correctly execute movement persist over time without practice?" The teacher will observe consistency in movement performance and persistence in effort from students when learning has occurred. This characteristic speaks to the relatively permanent results of learning.

UNDERSTANDING MEMORY

Memory is a fundamental component within the learning process. Memory allows an individual to store and retrieve information within the brain. During a dance class, a student continually learns new skills, patterns of movement, and more effective strategies of executing movement. As this information is learned, it must be retained by the student and then easily recalled so that skill and artistic progression can occur. It is important for the dance teacher to understand the functional aspects of memory and how to enhance a student's learning through memory. As highlighted in Chapters 4 and 5, individuals rely on the various forms of memory as information is processed, retrieved, and stored. Instructional strategies can assist the teacher in helping students to retrieve and retain information, boosting the likelihood of success within the learning process.

Information gained from the environment through our senses is first contained within our short-term sensory memory. This stage of memory serves as a precursor to short-term memory and encompasses a large capacity of information, yet information only remains for literally a second at a time.[4] When driving down the street, we see all the billboards, street signs, businesses, and other cars around us, yet very little of that information remains with us once we see it. A similar scenario unfolds within the dance studio. During any given point of the class, the student may take in the reflection of the sun as it shines on the floor, hear the sound of the teacher's voice, sense the child next to them jumping, notice the parents in the waiting area, and feel the rush of air from the fan overhead. Yet, in the next second, the student has dismissed the teacher's voice, and their other senses have moved on to gather new information.

Recall from Chapter 4 that short-term memory, which also encompasses working memory, is where information is processed. The sensory information that one collects is either dismissed or moves to short-term memory and can then be processed. This memory space allows for the integration of the newly acquired material with information retrieved from long-term memory. However, only a limited capacity of data is held in short-term memory and for a limited amount of time. Research indicates that short-term memory holds only five to nine pieces of information at a time.[5] Authors Krasnow and Wilmerding suggest that elite athletes, including dancers, can store more than nine items in their short-term memory during sports practice yet most likely cannot reproduce this capacity in their everyday life.[6] Individuals are able to retain information within their working memory for 20–30 seconds.[7] It is within the short-term memory that the dance student holds on to newly taught movement and assimilates it with previously learned material. As the student is learning a reverse leap in jazz dance, the student may recall the body mechanics of a regular split leap along with the actions required to quickly change the body's facing while in the air. The student may even connect the action to an *arabesque fouetté sauté*, should they also have that experience. The connections made within the short-term memory become the first step in developing near-term and far-term transfer of movement ideas.

Long-term memory is the function of memory where information is accumulated and permanently stored. Dance terminology, past movement attempts, and similar experiences are retained here, enabling the dance student to recall how to execute the movement. Unlike short-term memory, long-term memory has an increased capacity and duration for information. Through the combination of the devised lesson plan and use of instructional strategies, the dance teacher encourages learned principles to transfer from the students' working memory to their long-term memory. As the teacher demonstrates the back-side-front pathway of a basic *pas de bourrée* and then provides practice, they assist in the transfer of this movement pattern to the students' long-term memory. This learned sequence can be recalled later when the teacher offers the movement in various approaches and settings.

Students sometimes have difficulty in transferring learned movement as interference can deter the learning process. Information introduced before or after a learning session can hinder an individual's ability to learn a skill or concept. For example, if a student learns and practices an exercise that includes turns in one direction, such as outward turns, yet the next exercise requires inward turns, the student may struggle to learn the new turning approach. The original direction of turning has been patterned into the student's movement, and this experience can then interfere with their ability to now turn in a different direction. In another example, a student learns a combination and successfully performs it. They are then taught a new combination. When asked to reproduce the original movement, they may demonstrate difficulty because the new movement ideas have interfered with their recall of the original combination. This understanding of the stages of memory and risk of interference reminds the dance teacher of the importance of organizing information and making connections as they teach new skills and movement concepts to students.

Forgetting information may be the result of memory loss over time – also referred to as trace decay – yet there may be other reasons why a student forgets learned movement and concepts. When an individual forgets information stored in long-term memory, it is often not that the information is gone from memory, but rather the individual is simply not able to locate and recall it. In some instances, the information may not have been fully learned and transferred to long-term memory. Consider the scenario where students learn a phrase of choreography. After teaching the movement and then having the students practice, the teacher gives the class a break. The students disperse to the water fountain, restroom, or to engage in social conversation with their peers. The teacher then calls the students back and shares a quick unrelated story with the students before revisiting the choreography. If the students did not fully learn the movement, they will have difficulty in reproducing the phrase after the break and idle conversations.

When a student commits information to their long-term memory, habits begin to form. If information or movement patterns are learned incorrectly, poor movement habits will form. Because these habits are embedded into the long-term memory, they become hard to break. Consider the student who is taught to shuffle with the upper leg held still, the ankle tense, and the toes clenched. This student will then have difficulty changing their physical approach to the shuffle. Even if a student learns movement correctly, they can still struggle to change their style or approach because of how the movement has been transferred to their long-term memory. For example, a student is taught to execute a *pas de bourrée*, or triplet, in a jazz dance class with an up-up-down movement pattern. In a later class, a different jazz dance teacher may ask the student to remain grounded with the knees bent throughout the *pas de bourrée*. The student has already committed the up-up-down spatial aspect into their long-term and muscle memory. Remaining low and grounded during the movement execution may prove difficult and take an adjustment period to learn the new approach.

To help students appropriately prepare their short-term working memory and recall movement ideas from their long-term memory, the dance teacher considers the way in which material is presented and conveyed to students. These instructional strategies range from mode of presentation to division of movement into parts to specific use of cueing and pacing. The following sections of this chapter provide further information the dance teacher may consider to enhance the learning process.

THEORIES OF MOTOR LEARNING

There are several theories of motor learning that researchers and behaviorists have developed over the years. The authors have chosen to isolate Adams' closed-loop theory, Schmidt's schema theory, and the constraints-led approach within this section. Each correlate to the learning of dance movement and can assist the dance teacher in determining how students may approach the learning of dance.

Adams' Closed-Loop Theory

In 1971, Jack Adams developed the first motor learning theory. Recall from Chapter 4 the discussion of motor control and closed-loop systems. Based on the closed-loop system of motor control, Adams' closed-loop theory of motor learning relies on the use of sensory feedback in navigating movement results and incorporates the component of memory within the learning process. This motor learning theory encompasses two unique aspects of memory: memory trace and perceptual trace. As a student learns a skill, they generate a memory trace through their initial attempts of the skill. In subsequent attempts, the comparison between the feedback received from the current movement attempt and the memory or reference of the movement's correct version creates a perceptual trace within the CNS. Feedback of the movement attempt "leaves a trace" within the individual's neural pathways and brain.[8] Each time the student attempts to perform the skill, the perceptual trace gets closer to the correct version of the movement; therefore, the student's skill accuracy is improved.

At the core, a student is provided with a movement task and utilizes the instructions (visual demonstration or image, verbal cues, etc.) to attempt the movement. The student then recalls the original demonstration for error detection and practices again. Through repeated practice and correction of errors, execution becomes more accurate. Learning is strengthened through repetitive practice and sensory feedback. The two memory states within this theory work best with slower movements where students are afforded more time for cognitive processing. As with all movement learning, a teacher's watchful eye is required for further guidance.

Adam's closed-loop theory is a memory-based explanation of learning. This theory is limited due in part to its reliance on feedback. It does not allow for the intentional choices that humans may make during movement execution, nor does it account for learning that can occur void of sensory feedback. There is additional concern that this theory can be harmful to learning. Through poor visual demonstration or without appropriate teacher-guided feedback, there is great opportunity for incorrect perceptual traces to be made. In this case, the student may develop bad habits or incorrectly learn skills.

This theory does emphasize the need for the dance teacher to provide correct and adequate visual demonstrations and clear verbal instructions of movement. Without appropriate instructions, students can easily misconstrue directions and/or movement execution and risk injury or the development of poor habits.

Schmidt's Schema Theory

In 1975, Richard Schmidt presented his schema theory, a contrasting theory to Adams' work. His theory emphasizes the open-loop process of motor control and utilizes general motor programs. General motor programs were identified in Chapter 4. A general motor program (GMP) is a grouping of commands stored in the memory that inform the musculature to execute a given movement or pattern of movements. GMPs are particularly useful when considering classes of actions that are similar, such as the many types of *sissonne* in ballet or *shuffle* in tap dance.

There are two additional aspects of a GMP for us to now consider, parameter and invariant feature. The component of the GMP that does not change is called the **invariant feature**. A *sissonne* is always a jump from two feet and landing on one foot. The movement may then be performed in different directions, at altering tempos, and with opposing body lines. These variations in execution are called the **parameters**. As the dancer prepares to execute a *sissonne*, they must consider how to execute the motor program. What will be the starting position of the feet? In which direction will the jump travel? What will be the position/line of the upper body? The dancer then decides to set the parameters for the jump accordingly. In a separate example, the invariant feature of the shuffle is the swing of the leg to strike the foot to the floor twice. The parameters of the shuffle's GMP can include aspects such as the line of direction (front, side, back, crossing the other foot, etc.) or the part of the foot that strikes the floor (i.e., ball, heel, edge of the shoe, etc.).

Central to Schmidt's theory is the concept of a **schema**, or set of rules, for a movement. A GMP may have been generated for a movement skill; however, the concept of a schema allows the individual to apply a specific set of criteria to further adapt the GMP. A schema enables the individual to take a GMP and apply specific information to it to assist in motor learning. When a movement is learned and attempted, an individual places five types of information into their short-term memory.[9]

- **Basic general motor program** (GMP) of the movement
- **Invariant features of the movement** (aspects of the movement that will not change)
- **Parameters of the GMP** (aspects of the movement that can be varied)
- **Outcome of the movement** (knowledge of the results)
- **Sensory feedback of the movement outcome** (feeling, appearance, sound of the movement, etc.)

This information is then summarized within Schmidt's schema theory in two sections. First, the student uses the recall schema to call on the GMP to prepare and produce the movement. Next, the recognition schema evaluates the movement outcome and incorporates feedback after the fact to detect errors.[10] Schmidt's theory emphasizes variability of practice rather than practicing the movement in the exact same manner repeatedly. The variability enhances the movement's schema that is stored in long-term memory.

Schmidt's theory encourages students to develop associations among movements. This theory then suggests that a student can learn a new skill that has never been attempted based on the rules that the student has already established. For example, consider the student who practices and learns the standard time step in tap dance. They can then apply variations to the time step and execute double, triple, etc. time steps without much difficulty because they have already established the schema for the fundamental weight change and rhythmic pattern of the step. This theory can also explain why some students find it difficult to apply feedback. The student who consistently turns with their arms held too low will have difficulty re-training their recall schema to turn with their arms held in a higher position.

As the dance teacher approaches curriculum design and lesson planning, they should consider the way in which they are scaffolding movement. Fundamental movements are introduced first, and variations can then be taught and explored. The effective dance teacher instructs students in basic movement patterns, where a GMP is established, and then offers variations for the student to learn. Students' motor learning is facilitated because the GMP has been established and connections are made between movement developments. For example, the dance teacher can teach a basic shuffle and help the student development a schema to then adapt the movement within various parameters.

Constraints-Led Approach

The constraints-led approach contrasts the earlier memory-based theories in that it focuses on the relationship between perception and the environment. This perspective stems from the dynamic systems approach (discussed in Chapter 4), which looks at the interaction between the individual, the nature of the task, and the environment. The synergy between the learner's perception of the task and the surrounding environment creates a dynamic learning process focused on problem-solving and generating a movement solution.

The constraints-led approach follows a nonlinear mode of instruction allowing for individual learning pathways within a single classroom. These include individual-based, task-based, and environment-based constraints. The student's physical body can create obstacles that restrict the learning of a movement. The student who struggled in their development of basic motor patterns may present difficulty in learning dance movement patterns. For example, a student may have difficulty in executing a *chassé* step exercise. They may consistently and inappropriately switch their leading foot. The complexities of the task itself could provide a learning barrier. For example, the jumping action and "hang time" required of a single wing in tap dance could restrict the student learner. An environment-based constraint may be physical or social aspects that discourage or intimidate student participation, thus hindering motor learning and development.

Through verbal instructions and visual demonstrations, the teacher restricts the movement to facilitate the student's learning and adaptability. Rather than encouraging students to focus on multiple aspects of a prance in a modern dance class, the teacher encourages students to release their weight into the floor, which affects their movement quality and execution. This quality is then incorporated in other movement patterns throughout the class.

The constraints-led approach requires students to be active participants in the learning process, often referred to as discovery learning, and encourages students to adapt to the constraints as they explore movement options and strategize new action plans to reach the movement goal. Through varied practice opportunities and trial-and-error, students make individual action plans based on their perceptions of the information they are provided. In this method, teachers may be more "hands-off" in their interaction with students.

The dance class often provides an opportunity for students to take time and explore a movement idea after a skill or concept has been introduced. It is in these moments that the students are engaged in discovery learning and focused on individual and task-based constraints. In an improvisation class, the teacher will frequently establish constraints during an activity. Movement that remains in a low level may be explored, movement may be limited to only one body part, or a specific rhythm might be reproduced through spontaneous locomotor actions. In a modern dance class, students executing the Horton Lateral T may struggle with flexibility in the hamstring of the supporting leg to achieve optimal position. The movement is constrained in the position of the straight and lengthened position of the standing leg into a bent position. The dancers will learn to emphasize the strong supporting leg and continue to build flexibility. The goal of these exercises is for the student to problem-solve and self-organize their muscles into the prime manner for their body in facilitating the action goal.

The three motor learning theories discussed have their advantages and disadvantages. They each emphasize the need for practice. Adams' closed-loop theory makes use of blocked practice, or repeatedly practicing the same skill in the same manner, while Schmidt's schema theory and the constraints-led approach emphasize variability in practice. Adams' closed-loop theory is best applied to slower movements that allow time for sensory feedback. Schmidt's schema theory better identifies with movements that must be pre-programmed upon execution. The constraints-led approach encourages students to take a more active role in the learning process as they navigate imposing constraints. Each motor learning theory requires a teacher's careful guidance to fully support the students' acquisition of skill.

LEARNING STYLES

Each individual approaches the learning environment in unique ways. It is important that the teacher recognizes the different ways in which students approach learning – their **learning style** – and seek to teach to those learning preferences. In a class of many students with a variety of learning styles, this can prove challenging. Yet, through understanding the distinct learning styles, the teacher becomes better equipped to engage all students and communicate effectively.

The VARK Method

When considering learning styles, dancers often immediately think of visual, auditory, and kinesthetic learning approaches. These types of learning preferences are abundantly inherent within the dance setting and become automatic in the dancer's mind. Neil Fleming identified this learning style as the VARK (Visual, Auditory, Reading, Kinesthetic) method. See Figure 5.2.

Dancers may have a preference for one style over another; however, they will typically blend and balance learning through the visual, auditory, and kinesthetic cues (discussed in Chapter 13) within the dance class. It is important that the dance teacher encourage all

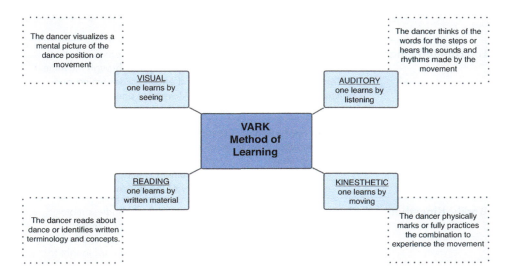

FIGURE 5.2 Diagram of the VARK method of learning with dance-based applications.

98 Motor and Cognitive Learning Processes

three styles (or four as appropriate) with students. Relying on only one style can hinder one's learning. If a student only develops the ability to learn through using their visual sense, then their ability to understand timing or musical phrasing may suffer. Some students rely solely on listening to the instructional cues rather than attempting to experience the movement physically. When placed in a new setting with a different instructor, they may find it difficult to learn movement of a different style or pattern construction. The dance teacher should be mindful to help students recognize their preferred learning style but also emphasize the importance of developing learning through other means. Chapters 13 and 14 discuss instructional and practice strategies.

Gardner's Theory of Multiple Intelligences

In the 1980s, Howard Gardner presented his research in the theory of multiple intelligences. Gardner's theory proposes that an individual does not just rely on one type of intelligence to process information, but rather may make use of a range of intelligences. He believes there are eight different intelligences that an individual may encompass during learning and problem-solving settings. See Table 5.1.

Gardner claims that his eight intelligences comprise the entire spectrum of human understanding and cognition.[11] Yet, each person is designed with their own blend of the intelligences. Some individuals may be a mix of linguistic, musical, and intrapersonal, and

TABLE 5.1 Gardner's Theory of Multiple Intelligences and its correlation to dance training.

Gardner's Theory of Multiple Intelligences

Intelligence	Description	Dance Application
Linguistic	Understanding and utilizing words, spoken or written	Dance classes utilize terminology and often provide historical context through stories of significant events and influential individuals.
Logical-Mathematical	Capacity to reason and analyze abstractly, discern logical number patterns	Choreography encompasses abstract ideas made tangible through movement. Movement encompasses timing and rhythm. Movement phrases often consist of logical patterns and sequences.
Musical	Ability to appreciate or produce musical theory and composition	There is an inherent relationship between musical structure and movement phrases. Rhythm is key in many forms of dance, and movement is enhanced through the musicality of the dancer.
Bodily-Kinesthetic	Capacity for movement of the body	Dance is more than mindless motor movements of the body. There is expression and technique applied to the movement. Dancers are taught to be fully attuned to their bodies and to the movement, moving aesthetically, efficiently, and safely.

Gardner's Theory of Multiple Intelligences

Intelligence	Description	Dance Application
Visual-Spatial	Understanding in pictures and capacity to sense the space and the self within the space	The dance teacher employs visual demonstrations, and then dancers replicate the movement they see. Dance phrases and choreography require the use of space. The positive, negative, and stage space must be navigated by the dancers.
Interpersonal	Capacity for social interaction	Dance requires collaboration and communication with others. Through feedback, partner work, discussion, and problem-solving within rehearsals, the dance setting provides opportunity for individuals to connect and exchange ideas with those around them.
Intrapersonal	Capacity for self-awareness	Dance can organically offer individuals an opportunity to release emotion and connect to themselves. Choreography often dives into personal reflection, themes, or stories.
Naturalistic	Capacity to categorize objects in nature	Children often learn dance movement through nature-based imagery. "Scurry like leaves in the wind," "Move your arms as though you are floating in water," or "Hop like a bunny." Choreography often encompasses themes of nature as well.

it is through these areas that they tend to learn and operate best. Regardless of the blend of intelligences, "an individual's capacity in a particular intelligence will have a direct bearing on the way they learn."[12] For example, if a student has a high ability to discern number patterns and think logically, the student will appreciate knowing the counts for a movement pattern or exercise.

Teachers should recognize that students will learn movement differently depending on their learning strengths. Regardless of the theories of learning styles or approaches considered, the dance teacher should strive to vary their teaching style to reach the spectrum of learners. Not only will this ensure that all students are learning but also enhance the scope of approaches in which the students can learn.

STAGES OF MOTOR LEARNING

Regardless of age, individuals progress through stages of learning as they are introduced to and improve upon motor skills. These stages of learning apply to the teacher's approach to lesson planning and in assisting students' progression of dance technique. This section identifies two learning models: Fitts and Posner's three-stage theory and Gentile's two-stage theory. Recognizing the characteristics of the learning stages can enable the dance teacher to better identify the behavioral, cognitive, and physical needs of students within each phase of the learning process.

Fitts and Posner's Three-Stage Theory

In 1967, psychologists and researchers Paul Fitts and Michael Posner presented a three-stage model for motor learning that is still used by researchers and educators today. Fitts and Posner identify these stages as the cognitive stage, the associative stage, and the autonomous stage. The stages, which are based around observed behavioral changes within the learner, advance from novice to expert. Within each stage, the teacher plays a specific role.

The Cognitive Stage

The cognitive stage can be considered a beginning learning level. In the **cognitive stage**, the learner is focused on understanding the basic elements of the moment. The student uncovers the nature of the task or movement, develops mechanisms to accomplish the skill, and discerns the best strategies to execute movement. It is in this stage that students learn the basics of the dance form and develop a foundation for dance technique. The novice dancer falls into the cognitive learning stage.

During this stage, the student expends a lot of mental focus and requires sensory information during movement execution. The student will visualize movement, often saying the steps aloud or to themselves as they dance, and they will ask a lot of questions. Students in this stage may become easily confused in simple tasks as they may feel inundated with information. Students experiment with trial-and-error as their body navigates coordination and control. Their movement will be uncoordinated and may appear awkward or clunky. Students may be aware of their errors but unknowing in how to make corrections on their own. Performance will be inconsistent in this stage; however, students will experience the largest amount of gain in skill improvement during this stage.

The dance teacher should provide verbal and visual instruction and demonstration. The teacher will find offering targeted feedback and reinforcement to be effective. Additionally, the teacher should model the behavior they expect and be quick to encourage students.

The Associative Stage

The associative stage can be considered an intermediate learning level. Students now have a basic understanding and comprehension of what to do regarding the dance technique. In the **associative stage**, students begin to refine their actions, focusing on the how of the movement. Students tend to rely less on visual and verbal cues and begin to tune in to the kinesthetic sense more. Because students can already execute dance movements, improvement will be smaller and more gradual. Students will make fewer errors, and performance will be more consistent. The student will slowly develop the ability to self-cue, which they will begin to employ. They will recognize errors and demonstrate the ability to apply and maintain instructor-guided feedback.

The dance teacher should now focus more on the composition of exercises and the construction of the lesson plan in a way that will challenge and further develop the students' learning and practice opportunities. Rather than introducing vocabulary, the teacher devises creative exercises for students to enhance and refine their abilities. The teacher still needs to offer feedback and reinforcement. They will find proprioceptive cues to be helpful to the student. These are instructional cues that emphasize body awareness and the sensation within the body during movement execution.

The Autonomous Stage

The autonomous stage can be considered an advanced learning level. A professional dancer is in the **autonomous stage**. It takes significant practice for a student to reach this stage; not all dancers advance to this level. In this stage, the student's movement can appear effortless or automatic as though it is performed without conscious thought. The student has the ability to execute movement while focusing elsewhere, such as on the artistry of the performance. The student no longer needs to worry about the what or how of the steps. Instead, they can consider decision-making strategies in their overall performance. They make minimal errors, resulting in a strong and consistent performance of movement. Improvement may not be blatantly visible because of the skill level of the student, although they will continually work to fine-tune their abilities. The student in this stage can reliably self-cue and is committed to developing proficiency in their technique and artistry and consistently performing at a high level.

The dance teacher's goal with a student in this learning stage is to motivate students and help them maintain their skill level. The teacher should provide variability in practice so that skills are approached in a variety of manners and conditions. The dance teacher recognizes that students may not achieve the autonomous stage in all forms of dance. A student's achievement of this high learning level is dependent upon the quality of their instruction and the quantity and quality of their practice.

TABLE 5.2 Details of the features of Fitts and Posner's three-stage theory of motor learning.

Fitts and Posner's Three-Stage Theory of Motor Learning

Stage	Student	Teacher
Cognitive Stage	• Focuses on gathering information • Demonstrates large gains in improvement yet is inconsistent in performance	• Breaks down the movement and conveys to students how to execute the skills • Uses verbal and visual instruction and demonstrations
Associative Stage	• Focuses on assimilating and integrating movement • Demonstrates small gains in improvement and may be disjointed in movement execution, yet conscious effort	• Creates exercises to help students refine their skills and make connections between movement ideas • Offers feedback and reinforcement • Utilizes instructional cues to help students' proprioception
Autonomous Stage	• Focuses on varied practice • Demonstrates automatic execution and ease in effort	• Offers appropriate feedback and fosters opportunity for students to self-cue • Incorporates variable practice conditions

Gentile's Two-Stage Theory

Antoinette Gentile created a two-stage learning model in the 1970s. Her theory looks at the movement as well as instructional strategies to facilitate the student's progress in learning the movement.

Initial Stage

In the first stage, the goal of the student is "getting the idea of the movement." This initial stage parallels Fitts and Posner's cognitive stage. Here, the learner is focused on two goals: figure out the coordination of the movement and distinguish between the regulatory and nonregulatory conditions of the movement. **Regulatory condition** is a term used by Gentile to describe the aspect of the skill and environment that are relevant to the movement. For example, the student needs to know how much space in which they have to move and the tempo of the music. In some choreography, the spacing or timing of other moving dancers might be part of the regulatory conditions. The **nonregulatory conditions** are those aspects that distract the learner from successfully attaining the movement skill. Movement outside of an observation window can catch a child's eye during class, or the creaky sound of a fan propped in the corner of the studio can easily distract a young dancer. Students must learn to tune out nonregulatory conditions while dancing and focus on only those aspects that are essential to the task at hand.

The student employs mental focus and uses trial-and-error strategies as they learn how to execute movement skills. At the end of this stage, the student can do the movement but not efficiently, and performance is not consistent. The primary focus of the dance teacher in this stage is to break down the movement and convey to students how to execute the skills. Similar to the cognitive stage, the teacher should use verbal and visual instruction and demonstrations. To maximize the learning process, the teacher should emphasize the regulatory conditions to avoid opportunities for students to focus on bad habits.

Later Stage

The fixation and diversification stage, known as the later stage, of Gentile's learning model connects to Fitts and Posner's associative and autonomous stages. In this stage, movement is refined, and consistent performance is developed. The student focuses on efficient execution of movement and then fixates on consistent application in performance. To allow for variability and enhance true learning, it is important for the student to also practice the skill under a range of conditions. This diversifies the student's abilities.

In order for skill improvement to continue, Gentile's later stage aims for the characteristics of consistency, economy of effort, and adaptability. The student should demonstrate consistency in performance from one day to the next or one week to the next. When a dancer learns choreography, they must be able to consistently execute it with precision in each performance. The student that displays economy of effort is demonstrating efficiency in their movement. They are not using more muscle effort than needed to complete a skill. Finally, the student should demonstrate adaptability within their skill execution; they should be able to take what they have learned regarding a movement skill and apply that knowledge to meet any performance demands for that skill. If a student is able to do *jeté battu*, they should be able to execute the skill within any allegro combination.

The earlier text offers two theories for discerning stages in motor learning. The dance teacher could choose to follow either, or perhaps even a blending of the two. They are

TABLE 5.3 Details of Gentile's two-stage theory of motor learning.

Gentile's Two-Stage Theory of Motor Learning

Stage	Student	Teacher
Initial Stage	• Utilizes trial-and-error strategies as they learn • Movement execution lacks efficiency and consistency	• Breaks down the movement and conveys to students how to execute the skills • Uses verbal and visual instruction and demonstrations
Later Stage	• Achieves consistency in performance • Displays economy of effort/movement efficiency • Demonstrates adaptability within their skill execution	• Offers appropriate feedback and fosters opportunity for students to self-cue • Incorporates variable practice conditions

both helpful in reminding the teacher of the cognitive and behavioral processes that occur during learning. It is important to note that a student could be in different learning stages in different forms of dance. A dancer could be in an autonomous learning stage in tap dance yet be a novice ballet dancer. Additionally, some dancers demonstrate advanced, or high-level, cognitive learning skills yet are not able to physically produce the movement due to individual constraints. Some dancers naturally excel at turning but struggle in elevation movements. Other dancers are naturally inclined to perform ballistic type movements but have trouble in executing turning movements. A dancer may be constrained in leg extension work due to limitations in leg, hip, or back flexibility. Another dancer may not be able to execute correct ballet movement with clear turnout control due to constrained rotation in the hip socket. These situations may not imply that the dancer has not "learned" the movement, but rather the dancer does not have the physical capacity to perform the movement with the desired aesthetic execution. By highlighting the variables that are at play during the learning process, the dance teacher can better prepare, in both curriculum design and instructional strategies, for the dance class.

Box 5.4 The Speed-Accuracy Trade-Off

In the late 1800s, psychologist Robert Woodworth conducted early research in motor behavior, exploring the inverse relationship between speed and accuracy. In 1954, psychologist Paul Fitts devised a mathematical law, Fitt's Law, to explain the findings. Ultimately, this law identifies that the degree of difficulty of a movement affects the speed of execution.[13] As an individual increases their speed in executing a motor skill, their accuracy in the skill will diminish. When an individual focuses on accuracy of a motor skill, their speed will diminish. The dance teacher will notice the same results in the dance class. Students will demonstrate greater technical errors as they increase their movement speed. As students focus on specificity and accuracy in movement, their speed will decrease. Can you think of times in the dance class when a teacher may want to focus more on speed or accuracy? How could a teacher help the dance student improve in both areas?

Characteristics of Learning

It is clear that learning occurs in some form of stages and that changes occur in an individual's ability and performance as they progress through the stages from a novice to an expert. Recall the indicators of learning discussed in the beginning of this chapter. As a student learns, the dancer teacher will notice a marked rate of improvement, consistency in performance, efficiency in movement effort and energy, application of attention, and ability to adapt skills through different approaches and conditions. Recognizing characteristics that the student will display as they move through the stages of learning can be useful to the dance educator as they guide and encourage the student's development of skill and artistry. It is unfair for a dance teacher to expect the same rate of improvement from a higher-level dancer as a beginning level student or anticipate the novice student to demonstrate fluid and controlled movement execution by week two.

CHAPTER SUMMARY

This chapter explores the learning process with focus given to the styles, theories, and stages that students may experience as they grapple with skill acquisition. Whether learned implicitly or explicitly, motor learning is a process that requires practice and experience. Its inferred results are relatively permanent and can often be transferred among similar skills.

Adams' closed-loop theory and Schmidt's schema theory offer memory-based learning perspectives for slower, closed skills and more rapid, open skills, respectively. The constraints-led approach provides a discovery-based learning experience that enables the student to problem-solve while devising action plans for optimal results. Students approach the learning process with distinct preferences, or learning styles, that the dance teacher should strive to recognize. The awareness of how students approach the learning process prepares the educator to be better equipped to engage and communicate effectively with all students.

In addition to individual learning styles, the effective dance teacher should be aware of the learning stages through which a student will progress. This chapter discusses the three-stage theory of Fitts and Posner's and Gentile's two-stage theory. Both theories bring awareness to the behavioral, cognitive, and physical changes of the student inherent within the learning process.

PRACTICAL APPLICATIONS

1   Distinguish between the three theories of motor learning.

2   Which learning style do you find you relate to most within the dance class? Why?

3   Describe the ways in which a dance teacher might engage with students possessing a particular intelligence. (Choose any.)

4   Compose a movement exercise for a student in each stage of Fitts and Posner's three-stage theory of motor learning.

5   Provide details of how the teacher might instruct the exercises created in the previous question and what might be expected of the student's performance.

6   Consider the characteristics of learning. How have you observed these characteristics manifest as you learn a new movement skill?

NOTES

1 Donna Krasnow and Virginia Wilmerding, *Motor Learning and Control for Dance: Principles and Practices for Performers and Teachers* (Champaign, IL: Human Kinetics, 2015), 177.
2 Krasnow and Wilmerding, *Motor Learning and Control for Dance*, 177.
3 Richard A., Schmidt and Timothy Donald Lee, *Motor Control and Learning: A Behavioral Emphasis* (Champaign, IL: Human Kinetics, 1999), 302.
4 Krasnow and Wilmerding, *Motor Learning and Control for Dance*, 247.
5 Pamela S. Haibach-Beach, Greg Reid and Douglas Holden Collier, *Motor Learning and Development*, 2nd ed. (Champaign, IL: Human Kinetics, 2018), 43.
6 Krasnow and Wilmerding, *Motor Learning and Control for Dance*, 248.
7 Krasnow and Wilmerding, *Motor Learning and Control for Dance*, 250.
8 Schmidt and Lee, *Motor Control and Learning*, 411.
9 Schmidt and Lee, *Motor Control and Learning*, 414.
10 Schmidt and Lee, *Motor Control and Learning*, 414–415.
11 Bob Bates, *Learning Theories Simplified . . . and How to Apply Them to Teaching* (Los Angeles: SAGE, 2019), 84.
12 Bates, *Learning Theories Simplified*, 84.
13 Schmidt and Lee, *Motor Control and Learning*, 212.

BIBLIOGRAPHY

Bransford, John D., Ann L. Brown, and Rodney R. Cocking. *How People Learn: Brain, Mind, Experience and School.* Washington, DC: National Academy Press, 1999.
Humphrey, James Harry. *Child Development and Learning through Dance.* New York: AMS Press, 1987.
Krasnow, Donna, and Virginia Wilmerding. *Motor Learning and Control for Dance: Principles and Practices for Performers and Teachers.* Champaign, IL: Human Kinetics, 2015.
Magill, Richard A. *Motor Learning: Concepts and Applications.* Boston: McGraw-Hill, 2007.
Magill, Richard A., and David Anderson. *Motor Learning and Control: Concepts and Applications.* 11th ed. Boston: McGraw Hill, 2016.
Rose, Debra J., and Robert W. Christina. *A Multilevel Approach to the Study of Motor Control and Learning.* San Francisco, CA: Benjamin Cummings, 2008.
Schmidt, Richard A., and Timothy Donald Lee. *Motor Control and Learning: A Behavioral Emphasis.* Champaign, IL: Human Kinetics, 1999.
Sigmundsson, Hermundur, Leif Trana, Remco Polman, and Monika Haga. "What is Trained Develops! Theoretical Perspective on Skill Learning." *Sports* 5, no. 2 (2017): 38. https://doi.org/10.3390/sports5020038
Wulf, Gabriele. *Attention and Motor Skill Learning.* Champaign, IL: Human Kinetics, 2007.

UNIT 3

Factors That Affect the Learning Environment

CHAPTER 6

Motivation

Box 6.1 Chapter Objectives

After reading this chapter, you will be able to:

- Define motivation
- Distinguish between the theoretical differences of intrinsic and extrinsic motivation
- Articulate how the theories of self-determination, goal orientation, and flow can affect a dancer's motivation during training
- Recognize the ways in which dance teachers can employ motivational strategies to enhance students' progression in technique and artistry

Box 6.2 Chapter Vocabulary

arousal
extrinsic motivation
goal orientation theory
intrinsic motivation
mastery goal
motivation
performance goal
self-determination theory
self-efficacy
self-esteem

Motivation is an internal process that propels one to behave in a certain way or accomplish specific tasks during a determined length of time. It is this internal process that drives us to move, act, speak, etc. Nearly all that we do in our daily lives requires a degree of motivation. Sometimes our motivation may simply be "this must get done." We brush our teeth so that we maintain good dental hygiene and do not get cavities. We watch our favorite

DOI: 10.4324/b22952-10

television show because we desire to be entertained. We eat to quiet our stomachs and feel energized. Yet, there are aspects of our days that require an extra push in which to find the motivation to complete a task or activity. We could wash the dishes today or tomorrow. They will get clean either way, so what motivates us to buckle down and do it today? These same attitudes are present within any learning environment, including the dance class.

The best learning environments allow for a range of motivational tactics as the teacher considers the students' ages, level variations, and the dance form being taught. A dance teacher may approach a ballet class of 8-year-old students in a completely different manner than a hip-hop class for teenagers. Additionally, it is helpful for teachers to realize that each individual student may be motivated to participate by distinct factors. Some students strive to become professional dancers and are inherently driven within the dance class. Many students often participate for social or recreational gains. Further, some students may lack a desire to learn dance but have been signed up for the class, nonetheless. Additionally, the student who is usually driven and engaged may have experienced a terrible day at school which can then affect their stimulation during their evening dance class. What strategic shifts does the teacher then employ to help each student achieve their goals and keep everyone actively engaged? How does the teacher design their classes and tailor their teaching in such a way as to properly prepare pre-professional students while still inspiring the students who are there for purely recreational benefit?

CATEGORIES OF MOTIVATION

An effective dance teacher understands the reason behind a student's motivation, which in turn helps the teacher direct the student's focus in specific ways as they learn, practice, attain movement skills, and meet goals. Motivation can be divided into two broad categories: intrinsic and extrinsic. Reward lies at the heart of both types of motivation. Does one gain an internally based reward through their participation, or does the desired behavior merit reward through external means? Individuals may require a particular mode of motivation within the learning environment, or different situations within the class may necessitate a certain form of motivation.

Intrinsic Motivation

Consider the following statements:

> *I love the freedom and energy that dancing gives me.*
> *I really hope to have a solo someday, so I'm going to keep working hard.*
> *I love the feeling that I gain when I finally master a difficult step.*
> *I know that I am a perfectionist, but if I keep practicing, I really think I can be more consistent in my execution.*

Perhaps you can relate to one of these statements. When the motivation to engage in activity or focus your attention stirs from inside you – or is personally driven – it is labeled as **intrinsic motivation**. This category of motivation encompasses rewards for behavior that emanates from an internal place or out of personal interest. When we take part in an activity because of the positive way it makes us feel despite any external reward, we are said to be intrinsically motivated. Students who are intrinsically motivated reflect inward and are often driven by a sense of mastery in skill or performance, the ability to control and exert autonomy within their learning, the challenge of learning something new, and/or the enjoyment and curiosity in the activity. Oftentimes, the joy and satisfaction alone of engaging in the activity is enough to motivate one to continue.

Dance studios and performing arts schools often include performance opportunities to showcase their students' abilities and to further develop the artistic component of the students' dancing. K–12 dance training regularly uses this vehicle to motivate students during community events, school assemblies, and sports gatherings. However, these performances often provide an additional benefit as well: they can serve as a driving force for the continued enrollment and motivation of the student dancer. You have probably experienced the artistic "high" that performing can bring. After weeks of classwork and rehearsal, successfully executing movements in front of an audience, in a dazzling costume, with stage makeup and lights can offer a dancer of any age a dynamically satisfying feeling. In addition to this euphoric feeling, we can be internally motivated by our own sense of autonomy and control in our learning or fueled by personal or group goals. Our self-esteem, self-efficacy, and/or arousal within the learning environment can further contribute to our intrinsic motivation positively or negatively.

Extrinsic Motivation

Unlike intrinsic motivation, the motivating factors of extrinsic motivation extend outside of the individual's internal awareness. **Extrinsic motivation** is externally driven or focused on a consequence outside of the individual. In this design, motivation is prompted by various forms of rewards which can be verbal, tangible, or abstract in nature.

Extrinsic motivation can be offered in the forms of praise, feedback, rewards, or incentives. Many students find motivation to continue their engagement when offered praise and positive, uplifting remarks from their teacher. A simple comment from someone else, such as "That was much better!" or "Good focus," can inspire students in their efforts. The various forms of feedback that a teacher may offer can create within a student a drive or desire to continue their efforts. When applied as a motivational tool, instructor feedback recognizes a student's strength, improvement, or effort as it offers direction for achieving the movement goal. If feedback is delivered in a condescending or hurtful manner or focuses solely on negative aspects of the movement attempt, a dancer may be discouraged to continue. Chapter 15 is dedicated to the forms and application of feedback within the dance class.

Dance teachers often offer rewards to primary age students (3 to 5 years of age) to encourage motivation and participation. These items should be something that the children look forward to, will help sustain their attention, are fun and enjoyable, and encourage them to return to the class. Children may look forward to receiving a sticker, handstamp, or candy from the teacher at the conclusion of a class. The incorporation of games throughout the lesson plan can persuade younger dancers to pay attention during "work" portions of the class. Fun or silly songs can also drive students' attention and motivation. Oftentimes, these games or songs have a movement component as well, enabling

FIGURE 6.1 Three young dancers enjoy participating in a ballet class.
Source: Photo by Jeffrey Smith/Western Kentucky University.

the students to continue to practice a certain concept or skill, while the focus remains on the amusing aspect of the activity. Having their picture included on a photo "wall of fame" or being invited to lead the line in a specific activity can also encourage motivation. A special prize awarded to dancers when they attain a specific movement skill or goal, such as a full split or successful execution of a turn, entices the dancer to continue their effort and practice over an extended period of time.

Incentives are similar to rewards; however, incentives do not include a tangible item. A student may be motivated to be "the first dancer in the class" to execute a particular jump or tap step or may be incentivized to fully perform so that they might be chosen for a particular part. Here, the student desires external recognition from others. Older dancers may be extrinsically motivated by peer feedback. When peers appropriately offer critical reflection and recommendation of student performance, the student may become incentivized to continue their practice or creative work. For example, a teacher may have students practice in pairs. The partner can provide feedback following their peer's movement attempt. Or, the teacher may split the class into two groups during practice runs of a recital dance. The non-dancing group can offer encouraging reaction to the dancing group's performance. Both activities can provide motivation for a student to perform their best.

The dance teacher considers the individual and/or group of students as well as the desired result when making the decision to offer rewards or incentives. It is important to note that intrinsic and extrinsic motivators do not occur separately or independently. If a reward is used as an outcome – for example, "learn this movement or attain this skill, and you will get a prize" – the intrinsic reward (enhanced feeling of self-worth, deeper understanding, sense of agency) will be reduced. As the product/result becomes the focus, students strive toward receiving the reward, often negating or providing little effort toward the thought and learning components of the task.[1] Should a reward be repeatedly used, the dancer may no longer feel a sense of control in the learning or may feel as though they have been manipulated.[2] Consider a teacher that routinely promises a sticker for each student that works hard during a class, yet at the end of each class, offers a sticker to all dancers regardless of their effort or behavior during the class. An unmotivated student may recognize that they will still receive a reward regardless of their participation. A motivated student who consistently applies full attention and effort may feel as though their work in class does not truly matter. Further, some students may come to expect a reward for every performed behavior or attained skill.

In contrast, students may not perceive a reward as the teacher intends. Rewards may humiliate or even negate student effort as emphasis becomes placed on a particular physical outcome, ignoring cognitive learning and efforts. For example, if a class consists of varying skill or learning levels, students may feel as though the reward structure leans a certain way, thus creating an unfair competitive field. As a result, students unable to attain the goal and thus not rewarded may feel devalued or unable to reach their potential.[3] The effective dance teacher considers the perception of the reward while also incorporating further extrinsic motivation through verbal praise.

Additional factors can also affect intrinsic and extrinsic motivation. The students' agency over their learning can directly affect their effort and focus within the learning environment. Autonomy for one's learning (discussed later in this chapter) has great power in regard to motivation. Some dancers work hard simply because they are self-driven. Unfortunately, other dancers may be motivated to work hard or attain a goal out of fear of the consequences, which could include personal humiliation or degradation of the student by the teacher. Teachers who are over-demanding or insensitive toward students may incite fear among their students. Humiliation among peers could prohibit motivational attention or effort. The use of feedback becomes crucial in supporting motivation.

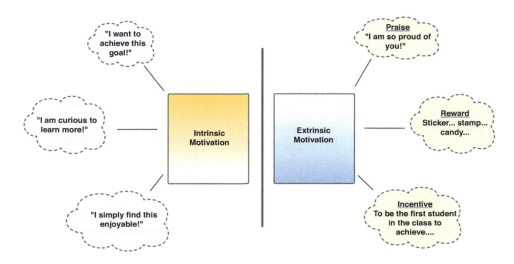

FIGURE 6.2 Diagram distinguishes between examples of intrinsic and extrinsic motivation within the dance learning environment.

THEORIES OF MOTIVATION

The relationship between motivation and human behavior has been studied through the lens of educators, employers, and psychologists as they consider the inner drive of students, workers, and individuals in general. Yet, what theories of motivation are integral when the topic is learning movement and the outcome includes a blend of cognitive and physical products?

Maslow's Hierarchy of Needs

In 1943, revered psychologist Abraham Maslow developed his five-stage model of hierarchy of needs, emphasizing that one's basic needs must be met before those at a higher level could contribute to motivated behavior. He later expanded his theory to encompass additional levels as society and culture developed and changed over time. The first four levels represent deficiency needs, those that must be satisfied before one can be motivated "to seek the experiences that relate to the upper levels," known as growth needs.[4] Maslow's current model includes the eight stages seen in Table 6.1.[5]

TABLE 6.1 Abraham Maslow's eight-stage model of hierarchy of needs.

Stage	Need	Examples	Application to Dance
Deficiency Needs			
One	**Biological and physiological needs**	basic needs of sleep, food, water	The well-rested and nourished student can better focus on the task at hand and be more motivated to learn.
Two	**Safety**	shelter, protection from extreme temperatures, free from anger and threat	The student who feels safe and secure can relax and better engage within the dance class.
Three	**Love and belongingness**	friendship, trust, acceptance into a group	Some students value and are motivated by the social aspect and sense of belonging that a dance class setting can provide.
Four	**Esteem**	dignity, independence, acceptance	Dancers become motivated when they believe they contribute to the dance environment, have a healthy body image, etc.
Growth Needs			
Five	**Cognitive**	understanding, logic, predictability	Some students are motivated by the intellectual and conceptual aspect of movement. They are inspired by the act of learning.

Stage	Need	Examples	Application to Dance
Six	**Aesthetic**	appreciation for beauty and form	Some students are motivated by the physicality of the movement and enjoy the aesthetical aspects of the dance.
Seven	**Self-actualization**	self-fulfillment, personal growth	Students can be motivated as they acquire skills and attain self-determined goals.
Eight	**Transcendence**	search for deeper meaning beyond the physical self	Some students find that dance brings new meaning within their life and feel motivated when they believe they are contributing to society by sharing art.

If we consider Maslow's original theory, the dance student must be well-nourished and rested and feel safe, accepted, and confident before becoming motivated to learn. You may recognize a relationship between this theory and your own behavior patterns. For example, you have trouble motivating yourself in a learning environment when your stomach is constantly growling from hunger and the mind continuously wanders to when and what your next meal will be. Or, perhaps you recall an intimidating dance teacher whose negative body language, harsh tone, or extreme expectations prevented you from discovering the motivation to find the joy throughout the class.

This theory, however, does have limitations. First, Maslow's research was based, in part, on biographical analysis, a research method that can be subjective and include biases. Second, many argue that human needs, specifically in this order, are not universal. For example, although some artists may often live in poverty and lack in their first two needs, they remain highly motivated within their art form. Yet, the theory offers dance teachers a reminder of the various needs that students may require in order to become motivated to learn something new or continue in practice or rehearsal.

In addition to Maslow's findings, other researchers have suggested that autonomy, mastery, and purpose are primary and specific motivating factors within the learning environment.[6] These align in many ways with Maslow's designated needs. Human beings are driven with an innate desire to make their own decisions. Freedom to choose, control, or determine their own path is often at the heart of human behavior. The challenge for the dance teacher is then discerning how to maintain the desired environment and attain the goals of a lesson plan while providing students the opportunity to feel as though they are contributing to the class setting and their own learning. Mastery of skill often brings continued motivation, meaning that when one achieves their goals, they gain a sense of fulfillment and are more inspired to continue within the learning process, similar to Maslow's seventh need of self-actualization. Finally, and adjacent to Maslow's eighth stage, many individuals need a reason to focus, concentrate, pay attention, and work hard. When the purpose of the task is clear, one often becomes motivated to work toward a goal. These ideas are further expressed in the following theories.

Self-Determination Theory

In 1985, researchers Edward Deci and Richard Ryan developed the self-determination theory, which contrasts the idea that motivation is a result of rewards. The **self-determination theory** suggests that individuals are motivated by a sense of agency within their learning. Here, the students' freedom to make choices or be in control of their learning is paramount to their attention and effort.[7] This theory emphasizes the value of intrinsic motivation to an individual and views the potential for extrinsic motivation to devalue or taint the experience.

The self-determination theory ascribes three innate psychological needs on which an individual will focus: autonomy, competence, and relatedness. Autonomy refers to the students' ability to decide what and how to do something. Competence relates to the students' perceived ability to complete a task. As students feel skilled or capable of attaining goals, they are inspired to work hard and continue their training.[8] Relatedness deals with the connections that are established through social relationships to others in the classroom. One's sense of belonging can encourage participation.

The self-determination theory suggests that when a student feels agency, competence in their ability to move and interact within the environment, and a connection to others involved, they will be motivated to learn. These factors lead to the student's self-determination to engage in the learning environment. It is helpful to note that self-determination does not necessarily occur in the absence of extrinsic motivation. For example, if a dance teacher offers an incentive (external reward) for learning a new skill, the student may become self-determined to practice the skill, taking ownership over their effort and progress. In another example, a student may listen to directions and attend to movement practice because they have decided that they should (an internal choice). Perhaps they recognize the importance of learning the skill or realize they will feel guilty if they do not practice. This student is then motivated by external conditions but has made the individual choice to participate.[9]

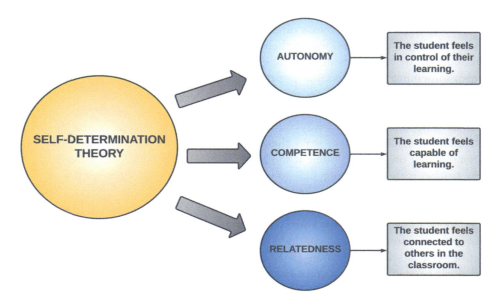

FIGURE 6.3 Diagram of the self-determination theory, which emphasizes intrinsic motivation.

The dance teacher can generate motivation among students by considering the self-determination theory within their teaching and asking questions of themselves such as "What do the students like? When do their eyes light up?" The teacher can then lean into that excitement and build on the students' existing motivation. For example, the dance teacher may discover that consideration of the students' perspective when preparing lesson plans and teaching strategies can increase autonomy among students. The teacher can ask for the students' opinions, as appropriate, and provide room for students to self-select options or self-cue as learning occurs. Allowing students time to practice on their own or creating space for the students to arrive at an answer on their own can assist students in realizing their control over their effort, learning, and movement outcomes. Recognizing a student's accomplishments can lead to increased feelings of competency within a student. Finally, the dance teacher can establish a supportive and encouraging environment for all students and foster cohesion within the group of students by recognizing the students as individuals, acknowledging their unique differences and strengths, and emphasizing community among students.

Goal Orientation Theory

The goal orientation theory examines the relationship between an individual and their goals along with the resulting effect on motivation. The **goal orientation theory** contends that individuals are often driven by goals, whether they are set by themselves or established by someone else. The individual's pursuit of an attainable goal can stimulate their desire to engage in an activity. An established concept, movement, or behavior is learned cognitively and physically. Goals can inspire students to pay attention to direction, focus during movement execution, and thus fully engage in learning movement. Effective dance teachers recognize that as students relate to a goal and strive to achieve it, they are often more motivated to engage in the learning environment.

Goals may be short-term or long-term as well as mastery-focused or performance-focused. **Mastery goals** are those that add to an individual's knowledge bank and/or skill ability. In this instance, a dancer will be driven to acquire the ability to correctly execute or fully comprehend a specific movement. Their ability to reproduce the technique and execution is at the core of the goal. Here, learning takes precedence for the student, and the emphasis becomes placed on the process. They strive to understand and attain an increased skill level. Students sometimes make the assumption "that outcomes are a result of effort."[10] In many instances, this theory is true. However, a student may assume that their effort has helped them complete three revolutions of a turn and that they have, in fact, mastered the turn. However, they fail to realize that they are simply spinning but are not in control of the turning skill. Their natural turning ability is facilitating the movement rather than their applied effort. The student has not truly learned how to turn (mastery goal).

Performance goals reflect the desire of a student to demonstrate their ability and competence to others and often encompass an external assessment or judgment. These types of goals place focus on the end result or outcome. For example, during a dance class, the student aims to receive complimentary feedback or praise from the teacher. Performance goals are outcome-driven, whereas mastery goals emphasize learning. Mastery goals often lead to more positive outcomes in the individual's overall physical and cognitive learning than performance goals because the student is focused on the process rather than the outcome and in increasing one's abilities.

FIGURE 6.4 Diagram distinguishes between mastery goals and performance goals.

It is necessary to realize that goals can also adversely affect a student's motivation and inhibit learning. For example, a student may want to remove themselves from situations in which they feel they are negatively judged or compared to others. A student who feels they are constantly berated in the dance studio or viewed critically by peers for reaching or missing goals may be unmotivated or fearful to participate. In this instance, the student may avoid fully engaging or focusing during class as their negative emotions distract them from putting forth effort. In an additional instance, some dance teachers may contend that students must approach skills or movement in a distinct manner that contradicts what their physical facility may allow. As a result, the student may feel compelled to give up.

Concept of Flow

The dance class and dance performance opportunities can offer a flood of positive emotions, sometimes even providing an escape from reality for an individual. This artistic "high" was discussed earlier in the section on intrinsic motivation. Psychologist Mihaly Csikszentmihalyi labeled this feeling as the concept of flow.[11] In this instance, there is a rush of adrenaline accompanied with accomplishing skill and performance-based activities. During these periods, the individual enjoys performing and finds themself lost in the moment of movement. They are fully absorbed in the task at hand. In a sense, "action and awareness merge; we experience one-pointedness of mind."[12] Any other worries, concerns, or problems dissipate for a period of time. The dancer feels empowered and in control. They transcend from their everyday selves and feel a powerful potential of autonomy and enjoyment as time seems to stand still. All the hard work that has been put in is suddenly perceived to be well worth the sense of accomplishment and joy that is felt in that performance moment. The task then becomes how the dance teacher can capture and sustain this sense of flow and energized feeling throughout the semester or term. The dance teacher should be aware of these moments of energy flow experienced by students so that they can encourage and reproduce these instances throughout classes.

SELF-ESTEEM, SELF-EFFICACY, AND AROUSAL

Self-esteem, self-efficacy, and arousal are internal factors that may have a positive or adverse effect on motivated behavior or the learning process and can play a role in the effect of intrinsic and extrinsic motivation strategies that the dance teacher may employ.

Self-esteem is the value and worth that one feels about themself and may be correlated to self-confidence. A dancer's self-esteem will directly affect their motivation in class. For example, students may consistently question their body image and self-worth. A student's self-esteem can also be affected by social acceptance within the class. Will the other kids want to be my partner or stand next to me, or laugh at me while I attempt a skill? A child's behavior or physical appearance can likewise influence their feelings of self-worth.[13] A child may feel too quiet or too loud, smaller or bigger, or that they act or look different from their peers. As a result, they may withdraw from class engagement or act out to compensate for these feelings.

In contrast, **self-efficacy** is one's belief in their competence and skill. Students who have a positive view of their abilities often demonstrate eagerness in setting goals and striving toward skill attainment. On the contrary, dancers who lack belief in their abilities may be less motivated to pursue goals or remain focused in class. Self-efficacy can serve as a predictor of successful achievement within the class.[14] Albert Bandura, prominent psychologist, coined the term self-efficacy in 1977. His research shows that humans are motivated to do what they believe they can do. When a student regards themself as capable of successfully completing a task or skill, they will naturally envision positive outcomes and be driven toward that positive performance. The student who does not believe they are capable will be less likely to pursue goals or pay attention in class. Conversely, students with high efficacy may overestimate their abilities. This inflation of belief in abilities or personal progress could have an adverse effect on future performance.[15] Students may take it upon themselves to practice a movement that they have not yet been taught, such as *fouetté* turns or a specialized leap, before or after class. In this instance, the result for the student could be physical injury, embarrassment, or fear of failure.

Box 6.3 Teacher Efficacy

Students are not the only individuals within the classroom whose sense of self-efficacy affects the learning process. A teacher's self-efficacy is the confidence and assurance that they possess in their teaching abilities to facilitate the desired cognitive and physical learning within their students. Children can sense whether a teacher is confident in their teaching practices. Teachers who have positive beliefs in their teaching capabilities will instruct with more confidence and self-assurance. Conversely, teachers who demonstrate doubt in their ability to effectively lead and instruct the class will yield skepticism among their students. Further, it is believed that teachers with high self-efficacy will be more open to experimentation within their teaching methods and demonstrate flexibility with their students, which in turn can garner a level of autonomy among students.[16]

Arousal is a physiological and psychological state that relates to the student's level of stimulation. Arousal can refer to the student's desire to participate within the learning process. Motivation can be affected by too much or too little stimulation within the classroom. This stimulation can affect heart rates, breathing rates, and ability to focus in positive or negative manners. These effects are manifested in the emotion displayed by the student and in their muscular tension. Arousal levels are individual to each student. Activities that introduce new movements or concepts, incorporation of complex material, or unfamiliar scenarios within class can incite positive or negative levels of arousal. A state of positive arousal in students may lead them to be highly excited to learn new, more difficult movements or engage in a performance opportunity. Negative arousal may cause other students to feel threatened and stressed by the activity. When a student becomes anxious, their arousal state is increased. Anxiety is a negative arousal state in response to stress. Students may demonstrate nervousness, tension, worry, or fear when they become anxious. The dance teacher must be aware of the various states of arousal and their effect on motivation and performance. Additional encouragement or discussion may be required by the teacher. The teacher may emphasize to student that the new skill introduced is a challenge, yet the students are well-prepared for the challenge. The teacher may further discuss with students why the learning of or attempt of a particular skill is necessary. Finally, the teacher should encourage the student's effort even if skill attainment is not yet achieved.

Students with high self-efficacy or high arousal often demonstrate intrinsic motivation toward an activity, whereas students with low efficacy or low arousal may experience fear of failure or judgment. When a student feels good about themselves and capable, they are more likely to demonstrate a drive to learn. If a student is concerned that they will not be able to do a movement or exercise, they are often less stimulated to put forth effort. Goals also relate to and can be affected by a student's self-efficacy. Psychologist Albert Bandura argued that individuals with high levels of self-efficacy often create "more challenging goals, are more committed to those goals, and exert greater efforts in pursuit of those goals," whereas those with lower levels of self-efficacy may set goals that are easier to accomplish or have a greater inclination to give up on their goals.[17]

FIGURE 6.5 A dance teacher positively communicates feedback to tap dance students, encouraging their motivation to learn and perform.

Source: Photo by Clinton Lewis/Western Kentucky University.

ROLE OF THE DANCE TEACHER

It is important for the teacher to realize their role in a student's motivation to learn and engage in activity. While teachers often expect students to focus and pay attention, simply expecting those behaviors can be futile. Learning is often a two-way street. Students are responsible for their work ethic, which includes paying attention in class and working outside of class; however, the teacher must recognize the part they play in motivating a student's full engagement in the learning process. The teacher bears a large portion of this responsibility in both initiating and maintaining motivation within a student. The teacher should be wary of both their own behavior and the structure they establish within the classroom as these can both directly influence motivation. In fact, the teacher can be the single most powerful motivating tool within the classroom.

The dance teacher's personality and behavior within the class setting has the ability to motivate or discourage students from learning. For example, consider how you might approach speaking to a class of second-grade dancers. One's tone of voice, the language used, and the personal characteristics emphasized can encourage a group of young students to not only listen but become inspired to try a new movement exercise. Now if one used the exact same voice, words, and mannerisms with a class of high school students, they would not only roll their eyes but they would most likely tune out anything that was taught to them. The way in which we communicate to students – both verbally and non-verbally – and the behavior we model are essential in motivating desired behavior.

As the dance teacher considers intrinsic and extrinsic motivation and the theories of self-determination, goal orientation, and the concept of flow, they can devise strategies to best engage their students within a given class. Perhaps the teacher will focus on the incorporation of rewards or the extent to which they will employ praise. Or, the dance teacher may recognize the power of enabling students to determine their path in learning a particular skill or concept. With the earlier theories in mind, let us shift to two approaches that dance teachers can consider in inciting motivation among their students.

Keller's ARCS-V Model

The ARCS-V model was developed in the 1980s by educational psychologist John M. Keller.[18] The integral components of the acronym-labeled model can offer benefits to the dance educator in understanding learner motivation. ARCS-V stands for *attention, relevance, confidence, satisfaction,* and *volition.* When in the dance class environment, a teacher can quickly recognize the concepts of each as they relate to a dancer's motivation to learn.

The teacher must first capture the student's attention. This might be done through the teacher's physical energy associated with the activity presented by the teacher. The dance teacher physically and/or verbally captures the student's interest and curiosity, and thus many students become interested in and curious of the activity. Relevancy is accomplished when the dance teacher connects movement ideas from one part of class to another or from one class to another. For example, during the warm-up, the teacher may remind students that the foot articulation exercise they are doing is preparing them to properly use their feet later in class when they jump. Or, students can be encouraged to focus on stretching their legs to improve their extensions and leaps. As students recognize how movement ideas connect and understand the benefit, they will be more motivated to learn and engage.

122 Factors That Affect the Learning Environment

TABLE 6.2 The five components of Keller's ARCS-V model along with its application to teaching dance.

Keller's ARCS-V Model for Motivation	Teaching Application
Attention	The students' curiosity is sparked as the teacher excitedly explains that the students are ready to tackle a new movement skill.
Relevance	The teacher identifies how previously learned movement has prepared the students for this new skill. Students become aware that as they learn this new skill, they will now also get to work on more complex patterns.
Confidence	The teacher has appropriately progressed students so that they can attain the new skill with practice. The students realize they are capable of performing the skill.
Satisfaction	Performing the newly achieved movement skill provides a sense of enjoyment and satisfaction among the students.
Volition	As the students' skill level develops, they become more determined to continue their progress in dance.

The next step for the teacher is to build confidence and enhance self-esteem and self-efficacy. Students who find themselves capable of executing a movement or see the potential for success begin to accomplish goals that have been set, which leads to enjoyment and satisfaction in the movement practice. The teacher can use positive verbal and non-verbal feedback as a form of praise to encourage students. Satisfied students tend to remain motivated in an activity. Finally, Keller added volition to his model to account for an individual's moxie, or power and perseverance, as it relates to learning. Dancers who have that inner dedication and determination will be more likely to remain motivated in the dance class.[19]

The Six C's

Professor Emeritus Mark Lepper of Stanford University has researched the effects of intrinsic and extrinsic motivation. Through his work, he established the five C's, which he believes promote intrinsic motivation within learners: *challenge, curiosity, control, context,* and *competence*. These components are similar to those published by Keller. Central to both models is the expressed need for the teacher to capture students' attention and curiosity, provide context and relevancy, develop students' awareness of abilities, and encourage their individual power in their learning.

Upon consideration of Lepper's five C's, the author has chosen to include a sixth "C" to this list: *community*. Learning requires interaction between an individual and their environment, which often includes a teacher and peers. Building cooperation and community within the class encourages a student to work hard and helps to drive motivation. Students often do not want to miss a class because they will then not see their friends, they realize they will be missed by those in the class, they do not want to disappoint the teacher or other dancers, or they do not want to get behind their peers in the learning process.

TABLE 6.3 The six C's along with a practical application to teaching dance.

The Six C's of Promoting Intrinsic Motivation	Teaching Application
Challenge	The teacher provides material that is appropriate for the student and presents it in a manner that enables students to learn yet feel appropriately challenged.
Curiosity	The teacher eagerly announces that the students are going to learn the teacher's favorite combination. The teacher enthusiastically demonstrates the combination.
Control	Students are asked questions and gently guided through problem-solving activities. As a result, they feel more responsible for their own learning.
Context	Students learn the why behind the movement and the reason that repetition is necessary. Students are then more willing to practice the movement as they work to enhance their technique.
Competence	The teacher helps students establish appropriate goals and provided a path to achieve those goals. As students reach their goals, they feel capable in their abilities.
Community	The teacher engages the entire class, creates a sense of belonging for each student, and encourages the collaborative spirit within the class.

Challenge

The material provided to students should be appropriate to their learning and skill level; however, it should also provide an adequate challenge. If the movement exercises are too simplistic, taught too slowly, or repetition is overused, dancers will become bored and lose their motivation to engage. In contrast, teaching practices that incorporate overly complex exercises, lack clarity in instruction, or are taught too quickly can deter a student's motivation. If the student feels that the content of the class is overly simplistic in nature, the student may feel as though a) the teacher does not believe they are capable of anything harder, or b) they will not continue to grow in their capabilities because they are not being provided with more opportunity to develop their skills.

Challenge connects to the goal orientation theory. The dance teacher should establish clear goals for the class and individual dancers. By having direct, level/age-appropriate goals, students will be more aware of their progression and be motivated as they work toward attaining those goals.

The way in which the dance teacher presents exercises to students connects to not only the students' attention capacity but their motivational drive to learn. Is material taught so slowly that the student becomes bored while learning? Are the verbal or visual instructions muddled and confusing, thus causing the dancer to lose interest in the exercise? Are students being asked to do the exact same sequence of movements class after class without any creativity, originality, or variety? Exercises should be designed to appropriately address an objective, but in a manner that will further engage the student. They must then be presented in a clear, exciting, and encouraging manner. Composition and presentation of movement exercises are detailed in later chapters.

Finally, mistakes and errors should be encouraged as a learning opportunity to challenge the dancer to continue to pursue skill and knowledge. Mistakes are human and part of the learning process. The teacher can then challenge students to learn from mistakes in order to progress and grow in their skill and knowledge. The learning environment can also be stressful or intimidating for some students. Helping students to realize that these feelings are normal and providing strategies and steps for them to take to work toward their goals enables the student to persevere through challenges. Teachers can explain the cause of errors, offer smaller goals to help the student work through trouble spots, redirect focus to a different aspect of the movement, and encourage equality and support among the class.

Curiosity

A teacher who conveys their passion for dance within their instruction and excitement for the progress of their students as well as demonstrates curiosity in movement possibilities and learning can inspire their students' curiosity and willingness to engage in the learning process. This is most often accomplished through the concept of modeling. The dance teacher should demonstrate the behavior that they wish to see in students. While this can apply to general class etiquette, it also speaks to motivation. If a teacher is eager and interested in movement, their students will most likely be eager and interested as well. The dance teacher that arrives to class prepared with a lesson plan, focused on the students, and excited to share movement ideas will encourage motivation within the students. We have heard the phrase "Monkey see, monkey do." Students in a classroom are no different. If the teacher is enthusiastic about an activity or learning goal, this will seep into the student's spirit as well.

Consider this – a teacher enters the classroom looking frazzled with an enormous sigh. They then continue to teach a class that has clearly not been planned and do so in a monotone or exasperated tone. The students will most likely also feel anxious or disengaged. Yet, when a teacher arrives, is happy to see the students, and teaches a fully prepped class – proving that they cared enough to invest the time in preparation – students will be more likely to engage in earnest.

One's enthusiasm for teaching should be apparent to students. Remember that the tone of your voice and non-verbal body cues will project your motivation for teaching as well as your perspective of the students in front of you. Standing with arms crossed, head tipped down, and eyes in a piercing fixed stare will leave students feeling threatened or discouraged. Additionally, the language that you use can enable students to see value for or develop an interest in the movement task. For example, rather than saying "Alright, it is time to work on X again," try one of the following:

- "Dancers, this is exciting, we are going to . . ."
- "Dancers, this will be challenging, but I know you can do it."
- "We're going to do one of my favorite phrases next!"

Control

When a dancer feels like they have some control, power, and decision-making ability in their learning, they will be more motivated to engage in class and practice movement independently. Dance teachers can help facilitate learning through their approach and the incorporation of student-centered learning opportunities within the class. It may prove more effective for the teacher to avoid constantly dictating to the student what the goal is or what will be worked on. Instead, the teacher can offer students the opportunity to establish their own goals and allow them to select from an option of activities as means to provide autonomy within student learning. Remind them that they are in control of their learning. Their focus and practice efforts will determine how quickly they may learn a movement, skill, or combination. Additionally, they must become their own problem solvers. Ask them questions, so that they feel empowered to answer, thus realizing they have the autonomy in their movement to apply that feedback. Incorporate opportunities for students to self-cue, a skill that must be taught to students so that they can recognize their own errors and provide autonomy in how they can correct or continue appropriately. Pose questions to students during group work so they realize that their feedback is valuable within the class setting. Conversely, encourage peer feedback as appropriate. This can be an optimal method for challenging students to offer their own perceptions and can serve as an observable indicator as to whether or not the student has learned the concepts inherent within the lesson. When students feel in control of their learning, they are more likely to be engaged, motivated participants.

Context

Context refers to providing reasons for engaging in a particular movement activity and offering connection to other movements, skills, concepts, or even other genres or classes in which the student may be participating. Dancers are often more motivated to learn material, practice exercises, or grasp new concepts when they understand how the learned material will apply to what they already know, enhance their current skill level and abilities, or enable them to transition to more advanced movement skills. It is often within the framework of context that good teaching begins and ends. Later chapters of this textbook discuss how the effective teacher approaches curriculum development and lesson planning, delivers information, and presents material. Together, these topics can provide context for the student.

The teacher is knowledgeable of the big picture when learning dance. They know why it is important to learn an efficient and safe method of bending the knees and how movements build upon one another. Yet, students may not recognize the importance behind certain skills or concepts or the connection between a mundane rolling through the foot exercise and safely landing a large, advanced leap. Students may roll their eyes at a slow-paced or perceived "elementary" undulation of the spine exercise, but the teacher recognizes how the fluid spine articulation inherent within the exercise will lead into the contemporary-rooted center combination that is yet to come. Context is provided in the way the teacher scaffolds movements and designs curriculum (Chapter 9) and in the instructional strategies (Chapter 13) employed throughout the class.

By providing context for the movement or exercise, the dance teacher can help the student discover purpose, and thus motivation, in the exercise. The teacher can reference how stretching the feet during a *changement* will help them progress to small jumps with beats (such as *entrechat or royale)*. Or, the teacher may reiterate to young tap dancers that consecutive hop shuffles will help them build strength to soon incorporate the pick-up or grab off sounds into various tap dance vocabulary. This knowledge will then motivate them to endure all the way across the floor during the repetitive hop shuffle exercise. Rather than solely focusing on completing an exercise or the technical execution, dance teachers should emphasize the concepts inherent within the exercise. For a choreography class, providing context can facilitate the students' ability to create developed compositions. When the students understand the why behind an exercise and how concepts connect, they are better motivated to practice and/or to advance in their abilities. In these ways, the teacher truly teaches students rather than just giving them exercises.

Competence

Individuals feel competent when they have the knowledge and ability to master skills. Effective teachers establish or help students to create goals and then provide a path for students to reach those goals. As a result, students can develop competence in their abilities. Exercises can be presented in a manner that encourages each student and makes them feel as though "yes, I can do this!" Appropriate opportunity and time to practice movement is essential in developing competent students. Additionally, adequate feedback can encourage and guide student progress. Supportive feedback may acknowledge a student's improvement or effort or provide further direction for comprehension.

Plateaus in skill acquisition are a normal part of the learning process. The dance teacher should be mindful of potential plateaus that students may occasionally encounter. Chapter 4 documents the nonlinear process in which students attain motor control and development and brings attention to the ways in which growth spurts can interfere with dance progress. The effective dance teacher helps students recognize that this curve in learning does not equate to their competence. Rather, they will continue to develop and progress in time. The teacher can shift the students' focus to other aspects of learning, including appropriate short-term goals. Students can be motivated to participate in spite of progress plateaus.

Community

Dance is an art form as well as a communicative sport. Dance is not a discipline intended to be studied or performed in isolation of others. Rather, initial dance forms derived as celebration and communication where the practitioners did not dance in isolation, but rather with or for others. Dancers tend to thrive when they are engaged with others. The dance teacher strives to connect with students. Performers desire to move an audience. Dance therapists focus on affecting their patients. Dancers gain motivation when in community with others within the classroom. How, then, can the dance teacher utilize this knowledge within the class setting?

By incorporating collective activities, the dance teacher can emphasize the community spirit within the dance class and in dance itself. Partner work or group work is a great example of this. The teacher should be careful not to compare students, or negatively call out a student during class, but rather strive to establish a safe environment that demonstrates trust and respect with and for students. Additionally, teachers should make eye contact with students, encourage dancers to support each other, celebrate individual efforts and accomplishments, let students know they were missed if they were absent from class, or simply acknowledge students within class. These actions will foster a sense of belonging, care, and respect among students. Knowing the students' names, making direct eye contact with each, and offering some type of feedback to each student can go a long way in motivating students to learn and continue with the art form.

The teacher who incorporates competition can inspire select students to do their best; however, there will be another group of students who shut down in response. While some students become motivated to work hard as they compete with their peers, other students may be reminded of their weaknesses, feel inadequate, and deem themselves unable to measure up. These students will quickly disengage from the class. The dance teacher may find that focusing on cooperation and community rather than competition will prove more effective. Here, teaching efforts encourage the class as a whole, rather than dividing students against one another.

CHAPTER SUMMARY

There is a cycle of motivation, the inner drive to persist, that can be observed within a class. A student's self-esteem, self-efficacy, and arousal levels can factor into their level of motivation to learn. While some students may be inspired through intrinsic motivation, other students may require forms of extrinsic motivation in order for them to engage and work hard. The environment established by the teacher can be a catalyst for enthusiastic attentive learning. When the teacher themself is motivated and enthusiastic about the material, their instructional practices will be positively affected, and student learning and engagement can increase.

Various theories, such as self-determination, goal orientation, and the concept of flow, can account for students' motivation within the dance class. By devising challenging and interesting lesson plans, providing students with a level of autonomy in the learning, and making movement ideas relevant to one another, the teacher can instill motivation within students. The teacher's positive feelings and behaviors can be reflected in the students they instruct. When students feel cared for and respected by their teacher, they will be more committed to the learning environment. Their own sense of competence will increase along with their desire to continue learning. The teacher who offers constructive feedback enables students to recognize their potential and their autonomy over their learning. Above all, the dance teacher should lead by example, help all students to feel valued and capable, and create pathways for students to attain teacher-driven and student-established goals.

PRACTICAL APPLICATIONS

1   Consider a recent dance class in which you have found yourself with a high level of motivation to engage. Identify the factors that influenced your motivation in that class.

2   In what areas of study or settings do you find yourself to be intrinsically motivated? Extrinsically motivated? Why do you think you demonstrate different forms of motivation?

3 Reflect on the six C's that promote intrinsic motivation within learners. Identify ways in which you could provide for each area within your own teaching.

4 Observe several dance classes (or other motor-based classes) that feature students of various ages and levels.

   a Can you recognize the students that are highly motivated to learn and those that lack motivation?

   b In what ways does the teacher attempt to motivate students?

NOTES

1 Mark R. Lepper, "Motivational Considerations in the Study of Instruction," *Cognition and Instruction* 5, no. 4 (1988): 295.

2 Ellen Criss, "Dance All Night: Motivation in Education," *Music Educators Journal* 97, no. 3 (2011): 62.

3 Criss, "Dance All Night: Motivation in Education," 62.

4 Tristan Coulter, Megan Gilchrist, Clifford Mallet and Adam Carey, "Abraham Maslow: Hierarchy of Coach and Athlete Needs," In *Learning in Sports Coaching* (New York: Routledge, 2016), 66.

5 Tristan Coulter, et al., "Abraham Maslow," 66–67.

6 Sandra C. Minton and Rima Faber, *Thinking with the Dancing Brain: Embodying Neuroscience* (Lanham: Rowman & Littlefield, 2016), 44–45.

7 Jere E. Brophy, *Motivating Students to Learn*, 3rd ed. (New York: Routledge, 2010), 161.

8 Brophy, *Motivating Students to Learn*, 7.

9 Brophy, *Motivating Students to Learn*, 155.

10 Carey E. Andrzejewski, Adrienne M. Wilson and Daniel J. Henry, "Considering Motivation, Goals, and Mastery Orientation in Dance Technique," *Research in Dance Education* 14, no. 2 (2013): 164.

11 Brophy, *Motivating Students to Learn*, 154.

12 Brophy, *Motivating Students to Learn*, 8.

13 Jennie Lindon, *Child Development from Birth to Eight a Practical Focus* (London: National Children's Bureau, 1993), 101.

14 Donna Krasnow and Virginia Wilmerding, *Motor Learning and Control for Dance: Principles and Practices for Performers and Teachers* (Champaign, IL: Human Kinetics, 2015), 205.

15 Mark R. Beauchamp, Kaitlin L. Crawford and Ben Jackson, "Social Cognitive Theory and Physical Activity: Mechanisms of Behavior Change, Critique, and Legacy," *Psychology of Sport and Exercise* 42 (2019): 114.

16 Fani, Lauermann and Jean-Louis Berger, "Linking Teacher Self-Efficacy and Responsibility with Teachers' Self-Reported and Student-Reported Motivating Styles and Student Engagement," *Learning and Instruction* 76 (2021): 3.

17 Beauchamp, et al., "Social Cognitive Theory and Physical Activity," 112.

18 Krista M. Reynolds, Lindsay Michelle Roberts and Janet Hauck, "Exploring Motivation: Integrating the ARCS Model with Instruction," *Reference Services Review* 45, no. 2 (2017): 150.

19 Thomas A. Angelo, "Assessing Motivation to Improve Learning: Practical Applications of Keller's MVP Model and ARCS-V Design Process: Assessing Motivation to Improve Learning," *New Directions for Teaching and Learning*, no. 152 (2017): 106.

BIBLIOGRAPHY

Anderson, Steven David, Sandra Darkings Leyland, and Jonathan Ling. "Gender Differences in Motivation for Participation in Extra-Curricular Dance: Application of the Theory of Planned Behaviour." *Research in Dance Education* 18, no. 2 (2017): 150–160.

Andrzejewski, Carey E., Adrienne M. Wilson, and Daniel J. Henry. "Considering Motivation, Goals, and Mastery Orientation in Dance Technique." *Research in Dance Education* 14, no. 2 (2013): 162–175.

Angelo, Thomas A. "Assessing Motivation to Improve Learning: Practical Applications of Keller's MVP Model and ARCS-V Design Process: Assessing Motivation to Improve Learning." *New Directions for Teaching and Learning*, no. 152 (2017): 99–108.

Bandura, Albert. "Human Agency in Social Cognitive Theory." *The American Psychologist* 44, no. 9 (1989): 1175–1184.

Beauchamp, Mark R., Kaitlin L. Crawford, and Ben Jackson. "Social Cognitive Theory and Physical Activity: Mechanisms of Behavior Change, Critique, and Legacy." *Psychology of Sport and Exercise* 42 (2019): 110–117.

Brophy, Jere E. *Motivating Students to Learn*. 3rd ed. New York: Routledge, 2010.

Coulter, Tristan, Megan Gilchrist, Clifford Mallet, and Adam Carey. "Abraham Maslow: Hierarchy of Coach and Athlete Needs." In *Learning in Sports Coaching*, 79–90. London: Routledge, 2016.

Criss, Ellen. "Dance All Night: Motivation in Education." *Music Educators Journal* 97, no. 3 (2011): 61–66.

Giguere, Miriam. "Dance Trends: Assessing Students on Motivation and Professionalism: Encouraging a More Positive Atmosphere." *Dance Education in Practice* 5, no. 2 (2019): 26–28.

Gillet, Nicolas, Robert J. Vallerand, Sofiane Amoura, and Brice Baldes. "Influence of Coaches' Autonomy Support on Athletes' Motivation and Sport Performance: A Test of the Hierarchical Model of Intrinsic and Extrinsic Motivation." *Psychology of Sport and Exercise* 11, no. 2 (2010): 155–161.

Hsia, Lu-Ho, Iwen Huang, and Gwo-Jen Hwang. "Effects of Different Online Peer-Feedback Approaches on Students' Performance Skills, Motivation and Self-Efficacy in a Dance Course." *Computers and Education* 96 (2016): 55–71.

Koltko-Rivera, Mark E. "Rediscovering the Later Version of Maslow's Hierarchy of Needs: Self-Transcendence and Opportunities for Theory, Research, and Unification." *Review of General Psychology* 10, no. 4 (2006): 302–317.

Krasnow, Donna, and Virginia Wilmerding. *Motor Learning and Control for Dance: Principles and Practices for Performers and Teachers*. Champaign, IL: Human Kinetics, 2015.

Lauermann, Fani, and Jean-Louis Berger. "Linking Teacher Self-Efficacy and Responsibility with Teachers' Self-Reported and Student-Reported Motivating Styles and Student Engagement." *Learning and Instruction* 76 (2021): 101441.

Lazaroff, Elizabeth M. "Performance and Motivation in Dance Education." *Arts Education Policy Review* 103, no. 2 (2001): 23–29.

Lepper, Mark R. "Motivational Considerations in the Study of Instruction." *Cognition and Instruction* 5, no. 4 (1988): 289–309.

Lepper, Mark R., Mark Keavney, and Michael Drake. "Intrinsic Motivation and Extrinsic Rewards: A Commentary on Cameron and Pierce's Meta-Analysis." *Review of Educational Research* 66, no. 1 (1996): 5–32.

Lindon, Jennie. *Child Development from Birth to Eight a Practical Focus*. London: National Children's Bureau, 1993.

Lüftenegger, Marko, Ulrich S. Tran, Lisa Bardach, Barbara Schober, and Christiane Spiel. "Measuring a Mastery Goal Structure Using the TARGET Framework: Development and Validation of a Classroom Goal Structure Questionnaire." *Zeitschrift für Psychologie* 225, no. 1 (2017): 64–75.

Mcleod, Saul. "Maslow's Hierarchy of Needs." www.simplypsychology.org/maslow. html#:~:text=There%20are%20five%20levels%20in,esteem%2C%20and%20 self%2Dactualization, Last updated April 4, 2022.

Mertens, Niels, Filip Boen, Gert Vande Broek, Maarten Vansteenkiste, and Katrien Fransen. "An Experiment on the Impact of Coaches' and Athlete Leaders' Competence Support on Athletes' Motivation and Performance." *Scandinavian Journal of Medicine & Science in Sports* 28, no. 12 (2018): 2734–2750.

Minton, Sandra C., and Rima Faber. *Thinking with the Dancing Brain: Embodying Neuroscience*. Lanham: Rowman & Littlefield, 2016.

Nordin-Bates, Sanna M., Thomas D. Raedeke, and Daniel J. Madigan. "Perfectionism, Burnout, and Motivation in Dance: A Replication and Test of the 2×2 Model of Perfectionism." *Journal of Dance Medicine & Science* 21, no. 3 (2017): 115–122.

Oliver, Wendy. "Body Image in the Dance Class." *Journal of Physical Education, Recreation & Dance* 79, no. 5 (2008): 18–41.

Quested, Eleanor, and Joan L. Duda. "Perceived Autonomy Support, Motivation Regulations and the Self-Evaluative Tendencies of Student Dancers." *Journal of Dance Medicine & Science* 15, no. 1 (2011): 3–14.

Reynolds, Krista M., Lindsay Michelle Roberts, and Janet Hauck. "Exploring Motivation: Integrating the ARCS Model with Instruction." *Reference Services Review* 45, no. 2 (2017): 149–165.

Wulf, Gabriele, and Rebecca Lewthwaite. "Optimizing Performance through Intrinsic Motivation and Attention for Learning: The OPTIMAL Theory of Motor Learning." *Psychonomic Bulletin & Review* 23, no. 5 (2016): 1382–1414.

CHAPTER 7

Understanding the Student Population

Box 7.1 Chapter Objectives

After reading this chapter, you will be able to:

- Identify the holistic approach in teaching dance
- Identify potential and distinct motor, cognitive, behavioral, and social characteristics among learners of different age ranges
- Recognize sociocultural considerations that may influence student performance within the dance class
- Articulate the effect of stereotypes and bias in teaching dance

Box 7.2 Chapter Vocabulary

cultural sensitivity
hidden curriculum
holistic approach
implicit bias
self-fulfilling prophecy
stereotype
stereotype threat

Teaching the art of dance requires more than the instruction of dance steps. Chapter 2 highlighted the role of the dance teacher, which extends beyond a facilitator of movement technique and possibilities but also includes mentoring and guiding students in the pursuit of their goals and in the development of students as creative, confident, and productive individuals. To effectively teach students, it is imperative that the dance teacher understands their students. The role of the dance teacher would be much easier if all students walked into the studio with the same behaviors, aspirations, and abilities; however, this is not reality.

DOI: 10.4324/b22952-11

Each student possesses different motivations for their studies in dance. Many factors can contribute to their participation – and sometimes lack thereof – within the classroom. Some students take dance classes because of their individual desire to train in dance. Some students attend classes because of parental wishes or peer influences. These various intentions behind enrollment can greatly influence the student's participation level and behavior during the class. Further, other factors, such as age, gender, socioeconomic, and cultural connections, can influence student motivation and learning.

This chapter explores the holistic approach taken by effective dance teachers and the potential areas that can affect a student's motivation within the classroom. It is helpful for the dance educator to consider these aspects as they approach lesson planning, classroom management, and instructional strategies. Knowledge of the factors that impact the student's participation and behavior in class strengthen the teacher's ability to communicate with and instruct the student appropriately and effectively. Awareness and understanding of these diverse influences can help the teacher prepare a dance space that is inviting and appropriately challenges all students.

THE HOLISTIC TEACHER

The **holistic approach** in teaching considers each student as an individual and focuses on the education of the whole student. The holistic dance teacher seeks to engage all aspects of a student. Rather than focusing only on motor learning, the holistic teacher also considers the individual's cognitive, emotional, and social development. This approach recognizes one's life experiences and the way in which these can influence the student's motivation and learning process. The holistic dance teacher incorporates student-centered learning opportunities, rather than a command approach, and varies their teaching strategies based upon the students within the class. Emphasis is placed on respect for and acceptance and encouragement of each learner. This requires the teacher to take time to know their students, which includes the students' experiences and values. In turn, the teacher will recognize how to best communicate with and motivate each student dancer.

The holistic dance teacher strives to build relationships with students that are based on trust and respect. They recognize and support each student as an individual, validate students' viewpoints and feelings, and are honest with students when they, themselves, make a mistake. The environment that is then created enables students to feel welcome, valued, and secure in their learning. Students feel encouraged to take risks as they trust the teacher and feel a part of the class community. The holistic dance teacher helps each student realize their distinct potential and worth. Students are treated fairly, and their individuality is embraced within the classroom. Students feel challenged to set goals and motivated to pursue them. Finally, the holistic dance teacher takes time to reflect on their personal teaching philosophy and the outcome of the class experience. The teacher evaluates their objectives as a teacher and analyzes their teaching effectiveness. They are mindful of the classroom environment they foster and the way in which it affects student learning. They are keenly aware of each student's development and are willing to make changes in their instruction as necessary.

TABLE 7.1 Identifying the primary aspects of the holistic dance teacher.

The Holistic Dance Teacher . . .
strives to build a relationship with students based on trust and respect.
helps each student to realize their potential and worth as an individual.
takes time to reflect on their teaching philosophy, on their experience in the classroom, and or each student's development.

Individuals can embrace characteristics and viewpoints that contrast one another due to a myriad of factors. The holistic dance teacher appreciates the differences between self and students as well as among the students and accommodates these distinctions as appropriate within the learning environment. Age, gender, socioeconomic status, and cultural connections are often factors that can contribute to contrasting perspectives and behaviors among individuals. The following sections considers the ways in which the holistic teacher can be mindful of such distinctions.

AGE EFFECT

Students of various ages typically present differing characteristics. For example, a 5-year-old child behaves considerably different than when the child is age 15; the 18-year-old student demonstrates more advanced cognitive skills than they did at age 10; a 3-year-old socializes in a contradictory manner from a 12-year-old. Children acquire new skills and deeper understanding as they mature in age, and the teacher can often connect behavior patterns to a child's age. In turn, this knowledge enables the dance teacher to understand possible reasons for certain behaviors and anticipate actions and patterns before they occur. This awareness becomes critical as the dance teacher crafts effective lesson plans and prepares instructional strategies.

Psychologists research the motor, cognitive, behavioral, and social characteristics an individual typically presents at each stage of their development. These generalized observations can offer a teacher insight into a child's behavior and needs within the learning environment. Table 7.2 divides children into three broad age ranges and includes basic developmental characteristics at each stage. The reader should keep in mind that these are expansive categories, and not every child will demonstrate these characteristics or in this order. Students in each age category present their own joys and challenges within the learning environment. It is up to the dance teacher to discern how the student's age may affect their willingness or ability to engage and then apply the most effective modes of instruction, guidance, and feedback.

Recognizable behaviors and instructional needs often emerge within the age groups. The preschool-age dancer will be quite limited in their motor and cognitive abilities. The dance teacher will find that creative play can help enhance student learning. The use of rhymes and songs proves effective in engaging this group of students and provides

134 Factors That Affect the Learning Environment

TABLE 7.2 Identifying the general developmental characteristics of preschool, elementary, and middle/high school–age children.

Preschool	Motor	• Fundamental motor skills progress, including running, jumping, galloping, hopping, skipping, and early kicking and throwing motions
	Cognitive	• Thinks in simple thoughts, uses short sentences • May use silly words and exaggerate stories • Understands basic concepts • Recognizes colors and numbers • Enjoys rhymes, songs, and imaginative play
	Behavioral	• Focus is on "me" • Independent, wants to do tasks by themselves • Learning how to follow rules and directions • Behavior can be erratic, may test behavioral and emotional limits • Talkative and inquisitive
	Social	• Playful and interactive • Learning social skills (sharing, cooperating, etc.) • Enjoys playing in groups • Eager to please • Demonstrates attachment, may cry when separated from parents/guardians
Elementary	Motor	• Develops body awareness • Progresses in gross motor skills • Improves in coordination, balance, and endurance abilities, which may vary
	Cognitive	• Shifts from an egocentric perspective to understanding the perspective of others • Can focus for a longer duration of time • Understanding of the concept of world around them • Demonstrates ability to remember, reason, and process information • Language skills develop • Motivation transitions from play-inspired to skill-inspired
	Behavioral	• Adapts to the school setting • Demonstrates increased interest in activities • Exhibits motivation and the desire to improve in ability • Develops a sense of competition with peers • Talkative
	Social	• Focuses on friendships; gravitates toward same gender • Transitions from playing in groups to true interest in social groups
Middle/ High School	Motor	• Demonstrates enhanced skill level • Develops the ability to control finite muscles
	Cognitive	• Understands abstract ideas • Thinks conceptually and independently • Establishes goals • Develops morals and values

Behavioral	• Develops their own identity • May be self-conscious, especially regarding body image and abilities • May have emotional outbursts • May be self-centered • Demonstrates desire for independence and control
Social	• Influenced by peers • Values acceptance by others • Self-esteem easily affected, needs positive reinforcement

learning connections. Students this age tend to focus on the "me" in learning and interactive environments and often respond to rewards and other incentives. Behavioral expectations will need to be consistently reinforced. The dance teacher will discover that facing the students while teaching is often most effective as the direct eye contact and communication helps maintain the students' attention. The stature of an adult teacher towering over them can be intimidating to a young child. When speaking directly to a preschool-age student, the teacher can kneel or stoop down so that they become face-to-face with the dancer.

The elementary-age dancer transitions from foundational motor skills to more developed dance movement; vocabulary and movement exercises become rooted in dance terminology and concepts rather than creative play. As their connection to the academic school setting increases, their ability to focus, process, and reason develops. Their motivation expands from creative play to skill acquisition, which sometimes corresponds to a competitiveness among their peers. The elementary-age student acquires self-awareness, yet they range in their abilities to coordinate their bodies. The dance teacher can incorporate variety in how movement skills and vocabulary are taught and practiced. Dance improvisation exercises become a useful tool in enhancing coordination and control and exploration of the body in space. These students often possess an eagerness to socialize, which can cause disruptions in the class. Group work within the class can provide an appropriate outlet for this. It is important that the dance teacher be consistent in their application of classroom policies and behavior management as they build trust and respect with their students.

Middle and high school–age dancers encompass a unique challenge: adolescence. Puberty can begin as early as age 8 or 9 and last up to two years; however, the typical age range is 11–14 years, with females beginning puberty before males.[1] It is during this period that the dancer will endure growth spurts and physical and hormonal changes within their body. During adolescence, the dancer may be challenged by body-image concerns as well as the desire for their peers to approve or accept them. Self-esteem and self-efficacy can be easily affected during this transition toward maturity and adulthood. Despite growth changes, students encompass finite motor control and enhanced abilities. As these students develop their own identity and autonomy, they also think conceptually and embrace goals. The dance teacher devises movement exercises that challenge the students' physical skill and conceptual thinking. The effective teacher will encourage self-cueing and continue to support the individuality of each student.

Adults can demonstrate a combination of the earlier-mentioned motor, cognitive, behavioral, and social characteristics drawn from all three age categories. While they are more advanced in their language and communication skills as well as their cognitive understanding of concrete and abstract thoughts, adults may struggle with motor skills based on their previous development in this area, experience with motor-based activities, or effects of aging. Some adults display strong athletic ability. Yet, as individuals age, many may demonstrate weakened strength, diminished flexibility, poor coordination, balance difficulties, and/or reduced endurance. As a result, the dance teacher may need to incorporate balance support mechanisms, a modified instruction pace, or motivational strategies that support the natural effects of aging. Individuals who have been continually active and devote attention to strength and flexibility may exhibit favorable tendencies and abilities in the dance studio.

Adults are often laden with many responsibilities and demands on their time. They may have work schedules and/or parenting schedules that prevent them from regularly attending dance class. It can be common for adult dance students to maintain sporadic attendance or eventually cease attending due to their work, home, or family commitments. Adults often engage in a dance class out of a curiosity to learn and for the social aspect. When present, adults may be chatty, prefer to dance in a group rather than individually, or be self-conscious about their bodies or abilities. They are often quick to celebrate achievements and are supportive of one another within the class. The young dance teacher should be mindful of these various facets and aware of the needs, intentions, and motivations of each adult learner.

FIGURE 7.1 A dance teacher engages with a diverse class of students.
Source: Photo by Jeffrey Smith/Western Kentucky University.

SOCIOCULTURAL CONSIDERATIONS

Individuals are unique beings. Our experiences, personal qualities, and learned traits contribute to the complexity and distinctiveness of our individual behavior patterns and thought processes. This singularity is often an expression of the social and cultural world in which we live. Behavioral interactions and learning patterns can be shaped by one's social and cultural way of life. These experiences can influence the student's degree of motivation and provide context for the teacher to better understand the individual student.

Social factors that may influence a student's behavior in the classroom can include family background, social pressure, socioeconomic status, and cultural customs. Acknowledging and understanding the cultures of the students provides opportunity for the dance teacher to embrace diversity within the classroom and celebrate differences. Promoting uniqueness enables students to discover their own expression within the learning environment and confidently and creatively contribute to problem-solving activities.

It is important to note that the generalizations and observations made in the following sections are based on research in the field and the experience of the authors. One should not presume that each situation automatically yields certain characteristics. Rather, these social and cultural factors are included within this chapter to provide potential insight for the dance teacher.

Family and Peer Influence

A student's home life plays a substantial role in the development of their morals, values, behavioral patterns, and emotional state. Children are first socialized within the home, and their family unit serves as their primary model for social and behavioral development. There are many family dynamics that a child may experience. A child may have a home life with two parents, or the parents may be separated or divorced; families may be blended, or the parents may be absent altogether from a child's life. The family unit may be closely connected throughout each day; yet in some instances, guardians may not pay much attention to the child. The home may be a supportive and loving environment, or there could be a presence of emotional or physical abuse.

The dynamics and interactions that occur in the student's household can have a direct positive or negative affect on the student's behavior and performance in the dance studio. It is helpful for the teacher to be cognizant of a student's family structure so to anticipate or recognize behaviors and attitudes that may affect a student's demeanor and motivation. A child may act defiant, withdrawn, joyful, timid, or confident as a result of family dynamics and lifestyle. The teacher should never stereotype families. Rather, the effective teacher recognizes and discerns potential connections between family influence and student behavior and strives to provide a positive and safe learning environment within the dance studio.

Family expectations of behavior may contrast greatly with the teacher's expectations of a student's etiquette in class. Consider the following questions:

- How is authority established and treated within the home?
- How are tasks given to the child, and what are the ways in which the child is expected to complete the task?

- How does the family value rewards (intrinsic or extrinsic)?
- How does the child tend to collaborate and cooperate with others, both inside and outside of the home?
- How does the family prioritize and structure their time?
- How does the family define success?
- How does the family celebrate success?

The varying answers to these questions can offer insight to the student's reaction to differing situations within the dance studio. For example, a child may not receive discipline in the home and may therefore defy the teacher in class. Or, a child may be continually reprimanded and degraded at home and is then afraid to speak or make a mistake in the studio. A child that spends the majority of their time in the home and away from other children may be shy and withdrawn among the other students in the class. A child accustomed to celebrating and supporting the achievement of family members may cheer on their peers during class. Even sibling order, or lack of siblings, can reveal insight to a student's personality and behavioral and social patterns. Perhaps the student is accustomed to someone else routinely doing things for them, or they may be entirely self-sufficient. Helpful questions, such as those previously listed, could be asked of the family adult in a questionnaire to lend insight into the student and to aid the teacher in developing lesson plans and behavior management strategies.

Family influence is most helpful when the parents or guardians are involved in the student's activities and can actively encourage their child. The dance teacher may notice differing attitudes and behaviors that stem from parental/guardian encouragement or pressure. The Center on Education Policy (CEP) provides research that shows children often tend to enjoy an activity more, demonstrate confidence, and perform better when their family takes a sincere interest in their participation and efforts.[2] Children will often reflect characteristics such as confidence, leadership, or perseverance when those are modeled within their families. If the child feels supported at home, they bring this comfort and assurance with them to the studio. The CEP also notes that immigrant families tend to emphasize hard work and perseverance as a result of their own immigration experience.[3] Children often carry this strong work ethic into their school and extracurricular activities.

While some children may not receive support from their families regarding their dance training, others may feel pressure applied on them from family members. If the family does not take an interest in dance or the child's involvement and progression, the child may be less motivated to engage in class. The child may feel as though their efforts or achievements in class will not be recognized or celebrated at home, so why should they bother working in class? Yet, some families may set high demands and expectations on a child. With this pressure, the child may exhibit low motivation and perform poorly.[4] The child may present negative behavior in the classroom or lose interest in dance altogether.

Pressure does not extend only from parents. Children, especially adolescents, can also face pressure from their peers. At times, children may feel as though they are missing out on other social activities and experiences in which their friends get to participate. They may then demonstrate reduced motivation and engagement within the classroom. Additionally, children may compel others their age to feel as though they should behave in a certain manner, demonstrate specific attitudes, or share values and viewpoints. Notably, boys who dance are often bullied or ridiculed by their peers as they deem the sport too effeminate. As a result, this stress may cause boys to demonstrate low motivation and effort within class or quit dancing altogether. The physical effects of adolescence are discussed in Chapters 3 and 4.

Peer influence may also emerge in the form of competition. Adolescent and older dancers may perceive, whether real or not, a competition between the performance of their peers and their own movement attempts. As a student makes a determination regarding their own success or failure in comparison to that of their peers, the student's attitude, motivation, and effort can be positively or negatively affected. When aware of these affects, the teacher can guard against or appropriately incorporate competitive activities.

Finally, gender can also affect a dancer's motivation, attention, and performance as they journey through growth spurts and puberty. Peer and cultural pressures regarding gender identity and the natural biological developments of an individual may cause reduced self-esteem, temporary decline of physical abilities, increased fatigue, or anxiety. The effective dance teacher understands physical human growth and development and considers the accompanying challenges in their instruction, while offering encouragement and support to the student.

Socioeconomic Status

Socioeconomic climates can affect family dynamics and also influence a child's attitude. Financial stress or time constraints can factor into the family dynamic and child behavior. Such factors may limit the opportunity for interaction within the home. As a result, the child may not have support as they work toward goals and skill attainment. Such students may struggle with feelings of competence, or they may fail to realize the value in learning and their developed abilities.[5]

Means, opportunity, and family support can contribute to a student's behavior in the classroom and overall approach to learning. A child's socioeconomic circumstances, coupled with family dynamics, can cause a child to respond in various ways. Some children may perceive themselves as inadequate or inferior to others, become withdrawn, demonstrate embarrassment, or act out to get attention. Conversely, other children might exhibit determination and motivation toward their individual learning or show sensitivity and generosity to the needs of others. Yet, some children may demonstrate attitudes of superiority or even deference to authority. They may bully others or fail to include those they deem unworthy or unequal. It is important to realize that socioeconomic status alone does not elicit certain behaviors among children. The interaction with the family unit, range of personal life experiences, and the child's individual personality and traits also shape the way in which they behave and learn.

Cultural Considerations

Cultural sensitivity – the awareness and acceptance of cultural differences – is important within any environment. The way in which the student may communicate, act, or react is related to the culture with which they identify. Different cultures encompass varied forms of communication, customs, behaviors, attitudes, and values. These cultural patterns may vary from the expectations of the dance teacher who is of a different ethnicity or cultural group. In the dance studio, the effective dance teacher should consider the cultural influences within communication and social and physical interaction and display respect toward any differences.

Communication

Language barriers can cause confusion and conflict within the dance learning environment. Such difficulties can occur when two people speak different languages and even when they share the same language. Accents and dialects can affect the way in which one might interpret conversations, lead to frustration between individuals, or even cause individuals to avoid speaking to one another. The dance teacher should foster patience, respect, and kindness within interactions.

Language barriers can also result when individuals or groups have different communication patterns. For example, consider who, within a given culture, is allowed or encouraged to speak. Within some groups, only the authority figure in the family engages in dialogue with other leaders, such as a teacher. Here, a specific method of who should talk and when is delineated, and this may mean that only one parent communicates with the teacher, never the other. In another example, a child speaking when adults are present may be frowned upon. As a result, the student may feel uncomfortable answering questions or addressing the teacher with inquiries.

The manner in which one speaks and communicates can also create confusion for the teacher or among students. The teacher will find that students interact with them in distinct ways. Some groups may view an interruption of others who are speaking as a sign of interest, yet this behavior may be considered rude in other cultures. This knowledge could explain why a specific student often interrupts the teacher when they are speaking; they are displaying enthusiasm toward the topic. Some students may avoid eye contact as a form of respect, yet they are paying attention to the instruction. The teacher may assume that the nodding of the head indicates that the individual understands and agrees with what the teacher is saying. However, in some groups, nodding means only that they are listening, and they may not necessarily understand the information being conveyed. This confusion can occur between teacher and student and teacher and parent. Additionally, children may not let the teacher know when questions or concerns arise but remain quiet instead, simply out of an uncertainty in how to communicate or due to embarrassment.[6]

The dance teacher should never be dismissive of the way a student acts and responds. Rather, they should be attentive to the communication patterns of each student, striving to uncover the distinct manners in which students interact and their connection needs. Certain behavior and communication may be taught and encouraged within the classroom, yet allowances for and acceptance of cultural patterns should always be present. The dance teacher should be prepared to alter the instructional approach if the response of the student is different than anticipated or desired. They could phrase questions differently or word directions in a new way. Most importantly, the teacher should find ways to let the student know that they support them and are making an effort to understand them.

Social Interaction

The dance teacher may also observe distinctions in the social interactions among students. The customary focus of a culture may be given to the individual or the group. For example, a specific culture may emphasize the extended family, wherein siblings, grandparents, and other family members may often be present to observe class, talk with the teacher, or attend performances. Awareness of the cultural family dynamic enables the teacher to better support child and familial needs. In the United States, mainstream culture focuses on the individual. Self-reliance and independence are often emphasized, which can lead to a sense of competition between individuals. Individuals often desire and become empowered by autonomy. Other cultures tend to concentrate on the collective group. As students interact socially and engage in cooperative learning, a desire for cohesion among the group is instilled.[7]

It can be helpful for the teacher to observe if focus is given to an individual or if it is customary for a culture to work together or engage as a group. Often a teacher may include partner or group work within the lesson plan. Students may display contrasting responses in these situations. One child may be excited to work with a partner or in a group because focusing on the group as a whole is quite normal to them. However, another child may prefer to work on their own. Further, a child may be uncomfortable to offer individual responses and shy away from questions directed to them yet may be content to answer along with the group.

Physical Space and Touch

A student often learns behavioral patterns and develops preferences regarding space and touch through their cultural customs. These approaches and attitudes can vary greatly among differing cultures. Consideration should be given to the ways in which individuals physically interact with each other. Are they constrained and reserved in their interaction, or do they eagerly participate both verbally and nonverbally? This information, gleaned through conversation or non-verbal cues, can guide the dance teacher in the way they engage with a student and facilitate group work and interaction among the students.

When considering physical space, individuals may stand or move in close proximity with others, or they may establish clear boundaries when around others. Some students may feel comfortable standing close to others while in conversation, whereas others may prefer substantial distance between themselves and those with whom they are speaking. A dance teacher may draw the class's attention to an individual student to highlight something that that student has done well; this is intended to be a positive action. However, for some students, being singled out is a negative teaching response.[8] The effective dance teacher considers their expectations regarding how personal space is approached within the learning environment yet recognizes the comfort and needs of their students. It may be necessary for teachers to guide students through boundaries of personal space or reconsider how students are situated within the studio.

Individuals often have strict boundaries regarding physical touch. These views may extend from one's personal characteristics and preferences yet can also result from the interactions developed within one's culture. Children within some cultures may employ a greater use of physical contact among their peers, such as touching a shoulder or arm of another, playing with a friend's hair, or offering hugs. This physical contact serves as a mode of communication as they engage with others.[9] Meanwhile, another culture may be reserved with their bodies and frown upon physical touch. It is always important for the teacher to ask before utilizing physical touch as a form of instruction or feedback.

The way that students communicate and socially interact may also be independent from cultural patterns. The religious beliefs, past experiences, and/or individual personality and characteristics of a student – separate from their cultural or family dynamics – can

142 Factors That Affect the Learning Environment

contribute to a student's motivation and behavior patterns. Some individuals are natural introverts or extroverts, hesitant or eager to try to new things, or display worry or confidence in the classroom. The effective dance teacher becomes aware of these distinctions, recognizes the need to interact with each student as an individual, and discovers ways to best communicate and teach each student.

AVOIDING STEREOTYPES AND BIAS

Everyone encompasses some degree of bias, and it can become all too easy to apply stereotypes to different groups of students. Society often creates ideas and notions of how a given group will behave, also known as **stereotypes**. A stereotype becomes a broad generalization regarding a specific group that has been frequently used without consideration of the distinct differences the group may actually embrace. A stereotype may be complimentary or derogatory, both of which can be harmful to others.

Unfortunately, individuals often make incorrect assumptions of others based on preconceived stereotypes. Such stereotypes may relate to age, gender, race, or social class. For example, a common stereotype of all male-identifying dancers is that they must be gay. Such a statement incorrectly categorizes an entire group of individuals based on their gender and hobby/profession. Another example is the assumption that all African American individuals are strong athletes. While many might be, there may be equally as many that are not athletic.

The dance teacher should be mindful of the effects of stereotype threat and self-fulfilling prophecy, both of which can influence the behavior and performance of a student. For example, children in certain socioeconomic situations may be given a stereotype of behaving poorly, or it may be assumed that their attendance and effort will be inconsistent. Because of this viewpoint, these children may become so worried about demonstrating or confirming this stereotype that anxiety takes over and they end up displaying the negative behavior attached to the stereotype. This is known as **stereotype threat**. The performance of an individual can be lowered simply because they are expected to perform poorly due to the generalization made about their social class, financial background, or cultural association. For example, the dance teacher could look at the class roster and make judgment calls on the behavior and abilities of a particular student before even meeting them based on their name alone. Connecting a name to a previously known individual with certain behavioral characteristics or the stereotype of the perceived culture can be extremely damaging to the interaction between teacher and student. Age, gender, and body type can also generate stereotype threats. For instance, a teacher may adopt the incorrect belief that only slender and lean students are capable of producing strong dance technique. Students who do not fit that body type standard may recognize this attitude and, in their effort to avoid that stereotype, overcompensate in their movement efforts and demonstrate poor technique or turn to eating disorders.

In a similar instance, the teacher can contribute to a **self-fulfilling prophecy,** wherein an individual takes on the characteristics of the expectations placed upon them. The teacher's view and assumptions of a student's behavior or skill level can hinder or enhance the student's cognitive and physical abilities, behavior and motivation, and overall learning. If the student is treated with low expectations, they can begin to believe they are only capable of attaining a certain degree of skill or behavior and will then set lower goals, failing to achieve their full potential. Conversely, the determination that a student will excel in class simply because of natural facility and ability can create a boost for the student's performance.[10]

Each individual encompasses a degree of **implicit bias**, the automatic and often unintentional judgment, decision, or attitude embraced by an individual. A person can adopt a bias from circumstances such as their upbringing or learning environment. These subconscious values can affect the interaction that a person has with others, often in a negative manner. For example, a teacher has unknowingly discerned, through their personal training, cultural connections, or social discourse, that dancers must be thin to be successful. Unknowingly to them, they maintain this assumption, which can manifest in their interaction with students of varying body types and sizes. Perhaps they ignore them in class because they assume they will not be able to do develop in their movement abilities or will not pursue a career in dance. Implicit bias can influence the way the teacher approaches lesson planning, interacts with others, and assesses students.

During instruction, the teacher's communication with a student can reflect their perspective of the student. Children are often quick to pick up on an authority figure's attitude, tone, or certain treatment, such as avoiding eye contact with the student or consistently calling on certain dancers, and will then respond either positively or negatively. Chapter 9 discusses curriculum development for the dance class. A curriculum is intended to help students develop their cognitive and physical abilities in dance and achieve movement goals. However, the dance teacher should be mindful of hidden curriculum as they prepare for and instruct their classes. A **hidden curriculum** consists of the assumptions a teacher makes regarding how students will behave or the skills they have acquired prior to attending their class. For instance, a teacher may believe that a student has no coordination or body control based on the student's performance the previous year. For the new term, the teacher then plans simplistic lesson plans with lower expectations and goals. The teacher fails to realize that the student is now older in age and has physically and cognitively developed. Dance technique and concepts now make sense to the student. They have discovered physical control and coordination, are able to perform at a new level, and need more challenging goals.

Before the dance teacher can determine the appropriate and effective lesson plan, instructional strategies, and delivery methods, it is helpful for them to know and understand their own prejudices and preconceived notions of what, how, and to whom a dance lesson plan is created. The effective dance teacher takes time to consider this as well as learn who their students are. The teacher who does not know and understand their students can be left confused, annoyed, or frustrated with students' reactions and conduct that do not match their expectations. Further, students are then forced to either adapt to their teacher's expectations or resist. This becomes a nightmare situation with the dance classroom.

Self-awareness is key when acknowledging and addressing bias, as one should never assume they are exempt. The effective dance teacher takes time to reflect on their implicit bias, reasons for these assumptions, and how this thought process can affect their teaching abilities as well as those they teach. The instructor considers how their assumptions may help or hinder their students' learning and the steps they can take to address their bias. They should never label students or assume how a student will engage in class. Rather, they should look at students as individuals, encourage all students, and create a sense of

144 Factors That Affect the Learning Environment

belonging in the classroom. The holistic approach to teaching can help the dance teacher avoid such pitfalls related to stereotypes and bias.

CHAPTER SUMMARY

The dance classroom can include a wide-ranging population of students each unique with their own behaviors, circumstances, and experiences. Some distinctions may be immediately observable; however, many contrasts will be derived upon a deeper knowledge and understanding of the individual students. The holistic dance teacher strives to teach the whole student, with attention given to the student's motor, cognitive, behavioral, emotional, and social development. The dance teacher is mindful that one's age and sociocultural connections can influence their behavior and motivation within the dance class. As a teacher uncovers a student's family and peer dynamics, socioeconomic background, and cultural connections, they can better relate to and discern the attitudes and behaviors of the student. It is important that the teacher recognize societal stereotypes and their own bias when planning for and teaching the dance class. The holistic dance teacher can help each student toward their full potential within the classroom and perhaps in their life by acknowledging and appreciating differences, establishing trust and respect for all students, varying communication approaches, and reflecting on the experience.

PRACTICAL APPLICATIONS

1   Identify the way/s in which the dance teacher can practice holistic teaching.

2   Reflect on the various age groups and characteristics listed in Table 7.2. How might a dance teacher approach communicating with and instructing each age group?

3   How can a dance teacher demonstrate cultural sensitivity within the classroom?

4   Consider the various stereotypes with which you may be familiar. How might this knowledge affect your views of or interactions with individuals who society may label with these stereotypes?

5   Reflect on your own personality and character traits. As a student, what are your behavioral tendencies in the classroom? How might the dance teacher vary their communication approach with introverted students compared to extroverted students?

6   Observe some classes at a local dance studio (or even gymnastic or karate studio).

   a   What differences do you immediately notice among the participating students?

   b   Does the teacher interact with each student in the same way?

   c   In what ways is the teacher's interaction with students effective or ineffective?

NOTES

1 Kathryn Daniels, "The Challenges of the Adolescent Dancer," *International Association of Dance Medicine and Science*, Accessed August 2023, 2, https://iadms.org/research-publications/resources-paper/.

2 Alexandra Usher and Nancy Kober, "4. What Roles Do Parent Involvement, Family Background, and Culture Play in Student Motivation?," *Center on Education Policy*, 2012, 2, https://files.eric.ed.gov/fulltext/ED532667.pdf.

3 Usher and Kober, "4. What Roles Do Parent Involvement, Family Background, and Culture Play in Student Motivation?," 8.

4 M. Gohin, D. Dubrov, S. Kosaretsky and Dmitry Grigoryev, "The Strategies of Parental Involvement in Adolescents' Education and Extracurricular Activities," *Youth Adolescence* 50 (2021): 906. https://doi.org/10.1007/s10964-021-01399-y.

5 Usher and Kober, "4. What Roles Do Parent Involvement, Family Background, and Culture Play in Student Motivation?," 5.

6 Gregory A. Cheatham and Rosa Milagros Santos, "A-B-Cs of Bridging Home and School Expectations: For Children and Families of Diverse Backgrounds," *Young Exceptional Children* 8, no. 3 (2005): 7.

7 Steven P. Chamberlain, "Recognizing and Responding to Cultural Differences in the Education of Culturally and Linguistically Diverse Learners," *Intervention in School and Clinic* 40, no. 4 (2005): 203.

8 Muriel Saville-Troike, "A Guide to Culture in the Classroom," Published 1978, Accessed September 2023, www.academia.edu/43863272/A_Guide_to_Culture_in_the_Classroom_by_Muriel_Saville_Troike_National_Clearinghouse_for_Bilingual_Education_1978.

9 Gregory A. Cheatham and Rosa Milagros Santos. "A-B-Cs of Bridging Home and School Expectations: For Children and Families of Diverse Backgrounds," 6.

10 Jere E. Brophy, *Motivating Students to Learn*, 3rd ed. (New York: Routledge, 2010), 294–295.

BIBLIOGRAPHY

"Adolescent Development." *Medline Plus*. National Library of Medicine. https://medlineplus.gov/ency/article/002003.htm, accessed December 2022.

Brophy, Jere E. *Motivating Students to Learn*. 3rd ed. New York: Routledge, 2010.

Chamberlain, Steven P. "Recognizing and Responding to Cultural Differences in the Education of Culturally and Linguistically Diverse Learners." *Intervention in School and Clinic* 40, no. 4 (2005): 195–211.

Cheatham, Gregory A., and Rosa Milagros Santos. "A-B-Cs of Bridging Home and School Expectations: For Children and Families of Diverse Backgrounds." *Young Exceptional Children* 8, no. 3 (2005): 3–11.

"Child Development Guide." Published 2015. https://ocfs.ny.gov/programs/fostercare/assets/docs/Child-Development-Guide.pdf.

Christenson, Sandra L., Theresa Rounds, and Deborah Gorney. "Family Factors and Student Achievement: An Avenue to Increase Students' Success." *School Psychology Quarterly* 7, no. 3 (1992): 178–206.

Daniels, Kathryn. "The Challenges of the Adolescent Dancer." *International Association of Dance Medicine and Science*. https://iadms.org/research-publications/resources-paper/, accessed August 2023.

Davies, Douglas, and Michael F. Troy. *Child Development: A Practitioner's Guide*. 4th ed. New York: The Guilford Press, 2020.

Davis, Crystal U. *Dance and Belonging: Implicit Bias and Inclusion in Dance Education*. North Carolina: McFarland & Company, Inc. Publishers, 2022.

"Developmental Milestones: 4–5 Year Olds (Preschool)." www.choc.org/primary-care/ages-stages/4-to-5-years/, accessed December 2022.

Dweck, Carol S. "Motivational Processes Affecting Learning." *The American Psychologist* 41, no. 10 (1986): 1040–1048.

Gonzalez-DeHass, Alyssa R., Patricia P. Willems, and Marie F. Doan Holbein. "Examining the Relationship Between Parental Involvement and Student Motivation." *Educational Psychology Review* 17, no. 2 (2005): 99–123.

Goshin, M., D. Dubrov, S. Kosaretsky, and D. Grigoryev. "The Strategies of Parental Involvement in Adolescents' Education and Extracurricular Activities." *Youth Adolescence* 50 (2021): 906–920. https://doi.org/10.1007/s10964-021-01399-y.

"Growth and Development: 6–12 Years (School Age)." *Children's Health of Orange County*. www.choc.org/primary-care/ages-stages/6-to-12-years/, accessed December 2022.

Halawah, Ibtesam. "The Effect of Motivation, Family Environment, and Student Characteristics on Academic Achievement." *Journal of Instructional Psychology* 33, no. 2 (2006): 91–99.

Krasnow, Donna, and Virginia Wilmerding. *Motor Learning and Control for Dance: Principles and Practices for Performers and Teachers*. Champaign, IL: Human Kinetics, 2015.

Lee, Jihuyum, and Valerie J. Shute. "Personal and Social-Contextual Factors in K-12 Academic Performance: An Integrative Perspective on Student Learning." *Educational Psychologist* 45, no. 3 (2010): 185–202.

McCarthy-Brown, Nyama. "The Need for Culturally Relevant Dance Education." *Journal of Dance Education* 9, no. 4 (2009): 120–125.

"Preschooler Development." *Medline Plus* (National Library of Medicine). https://medlineplus.gov/ency/article/002013.htm, accessed December 2022.

Saville-Troike, Muriel. "A Guide to Culture in the Classroom." Published 1978. www.academia.edu/43863272/A_Guide_to_Culture_in_the_Classroom_by_Muriel_Saville_Troike_National_Clearinghouse_for_Bilingual_Education_1978, accessed September 2023.

Saygili, Gizem. "Factors Affecting Students' Learning Motivation." *European Researcher* 9, no. 2 (2018).

"School-Age Children Development." *Medline Plus* (National Library of Medicine). https://medlineplus.gov/ency/article/002017.htm, accessed December 2022.

Sööt, Anu, and Ele Viskus. "Teaching Dance in the 21st Century: A Literature Review." *The European Journal of Social and Behavioural Sciences* 7, no. 4 (2013): 624–640. https://doi.org/10.15405/ejsbs.99.

"Teenager Growth and Development: 13–18 Years (Adolescent)." *Children's Health of Orange County*. www.choc.org/primary-care/ages-stages/13-to-18-years/, accessed December 2022.

Usher, Alexandra, and Nancy Kober. "4. What Roles Do Parent Involvement, Family Background, and Culture Play in Student Motivation?." *Center on Education Policy*. Published 2012. https://files.eric.ed.gov/fulltext/ED532667.pdf.

CHAPTER 8

Inclusion, Diversity, Equity, and Accessibility

Sara Pecina

> **Box 8.1 Chapter Objectives**
>
> After reading this chapter, you will be able to:
>
> - Apply culturally relevant teaching within the dance instruction environment
> - Define each term in IDEA and situate its application in the dance class

> **Box 8.2 Chapter Vocabulary**
>
> accessibility
> critical dance pedagogy
> culturally relevant teaching
> culture
> diversity
> equity
> inclusion

Dance is a human experience. The ability to express oneself through movement should be celebrated in its diversity and be accessible to all, yet challenges arise in implementing this simple statement. Issues in inclusion, diversity, equity, and accessibility exist in all sectors of dance education. The holistic dance teacher is mindful of each of these ideals in their dance class. In this chapter, culturally relevant teaching is defined, and the aspects of inclusion, diversity, equity, and accessibility within dance are considered. Knowledge in each of these areas equips the effective dance teacher to be an advocate for all students and forms of dance.

CULTURALLY RELEVANT TEACHING

Chapter 7 discussed holistic teaching with attention to cultural considerations that may affect the way in which students conduct themselves in the classroom. Let us now examine the ways in which the dance teacher may utilize cultural understanding to help their

DOI: 10.4324/b22952-12

students learn through culturally relevant teaching. First described by Gloria Ladson Billings in the 1990s, **culturally relevant teaching** is a teaching methodology in which the educator adapts their instructional strategies in consideration of the cultural affinities of the students.[1] Students learn more effectively when they feel safe, welcome, and appreciated, and can relate to course content. Culturally relevant teaching provides insight for dance teachers to achieve these goals.

Culture can be described as a collection of customs shared by a group of people. Such customs could include matter such as holidays, celebrations, coming-of-age rituals, societal structure, religion, language, food, music, fashion, dance, and countless other unifying systems. An individual most likely identifies with multiple cultures. For instance, someone may identify with their black ethnicity, ancestral heritage in Brazil, the LGBTQ community, and Generation Z. Along with different identities, there are countless ways in which each person practices any culture. In any geographic location, there is a dominant culture, which is practiced by either a majority of the population or the portion of population that holds power. It is not uncommon for those of the dominant culture to fail to recognize their culture, especially at a young age. On the other hand, those of any minority culture are often aware of their differences from what is considered mainstream in their region.

The dance class itself is a community with its own culture. Additionally, different dance classrooms, or genres, have their own subcultures. These subcultures have distinct preferences in aesthetics, performance practices, class structure, costuming, music, how to enter the dance space, the method of thanking the teacher, etc. For example, tap dance, classical Indian dance, ballet, competition dance, musical theatre, and hip-hop all have differing value systems in what students aim to achieve, how dancers interact, classroom structure, and performance setting. It is paramount for dance teachers to note that they must not discriminate against dance cultures different from their own. Naturally, holistically trained dance instructors will uphold the customs of the dance form they are teaching, while recognizing and celebrating students that come from another dance culture or practice multiple forms of dance.

Implementation

In order to implement culturally relevant teaching, dance teachers must first get to know their students. It is impossible to relate to students without knowing who they are. A practical way to achieve this information is through a survey. Rather than asking dry demographic questions, use this as an opportunity to learn about what motivates your students. Pose questions such as the following: "What do you do on the weekends? What are three goals you hope to achieve in this class by the end of the semester/year? Who inspires you? Where is your family from? Do you dance at home? How do you celebrate your birthday? Who is your favorite dance artist?" Questions like these can give valuable insights that simple data like age and race cannot provide. Reaching out to students in this manner also helps them feel cared for in the classroom for no other reason than the teacher attempting to learn about the individuals in the room. Questions should be tailored to the ages of the students. For example, in classes with more mature students, teachers can include questions like "what are your preferred pronouns?" Note that one piece of paper with a few

Inclusion, Diversity, Equity, and Accessibility **149**

questions will not provide all the needed insight. This is a good starting point, but teachers should actively learn about their students throughout the term.

Once there is a general understanding of the student population, lesson plans can be tailored to connect with the students' cultures and previous experiences. Intentional design of class rituals, exercises, and activities can help the students connect to class content and become more actively engaged in their learning. For example, at the beginning of class, students may introduce themselves or express how they are feeling that day with a movement of their choice. Students of East Asian heritage may be accustomed to meditation as a part of their daily lives; this practice could be utilized at the beginning or end of class sessions. Improvisation frees the body to express itself through each student's embodied history. The dance teacher could use a variety of music styles to accompany improvisation to aid students in their self-expression or allow them to create the rhythm themselves with their bodies or instruments in class.

As the students share in the experience of the dance class, a micro community is created. Singular experiences in the dance studio can also help strengthen these bonds. One such experience could be allowing the students to name an exercise that is regularly included with weekly lesson plans. For example, the students could select a name for the composed *barre* stretch that is done during each ballet class. Names or titles could include anything the students agree upon (excluding any inappropriate or harmful language, of course). Or, students could work together to create a short greeting or parting phrase that is done at the beginning or end of each class, almost like a secret handshake. These and many other applications of culturally relevant teaching are discussed at length in Nyama McCarthy-Brown's text *Dance Pedagogy for a Diverse World*.

IDEA

Presently and more than ever before, dance schools, companies, and organizations across disciplines include diversity, equity, and inclusion in their missions and strive to reach and maintain new standards in these ideals. It is common to see the acronym DEI (for diversity, equity, and inclusion) on advertising materials, job listings, websites, curricula, lesson plans, etc. The concepts that make up DEI have little impact if they are not accessible to all. Therefore, for the purpose of this text, the author has chosen to expand this to IDEA – for inclusion, diversity, equity, and accessibility. For clarity, each of these topics is discussed individually in the following sections.

Inclusion

Inclusion is the act of intentionally creating a dance space in which people from any background feel welcomed, supported, and valued. Age, gender, nationality, religion, socioeconomic status, race, language, ability, marital status, sexual orientation, and profession are all examples of various types of backgrounds with which people may identify. In an inclusive dance environment, students from across any of these spectrums feel able to participate fully in programming.

Society anticipates that leaders in a business, organization, or school will responsibly establish an inclusive environment. Likewise, dance teachers should make this effort in their classrooms. One way to do this is to avoid stereotypes, as described in Chapter 7. The holistic dance teacher values each individual in the room, models inclusive behavior for students, and manages any conduct from students who display stereotyping or exclusive treatment of others.

Diversity

Diversity is the spectrum of differences between people and cultures. Each type of identity listed earlier marks ways in which individuals may be different or similar to others. Generally, the ideals of the dominant culture may be reflected in educational programming. When handled correctly, proffering diversity in curricula broadens the perspectives of the students and strengthens their abilities to critically analyze information.

Dance studios and programs may offer a variety of technique classes to provide students a diverse curriculum. Dance teachers recognize the benefit of training in multiple dance genres. Motor development and learning may be enhanced, and skill and performance may become more fully developed. The design of these programs also helps prepare students to meet the demands of professional dance careers. Versatility of a dancer pursuing a professional career is paramount nowadays with companies collaborating across genres and presenting diverse performances while the ever-growing blend of styles in contemporary dance continues to evolve. A dancer pursuing a Broadway career should be advanced in jazz and tap dance techniques while also having experience in ballroom movements, hip-hop, ballet, and acrobatics plus training in singing and acting if they wish to remain competitive in the job market. The effective dance teacher recognizes this need within the performing world.

The dance teacher is also cognizant that, regardless of their chosen career paths, students will develop into adults within a diverse society. The dance teacher can best serve their students as dancers and prepare them to engage in a global society when they offer diversity within their classes. They may use a range of musical genres and styles as accompaniment. This can enhance the way that students hear and listen to musical accompaniment and approach movement style and quality. The dance teacher may discuss a variety of influential historical figures and events that have impacted the art form. This can help provide conceptual connections and inspiration for students. The teacher should, of course, be mindful to include a diverse collection of examples. Knowledge of dance forms from an array of distinct cultures could be shared with students through conversation and discussion, video recordings, or movement explorations. This exposure can broaden the students' awareness and appreciation not only for dance but various cultures as well. Additionally, the dance teacher might invite guest teachers that embrace diverse perspectives to instruct their students. This experience can expand the students' ability to learn or collaborate in new ways.

In the United States, the Eurocentric ideals of the founding fathers and ruling class still dominate the majority of dance studios and academic programming. These concepts can include the perspective that European, or White, individuals or practices are superior to others, specifically those from non-Western cultures. In her book, McCarthy-Brown introduces the term critical dance pedagogy (CDP). **Critical dance pedagogy** is an approach to dance education that invites questioning the power structures at play that determine what is taught to whom and how the dancing body is valued. McCarthy-Brown elaborates that investigation should include:

> the systems of power that dictates who performs, when, and where; who receives Dance Education, when, where, what genre, what levels, with what types of resources . . . who is included in Dance History; who is pictured in our textbooks; who is funded; who is excluded from the main concert stage; and who decides the value of dance.[2]

For example, an unfortunately common phenomenon is for someone from ballet or modern dance background to see a Black dancer performing a style in the Africanist aesthetic and say, "They are so talented. Now they just need some technique to become a real dancer." Here, "technique" is believed to be ballet or classical modern dance training. This statement is troublesome in multiple ways. First, it suggests the individual's talent becomes more valuable when applied to a Eurocentric dance form. It also negates the hours of training and learning techniques that go into forms of dance other than ballet or modern, implying these other forms lack rigor and a well-developed approach to movement simply because it does not match their preferred aesthetic. Similarly, suggesting they are not a "real" dancer until gaining command of a Eurocentric dance form dissociates other forms of dance from being valuable.

Box 8.3 The "Root" of Technique

Many dance studios and higher education programs across the United States perpetuate the idea that ballet and/or modern dance are to be considered the "real" dance techniques, even going so far as to require students to enroll in ballet class in order to be eligible to sign up for tap, jazz, or hip-hop. Teachers also have a tendency to say, "Ballet is the root of all dance technique." This is a grossly misguided statement. All dance forms around the globe are developed over decades or centuries, refining the technique and training. Technique is relevant to the individual dance aesthetic. The proper carriage of the body in ballet with an erect spine and lengthened torso while pulling up through the legs does nothing to aid the tap dancer in learning to drop their weight into the floor to create more resonant sounds. It is true that training in a variety of styles benefits the dance student. Not only do they become a more versatile performer but also the differing physicality of the movement vocabularies can help prevent injury. For instance, ballet dancers regularly extend the front of the ankles to the extreme by pointing their feet, especially when *en pointe*. The muscularity of rhythm tap with the use of toe drops, and various other steps strengthens the front (or anterior) portion of the ankle that is overstretched in ballet; thus, tap dance can aid in providing stronger support on *relevé* or *en pointe*.

Dance teachers should encourage students to train in any variety of dance forms that interest them. All dance forms will enhance a student's coordination, balance, musicality, etc. However, teachers should never perpetuate the falsehood of any technique being more important than another or being the foundation of all other dance forms.

The dance studio or school's curricular offerings should be reviewed through the CDP lens, with consideration given to the why behind curricular offerings and program design. Why are certain dance forms offered? Why are other dance forms excluded? Is preference given to certain classes or genres, and if so, why and in what ways? Are restrictions placed on student enrollment in select dance forms, and if so, why and to what extent? While different programs may focus on or specialize in certain dance forms, the effective dance teacher is mindful of their language and attitude toward all styles and genres.

Equity

Equity is fair treatment and opportunity for all people, including their ability to participate, adequate representation, respectful treatment, and access to resources. It is important to note that equality and equity are not the same, nor are they interchangeable terms. Equality focuses on everyone receiving the same amount or type of something. Equity recognizes that not everyone has the same starting point, and individual needs must be met in order to provide the same experience or opportunity for each person. Imagine a group of people are dividing a pie; some of the individuals have not eaten in a week, others' most recent meal was 24 hours ago, still others ate within the last hour. On the basis of equality, each individual gets the same size slice; it helps those who hunger marginally while not fulfilling much of a need for those who recently ate. With equity as the foundation, the slices of pie are measured relative to the need or hunger of the individual, with those who have not eaten recently receiving larger slices than those who just had a meal. In other words, equity effectively levels the playing field.

Equity in a dance instruction setting usually focuses on participation, success, retention, and access (addressed in the next section) while emphasizing minority populations and/or underserved community members. Publicly funded institutions must follow legislation that exists to provide equal opportunity employment and treatment. An example of equity issues within the field of dance can be noted in regard to gender and authority positions. By number, women dominate the field of dance with a vast majority of schools and companies enrolling and employing more female-identifying dancers than male. Yet, a majority of leadership positions – program director/chair, artistic director, executive

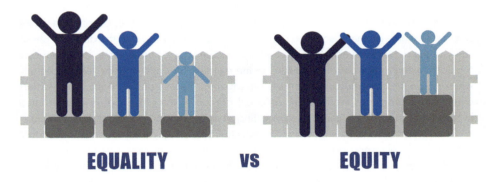

FIGURE 8.1 Image depicting the difference between equality and equity.
Source: Photo by iam2mai/Shutterstock.com

director, resident choreographer, etc. – are held by men.[3] Though, in theory, committee work often disperses power, the men still hold power over curricular, hiring, promotion, and artistic decisions. Assessing situations like this, designing solutions, and implementing plans strengthen the dance community by working to make the art form more equitable.

The holistic dance teacher considers equity within the way they lesson plan for the dance class and assess students. They should be mindful of the learning needs and stages of each student when establishing goals and objectives. For example, Student A may have significant experience executing a particular movement skill, whereas Student B has not yet learned the skill. The two students should not be expected to learn and perform a combination that includes the movement skill to the same degree of efficiency in a given time frame. Perhaps the goal for Student A may be to successfully complete the exercise during the class, while the goal for Student B might be to learn the skill and memorize the sequence of the exercise. The dance teacher should ensure that each student has opportunity and is encouraged to participate in all classes offered as appropriate to their age and level. They should assess the student as an individual, comparing learning and abilities in dance to the established curricular goals and the student's individual growth rather than comparing one student's development and abilities to that of another student.

Accessibility

Accessibility is the designing, building, and application of providing the means for all people of various backgrounds and abilities to engage and participate in dance. People of differing demographics and varying abilities face boundaries when pursuing dance. The focus of accessibility is to eliminate these obstacles so that anyone interested can participate in dance. This is a vast topic with extensive applied and qualitative research and more content than can fit in the scope of this book. Accessibility is no simple task. The following paragraphs provide preliminary insight into accessibility and dance and should spark interest in the reader's further research and advocacy.

A dance student with a developmental or physical disability faces both attitudinal and logistical barriers in pursuing the art form. Social barriers and stigmas can prevent these individuals from being widely accepted into the dance class. Some people perceive the participation in a dance class of a student with a disability as a mode of therapy rather than dance; this may partially be based in people's lack of understanding of disabilities and the notion that someone is automatically "suffering" from whatever condition with which they live. Dance is innately therapeutic for all participants, not just those perceived to be different from the traditional dancing body. This frame of mind is important for dance teachers and students to understand. Research demonstrates that when all bodies dance together, attitudes and beliefs about what dance is and who can dance changes for both able-bodied and disabled participants.[4]

Logistical barriers create even more roadblocks. The availability of programs that accept students with various disabilities in either separate or integrated classes is very low. Even with legislation surrounding building codes and accessibility, many studios may lack a ramp to the building or into the dance studio itself (if the classroom has a raised floor). Students with sensory issues require accommodation in brightness, volume, ambient noise, and crowds. Even if dancers have access to class, the majority of theatres and performance spaces pose architectural barriers lacking ramps and space for some dancers to enter the dressing rooms or backstage. Transportation and expense create additional logistical barriers.

In removing these obstacles and creating dance programs for all abilities, professionals have discovered best practices to aid success. Without studying occupational or dance/movement therapy, there are few training resources available. If teachers are unable to enroll and attend special training, such as Mark Morris Dance Group's Dance for PD® program, they should spend time with individuals with developmental and/or physical disabilities. Understanding physical limitations and behavioral tendencies is paramount. The dance teacher needs to be ready to adapt movement where necessary and deescalate behavioral situations. For example, a student may require an assistive device, such as a cane. The dance teacher should consider how the student can still participate in a ballet class, specifically during the center exercises. It can be challenging for the dance teacher to meet the needs of all students in a class. Utilizing volunteers in the room can prove extremely helpful. A recommendation might be to incorporate caregivers or other teaching assistants within the class. Their presence allows the teacher to proceed with the lesson for the class while a volunteer aids a specific student with adaptations, focus, or emotional distress. The use of assistants also reassures the parents that their child's needs will be met. Should a situation arise that the teacher or volunteers are unequipped to handle, it is always recommended to seek guidance from the student's parents or caregivers.

CHAPTER SUMMARY

Dance teachers hold a responsibility to be advocates for dance in all of its forms and for all people. Using the principle of culturally relevant teaching helps instructors connect with students and provide instructional strategies to make more successful learners. Thoughtful inclusion should be a cornerstone of all dance studios and schools. Diversity strengthens the abilities and character of students, and misinformed hierarchical beliefs on the value of different dance forms must be eliminated. Equitable practice provides fair opportunity, while accessibility removes barriers preventing people from experiencing dance training. Each of these aspects are paramount in the progression of dance education, building better communities, and strengthening dance as an art form.

PRACTICAL APPLICATIONS

1   With what cultures do you identify? How do these affect the ways in which you learn in the classroom or studio setting?

2   Go online and find a dance company or school's diversity statement (either a distinct statement or as part of their mission statement).

   a   Does this statement reflect the concepts discussed earlier?

   b   Explore the website. Does programming and leadership in this school reflect the ideals described in their statement? How so, or why not?

   c   Write your own statement of your dedication to IDEA in dance teaching.

3   Identify a time in your life in which you encountered obstacles with accessibility. What were those obstacles? What inspired you to overcome them? How was this achieved?

4   How do you predict the field of dance will grow in the areas of IDEA? What is an actionable step you can take to advocate for change?

NOTES

1   Nyama McCarthy-Brown, *Dance Pedagogy for a Diverse World*, 16.
2   Nyama McCarthy-Brown, *Dance Pedagogy for a Diverse World*, 10.
3   Doug Risner, "Equity in Dance Education: Where Are We Now?" *Journal of Dance Education* 6, no. 4 (2006): 105.
4   Michelle R. Zitomer and Greg Reid, "To Be or Not to Be – Able to Dance: Integrated Dance and Children's Perceptions of Dance Ability and Disability," *Research in Dance* 12, no. 2 (2011): 143–146.

BIBLIOGRAPHY

Albin, Chloe M. "The Benefit of Movement: Dance/Movement Therapy and Down Syndrome." *Journal of Dance Education* 16, no. 2 (2016): 58–61.

Aujla, Imogen J., and Emma Redding. "Barriers to Dance Training for Young People with Disabilities." *British Journal of Special Education* 40, no. 2 (2013): 80–85.

James, Tobin. "Calling for Cultural Humility in Ballet Academies and Companies." *Journal of Dance Education* 20, no. 3 (2020): 131–135.

Kane, Nancy. "Dance for All? A Rhapsody on Diversity, Equity, and Inclusion in Dance Education." *National Dance Society Journal* 7, no. 1 (2022): 5–14.

Matzner, J. "Sitting Ballet: A Pilot Program Designed to Include Children with Physical Disabilities in the Private Studio Environment." *Journal of Dance Education* 15, no. 3 (2015): 116–121.

McCarthy-Brown, Nyama. *Dance Pedagogy for a Diverse World*. North Carolina: McFarland & Company, Inc., 2017.

McGreevy-Nichols, Susan, and Shannon Dooling-Cain. "Cultivating Equity and Access: Focus on Men in Dance." *Journal on Dance Education* 17, no. 2 (2017): 86–87.

Morris, Merry Lynn. "Pushing the Limits: Making Dance Accessible to Different Bodies through Assistive Technology." *Journal of Dance Education* 15, no. 4 (2015): 142–151.

Morris, Merry Lynn, Marion Baldeon, and Dwayne Scheuneman. "Developing and Sustaining an Inclusive Dance Program: Strategic Tools and Methods." *Journal of Dance Education* 15, no. 3 (2015): 122–129.

Oliver, Wendy, and Doug Risner. *Dance and Gender*. Gainsville, FL: University Press of Florida, 2017.

Prichard, Robin. "From Color-Blind to Color-Conscious." *Journal of Dance Education* 19, no. 4 (2019): 168–177.

Reinders, Nicole J., Pamela J. Bryden, and Paula C. Fletcher. "'Dance Is Something That Anyone Can Do': Creating Dance Programs for All Abilities." *Research in Dance Education* 20, no. 2 (2019): 257–274.

Reinders, Nicole, Paula Fletcher, and Pam Bryden. "Dreams Do Come True: The Creation and Growth of a Recreational Dance Program for Children and Young Adults with Additional Needs." *Journal of Dance Education* 15, no. 3 (2015): 100–109.

Risner, Doug. "Equity in Dance Education: Momentum for Change." *Journal of Dance Education* 8, no. 3 (2008): 75–78.

Risner, Doug. "Equity in Dance Education: Where Are We Now?" *Journal of Dance Education* 6, no. 4 (2006): 105–108.

Sanderson, Patricia. "The Arts, Social Inclusion and Social Class: The Case of Dance." *British Educational Research Journal* 34, no. 4 (2008): 467–490.

Seham, Jenny, and Anna J. Yeo. "Extending Our Vision: Access to Inclusive Dance Education for People with Visual Impairment." *Journal of Dance Education* 15, no. 3 (2015): 91–99.

Wakamatsu, Kori. "Asian American Perspectives." *Journal of Dance Education* 20, no. 3 (2020): 121–125.

Zitomer, Michelle R., and Greg Reid. "To Be or Not to Be – Able to Dance: Integrated Dance and Children's Perceptions of Dance Ability and Disability." *Research in Dance Education* 12, no. 2 (2011): 137–156.

UNIT 4

Class Content and Preparation

CHAPTER 9

Curriculum Development and Lesson Planning

Box 9.1 Chapter Objectives

After reading this chapter, you will be able to:

- Understand the importance of planning for instruction
- Articulate the distinction between goals and objectives within the dance lesson plan
- Identify the components of Bloom's taxonomy and its application in the planning of dance training
- Develop a dance curriculum
- Prepare a lesson plan for the dance class

Box 9.2 Chapter Vocabulary

curriculum
goal
objective
sequential progression
taxonomy

Think back to dance classes that you have taken in the past or may currently be attending. Can you identify similarities in class structure? Are you able to recognize a theme within a class? How did the content of the class help you grow in your comprehension or execution of the dance form? Effective classes, in any discipline, require a level of preparation by the teacher. This preparation includes the teacher's training and studies in dance, but more specifically incorporates focused consideration for the specific class to be taught. How will the class be structured? What movement and exercises will be included? In what way/s will the material presented help students progress in their understanding and skill abilities?

A degree of planning should occur prior to the start of the class term. Before stepping into the classroom, the effective dance teacher examines a variety of factors that are

DOI: 10.4324/b22952-14

helpful in creating a productive and successful curriculum for the class. Consideration is given to the genre that will be taught, the age and level of the students, long- and short-term goals for the class, and the students' overall training needs.

This chapter considers the student's motor development and learning process, as discussed in Chapters 4 and 5, to help the dance teacher devise appropriate curricula and lesson plans. Planning strategies highlight the importance of developing goals and objectives and consideration of Bloom's taxonomy. Examination is given to the components of a dance curriculum and method for constructing effective lesson plans.

BASICS OF PLANNING

The dance teacher often has three primary considerations within a dance class: technique, artistry, and fostering the joy of movement. Teachers guide the students' learning of terminology and mechanics of the dance form and development of their expressiveness and performance quality, while also instilling a sense of enjoyment and personal satisfaction within their students. These overarching targets are best achieved when appropriate planning is inherent within teaching.

Planning the dance class can be a formidable task for the teacher. Where does one start when there are many movements, concepts, qualities, and activities that could be included? Once selections have been made, how does the teacher then best progress the curriculum throughout the term? The effective dance teacher recognizes that it takes more than simply instructing students in a variety of steps and concepts. Rather, a methodical progression of these ideas should occur. There are logical sequences that can be incorporated in the learning process. For example, a student does not learn math by beginning with advanced calculus. Rather, they first learn to count in sequential order and how to combine and subtract numbers. In time, with repetition, practice, and a logical development of the introduction of new ideas, students can progress in their understanding of mathematical concepts, achieving a higher level of knowledge. Learning within any dance form is no different.

Benefits of Planning

Planning affords the dance teacher three primary benefits. Firstly, planning can offer a sense of security for the dance teacher. It can be a daunting realization, especially to the novice teacher, to know that the students' dance training is in your hands. Inexperienced teachers may lack confidence in their abilities or a clear comprehension of how the pace of a lesson plan can change within different class environments. Students may learn faster than anticipated, or they may struggle unexpectedly in certain areas. Either situation will require the teacher to craft new or alternative exercises or activities on the spot. This can often waste time during the class. Having a plan means that the teacher has prepared material and considered potential situations or pitfalls, thus alleviating their stress and maintaining an effective class pace and content delivery. Although they may be nervous or uncertain how students will respond, they will have exercises prepared to teach and backup plans they can divert to when needed.

Secondly, planning includes goal setting, which is important to the development of the students' abilities. Students may not always be aware of every goal prepared by the

Curriculum Development and Lesson Planning 161

FIGURE 9.1 Image of a dance teacher leading young dancers in a jump exercise.
Source: Photo by Jeffrey Smith/Western Kentucky University.

teacher, yet clear goals and objectives within the lesson plan help students to progress appropriately. Without considering the lesson plan in advance, a dance class can easily lack direction or focus and consist of randomly selected movement and exercises. Planning helps the teacher create long- and short-term goals for the class, which leads to a clear path for the teacher and students to follow. As the teacher plans, a methodical approach toward the goals can be devised.

Finally, planning assists in narrowing the selection of material for a given dance class. Choosing movement and creating exercises for a class can feel overwhelming at times. The teacher must decide which vocabulary to include, what areas of focus will be most helpful for students, how to assemble creative and effective movement patterns, and in what sequence to teach the composed exercises. Planning reduces movement options and shifts the teacher's focus to the specific needs of the lesson plan. The developed goals and overall plan for the student's learning thus assists the dance teacher in choosing material for each class.

Amount of Planning

A devised curriculum for the dance training environment can facilitate one's planning process, yet the time spent in preparation may still vary from teacher to teacher. An experienced teacher may be equipped to quickly recognize student needs, understand distinctions in student levels and abilities, set appropriate goals, and select material for lesson plans, whereas a novice teacher may need to spend a greater amount of time preparing for the term and/or individual classes. The level of expertise in a specific genre of dance also affects the time spent on planning. If the teacher's strength lies in ballet, they may find that it takes them longer to plan for a modern dance class, even if they are competent in modern. Additionally, the dance teacher may be comfortable teaching older children, but find they need more thorough lesson plans when instructing younger children.

The amount of time spent planning differs between each class meeting as the quantity of material needed may vary. A chosen training goal might require that a significant portion of class time be spent on a single exercise or activity in order for the goal to be attained. Yet, a separate goal may rely on a series of varying exercises to help students in achieving the target skill, thus require more planning. Early in the term, the teacher may need to plan more options or exercises as they get to know the student's and their abilities. Yet at the end of the term, a class may demand less planning as a majority of the class time will be spent practicing the recital dance.

Finally, planning may look different among teachers and classes. Many excellent teachers require a fully prepared and notated plan prior to entering the studio, while other equally exceptional teachers can walk into the class setting with only general ideas in mind. The dance teacher may find they do not need to prepare as much material for an advanced hip-hop class as they do a beginning level class, or vice versa. With advanced students, they may have a clear goal for a class, yet are experienced enough that they can enter the studio with a few ideas and then immediately respond to the needs of the students. If the students struggle, they have "go-to" exercises that they can draw from and quickly switch gears to different material that will help students in that moment. Or perhaps the students catch onto the combination quickly with time remaining; the dance teacher can readily offer unplanned movement to further support the objectives of the class.

Not all teachers are able to improvise in the moment or plan on demand as they teach while maintaining the students' attention and still adhering to the goals for the term and focus of the class. Teachers in the early stages of their career often find it helpful to plan more material than they will reasonably need for a class. As challenges arise during the students' learning, they are then prepared with variations of exercises and options for alternate movement. Regardless of one's approach, effective teaching calls for some degree of planning.

Goals and Objectives

Effective dance classes include clear goals and objectives devised by the teacher and influenced by the curriculum. The goals and objectives help guide the lesson plan and effectively develop students' skill acquisition and artistic abilities. A **goal** is the broad area toward which one works, the outcome that one desires to achieve. Goals function best when objectives are also in place. An **objective** is a specific and measurable action that connects to the goal. Objectives clarify what one will learn and are the distinct steps that one takes to move toward the broad goal. Together, goals and objectives help ensure cohesion in the students' learning. At the curricular level, goals and objectives ensure logical progression of skills, concepts, and behaviors essential to the successful development of the dance student over a broad span of time. Within lesson plans, goals and objectives provide connection among the various exercises and activities, assist students' acquisition of skill and understanding, and provide a source of assessment for the teacher.

The dance teacher typically constructs curricula around general training goals that are broad in nature yet narrowed in focus by the objectives assigned with them. Training goals can include the following:

- Body awareness
- Body alignment
- Balance and control
- Strength and flexibility
- Coordination
- Movement vocabulary
- Elevation
- Speed and accuracy
- Weight change
- Movement style
- Musicality
- Artistry
- Historical knowledge
- Confidence and positive self-esteem
- Appreciation for dance

Objectives build toward the end results, which are the skills to be learned, attitudinal behaviors to acquire, or knowledge to be attained. When objectives are met, progress toward the training goal occurs. For example, the goal of balance and control could be pursued through the objectives of the preschool-age student successfully standing on one leg for a duration of time, the ballet student effectively executing an *adagio* exercise, or the hip-hop dancer successfully completing a shoulder freeze.

Bloom's Taxonomy

A **taxonomy** is a systematic method of classification into a structured framework. During the latter half of the 19th century, a taxonomy of learning objectives was developed by educational psychologist Benjamin Bloom along with colleagues. Bloom's taxonomy considers the three domains in which learning can occur (psychomotor, cognitive, and affective) and provides a hierarchical framework for each wherein learning objectives occur along a continuum. Objectives within each domain progress from simple to complex. The taxonomy of psychomotor domain, which relates to motor skill and ability, includes *imitation, manipulation, precision, articulation*, and *naturalization*. Within the cognitive, or thinking, domain, objectives of the taxonomy include *remembering, understanding, applying, analyzing, evaluating*, and *creating*. The affective domain is focused on attitudes and values. The taxonomy of the affective domain encompasses the objectives of *receiving, responding, valuing, organizing*, and *internalizing*. Tables 9.1–9.3 provide a summary of each domain's learning taxonomy as they relate to dance training.

164 Class Content and Preparation

TABLE 9.1 Summary of the taxonomy of the psychomotor domain.

Psychomotor Domain

Objective	Behavior	Dance Example
Imitation	Observe and replicate	Students watch the teacher demonstrate a movement and attempt to copy it.
Manipulation	Reproduce	Students continue to execute the movement with verbal direction from the teacher.
Precision	Skillfully perform	Students demonstrate proficiency in execution of the movement.
Articulation	Adapt and integrate	Students execute movement with new parameters and/or in varying exercises.
Naturalization	Automaticity	Students perform the learned movement with ease in a variety of approaches.

TABLE 9.2 Summary of the taxonomy of the cognitive domain.

Cognitive Domain

Objective	Behavior	Dance Example
Remembering	Recall information	Students demonstrate ability to label movement with correct terminology.
Understanding	Determine meaning	Students explain a movement concept.
Applying	Implement information	Students demonstrate application of knowledge in varying situations.
Analyzing	Differentiate	Students compare and contrast approaches to movement execution.
Evaluating	Make judgments	Students demonstrate the ability to self-cue as they perform movement.
Creating	Synthesize information to make a new product	Students produce original movement compositions.

SMART Planning

SMART (specific, measurable, age-appropriate, realistic, time-targeted) planning is a helpful guide in developing effective goals and objectives for a lesson plan. The effective teacher establishes specific objectives that are strategic, focused, and align with the curriculum. These objectives are measurable and able to be clearly evaluated. Rather than creating an objective of improving strength, the dance teacher devises a specific objective of completing ten push-ups. Objectives should be age-appropriate and realistic, meaning that behavior is comprehendible and attainable by the students. Gaining strength can be an ambiguous

TABLE 9.3 Summary of the taxonomy of the affective domain.

Affective Domain

Objective	Behavior	Dance Example
Receiving	Awareness	Students demonstrate awareness of self in relationship to others.
Responding	Willingness to respond	Students cooperate with peers.
Valuing	Acceptance, preference	Students gain an appreciation of dance.
Organizing	Values are organized internally	Students commit to practice outside of class.
Internalizing	Values are internalized and practiced	Students consistently display appropriate classroom etiquette.

TABLE 9.4 Breakdown of the SMART acronym.

Smart Planning

Specific	**M**easurable	**A**ge-appropriate	**R**ealistic	**T**ime-targeted

objective to students; however, completing ten push-ups is much more tangible. Finally, successful outcomes are time-targeted; a time frame is applied to the objective. For example, the objective may state that the student will complete ten push-ups at the conclusion of the semester. When the goals and objectives of a lesson plan are SMART, there is a greater likelihood that students will be able to demonstrate the objectives and achieve the goal. With this knowledge in mind, let us consider the preparation of curricula and lesson plans.

CREATING A CURRICULUM

A curriculum is necessary to help guide teachers in class preparation and assist students in understanding level progression. A **curriculum** is a body of knowledge and course of study divided among levels that a program follows and around which courses are planned. The curriculum contains the overarching collection of training goals and objectives that guide a student's path of study or training in a given setting. The dance teacher may be required to follow a curriculum already established within the school/studio, or they might be in a position to develop their own. A dance school or studio's curriculum will include a variety of classes offered in different levels that help a student to progress technically and artistically as a dancer. Each course is generally offered during a term. Terms may be an academic year, semester, or determined number of weeks. A curriculum allows the teacher and students to understand the progression of vocabulary and concepts throughout the learning process. With a curriculum in place, the teacher can generate individual lesson plans with greater ease.

When creating a curriculum, it is best to begin with consideration of the program and environment in which the curriculum will be used. What is the purpose of the school/

studio? Is it to prepare pre-professional dancers? Are classes for the recreational student? Are multiple genres of dance included and taught? In general, the dance class should encompass the primary teaching goals of technique, artistry, and joy of movement as a fundamental focus, yet will be guided by the appropriate training goals for the genre and school.

The dance teacher next considers the highest level of training that is offered and the division of levels and then reflects on what knowledge and abilities the students should acquire upon completion of or graduation from the program. These aspects become the training goals toward which the curriculum can be built. The dance teacher can then work backwards and establish objectives for each level. Charting the plan in reverse allows the teacher to ensure that all objectives lead toward the training goals. The complete curriculum should provide students with appropriate progression toward effective demonstration of the school's mission. Finally, appropriate time for students to mentally comprehend and physically attain level objectives should be woven into the curriculum. It is for this reason that research in motor development and the learning process, as discussed in Chapters 4 and 5, is beneficial knowledge for the dance teacher.

Curriculum development considers not only the individual vocabulary and movement concepts but also the students' age and cognitive abilities. Recall Bloom's taxonomy of learning in each domain. The dance teacher may find it helpful to consider the objectives included within the three learning domains. Then, the objectives at each level of the curriculum consist of a blend of psychomotor, cognitive, and affective aspects.

The curriculum should provide for the appropriate sequencing of vocabulary and concepts and allow for the progression of mental and physical learning. **Sequential progression**, or a logical advancement of skills and concepts, should be reflected throughout the curriculum. Students must first learn fundamental components before advancing to more complex material and expectations. Sequential progression is essential to properly develop appropriate muscular control and coordination, avoid injury, and aid in the students' comprehension of dance concepts and recognition of expected behavior. Consider the following examples of sequential progression:

- A ballet teacher would not teach students *changement* before *sauté*. Students need to demonstrate ability to properly maintain alignment and articulate through their feet in elevation before adding advanced changing positions of the feet. Prior to teaching *sauté*, the teacher would help students understand how to articulate through their feet and execute an effective *plié*.
- The jazz dance teacher would not introduce a full jazz layout until students have developed appropriate core muscular control. Exercises that strengthen the students' abdominals, gluteal muscles, and back would be practiced, and an upper body layout would be introduced before adding the leg extension.
- The tap dance teacher would not teach students how to execute a wing if they did not yet have knowledge of how to strike different parts of the shoe on the floor. The students would not be able to comprehend the mechanics of the movement if certain terminology – such as a brush – was not first introduced and practiced in various directions. Students would need to demonstrate enough strength in elevation to execute the movement.

Additionally, students learn behavioral aspects in a progression. For example, before a student can demonstrate a strong work ethic, they must first learn how to focus during class.

Before a student can self-cue their performance, they must develop cognitive awareness of movement concepts and experience appropriate feedback in conjunction with their movement attempts. The teacher should also deeply consider this when designing a curriculum and lesson planning.

The dance curriculum helps articulate the components that need to be accomplished before level progression can occur. The written curriculum should include, at minimum, vocabulary and course goals and objectives for each level offered. Additional components may include spatial and temporal aspects and performance expectations for students. (See Tables 9.5 and 9.6.) Finally, the teacher must help students realize that it is often appropriate and natural for students to remain in a specific level of dance training for multiple years. Students need time to physically and cognitively learn ideas and skills, and some students, at various ages, may need more time than others.

With a curriculum as a guide, the dance teacher is then ready to devise an overall blueprint or syllabus for a class as well as individualized lesson plans. The dance teacher prepares a strategy to help students enrolled in a course to work toward and/or achieve the appropriate criteria within the curriculum. Knowing the curriculum expectations for each level helps the teacher determine what the goals and objectives for the course should be, along with a focus for each class meeting.

TABLE 9.5 A basic sample curriculum for a creative movement course for preschool-age students.

Creative Movement for Preschool-Age Students

Training Goals	*Objectives*
Weight Shift (psychomotor)	Students will demonstrate ability to effectively shift weight.
Balance (psychomotor)	Students will demonstrate ability to momentarily balance on two feet and on one foot.
Locomotion (psychomotor)	Students will demonstrate ability to effectively execute fundamental locomotor movements.
Imagination (cognitive)	Students will connect movement ideas to creative themes.
Joy of Movement (affective)	Students will discover joy in class through the use of imagination and personal expression during movement.

Vocabulary	*Spatial Aspects*	*Temporal Aspects*
• Ball change • *Chassés* or gallops • Hops on one foot • Skips or step hops • Small jumps • Small knee bends or demi *pliés* • Step touch • Three step turn	*Arm placement:* • Hands on hips • Basic jazz positions • Relaxed *Feet positions:* • Parallel 1st and 2nd positions *Direction of travel:* • Forward • Sideways *Formations:* • Circles • Straight lines	• Moderate tempos • Use of whole, half, and quarter notes • Simple rhythms • Repetitive patterns

168 Class Content and Preparation

TABLE 9.6 A basic sample curriculum for beginning jazz dance. Sequential levels of jazz dance would build upon these fundamental skills.

Intermediate Level Jazz Dance

Training Goals	Objectives
Weight shift (psychomotor)	Students will demonstrate ability to effectively shift weight in a variety of directions.
Balance (psychomotor)	Students will demonstrate ability to balance on demi pointe on two feet and on one with correct alignment and placement.
Locomotion (psychomotor)	Students will demonstrate ability to effectively execute stylized locomotor movements.
Movement Sequence (cognitive)	Students will recall more complex movement sequences.
Personal Expression (affective)	Students will display enhanced performance quality and musicality during movement.

Vocabulary	Spatial Aspects	Temporal Aspects
• Ball change • *Battement*/kicks (with elevation) • *Chaîné* turns • *Chassés* • Drags and flicks • Fan kicks • Grapevine • Hinges • Hitch kick • Jazz slide • Lindy • *Pas de bourrée* (traveling, turning) • *Passé jump* • *Passé saute* (with tuck) • *Pirouette* • *Piqué* turn • Pivot turn • *Relevé* • Scissor step • Small jumps • Small knee bends or demi *pliés* • Split leap (forward and center) • Step touch • Sugar steps • Suzie Q • Three step turn • Triplets • Upper body layout	*Arm placement:* • Basic jazz dance positions • Hands on hips • Relaxed • Swinging *Feet positions:* • Parallel 1st, 2nd, 4th positions • Turned-out 1st, 2nd, 4th positions *Direction of travel:* • Backward • Diagonally • Forward • Sideways *Formations:* • Circles • Diagonals • Squares • Straight lines • Zigzag	• Moderate to quick tempos *Musical Notes:* • Whole • Half • Quarter • Eighth • Sixteenth • Repetitive and varied patterns • Simple to varied rhythms

DEVISING LESSON PLANS

A lesson plan is a road map for an individual class meeting. Similar to creating a curriculum, the teacher should first consider the genre, age, level, and individual group of students as they develop lesson plans. Not every class of 10-year old intermediate-level dancers will be the same. One class may be full of students on the cusp of moving to the next level, whereas another class may have just been promoted to the intermediate level. Or, a class of 10-year-old beginning level students who are in their second year of dance training may process material slower than the average class, thus requiring a slower pace and specific instructional strategies when learning movement ideas. Knowing the group of students and, their placement within the curricular levels and recognizing their needs is critical to developing effective lesson plans. What skills are the students ready to learn? What level-based knowledge in technique are they lacking? Are the students dealing with growth spurts or other physical and/or emotional challenges? These are all questions that can be considered when planning an outline for a class.

Establishing Class Learning Goals and Objectives

Goals and objectives are an essential part of curriculum development and the individual lesson plan. Whereas the dance curriculum guides the path of the student over many years and throughout various levels, the lesson plan focuses on an individual class meeting. When preparing for a new term, it is good practice for the teacher to reflect on the goals for the class as established within the curriculum. For example, a class of "level three" dancers should be working toward the specific skills and concepts identified within the curriculum for "level three." These curricular goals then shape the objectives/s the teacher sets for each class.

The goal within a lesson plan may be the focus or theme for the class. Perhaps a class meeting will focus on musicality. Or, a class may focus on learning and executing new vocabulary. It is important that these goals reflect reasonable expectations for the specific group of students. Perhaps, in the first year of "level three," students focus on understanding the mechanics of certain vocabulary, whereas in their second year at the same level, the emphasis switches to varied execution of the vocabulary in relation to musicality, tempo, or direction.

Once the teacher has established goals for the course as a whole, it is helpful to divide the term into smaller units, perhaps by months or weeks. This enables the teacher to then set short-term goals on which students can work. For example, if the long-term goal is for students in the class to execute a single-time step in tap dance, then a short-term goal might be to demonstrate effective weight change during the execution of a ball change performed in different directions.

The objectives within a lesson plan guide the composition of exercises for that class. Developing class objectives allows the teacher to design movement exercises that assist students in achieving the class goal. Consider the example within Table 9.7. Learning a split leap is the end goal for the class. The objectives are designed to assist students in achieving the goal. The individual exercises align with specific objectives. The teacher aims for the students to further develop their abilities and/or demonstrate the established goal.

170 Class Content and Preparation

TABLE 9.7 Identifying a devised goal and corresponding objectives for a dance class.

Lesson Plan Goal/Objectives Example

Goal	Objective	Exercise
Learn the basics of a split leap	**(1)** Students will recognize and practice the body line/position required of the leap.	Students will work on floor splits during the warm-up. **Connection will be made between the position required in the split leap and the importance of the flexibility of the legs and hips.*
	(2) Students will appropriately articulate through the feet with control and alignment.	Students will be taught a combination of basic jumps and prances. **Emphasis will be given to the push through the feet and the aligned use of plié in the preparation and the landing.*
	(3) Students will demonstrate a clean preparation for the leap.	Students will practice a *chassé* step across the floor. **Emphasis will be given to use of energy.*
	(4) Students will learn the mechanics of the split leap.	Students will be taught the mechanics of the split leap and practice the basic movement with a *chassé* preparation.

Consideration of Class Structure

Regardless of genre, all dance classes should include a warm-up and opportunity to practice skill and artistry. The format in which these tasks are accomplished can vary from class to class. The specific structure of the dance class can be dictated by genre. For example, a ballet class traditionally begins with *barre* work followed by center work. The preference of the teacher may influence the structure of the class. One modern dance instructor may choose to have dancers first locomote around the room, whereas another instructor may begin a class with the dancers lying on the floor. The goal of the class may also influence the structure of the class for a particular day. As recital time approaches, the structure may be designed to focus primarily on the recital dance. A ballet lesson plan that aims to increase dancers' stamina may skip the adagio and traveling combination and increase the quantity of allegro exercises. A lesson plan for a jazz dance class may focus on movement quality or musicality and include improvisational-based exercises throughout the duration of the class instead of its usual structure of warm-up, progressions, and center combination.

The following sections explore general class structures within the genres of ballet, jazz, tap dance. The dance teacher considers the structure of the class when creating lesson

Curriculum Development and Lesson Planning **171**

plans. With the class structure in mind, the dance teacher should work from the end of the class backwards when preparing the lesson plan. This will ensure that there is a logical, sequential progression of movement throughout the class and that students are fully prepared for the demands of each combination.

Ballet

A traditional classical ballet class includes *barre* work and center work and concludes with a *révérence*.

1) *Barre work*: In addition to warming up the dancer's body, *barre* work provides opportunity to practice placement and alignment. Fundamental positions and *port de bras* are practiced. The dancer is challenged by exercises that emphasize coordination, isolation, strength, and/or flexibility. *Barre* work includes a traditional set of exercises that are often performed in a routine sequence – although the teacher may choose to deviate from this order, adding or omitting exercises as needed according to the level and lesson plan. Specific exercises are designed to strengthen the dancer's body and prepare them for the center portion of class. Traditionally, exercises are composed utilizing the following vocabulary:

- *Plié*
- *Tendu*
- *Dégagé*
- *Rond de jambe*
- *Fondu*
- *Frappé*
- *Développé*
- *Grand battement*

2) *Center work*: Traditional center work also includes a prescribed set of exercises. The first exercise is typically a placement-based exercise that utilizes *tendu* and/or *dégagé* with focus on helping the dancer transition from the support of the *barre* to balance in the center. Following exercises include an adage, traveling waltz, and *petit*, medium, and grand allegro.

- Each exercise focuses on different aspects of ballet technique and performance. The *adage* exercise requires balance, control, fluidity, and leg extensions. A traveling waltz encourages students to use their space and often incorporates practice of various turns. The *allegro* portion of the class features jumps of various sizes. Dancers are challenged in stamina, endurance, strength, coordination, and movement quality.
- When considering the pacing of the ballet class, the rule of thumb is to devote one-third of the time to *barre* work, one-third to the first few exercises in the center, and the remaining one-third to allegro work.

172 Class Content and Preparation

Jazz Dance

The following description depicts an average jazz dance class taught throughout the United States. However, the style of jazz dance being taught may alter how this structure looks or is delivered. An authentic jazz dance class may begin with students traveling around the room in a walking pattern and transitioning into improvisation. From there, the students may practice new vocabulary and learn a center combination. Throughout the class, improvisation, rhythm, and a sense of community is ever-present. Other styles of jazz dance may incorporate ballet or modern-based vocabulary and movement throughout the class.

A classic jazz dance class often includes a warm-up, progressions, center combination, and cool-down. Each component of the class serves certain purposes.

1) *Warm-up*: The warm-up provides dancers with preparation, awareness, maintenance, and conditioning. This portion of the class prepares the students both physically and mentally for the rest of the class. Awareness is given to the concepts of the technique, which can include isolations, body positions, groundedness, rhythm, and dynamics. The warm-up includes opportunities for general body maintenance and injury prevention as well as body conditioning to enhance strength and flexibility.

2) *Across-the-floor progressions*: Progressions travel across the floor and utilize locomotor movements. Here, specific vocabulary, skills, and sequences are practiced. Students work toward the development of mental and muscle memory, coordination, proper technique, and movement style.

3) *Center combination*: Students are brought back to the center of the room where a lengthier movement combination is taught. The center combination (sometimes the recital dance) assimilates the skills practiced across the floor and emphasizes movement style, musicality, and performance. Students are encouraged to learn movement sequences quickly and improve memorization. The combinations also enhance the students' stamina.

4) *Cool-down*: The class concludes with a cool-down to lower heart rates and allow for gentle stretching of muscles.

Tap Dance

The structure of a tap dance class is determined by the preference of the teacher as well as the goal of the class. All tap classes will include some form of a warm-up. The content of the warm-up can differ. The warm-up could consist of basic or improvised locomotor patterns as the students weave around one another, or the teacher may lead the dancer through a series of steps and patterns, improvised or choreographed, with the students standing behind the teacher as they follow along.

The remainder of the class often varies. Some tap classes follow a structure similar to the jazz dance class in that progressions and a center combination follow the warm-up. Other tap class structures have students remain in the center for practice on exercises of varying lengths and objectives.

FIGURE 9.2 A circle of tap dance students engage in an improvisation exercise prompted by the instructor.
Source: Photo by Clinton Lewis/Western Kentucky University.

Selection of Class Material

The goal and objectives for a class narrow the scope of the material which the teacher may consider. In the final step of lesson preparation, the dance teacher uses the devised lesson objectives as a guide to choose specific movement material and compose class exercises. The teacher should select movements that contribute to the purpose of the class and will help students achieve the goal/s of the lesson plan. An effective lesson plan should be thoughtful in the composition of exercises. When creating movement patterns and exercises, it is helpful for the dance teacher to be mindful of the following ideas:

- **Build from slow to fast, small to big, and easy to complex.** A ballet *barre* would not begin with quick *frappés* that require fast action of finite and un-warmed muscles, nor would it begin with *grand battements* that stretch the hamstrings and place demands on the hip flexors and muscles of the leg. Rather, the class starts with slow, fluid movement that gently eases the dancer into the demands of the class. Additionally, combinations may focus on the fundamental element first before progressing to the most complex variation. If a lesson plan focuses on turning, then *relevés* and turning positions should be incorporated into the warm-up.

174 Class Content and Preparation

Exercises for beginning students will consist of slower speeds and simplistic patterns. Combinations for advanced students can vary in tempo and build to complex sequences.

- **Incorporate sequential progression.** Create lesson plans that demonstrate a logical sequence of exercises within a class. Then, build on material from the previous class. Help students make connections and recognize their progress by connecting each lesson plan in some way.
- **Approach the lesson plan in diverse ways.** Including the same movement in every single exercise can quickly become boring to students and will not help them fully learn a skill. Suppose that the teacher wants students to learn how to do an X roll. The introduction of the movement and its inclusion in subsequent exercises is always led by two walks. The students will learn to approach the movement by stepping and lowering into the roll but may not be able to comprehend how to complete the movement if already seated on the ground. Additionally, if the entire class only includes work on X rolls, then students can quickly become bored. Instead, the teacher should include some type of contrast within the plan to keep students engaged.
- **Design appropriately challenging material.** Students can remain motivated by combinations that provide challenges, but the effective dance teacher is careful not to make the material overwhelming as this can deter learning and hinder motivation.
- **Consider music options.** Select music that is engaging for students yet appropriate with the movement. Music selection is discussed in the next chapter.
- **Pay attention to pacing.** The dance teacher should think about how much time will be spent on each exercise. Students may lose interest if they are asked to work on the same exercise for too long. Yet, the plan should allow sufficient time for student progress.
- **Pay attention to spacing.** Younger dancers may become easily distracted if they remain in the same position of the room throughout the entire class. Also, how will the planned movement fit in the teaching space? Consider the size and dimensions of the studio.
- **Include variations.** Devise exercises that can progress over a span of weeks, or combinations that can be simplified or increase in difficulty.
- **Consider the learning rate.** Keep in mind that younger children and beginners will learn at a slower rate than older or more advanced students. Growth spurts can also slow learning rates. Allow appropriate time for students to learn content.

Table 9.8 provides a sample template for a lesson plan that a dance teacher may use. However, lesson plans can follow a range of templates. When notating the lesson plan, the dance teacher should include the goal and objectives along with description or notation of each exercise and/or activity. The teacher may also want to include a reminder of aspects they want to emphasize during each exercise or other elements they want to be sure to share with the students. Finally, lesson plans may also include an assessment method or criteria, which is discussed in detail in Chapter 15.

TABLE 9.8 A basic lesson plan template for the general dance class.

Lesson Plan Template

Title of Class:

Date of Class:

Focus/Theme of the Class:

Goals and Objectives for the Lesson (as appropriate to the age/level/genre)

Psychomotor	Description of goal/s	Students will be able to. . . .
Cognitive	Description of goal/s	Students will be able to. . . .
Affective	Description of goal/s	Students will be able to. . . .

Movement Exercises and Activities

Exercise 1: Description/Notation — **Teaching Notes:** *(may include components such as planned delivery method, instructional strategies to employ, cueing reminders, potential feedback, approximate time frame for exercise, etc.)*

Exercise 2: Description/Notation — **Teaching Notes:**

Exercise 3: Description/Notation — **Teaching Notes:**

Exercise 4: Description/Notation — **Teaching Notes:**

Etc.

CHAPTER SUMMARY

Planning is an important aspect of the dance class. It can ease the nerves of novice teachers, provide a clear path for instruction, and narrow the scope of material to be taught. Effective dance teachers consider the three domains of learning – psychomotor, cognitive, and affective – and their corresponding taxonomies throughout the planning process. Devised goals and objectives guide both the development of curriculum as well as individual lesson plans. It is best to approach both the curriculum and lesson plan by beginning with the end goals and exercises and working backward. This helps to ensure that sequential progression is inherent within each. Class structures may also influence the design of the lesson plan. While dance classes all include some form of warm-up and movement practice and exploration, the specific class structure can be determined by the genre, teacher preference, or the goal and theme of a class. Effective lesson plans are those that consider focus, diversity, pacing, challenge, and logical progression of ideas.

PRACTICAL APPLICATIONS

1. Observe a dance class. What goal or objectives can you identify? What do you notice about the structure of the class? How is sequential progression observed throughout the lesson plan?

2. Identify goals in the three learning domains that may be specific to certain ages or levels of dance students.

3. Devise a goal and objectives for a dance class of any genre. Compose exercises to help students meet each objective.

4. Select a movement from a specific dance genre. Identify the skills that must be learned before being able to execute the movement.

5. Create an advanced exercise in any genre. Identify the skills that the student must know before learning the exercise.

6. Create a movement exercise along with simple and complex variations of the exercise.

BIBLIOGRAPHY

Aceto, Melanie. "Developing the Dance Artist in Technique Class: The Alteration Task." *Journal of Dance Education* 12, no. 1 (2012): 14–20.

Adams, Nancy E. "Bloom's Taxonomy of Cognitive Learning Objectives." *Journal of the Medical Library Association* 103, no. 3 (2015): 152–153.

Anderson, Lorin W., David R. Krathwohl, and Benjamin Samuel Bloom. *A Taxonomy for Learning, Teaching, and Assessing: A Revision of Bloom's Taxonomy of Educational Objectives*. Complete ed. New York: Longman, 2001.

Conzemius, Anne, and Jan O'Neill. *The Power of SMART Goals: Using Goals to Improve Student Learning*. Bloomington, Indiana: Solution Tree Press, 2006.

Doran, G.T. "There's a SMART Way to Write Management's Goals and Objectives." *Management Review* 70 (1981): 35–36.

Foster, Rory. *Ballet Pedagogy: The Art of Teaching*. Gainesville, FL: University Press of Florida, 2010.

Harrow, Anita J. "The Behavioral Objectives Movement: Its Impact on Physical Education." *Educational Technology* 17, no. 6 (1977): 31–38.

Harrow, Anita J.A. *Taxonomy of the Psychomotor Domain; a Guide for Developing Behavioral Objectives*. New York: D. McKay Co., 1972.

Holt, Brett J., and James C. Hannon. "Teaching-Learning in the Affective Domain." *Strategies* 20, no. 1 (2006): 11–13.

Krathwohl, David R. "A Revision of Bloom's Taxonomy: An Overview." *Theory into Practice* 41, no. 4 (2002): 212–218.

Lawlor, K. Blaine. "SMART Goals: How the Application of SMART Goals can Contribute to Achievement of Student Learning Outcomes." *Developments in Business Simulation and Experiential Learning* (2012). https://absel-ojsttu.tdl.org/absel/article/view/90.

Mainwaring, Lynda M., and Donna H. Krasnow. "Teaching the Dance Class: Strategies to Enhance Skill Acquisition, Mastery and Positive Self-Image." *Journal of Dance Education* 10, no. 1 (2010): 14–21.

Schlaich, Joan, and Betty DuPont. *The Art of Teaching Dance Technique*. 1996.

Shannon, Tony, and Leong, Melvin. "Affective and Psychomotor Taxonomies." *International Journal for Business Education* (2023). https://ir.library.illinoisstate.edu/ijbe/vol164/iss1/14.

Willis, Cheryl M. *Dance Education Tips from the Trenches*. Champaign, IL: Human Kinetics, 2004.

Wilson, Leslie Owen. "The Three Domains of Learning: Cognitive, Affective, and Psychomotor/Kinesthetic." *The Second Principle*, 2023. http://thesecondprinciple.com/instructional-design/threedomainsoflearning/.

CHAPTER 10

Music Concepts for Dancers

Box 10.1 Chapter Objectives

After reading this chapter, you will be able to:

- Articulate the relationship between dance and music
- Understand basic music terminology as it relates to the dance class
- Identify successful methods of working with a dance accompanist
- Recognize essential considerations when selecting music for a dance class

Box 10.2 Chapter Vocabulary

bar
BPM
call and response
crescendo
decrescendo
eighth note
half note
legato
measure
meter
quarter note
rallentando
rhythm
sixteenth note
staccato
swung rhythm
syncopation

DOI: 10.4324/b22952-15

tempo
time signature
whole note

Dance and music are two art forms that often go hand in hand. Dance, in its various forms, is often performed with music. Similarly, the dance class typically makes use of some form of musical accompaniment, whether pre-recorded or played live. Both encompass the element of time; they each occur and extend through a duration of time. The effective dance teacher recognizes this aspect and organically or strategically includes the element of time within their teaching. Yet, they may not always discuss the resulting relationship that must occur between dance and music.

To best understand the direct relationship between dance and music, it is beneficial for the dance student to understand music fundamentals. When the dance teacher shares this knowledge with students, musicality and rhythmical accuracy can be encouraged and developed in the student's performance. These aspects are an important component in the relationship between dance and music, and they can influence movement execution. The tempo, established by the music or other means, can affect the dancer's physical and technical capabilities. For example, a dancer can only jump so slowly, yet discussion of timing and musical nuances challenges the dancer to remain in the air longer during the jump. A turn can only be performed so fast, but quickness of the spot can assist the dancer technically and keep them on time. The use of music can help students embody nuances of the movement desired by the teacher. Certain time signatures or forms of music lend themselves to certain types of movement or movement qualities. A dancer can feel the fluidity in and quality of a waltz step when performed to music composed in a 3/4-time signature. Musical phrasing can influence a dancer's use of breath within a movement combination. Music can also serve as a guide for the inclusion of accents and dynamics within the movement and increase the dancer's artistic expressiveness.

Not all dance teachers are musically inclined. Many did not grow up playing a musical instrument, singing in a choir, or participating in a music class where note values and basic music theory were introduced and practiced. This ability or experience does not negate the teacher's capability in conveying a relationship between dance and music. Yet, a dance teacher who encompasses a working knowledge of basic music terms and concepts will find they are then able to foster a clearer relationship between dance and music for themselves. This knowledge will increase the teacher's effectiveness in communicating the distinct relationship between the two art forms and enhance musicality among their students.

FUNDAMENTAL MUSIC TERMINOLOGY

Following are fundamental musical terms and concepts with which a dance teacher should be familiar.

Music Organization

Tempo, Measure, and Time Signature

Music encompasses a distinct tempo. The **tempo** refers to the speed of the music. This can be determined through the recurring beat, or pulse, that can be felt throughout the music, often referred to simply as the beat of the music. Tempo can be conveyed in various ways, including BPM (beats per minute), Italian terminology, or through contemporary language. **BPM,** sometimes referred to as metronome marks by musicians, identifies the precise number of beats that are played/heard within the time frame of 60 seconds. For instance, music with a tempo of 120 BPM indicates that two beats are played every second. This accurate detail of tempo is used to establish the speed when setting a metronome.

Tempo can also be discussed utilizing Italian terms. Western music was traditionally composed utilizing Italian-based terminology. There are many Italian terms, some of which are included in Table 10.1, that are used to depict tempo, including largo, andante, allegro, and presto. These terms can be helpful to know when working with a classical musician or when exploring Western classical compositions.

Music composition is divided into discernible measures. A **measure**, or **bar**, is a grouping of beats separated by a bar line within the written music. The grouping of beats follows the time signature noted at the beginning of the first line of the written music. Each new measure begins with count 1 and continues to a certain count as dictated by the time signature.

The time signature is written like a fraction and appears at the beginning of the staff. **Time signature** identifies both the number of beats in a measure (the top number) and which type of musical note equates to a single beat (the bottom number). For example, music in 4/4 time signature has four beats within the measure, and the quarter note receives the beat. (Musical notes are discussed later in this section.) For every bar of music, four beats occur, and a quarter note will take exactly one beat. In a 3/4 time signature, each measure contains three beats, with the quarter note taking one beat. In 6/8 time signature, there are six beats within each measure, and the eighth note takes one beat.

TABLE 10.1 Depicting select Italian terminology indicating tempo.

Largo	Adagio	Andante	Moderato	Allegro	Presto
Very slow, stately	Slow	At a walking pace	At a moderate speed	Quick and bright	Very fast
40–60 BPM	66–76 BPM	76–108 BPM	98–112 BPM	120–156 BPM	168–200 BPM

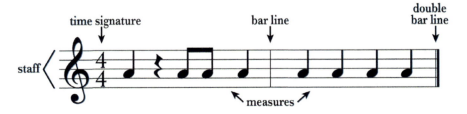

FIGURE 10.1 Diagram of a treble clef depicting certain music terminology and measures of different rhythms.

Meter

Meter is the regularly recurring pattern of strong and weak beats. This can be felt by counting the beats from one strong beat (where one often claps or taps their foot) to the next strong beat. Not all music has a meter, yet other music, such as West African drumming, may contain very complex meters. Commonly recognizable meters for the dancer are duple and triple. A duple meter includes two beats to a measure, and the first beat is typically the strong, or accented, beat (1 2, 1 2). A triple meter contains three beats to the measure. The accent is often on beat one or beat two (1–2–3, 1–2–3 or 1–2–3 1–2–3).

Meter can be further classified by the terms simple and compound. Whereas duple and triple meter refer to the number of beats within a measure, the categories of simple and compound distinguish the way in which the beats within a measure are subdivided. If an individual beat can be divided by two, then the meter is considered simple (1&, 2&, . . .). If an individual beat can be divided by three, the meter is called compound (1&a, 2&a, . . .). There are, of course, further distinguishing meters, such as mixed and polymeter, that the dance teacher can research. Some dance forms, such as African dance and modern dance, often incorporate more complex meters into compositions. Variations of simple duple and triple and compound duple and triple meters are delineated in Table 10.2.

Musicians and dancers often use separate language in regard to musical concepts. One primary distinction is in the reference to the music. While a musician uses the term "piece," the dancer often applies the term "song." Distinctions are also made when counting music. For example, a musician will refer to the "beat" of the music, whereas the dance teacher typically applies the term "count." Additionally, musicians recognize and consider the simple and compound meters while dancers often refer to meters with only the terms duple and triple. For example, the dancer may ask the accompanist for a duple meter because they are counting their movement 1&, 2&, 3&, 4& (a simple quadruple meter). The dancer often requests a triple meter when they count their movement using 1&a, or 1, 2, 3. The musician may then play music that is either a compound duple or triple meter. Experienced dance accompanists learn to recognize this distinction and select pieces in the appropriate meter and time signature to complement the movement. However, it is wise for the dance teacher to be aware of the distinction.

The dancer teacher will quickly discover that certain exercises are best suited for a specific meter. For example, a military time step in tap dance or basic march steps with young children are best suited for a simple duple meter. A basic waltz turn combination or grand allegro pattern is generally best suited for a simple triple meter. Modern dance

TABLE 10.2 Delineating simple to compound duple and triple meters with sample time signatures.

Meter	Musical Counts	Sample Time Signature
Simple duple	1 & 2 &	2/4
Simple triple	1 & 2 & 3 &	3/4
Compound duple	1 & a 2 & a	6/8
Compound triple	1 & a 2 & a 3 & a	9/8

182 Class Content and Preparation

phrases may often include mixed meters, but the division is usually clearly duple or triple. Oftentimes, the exact meter and time signature are not recognizable by just listening. Rather, one would need to see the written music.

Phrasing

The dance teacher should be cognizant of the phrasing of composed movement exercises. While the phrasing may be uneven or varying in some dance genres, some forms utilize certain groupings of counts. In classical ballet, movement is traditionally counted in 8's, and exercises are evenly grouped into phrases of 16, 32, 64, etc., counts. Occasionally, exercises may include a body stretch or balanced pose that extend beyond the traditional phrasing. A musical tag provides additional measures of music played at the end of the song to allow for the extra movement.

In tap dance, movement phrasing generally follows that of the music. Tap dance evolved alongside jazz music, so it only makes sense that the movement phrasing be similar to the music. Standard jazz tap patterns often follow a 32-bar format as detailed later in this section, although contemporary tap may utilize various phrasing patterns. By remaining mindful of the relationship of phrasing between music and dance, teachers help dance students to learn more efficiently and connect their movement performance with the musical accompaniment. The familiar and complementary phrasing assists dancers in sequencing movement and encourages their listening abilities.

Subdivision of the Beat

Each musical note is a subdivision of the beat. Musicians recognize both where the note falls on the staff, which identifies the pitch, along with its symbol, which denotes a certain value of time. Dancers are most concerned with note value. A beat of music can be subdivided in various ways. Note values are discussed with the quarter note, the most common note, taking a single beat within 4/4 time, also known as common time. With this in mind, let us consider five types of note values.

The **whole note** is an open-faced note without a stem and takes four beats, the entire measure. Each note value following is essentially divided in half of the preceding note type. This is best visualized and understood through the assistance of the rhythm tree diagram depicted in Figure 10.2. The **half note**, also an open-faced note but with a stem, equals two beats; there are two half notes within a measure. The **quarter note**, a filled in or black note with a stem, equals one beat; there are four quarter notes in a measure. If one claps on every beat of the music (in 4/4 time), they are clapping four quarter notes. The **eighth note** equals half of a single beat and is represented by a closed face note with a stem and flag; there are two eighth notes for every quarter note, or eight eighth notes in a measure. Two eighth notes are often connected by a line at the top of the stems. These can be played in even rhythm or in a pattern of short and long, which is often referred to as a swung rhythm. Finally, the **sixteenth note** equals half of an eighth note; there are four sixteenth notes for every quarter note, or 16 sixteenth notes in a measure. The sixteenth notes are represented by a closed face note with stem and two flags. Four sixteenth notes are connected by two lines at the top of the stems.

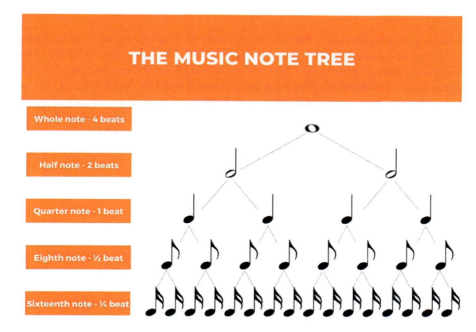

FIGURE 10.2 Depiction of the music note tree, also known as a rhythm tree, including note symbols.

Source: Image courtesy of hellomusictheory.com.

When counting dance movement in 4/4 time, the dancer moves in the various note values. A whole note would be represented by a single movement that is either held for four beats or takes four beats to complete. Holding movement for two beats reflects the half note. A dancer may simply walk in half notes, stepping on count 1 (hold count 2) and then count 3 (hold count 4). An example of eighth note movement is a shuffle in tap dance. The forward and backward strike of the ball of the foot on the floor is done in one beat, either evenly or swung. **Swung rhythm** is an uneven division of a beat that emphasizes the space between two sounds, producing long and short durations in rhythm. Rather than an even space between parts of a beat, the space is either shortened or lengthened. Even eighth notes are counted as "&1 &2." Swung eighth notes offer a short-long feel with the sounds that are executed and are counted as "a1, a2." For example, a single shuffle evenly executed is counted "&1." A swung shuffle is counted "a1." Finally, movement completed in a sixteenth note pattern could be counted "1e&a" or "e&a1." Isolations in a jazz dance exercise might be done in sixteenth notes.

Box 10.3 Musician Counts Versus Dancer Counts

In 4/4 or common time, musicians will count two bars as "1234, 1234;" however, dancers will often count the same two measures as "1234, 5678." Dancers choose to count in 8's rather than 4's as it helps them keep track of the movement and phrasing. As

> musicians are playing music, they can quickly refer to a specific measure by its number in the score or sheet music. However, it would be difficult and confusing for the dance teacher or choreographer to say, "Let's do the 7th and 8th set of 4 counts again." Instead, it may be more effective to refer to the same movement as "the fourth 8-count," or better yet, the measure number. Counting in 8's helps the dancer to sequence and quickly pattern movement. Tap dancers are one exception as they consider themselves musicians with their feet. Tap dancers typically count in 4's as opposed to 8's. When counting in the start of the movement, the tap dancer, like musicians, will say "and 1, 2, 3, 4" whereas other dancers tend to use "and 5, 6, 7, 8."

Rhythm

The various ways in which music utilizes the differing note values creates rhythm within the music. **Rhythm** is the specific arrangement of musical notes by duration, an inherent part of a musical composition. In dance, rhythm becomes the systematic arrangement of movement based on its duration of time. For example, the dancer steps to the side and pauses before executing a quick ball change followed by a clap versus the rhythm produced when the dancer steps to the side and immediately completes a slow ball change followed by a clap. These rhythms are depicted in Figure 10.1 and delineated by the following examples.

Version 1/Measure 1:

Movement:	Step	hold	ball change	clap
Counts:	1	(2)	&3	4

Version 2/Measure 2:

Movement:	Step	ball	change	clap
Counts:	1	2	3	4

A facet of rhythm that emphasizes the weak beats rather than the strong beats within music is referred to as **syncopation**. The meter feels disrupted as accents are placed on notes that are not typically accented. In 4/4 time, beats 1 and 3 are typically the strong beats. A syncopated rhythm will accent some of the eight notes, or "and" counts within a measure. Musicians and dancers often emphasize the weak beats, including the space between beats (i.e., the "&" count) as a way to make the rhythm of the music or movement more interesting.

Dynamics

When a dance teacher is teaching with an accompanist, knowledge of additional terminology can be helpful. For example, asking an accompanist for a **rallentando** in the music would provide a gradual decrease of the tempo. A teacher may ask for a **crescendo**, the gradual increase of volume within the music, or a **decrescendo**, a gradual decrease in volume within the music. Both influence the energy of the movement that is performed. Music can be played with different qualities. **Legato** suggests a smooth continuation of notes played without any breaks, whereas **staccato** in music leads to shortened, or punctuated, notes followed by silence between notes. A dance teacher may want dancers to perform movement with a very smooth, fluid, continuous quality. Therein, they would request a legato quality within the music. Yet, a teacher may want a sharp, percussive, stop-start quality within the music to match the movement. In this instance, a staccato quality would be requested.

FORM AND STRUCTURE

Musical form is the order in which musical phrases are arranged to give shape to the overall composition. In choreography, a choreographer establishes form by giving attention to the specific arrangement of movement phrases and sections. The forms utilized by a choreographer are often derived from music structures. Similarly, the dance teacher can follow music structures when composing exercises for the dance class. For example, through-composed (best recognized to dancers as linear), binary, ternary, rondo, and theme and variation, are all forms from Western classical music that may be adapted for the dance composition. We see these forms utilized in various notable choreography. For example, *The Prodigal Son*, a ballet created by George Balanchine, is composed in a linear, narrative structure. Twyla Tharp's *The Fugue* is an example of choreography encompassing the structure of theme and variation.

Jazz music also offers specific structures that can be helpful for the teacher to recognize and utilize when composing exercises. These structures were emphasized and incorporated in popular American music from the early to mid-20th century. Standard jazz music follows a 32-bar structure, also referred to by early jazz musicians as a chorus, divided into four 8-bar sections. The most popular 32-bar structure is the AABA format. Part A lasts 8 bars and establishes the melody. These 8 bars are repeated, perhaps with a subtle variation of the melody. Part B, also 8 bars, is a contrasting section sometimes known as the bridge. The music structure then returns to part A (8 bars). Standard jazz music often follows this structure in their *overall* form, not just in each 32-bar section. The form of the entire song is in the AABA structure delineated by 32 bars (A), 32 bars (A), 32 bars (B), 32 bars (A). In musical terms, part A, or the melody, of jazz music is often referred to as the head. Part B typically consists of instrumental solos.

32-bar Structure:	8 bars	8 bars	8 bars	8 bars
	A	**A**	**B**	**A**
Jazz Music Structure:	32 bars	32 bars	32 bars	32 bars
	A	**A**	**B**	**A**
	Head	Head	Solos	Head

Any standard version of the songs "On the Sunny Side of the Street" or "Take the A Train" are excellent examples of compositions written in this traditional jazz form and structure. We often hear a generalized structure of AABA in American popular music today. However, the dance teacher should note that popular music may not be consistent in measures and phrasing. For example, between verses, popular music may include an extra measure or two before shifting into the next verse. This can throw off the phrasing of an exercise designed to repeat every 16 or 32 measures.

Form:	**A**	**A**	**B**	**A**
Popular Music:	verse/chorus	verse/chorus	bridge	verse/chorus
Jazz Music:	head	head	solos	head

Table 10.3 identifies the manners in which musical forms relate to dance structures. The dance teacher can devise class material or choreography following these structures to create interesting exercises and offer variety in movement development. From creative movement for preschoolers to advanced movement in a specific dance genre, these patterns can help students learn movement sequence while also gaining awareness of

TABLE 10.3 Identifying common musical structures that can be adapted within the dance exercises and choreography.

Relationship between Musical Forms and Dance Composition

Music Form	Structure	Description	Dance Application
Through-Composed (linear, narrative)	ABCDE	The structure follows a sequential order.	• Sequenced exercises that consistently transition from one idea to a new idea
Three and a Break	AAAB	The structure follows a repetitive sequence with a contrasting break; an idea repeated three times followed by a separate idea.	• The first three patterns of the traditional *Shim Sham Shimmy* tap dance
Binary	AB	The structure is in two even parts with contrasting themes.	• A single grapevine followed by a three step turn, jump together
Ternary (cyclical)	ABA	The structure is in three equal parts; general idea, contrasting idea, return to original idea.	• A jazz dance progression of *chaîné* turns, axel turn, *chaîné* turns
Rondo	ABACADA . . .	The structure is an expansion of ternary form; contains several contrasting parts with a consistent repeat/ variation of the original part (A).	• A dance progression that alternates four prances with various other equally phrased movements
Theme and Variation	A, A^1, A^2, A^3 . . .	The structure begins with a theme followed by variations of the theme; each are similar in length and structure.	• Walk *battement* traveling across the floor; *battement sauté*; *battement sauté* with a tuck of the bottom leg

fundamental music theory. The dance teacher should note that music may encompass varying time signatures and contrast greatly to the forms listed. It is important that the dance teacher listens to the music and learns its distinct tempo, meter, and structure prior to use in class. When students understand the organization of the exercise or choreography and its connection to the music, they demonstrate better success in retaining the movement and accurate memorization of sequence.

Compositional Techniques

Dance teachers can borrow various forms from music as well as compositional techniques used by musicians. Two such examples include canon and call and response. The application of these techniques can assist the dance teacher as they compose movement exercises and combinations. They also provide students with interesting approaches for additional practice with certain movements or learning abilities.

Canon

A **canon** contains a melodic line that is imitated exactly at specified intervals of time. In dance, the teacher may begin a recital dance with the children facing upstage in a line across the stage. On each count of music, a dancer steps forward into a pivot turn to face downstage. Here, the same movement is repeated by a single dancer on each successive count. The movement could be performed at any spacing of counts. Canons could be several movements or counts in length. Three dancers could perform a canon in a variety of ways as listed subsequently:

Reverting Canon:

Dancer 1:	1	2	3		
Dancer 2:	hold	1	2	3	
Dancer 3:	hold	hold	1	2	3

Cumulative Canon:

Dancer 1:	1	2	3
Dancer 2:	hold	2	3
Dancer 3:	hold	hold	3

Simultaneous Canon:

Dancer 1:	1	2	3
Dancer 2:	2	3	1
Dancer 3:	3	1	2

The use of a canon can be an engaging way for students to practice classroom exercises. To provide variety in execution, groups of students may stagger the starting point or delay the starting count of an exercise during their practice. This also requires the students' concentration, focus, and awareness of tempo during movement execution.

Call and Response

Call and response is a structure wherein the leader performs a musical phrase, and the group echoes the same phrase. The leader calls; the group responds. This technique functions the same way with movement. Call and response is often utilized as a teaching

188 Class Content and Preparation

technique in a tap dance class. The teacher executes a movement or pattern, then the dancers recall the step(s). The movement response of the students should be in tempo. Students must listen to the timing and rhythm of the teacher's movement execution to accurately replicate the steps and rhythm. This compositional structure challenges dancers to use their visual and aural senses to quickly learn and embody correct movement sequence and accurate timing. Call and response can be incorporated within various dance genres during instruction and as a movement-based game.

WORKING WITH AN ACCOMPANIST

Accompanists are often utilized within the dance class and performance. An accompanist brings the energy of live music into the dance space and can engage dancers in a new way. The vibrant sound from a piano or *djembe* drum being played in the space as dancers move creates energy and motivation for many dancers. Use of an accompanist is an excellent way to incite the dancers' appreciation for and understanding of music. It also expedites the time spent by the teacher in planning for the class. While it can be an added expense to the dance teacher or studio/school, the benefits are well worth the cost.

Each musician, just like each dance teacher, is an individual. The relationship between dance teacher and musician must be developed. It can take time for the dance teacher to "speak the same language" with the accompanist and help them to understand the musical needs for each exercise. Clear and consistent communication is of utmost importance between the two individuals. Following are some helpful tips for the dance teacher when working with an accompanist:

- **Get to know one another prior to the first dance class.** The more information that the accompanist has in advance, the more effective their music choices and communication in class will be. The dance teacher should discuss with them their expectations and learn those of the accompanist. Lesson plans can be shared so that the accompanist can begin to recognize how exercises are phrased (meters used, number of measures/counts).
- **Understand their language.** The effective dance teacher should know basic music terminology and use it as appropriate. It is important to remember that accompanists are often not familiar with dance, or possibly the genre of the class. The teacher can help the musician by using terms with which they are familiar. Meter, measure, music time periods, tempo examples, etc. are all useful to the accompanist in selecting an appropriate song/piece for the movement.
- **Offer context prior to demonstration.** The dance teacher should offer pertinent information to the accompanist before teaching the demonstration to students. For example, the teacher may tell the pianist that the next exercise will be *rond de jambe* in a triple meter before they demonstrate for the students. This allows the accompanist to mentally transition to certain music that may be appropriate and locate a selection quickly while the teacher instructs the students.

Music Concepts for Dancers **189**

FIGURE 10.3 An image of accompanists and students listening to the dance teacher's instructions.
Source: Photo by Kyra Rookard/Western Kentucky University.

- **Clearly demonstrate each exercise.** There can be many ways that a dance teacher demonstrates. Regardless of whether the demonstration is verbal or visual, the dance teacher should stand where the musician can see them and dance/speak in tempo and rhythm. The musician will pay attention to the phrasing of the combination so that the music phrasing will also match. For example, a ballet teacher may always devise the first center exercise in 32 bars, but the next exercise may require 64 bars. Further, the teacher can use their voice to help convey movement accents or the quality desired or needed for the exercise to assist the musician's selection.
- **Have a specific way to cue the musician.** How will the accompanist know when the teacher is finished demonstrating and ready for the music to start? Some

dance teachers may motion to the musician with a nod of the head. Others may begin to count them in with "and 5, 6, 7, 8" or cue them with a phrase such as "here we go."

- **Avoid clapping or snapping over the music.** Consistently clapping or snapping while a musician is playing can be disruptive, irritating, and offensive to the musician. Of course, a snap here or there to draw students' attention to the timing may be appropriate and necessary.
- **Communicate appropriately when things do not work.** Occasionally, the music played by the accompanist simply will not work with the movement exercise. It is okay for the dance teacher to respectfully ask for a different song/piece. They should then follow up with the musician after the class to further clarify why a selection did or did not work for an exercise. The teacher should never belittle the musician, especially in front of students.

Live music in the dance class provides a wonderful experience for students. Dancers become uniquely aware of how music can enhance the musicality and artistry of the movement. Dancers also learn etiquette in working with musicians, including respect for both the musician and their instrument(s). For the teacher, the use of an accompanist allows them to focus on the goals of the lesson plan and their interaction with students.

SELECTING MUSIC

A vast majority of dance classes are taught with recorded music rather than an accompanist. Whether the dance teacher utilizes recorded music or an accompanist, the music can make or break the effectiveness of a movement exercise within the dance class. When utilized, music plays an essential part in helping students learn steps, skills, and concepts. It can help students connect to the movement, or it can hinder the students' ability to attain the learning objective of the exercise. Therefore, it is necessary that the dance teacher be mindful and thoughtful of the music chosen for use with an exercise and then help students develop the ability to listen to the music when dancing and understand the relationship between the two. When a movement combination fits with the music, the students are able to approach movement with correct timing and can better recognize the force, quality, dynamics, and emotion needed within the movement; both technique and artistry are enhanced.

While the dance teacher may want to use music that is in their preferred music genre or songs that they like and to which they feel comfortable dancing, it is important that the dance teacher incorporates a variety of music genres and styles, as appropriate, within the dance class. Listening to a range of musical styles will enhance the student's understanding of music and sense of musicality. Students may desire to dance to only popular music, yet giving in to their preferences will restrict their knowledge bank and appreciation for music. Further, popular music often offers a steady, driving pulse, or beat but leaves little room for nuances in rhythm or musicality. Not all movements or styles can be danced to popular music. Consider the swing musicality in some tap and jazz dance. Swing cannot be effectively accomplished with pop music.

A dance teacher should strive to use a variety of music within the dance class and help students appreciate and understand the relationship between dance and music. To do this effectively, the teacher can consider the following tips:

- **Listen to all kinds of music – not just the same two or three genres – in preparation for a class.** This will help expand awareness of differing music forms and styles.
- **Learn to recognize the meter and be able to count the music.** This will help the teacher to select a song that will match the timing of the composed exercise. Counting will clarify the rhythm of the movement and can aid in student comprehension and learning. Meter and counting are especially important when working with an accompanist.
- **Prepare options in music.** The teacher should prepare not just one song for an exercise but three: songs in a slow, medium, and fast tempo. If the preferred song is too slow or fast in tempo, options will be easily ready to use, and the teacher will not have to waste time searching for music.
- **Select music that matches the quality and style of the movement.** Imagine teaching a salsa combination and then playing swing music from the 1930s. The music should support the style of the movement as well as the movement quality. A flowing and waltzy ballet combination would not connect to bebop music or a dance remix.
- **Avoid chart topping songs.** Students are already listening to the most popular songs through their earbuds. They have heard this music and quite possibly observed dances to it on social media. As a result, students will not focus on the connection between the movement and music. Instead, they will sing the lyrics (inwardly or outwardly) while executing the exercise. The effective dance teacher chooses music that may not be known to the students and thus expands their music palate.
- **Consider the form and structure of the music.** The form of the song can help support a movement exercise that follows that same structure. Musical phrasing can enhance students' ability to memorize sequences when there is a connection to the dance phrasing. For example, extending a modern phrase beyond the music phrase may feel disruptive to the students as they are executing the movement. They may not garner a clear sense of movement phrasing when musical phrasing seems to contrast. The teacher should be cognizant of extra measures in the music. This often occurs with popular music. A typical 32-count exercise may not match the musical phrasing because the music includes an extra measure (4 counts) before transitioning into the next verse or section. This is not to say that one cannot compose an exercise that overlaps phrasing, but there should be a purpose for this choice, and the timing and phrasing should be clearly conveyed to the student.
- **Use age-appropriate music.** The dance teacher should be mindful of the lyrics and content of a song that is played for younger children or in certain settings or venues.
- **Know your playlist.** A playlist that is sequenced to follow the lesson plan reduces time wasted searching for a song. It is imperative that the teacher only put songs in a playlist that they know. This way the movement is sure to connect with the music, the teacher is prepared to cue and count with the music, and there are no surprises in style or lyrics.

Box 10.4 Music Games for the Dance Class

The dance teacher can incorporate various games into lesson plans designed to help students develop musicality. The following suggestions provide opportunity for the playful inclusion of musical awareness and understanding into the classroom.

Find the Beat: Introduce the idea of moving with the music during a basic "discover the beat" activity. This can be done with even young preschool-age students. The dance teacher selects a song that has a clearly defined pulse, then helps students clap on the beat. Instead of clapping, students could snap, slap, click their tongue, walk or hop on the beat, isolate a body part on the beat, etc. The use of drumsticks can also be fun for children.

- Once students can consistently clap on the beat, the teacher helps them identify the down beat and count to four while clapping. Dancers could practice accents on different beats beginning with a strong count 1.
- It is important to vary the music selections as appropriate to abilities and age.

Counting Music: It is best to begin this activity without music. Now that the dancers recognize the beat, they can transition to recognizing note lengths. The dance teacher should begin with whole notes and half notes especially with young students. Students clap on just the 1 count and keep their hands together during beats 2, 3, and 4, expressing a whole note. When ready, they can progress to claps on count 1 and 3 (keeping the hands closed on counts 2 and 4), expressing half notes. As students become familiar with the terms whole note and half note, the teacher can begin to vary the rhythm. Students could transition from claps to slaps on the thighs, or drumstick taps on the floor.

- Once students are comfortable, the activity can be repeated with quarter notes and then they can alternate between whole, half, and quarter notes. Elementary-age and older dancers can repeat with eighth notes and then sixteenth notes.
- The teacher should explain the distinction between the note values clearly. They might draw the notes and rhythm tree on a whiteboard or use flashcards to aid students in their learning of music notes.

Incorporating Silence: Next, the dance teacher has the students clap on the beat, counting either one through four or one through eight. Once the beat has been established, the teacher asks the students to hold a certain count. For example, the teacher may direct students to hold count 6; students will clap on 1, 2, 3, 4, 5, hold count 6, clap on 7, and 8. This should be repeated at least four times before changing the placement of the hold.

- Students can progress from clapping to walking around the room. The dance teacher should continue to give students a certain count (or let them pick!) to hold, or freeze their movement. Each pattern should be repeated several times so that students can achieve the freeze. This exercise will also help students with postural control and balance.

- This activity can then progress to holding multiple counts within the 8 counts (e.g., counts 2 and 7) and to alternate movements. For example, tap students could shuffle or flap. Other dancers might alternate arm reaches in a certain direction, prance around the room, or hit individual poses.

Call and Response: Now that recognition of the beat and note has been established, the teacher has students sit in a circle. The teacher claps a short 4-count rhythm (e.g., 1 2 (hold 3) 4), and students echo the rhythm with their own claps. Simple rhythms should be introduced first before complex rhythms.

- Each student can take turns being the leader while the group echoes their rhythm. Essentially, the leader is improvising a rhythm for the group to distinguish and repeat.
- This pattern is continued as the group transitions from making noise to moving a body part. Variations could include different body parts, striking poses, or executing specific movement. If appropriate, the teacher can have students repeat the leader's rhythm with their own movements of any type.

MUSIC LICENSING

When an individual purchases music through any platform, the individual owns the right to play that music as often as they wish for their own personal use. If an individual purchases music and uses the songs for public performance or in a manner in which a profit is made, then the individual must secure a music license in order to play the music. Essentially, any individual/business that uses the music for commercial gain or performance by others must secure a specific music license. This includes businesses such as restaurants, night clubs, gyms, and dance studios.

Dance studios are commercial entities that rely on the use of music as an instrumental component of the training process. Imagine if a tap or hip-hop class never utilized any music accompaniment. Students would not learn the relationship between the art forms, performance would be hindered, and business would decline. Dance teachers use music both in the classroom, which students pay tuition to attend, and during recitals and performances, which audience members typically pay a fee to view. According to the American Society of Composers, Authors, and Publishers (ASCAP), "Unlike playing a CD in the privacy of your home, when you play recorded music in a public setting, it is considered, by law, a public 'performance'."[1] Therefore, the dance studio must follow the U.S. Copyright Law, and secure music licensing to play the plethora of music throughout the year both in classes and performance, otherwise they risk facing hefty licensing fines.

There are three agencies, known as performing rights organizations, dedicated to protecting the copyright of musicians and publishers. The two agencies with which dance teachers in the United States must be concerned are the American Society of Composers, Authors, and Publishers (ASCAP) and Broadcast Music, Inc. (BMI). These two organizations hold the copyrights for the majority, if not all, of the music that dance teachers use within the United States. Teachers need to invest in licensing from both agencies to ensure that all the music used in their classes and performances is covered.

Music licensing is obtained on a 12-month basis, meaning it must be renewed annually. The fee for ASCAP is based upon the genres of dance taught and the number of students that attend weekly. It can range from an annual fee of $1 up to hundreds of dollars.[2] The fee for BMI is determined based upon the number of different students enrolled weekly, whether music is used for instructional use or background, and the number of levels within the building. Annual BMI fees range from $100 up to approximately $2000.[3]

Individual dance artists, such as freelance choreographers, must also obtain a music license if they use copyrighted music for their choreography. This includes live performance or streaming videos. It may be necessary to get a separate music license for both the song itself and the version you intend to use. For example, the song "At Last" would require a license, and if you are not using the original recording, you would also need a license for the new artist's recording.

Some music exists as public domain, meaning the intellectual rights to the song have expired. Typically, music that was recorded prior to 100 years ago from the present day is most likely in the public domain. However, the dance teacher should specifically check before assuming that music is in the public domain. For instance, as of 2024, all music written prior to 1924 is considered to be public domain; however, the performance of a song may not be if it was recorded after 1924. One can do a quick Google search to discern if the piece is in the public domain. If not, the individual will need to seek out permission to use rights from the composer and/or publisher. ASCAP or BMI can be a good place to locate the contact information for a composer or publisher. It is best for a choreographer to begin the process of securing music rights a minimum of three months prior to the performance. For dance studios, it is best that the teacher/studio owner secure annual licensing fees for the business through ASCAP and BMI to avoid the time spent searching for "free" music or securing individual music rights.

CHAPTER SUMMARY

Many forms of dance are performed with some form of musical accompaniment. Dance and music work together in performance, engaging both the dancer and the audience. In class, music can assist the dance student as they learn movement sequences, embody a movement quality, and discover musicality in execution. It is important for dance teachers and students to recognize and understand the connection between dance and music. Comprehension of basic music terminology, awareness of note values, ability to count music, and understanding musical phrasing become tools for the dance teacher in developing musicality and artistry among the students. The addition of an accompanist within the dance class or performance setting provides an added energy for the dancers, yet teachers should be mindful of effective communication with musicians. Selecting appropriate music for the style, quality, and rhythm of the movement, as well as age appropriateness, is also a critical component for consideration. Finally, dance teachers must be aware of the necessity in attaining appropriate music licensing to adhere to the law and avoid fines.

PRACTICAL APPLICATIONS

1 Challenge yourself to listen to a variety of music, including that which may be unfamiliar to you.

    a   Discern the form and phrasing of the music. Perhaps map it out.

    b   Collect a minimum of ten songs in varying genres that you could use in a dance class. Be sure that you really know each song so that you are prepared to use it in a class or movement composition.

2 Identify ways in which you could incorporate different musical forms within composed dance exercises.

3 Practice teaching a devised movement exercise and convey the rhythm utilizing counts. Other than counting, how else can you convey the desired rhythm and tempo?

4 Have you participated as a dancer in a class that included an accompanist? How did the experience differ for you as a dancer than classes that utilized pre-recorded music?

5 As a dance teacher, have you been afforded the opportunity to instruct with an accompanist? How did having a musician in the classroom alter your approach or the experience as a whole?

6 Observe a dance class that utilizes an accompanist. How do the dance teacher and the musician communicate? How does the music selected and played by the accompanist enhance the movement of the dancers?

NOTES

1 "ASCAP Keeps Your Dancers in Motion," Accessed December 2022, www.ascap.com/~/media/files/pdf/licensing/brochures/dancers.

2 "ASCAP Keeps Your Dancers in Motion," Accessed December 2022, www.ascap.com/~/media/files/pdf/licensing/brochures/dancers.

3 "Music License for Dance Class," *BMI.com*, Accessed December 2022, 3, www.bmi.com/forms/licensing/gl/40.pdf.

BIBLIOGRAPHY

Ahm, Naz. "Do Dance Studios Need Music Licensing?: Ultimate Guide." *Studio Growth*, August 3, 2022. https://studiogrowth.com/dance-studios-music-licensing/.

"ASCAP Keeps Your Dancers in Motion." www.ascap.com/~/media/files/pdf/licensing/brochures/dancers, accessed December 2022.

Brooks, Charles. *Practical Approach to Understanding Music Theory*. 1st ed. Collier Library: University of North Alabama, 2022.

Cavalli, Harriet. *Dance and Music: A Guide to Dance Accompaniment for Musicians and Dance Teachers*. Gainesville: University Press of Florida, 2001.

Ewell, Terry B., and Catherine Schmidt-Jones. *Music Fundamentals 2: Rhythm and Meter*. Houston, TX: Connexions, 2013.

Gilbert, Al. *Al Gilbert's Tapdance Dictionary*. Lake Oswego, OR: Stepping Tones, Ltd., 1998.

Holland, Nola Nolen. *Music Fundamentals for Dance*. Champaign, IL: Human Kinetics, 2013.

"Music License for Dance Class." *BMI.com*. www.bmi.com/forms/licensing/gl/40.pdf, accessed December 2022.

CHAPTER 11

Injury Prevention
Sara Pecina

Box 11.1 Chapter Objectives

After reading this chapter, you will be able to:

- Articulate the importance of understanding anatomy, kinesiology, nutrition, and mental health as a dance teacher
- Recognize the six dimensions of Hettler's wellness model
- Adequately advise students in seeking professional medical care
- Advocate for proper conditions in dance spaces
- Develop a healthy culture in the learning environment that fosters injury prevention
- Strategize safe training practices to empower students

Box 11.2 Chapter Vocabulary

anatomic variation
chrononutrition
kinesiology
periodization
relative energy deficiency in sport

Injuries are a risk in any type of physical training, and dance is no exception. Not every injury is preventable, but it is the responsibility of the teacher to design their environment and movement practice to reduce the risk of injury – both acute, or sudden, and overuse injuries – as much as possible. A dance teacher should remain proficient in not only the practice of the technique they teach but also in basic anatomy, biomechanics, nutrition, and general principles of physical training.

Historically, dance has not remained current with best practices for sports medicine. One of the reasons for this is holding on to traditions in various forms of dance. Additionally, in some dance cultures and environments, dancing through an injury and pain

DOI: 10.4324/b22952-16

is seen as a badge of honor and grit. When confronting an injury, the whole picture of the dancer, production, timeline, and overall physical and mental health must be considered.

KNOWLEDGE

Dance teachers are responsible for the safety and well-being of their students while they are in their classes or rehearsals. In addition to the expertise of the specific dance technique/s they teach, dance instructors should be familiar with basic knowledge that aids in injury prevention, including kinesiology, nutrition, mental health, and how to seek professional care. Work must be done to prevent injury; however, dance teachers are often a student's first point of contact when they do encounter an injury and should know how to react in the moment and advise students long term.

Physical

Dance is a physical art form; students move their bodies to learn skills and perform artistically. Any artist should be familiar with their instrument, whether that be plaster in sculpting, canvas and oil paints in painting, the clarinet in orchestration, or the vocal instruments in singing. For dancers, this means knowing the human body and how it generates movement. Dance teachers should have at least a basic understanding of human anatomy – particularly in regard to the skeletal and muscular systems – and **kinesiology**, the study of human movement. In this book, Chapter 3 covers essential information in these areas, yet is not exhaustive. Additionally, dance teachers should know about anatomic variation.

Anatomic variation is a deviation from the accepted classic or textbook standards of human anatomy. Examples include hypermobility, scoliosis, bowleggedness, and accessory bones such as an os trigonum on the posterior of the ankle. These each affect dancing in different ways. Dance teachers must understand that each individual student's body is built differently; some variations may be more noticeable than others, but all must be met with the dancer's safety in mind. Hyperextended knees are commonly admired in ballet and modern dance, but improper alignment in the lower leg while weight bearing can lead to a multitude of injuries and potentially the need for surgery. The alignment of a bowlegged student's upper and lower leg will look different from standard alignment, but teachers should not expect the dancer to change this as it usually requires surgery. Similarly, a student with scoliosis will present different alignment landmarks in the hips and/or spine; a dance teacher should understand this variation and not correct the student for a structure they cannot change, but rather teach the student to work safely within the parameters of their body. Dance teachers are not expected to know every type of possible anatomic variation. Nevertheless, when teaching a student who presents some type of variation, the dance teacher should learn what they can about the specific circumstance and consider consulting a doctor for professional guidance.

Box 11.3 Representation in Research

Since the early to mid-20th century, many scholars and doctors have completed research in athletic training and performance, including injury frequency, factors, and recovery. A large portion of this body of research has been done in traditional sports such as basketball or football. Research into dance medicine and science has grown immensely over the last few decades. However, the vast majority of these studies only look at ballet and/or modern dancers and training. A small number of studies on ballroom and Irish step dancing exist. Literature on biomechanics, injuries, and training methods in all other dance forms – including tap, jazz, and hip-hop – is extremely limited.

It is important to note that the details gleaned from research in one dance form does not inherently equate to other forms of dance. The nuances of how the mechanical systems work together, movement trajectory, weight bearing, and most other distinctions are unique to each dance form. For example, the biomechanics of various jumps in ballet and tap vary greatly in the positions in takeoff and landing, how the leg, ankle, and foot create force, and the movement done while in the air. The floorwork done in modern dance differs from hip-hop breaking in similar aspects. The dance profession is more versatile than ever. Supporting research in dance medicine and science requires growth and expansion to meet the needs of artists and students.

In training conservatories or university systems, dance students may be required to take anatomy and/or kinesiology classes. Sometimes these are offered by dance professors with specific focus on these topics' relation to dance. Other times professionals in these fields who do not dance may teach the courses. In the private studio setting, this knowledge is usually beyond the scope of the school; however, the dance teacher should still be familiar with the information themself. Additionally, some teachers incorporate awareness and discussion of this knowledge in their technique classes.

Dance teachers need to understand the mechanics of what they are asking their students to do. Anatomy and kinesiology are at the root of all dance and should inform curriculum development and lesson planning. The effective dance teacher is curious about how the human body works, is deeply familiar with the mechanics of the movements within the technique/s they are teaching, and shares this knowledge with students as appropriate.

Nutrition

Nutrition is extremely important in any physical activity; however, it can often be neglected in dance training. Many people align nutrition directly with weight and body image; though it is not the only factor related to these topics, this correlation can make nutrition and eating a sensitive subject. Put simply, dancers require fuel or energy for the body to be able to perform the physical demands of any form of dance, and nutrition is the fuel provided.

The dance teacher should be familiar with nutritional demands of a dancing body and provide a supportive environment. Besides the ever-essential water, the majority of our dietary needs are made up of carbohydrates, fats, and proteins. In order to provide our bodies with fuel for activity, we need all three of these nutrients; dancers are no exception to this rule. Carbohydrates are essential for both muscle performance and recovery; they provide energy to muscles and the brain as well as a storage form of energy. For dancers, it is important to consume carbohydrates during long class or rehearsal days so that the muscles do not run out of energy.

Fats or lipids provide fuel to most cells and for contracting muscles. They also protect vital organs, provide structure for cell membranes, and form the base of many hormones. In regard to activity, stored fat will be used to produce energy for muscle contraction. As the body's backup energy, fat is used for endurance and is also important for dancers on long rehearsal days or performance evenings.

Proteins are a part of everything. They provide structure to all cells in the human body, largely make up muscle, skin, and hair composition, and provide structure for the minerals that make up our bones and teeth. Proteins also help repair muscle breakdown and work as reserve fuel. On average, the dancer's diet should be split into about 55–60% carbohydrate, 12–15% protein, and 20–30% fat.[1] Any exact dietary needs and planning must be based on an individual with consideration of age, gender, current health status, body composition, goal, and physical activity.

Unfortunately, eating disorders are not uncommon in dance. Various factors heighten this risk for dancers to develop disordered eating. Several forms of dance have a history of favoring a very thin body to achieve a certain aesthetic. Based on the individual, this can be an unrealistic expectation and can lead to disorders such as anorexia nervosa (restriction of food intake) or bulimia nervosa (binging and then purging food). Additionally, dance training almost always requires dancers to stand in front of mirrors for long periods of time wearing tight clothing while looking at oneself in the mirror. This repetition and temptation to compare oneself to others can also be a contributing factor to eating disorders. Other eating disorders include avoidant-restrictive food intake disorder (being extremely selective or picky about food options to the point of causing harm to the body) and other specified eating feeding or eating disorder.

Relative energy deficiency in sport (RED-s) is a syndrome of impaired health and decreased performance resulting from insufficient caloric intake and/or over expenditure of energy. Multiple physiological systems can be affected by RED-s including metabolism, bone health, immunity, cardiovascular and psychological health, and (in women) menstrual health. RED-s can affect athletes of any gender and ability level. A dancer experiencing RED-s is at a higher risk of sustaining stress fractures, early onset osteoporosis, experiencing more illnesses or infections, dizziness, depression, and anxiety. Performance is impaired by a decreased muscle strength, endurance, coordination, and concentration, among other problems. In short, malnourishment results in increased risk of injury, suboptimum performance, and decreased mental health.

Symptoms of RED-s include fatigue, rapid weight loss, frequent illness, trouble focusing, irritability, and depression. Some patients also exhibit psychological mechanisms such as low self-worth/confidence that lead to a feeling of never working enough and/or overtraining. Diagnosis usually involves a discussion with a clinician of the individual's medical

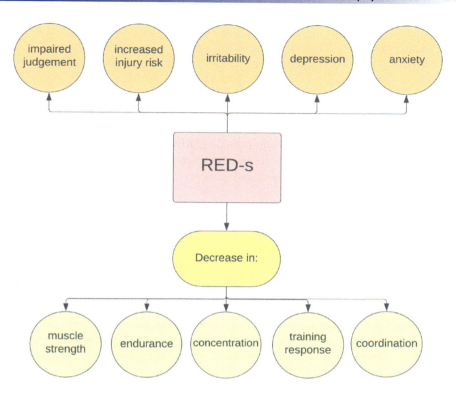

FIGURE 11.1 A diagram depicting effects of RED-s.

history, training history, and eating habits. Since RED-s is most often a combination of under fueling and over exercising, a multidisciplinary approach is necessary to treat it. Ideally multiple health professionals consult in a dancer's treatment including a physician, dietitian, psychotherapist or psychologist, and athletic trainer, which in dance can refer to the dance teacher or artistic director. Ultimately, food intake needs to be adjusted to adequately support the physical activity of the dancer, and overtraining must be avoided. Mental health and attitudes towards food also need to be addressed.

Additionally, diet culture or dieting fads are a dangerous phenomenon that often restricts necessary nutrients from a person's diet. There is no one answer to the correct way to eat, and the whole individual needs to be considered when making dietary decisions. **Chrononutrition** is the interaction between food and the circadian rhythm in the body. Each day our bodies cycle through various phases of rest and activity. Chrononutrition considers the *when* of a person's eating habits. Some nutrients are more beneficial when ingested at certain points in the day (e.g., soon after waking up, within two hours of physical activity, etc.). Dietitians and sports nutritionists continuously generate new literature in this area as more and more information becomes available. For example, ideal times to eat carbohydrates are at mealtimes and within about a two-hour window before activity (to provide energy) and about a two-hour window after activity (to help recovery). Like all nutritional concerns, there is no one right way to utilize chrononutrition; consideration must be given to the individual and their specific schedule.

While many schools and universities provide anatomy or kinesiology courses for dancers, very few offer or require a course in nutrition. It is problematic that so few educational offerings about nutrition are readily available for dancers. Just as a pilot must know how jet fuel affects flight and properly plan the amount before taking off, dancers need to know how to fuel their body to stay healthy and achieve optimum performance. Organizations like IADMS (see Box 11.4) do provide platforms for conversations about dancer nutrition. A wider range of available resources on this topic as it relates to dance would be extremely beneficial to dance teachers and students.

> ## Box 11.4 International Association of Dance Medicine and Science
>
> The International Association of Dance Medicine and Science (IADMS) was founded in 1990 by Allan Ryan, MD, and Justin Howse, MD. Their vision for the organization was to create a community of dancers, dance educators, directors, doctors, physical therapists, psychotherapists, dietitians, and other professionals to support dance health. Their programing includes resources for dance and health professionals, publication of the *Journal of Dance Medicine and Science*, webinars, networking opportunities, and an annual international conference. IADMS "is an inclusive organization for professionals who care for those who dance by evolving best practices in dance science, education, research, and medical care to support optimal health, well-being, training, and performance."[2]

Mental Health

When considering the health of dancers, it is imperative to recognize all aspects that comprise wellness. The National Wellness Institute promotes Bill Hettler's Six Dimensions of Wellness developed in 1976. This holistic model consists of six interdependent categories: *physical, occupational, emotional, social, intellectual,* and *spiritual wellness.*[3] *Physical wellness* includes maintaining the physical body through exercise, healthy eating habits, and proper care when experiencing illness or injury, all of which are described elsewhere in this chapter. *Occupational wellness* refers to the personal satisfaction and enrichment achieved through utilizing one's unique gifts and talents in work that they find rewarding and meaningful. For the dance student, this may include partaking in an art form that is bigger than the self and presenting that artistry in performance; for the dance teacher, this may be sharing the gift of dance with the next generation. *Emotional wellness* includes the ability to recognize and accept one's feelings as well as the amount of enthusiasm one has for their self and life. In the dance class, students must be able to express and cope with the many emotions they may experience in the learning and performing environments, such as frustration, confusion, worry, joy, comfort, or excitement. Dance can also help individuals cope with emotions experienced outside of the dance studio.

Social wellness recognizes the importance of contributing to a community and engaging in healthy communication. The dance class has a natural social component to it and should enable students to feel they are contributing to the class community, establish healthy communication patterns with peers and teachers, and develop a sense of camaraderie. *Intellectual wellness* refers to engaging in creative and stimulating activities. The dance class provides a creative outlet for students while arousing curiosity and learning in class content. *Spiritual wellness* recognizes the need to find meaning in life. Dancers can enjoy a spiritual experience through dance, practice religious worship in movement, or simply gain a new understanding of the world around them and their purpose in it. All six of these dimensions are codependent and exist on continuums of degree of wellness. Occupational wellness will have an effect on emotional wellness, physical wellness impacts social wellness, etc. Dance teachers should identify the ways in which their practices in class can affect each component of a student's health and strive to promote holistic health in class.

It is important to acknowledge that injury affects the mental health of dancers. Usually, dancers are upset and disappointed not to be participating in classes, rehearsals, or

FIGURE 11.2 A diagram of Hettler's Six Dimensions of Wellness.

performances. A student may experience a sense of loss of identity while unable to dance. Dance teachers should be sensitive to the sense of loss or even grief their students may feel when injured and patiently guide them through rest and recovery. Finding ways for an injured student to engage in class material – by engaging in discussion, providing feedback, etc. – rather than simply observing can aid in the student's ability to cope with the loss of physical activity.

In the 21st century, technology, and particularly social media, has a substantial effect on mental health. Dancers are influenced daily by online posts and content. Even individuals that may not have personal social media accounts hear about or see content via peers, and all media (television, news reports, etc.) are affected by social media trends. Dance has its own unique presence online. Often the flashier content gets the most circulation, which means young students are regularly seeing other dancers posing in positions that require extreme flexibility or executing tricks like falls to the floor, multiple turns, and acrobatics. This can shape a student's opinion of themself and what skills they believe they should be learning. For the safety of the students, dance teachers must structure their curriculum and lesson plans on a solid foundation of technique and artistry and not focus solely on teaching their students tricks. Furthermore, extreme content can lure those still learning into a falsely perceived lack of self-confidence or self-worth as a dancer. An effective dance teacher should be prepared to confront these challenges in students by reassuring them of their individual value and sharing the importance of knowing basic technique before attempting any advanced skills.

Professional Consultation

Injuries, nutrition deficiencies, and mental health concerns should be addressed by professionals in the respective fields. Dance teachers should never proffer an official diagnosis or treatment plan. It is common for dance teachers to give suggestions of care to a student or instruct them to modify movement, for example do not jump in class or avoid floorwork. However, the dance teacher should always pair this with a recommendation to visit a healthcare professional. A visit to the doctor's office can uncover underlying causes or hidden problems and provide diagnostic imaging to better understand what is happening in the affected area.

Communication on all fronts is key. An injured dancer and/or their parent or guardian needs to communicate with the dance teacher/s and doctor, the dance teacher must maintain communication with the dancer, and the doctor must communicate directly with the dancer. There exists a stereotype that dancers do not get along with medical professionals, either because dancers do not think the doctors understand dance as a sport or art form or dancers do not want to be told to stop dancing, even briefly. A solid foundation of trust and understanding can rectify these problems.

First, it helps for dancers and medical professionals to speak a common language with each other. This is where a dancer's basic understanding of anatomy and anatomical terms is helpful. Sometimes dancers feel a lack of respect when doctors or clinicians only speak in athletics terms or do not understand dance culture. However, just as dancers do not want to be expected to know all medical terminology, they should demonstrate the same patience with doctors. An effective health professional will listen to the patient's explanations and concerns regarding the cause of their visit.

On the other hand, dancers also need to be able to communicate with teachers without fear of retribution. Commonly dancers do not want teachers or choreographers to know they are injured because they are afraid it will affect their casting in current or future performances or that they will be perceived as weak or a complainer. It is the responsibility of the teacher to establish a culture in which dancers not only feel safe to communicate about injuries but also are encouraged to actively seek help. Young, and even professional, dancers learn from their teachers and peers. The dance teacher should demonstrate a priority to safely navigate and address all injuries and health concerns, including their own. Emphasis should be placed on taking care of injuries in order to heal better and faster, rather than pushing through pain, which would have longer and often more severe effects.

ENVIRONMENT

Dance teachers use their knowledge of anatomy, kinesiology, nutrition, and mental health to establish a healthy and nourishing environment for learning and artistic growth. The holistic teacher considers all of these factors when determining day-to-day practices in their classes and structure of the school. The physical space and culture must be thoughtfully constructed.

Space

Dancing requires space. Although monetary restrictions often limit the ability to control the physical space in which learning takes place, dance teachers should understand best practices to meet the needs of students as well as possible and advocate for better conditions when feasible. First, there must be enough square footage in a dance studio for students to be able to move comfortably and safely. Students need to be able to jump, turn, perform floorwork, and travel through the space without concerns of hitting objects or fellow dancers. This way they can focus on their learning and skill development. Ceilings should be a reasonable height, especially if lifts are being performed. If the size of the space is confining, then the maximum number of students able to enroll in each class should be adjusted accordingly. There also needs to be enough room to include any equipment that will be used regularly such as ballet *barres* and any sound equipment. The manner in which all equipment is stored must be well thought out to avoid collisions or items such as balls rolling out into the space while dancers are moving.

Flooring is essential in every dance setting. A proper surface to dance upon can help prevent many injuries. Dance spaces should have lightly sprung subflooring to accommodate the repeated force on joints that dancing requires. If the subfloor has too much spring, then when a dancer pushes off of it, it will spring up and hit them back as they land, rather than providing a giving surface. Concrete is never an acceptable flooring for dance classes. Additionally, the texture and composition of the flooring surface must be suitable for the type/s of dance it will be supporting. Ballet and modern dance are safest on a vinyl Marley flooring; there are a variety of specific types of Marley flooring, and the dance teacher should contact the manufacturer for detailed suggestions. Percussive dance, like tap dance, should be learned on a wood floor. In percussive dance, the floor is just as much an instrument as the shoes worn by the dancers. A student would not wear ballet slippers to tap class, nor should they be required to dance on incorrect flooring. Though many tap dance classes, competitions, and performance take place on Marley, it increases risk of injury because the dancers have to hit the floor with even more force than usual to produce their sounds.

It is not always possible to control flooring. Costs may prohibit best practices, or performance venues may control this variable. Whatever the conditions, dance teachers need to consider the circumstances they are in and adjust methods of teaching when possible. The flooring may not be ideal, but teachers do control the techniques they teach students, like proper jump mechanics, and the parameters of practice. For example, if the subfloor is not sprung, limit the repetitions of jumps in each class meeting, or if tap dancing on Marley, do not force the dancers to perform at full volume every time they rehearse a dance. Additionally, dance teachers should address any change in flooring when going from rehearsals in the studio to performance on stage at the local theatre or traveling to compete. The body will adapt to whatever conditions it is used to in the studio. When encountering a new floor, students should be encouraged to be aware of how the new surface feels and extra mindful of their technique to prevent injury.

Proper footwear should always be encouraged. This varies among dance forms, and the dance teacher should be aware of the options available for their classes and prepared to logistically aid students in obtaining the needed shoes. Students need to have the appropriate style of shoes and correct fit for each class. Parents should not be encouraged to buy shoes for their child that are too big to allow room to "grow into" them. This alters the mechanics of the way the student dances and increases risk of injury. When availability of resources is a concern, the teacher could consider incorporating a shoe "library" at the school from which children borrow shoes and then return them once they have moved up a size. Also, students should learn the technique and rehearse consistently in the assigned footwear. If dancers learn a piece of choreography and rehearse in socks for weeks but then are expected to wear jazz shoes in technical rehearsals and performances, they are put at greater risk of injury. Footwear changes the grip on the floor and affects the mechanics of all movement.

Culture

A dance teacher should be compassionate and prioritize their students' learning above all else. This priority should be reflected in the culture of the school. When encountering a student with an injury, the dance teacher must put the health and well-being of that individual above the casting of a performance or competition; in other words, let an understudy step in, or adjust bits of choreography as needed to allow that dancer to rest or perform safely. Friendly competition can be a motivational tool for some students, but it should never be overemphasized in class. Student obsession of outperforming one another or fear of underperforming creates an unhealthy learning environment and can cause students to push themselves well beyond their ability, resulting in injury.

The space and schedule of the studio should also promote healthy practices. Students often come straight from school or other activities to the dance studio, and older dancers tend to spend multiple hours in a row at the studio for classes and rehearsals. There should be space provided for students to eat on a table, not the floor. There should also be time in the schedule for dancers to eat at a healthy pace and digest large meals before engaging in physical activity. Rest should also be valued. A lack of rest or sleep causes delayed healing and decreased focus and slows down the learning process. Respect for the students' time should be reflected in scheduling by limiting back-to-back classes or rehearsals and avoiding late-night work on school nights. Lastly, cultivating a healthy environment is a continuous process. Teachers cannot expect to meet once with students and/or parents or guardians to explain protocols and proper conduct and expect everything to run smoothly and encounter no conflicts. Building a healthy culture takes day-to-day practice and is influenced by every decision made throughout the term.

MOVEMENT PRACTICES

Class Structure and Design

Each class meeting must follow safe practices in structure and design. This means every class should include a proper warm-up at the beginning of class and cool-down and the end of class. As discussed in Chapter 9, the structure of movements in class should be organized slow to fast, small to big, and simple to complex. This incrementally places greater demands on the body so that students are adequately prepared for the next segment of class. A cool-down allows the body to gradually return to its original state before activity, reduces risk of injury, and prevents dizziness, fainting, and muscle cramps and stiffness.

Periodization

Periodization is the division of training into phases or cycles to stimulate physical adaptations to improve performance. Studies have shown that strategically implementing periodization in athletic training reduces injury, strengthens the performance of athletes, and prevents overtraining. When utilizing periodization, training variables are manipulated to optimize performance. Training variables include frequency (how often one is training), duration (how long individual training sessions last), and intensity (repetitions, load, etc.). The goal is to adjust these variables to meet the needs of the athlete and their performance needs.

There are many types of periodization planning including linear and nonlinear. Linear planning can divide time in macro/large phases (e.g., twelve months), meso/medium phases (e.g., quarters of the year), and/or micro/small phases (e.g., a week or two). This planning model is not ideal for individuals who need to peak multiple times a year, like dancers, who have performances or competitions several times throughout a twelve-month period. Nonlinear planning alters variables more frequently and allows for several parameters to be addressed at one time. This allows consideration of how to best design a class at the beginning of the day to complement what will be asked of dancers in rehearsal a few hours later. In class, working supporting muscle groups and avoiding similar movement patterns that appear in the choreography can help reduce the risk or overuse injuries or even acute injuries caused by fatigue.

In dance, artists should reach peak performance just prior to a production or competition. In general, the intensity of training should gradually build up as volume goes down while leading up to a performance. As the body is being asked to do more demanding work, time spent in exertion should decrease to compensate. Dancers experience a significant loss of rest when transitioning from a training to performance phase; technical rehearsals are often long, end late at night, and require repetitive movement. Alterations of day-to-day scheduling and workload should be made correspondingly. A peak should be followed by an unloading or tapering phase that includes rest to allow the body time to recover. Rest is a crucial phase, but dance training tends to neglect it. For many athletes, a rest period would be their off season; however, many dancers do not experience this as they commonly train in the fall, perform in the winter, train and/or audition in the spring, perform in early summer, and then continue some type of training through the summer. Rest does not have to mean no physical activity, but exercise should be different than dance (see discussion of cross-training later).

There is no one way to utilize this design as individual circumstances must always be taken into consideration. In essence, the concept of periodization asks dance teachers to consider what should be added or removed from training to allow dancers to meet daily and annual performance needs safely. The discussion of integrating periodization into dance training is relatively new and has been met with some opposition. Many leaders in the field of dance prefer to hold onto the traditions long practiced in various dance forms. However, dancers are athletes as well as artists, and training should be strategized accordingly. Applying principles like periodization empowers dancers to be their best.

Cross-Training

Cross-training consists of engaging in physical activity different from one's primary activity. The goal is to exercise muscle groups not commonly used in the main activity to enhance strength, control, and coordination, thus also reducing risk of injury. Many athletes and artists are overspecialized at a young age, meaning that they focus excessively on one activity. This can lead to an increased risk of injury, burnout, and reduced long-term success. Cross-training provides an opportunity to train the body in movement patterns different from what a student regularly practices. For dancers, this could include weight training, swimming, or martial arts, among other activities. Since most dance classes are anaerobic, dancers also benefit from cardiovascular training. Class structure typically involves learning an exercise or sequence, performing it, and then listening to corrections before a second attempt, resulting in short bursts of energy. Cardiovascular training can improve a dancer's endurance, which is needed in performances. Activities such as Pilates or yoga can be helpful supplementary training, but they do not constitute true cross-training as these mostly utilize similar muscles and movement patterns as dance. Dance teachers should encourage students to cross-train and may even offer conditioning classes to help meet this need.

CHAPTER SUMMARY

Injuries are a risk for all dancers. Dance teachers should have fundamental knowledge of the human skeletal and muscle systems, nutrition, and mental health. When encountering an injured student, the teacher should recommend seeking professional care and maintain a line of communication with the dancer as they rest and recover. Dance teachers should recognize that injuries also affect mental health and be sensitive to this. Additionally, dance teachers are responsible for providing a safe environment for learning to take place. Adequate space and proper flooring and footwear are necessary. Lastly, the movement practices in class must support safe dancing. This requires warm-ups and cool-downs, periodization planning, and cross-training.

PRACTICAL APPLICATIONS

1 In what ways does an understanding of anatomy, nutrition, and mental health affect curriculum strategies and lesson planning?

2 Reflect on a time when you sought professional care for an injury or illness. How did you feel about the interaction with the medical professional? What did you learn from them that you would not have discovered without a meeting? How did your dance teacher react and how did this affect your recovery process?

3 Consider the intersection between injuries and mental health. How can the dance teacher contribute to fostering a supportive and empathetic environment that supports both aspects?

4 Evaluate your current dance studio or teaching space. What measures could be taken to make it safer for students?

5 Identify any challenges you foresee in implementing the recommendations of this chapter. What strategies can you develop to overcome these challenges and integrate these safety measures into your teaching practice?

6 Compose three cool-down exercises you could incorporate at the end of technique class.

7 Identify a form of cross-training you have done or would like to do. How did/would this activity directly impact your dancing?

NOTES

1 Clarkson, Priscilla, "Nutrition Fact Sheet: Fueling the Dancer," Factsheet #19, *International Association for Dance Medicine and Science*, 2005, Accessed November 28, 2023, http://hpri.fullerton.edu/Community/documents/dance_nutrition.pdf.
2 "Our Story," *International Association of Dance Medicine and Science*, Accessed November 28, 2023, https://iadms.org/our-story/.
3 "Six Dimensions of Wellness," *National Wellness Institute*, Accessed November 30, 2023, https://cdn.ymaws.com/members.nationalwellness.org/resource/resmgr/pdfs/sixdimensionsfactsheet.pdf.

BIBLIOGRAPHY

Allen, Nick. *Injury Prevention and Management for Dancers*. Wiltshire: The Crowood Press Ltd., 2019.
Clarkson, Priscilla. "Nutrition Fact Sheet: Fueling the Dancer." Factsheet #19. *International Association for Dance Medicine and Science*, 2005. https://www.yumpu.com/en/document/view/21846622/nutrition-fact-sheet-fueling-the-dancer-iadms, accessed November, 28, 2023.

Howse, Justin, and Moira McCormack. *Anatomy, Dance Technique and Injury Prevention.* 4th ed. London: Methuen Drama, 2009.

Langbein, Rachel K., Daniel Martin, Jacquelyn Allen-Collinson, Lee Crust, and Patricia C. Jackman. "'I'd got self-destruction down to a fine art': a qualitative exploration of relative energy deficiency in sport (RED-S) in endurance athletes." *Journal of Sports Sciences* 39, no. 14 (2021): 1555–1564.

"Our Story." *International Association of Dance Medicine and Science,* 2023. https://iadms .org/our-story/, accessed November 28.

"Six Dimensions of Wellness." *National Wellness Institute.* https://cdn.ymaws.com/ members.nationalwellness.org/resource/resmgr/pdfs/sixdimensionsfactsheet.pdf, accessed November, 30, 2023.

Statuta, Siobhan M., Irfan M. Asif, and Johnathon A. Drezner. "Relative Energy Deficiency in Sport (RED-S)." *British Journal of Sports Medicine* 51, no. 21 (2017): 1570–1571.

Welsh, Tom. *Conditioning for Dancers.* Gainesville, FL: University Press of Florida, 2009.

Wilmerding, M. Virginia, and Donna H. Krasnow. *Dancer Wellness.* Champaign, IL: Human Kinetics, 2017.

CHAPTER 12

Classroom Management

Box 12.1 Chapter Objectives

After reading this chapter, you will be able to:

- Articulate the importance of establishing guidelines and policies for the dance class
- Recognize the many aspects to consider when developing classroom expectations
- Develop effective procedures and strategies for managing the dance class
- Recognize strategies to address behavior modification

Box 12.2 Chapter Vocabulary

behavioral goal
classroom etiquette
classroom expectation
classroom management
classroom procedure
reflective listening

The learning environment encompasses more than the physical space of the dance studio. The dance teacher considers the actual studio space along with the social, intellectual, and emotional environments. This established environment then has influence over a student's ability and/or desire to learn. The manner in which the teacher shapes the learning atmosphere can boost student participation, promote trust, maximize students' development of skill, incite creativity, and ensure safety. This environment becomes the student's gateway to the art form. How, then, does the dance teacher manage the classroom in a way that creates a safe space in which respect and connection are cultivated and learning can occur?

The phrase "classroom management" often suggests approaches for control and discipline. However, classroom management encompasses much more than behavior modification

DOI: 10.4324/b22952-17

techniques. **Classroom management** is the approach a teacher follows to ensure that lesson plans are delivered and learning can occur with limited, if any, disruption to the learning process. How will the classroom or learning space be prepared? How will the interactions between teacher-student and student-student build a sense of belonging, trust, and respect? How can the teacher cultivate shared expectations within the classroom and develop the student's artistic voice? The effective dance teacher becomes mindful of the way in which they will connect to and communicate with students along with ensuring a safe space that will promote the students' growth and learning.

Upon considering classroom management strategies, the teacher aims to ensure an effective learning process for all. Some dance teachers may emphasize a behavioral approach, which focuses on the reinforcement of desired behaviors, often through the implementation of a reward system. Here, extrinsic motivation becomes central to the student's cooperation within the classroom and adherence to policies and behavioral expectations. However, a **relationship-based approach**, which emphasizes the way in which the teacher fosters connection with students, may prove more effective in establishing a successful learning environment. Through trust-building strategies, the teacher helps the students become intrinsically motivated to engage and contribute in a desired manner throughout the learning process.

Familiarity can build confidence which can lead to trust. This paradigm can work in both a positive and negative nature. Students become familiar with the teacher's response in how students meet expectations, and the students can then become confident in their abilities and how the teacher will react. Trust is established. A student may become comfortable with the structure of the class, which provides them with assurance. They then garner respect for and dependence upon their teacher to benefit their learning and growth. Yet, a student could also recognize the familiar outbursts of a dissatisfied teacher and, as a result, experience diminished confidence, and lose trust in the teacher.

In preparation for an effective learning environment, the dance teacher devises appropriate guidelines and policies for student behavior, procedures to follow during class instruction, and clear behavior management strategies. This chapter outlines the various approaches an effective dance teacher may take as they consider the dance learning environment and the ways in which their classroom policies, procedures, and actions can help students fully and positively engage in dance training.

FORMULATING GUIDELINES AND POLICIES

Order and structure can provide needed familiarity within the learning environment and therefore allow creativity to blossom. As a teacher prepares their curriculum and lesson plans, considerations are made regarding their expectations for student behavior and the necessary procedures that will lead to recognizable order within the classroom. Here, the teacher is devising a plan for classroom management. It is helpful to distinguish between expectations, procedures, and behavioral goals when strategizing classroom management. Classroom **expectations** are those aspects that *have to* be apparent within the class. These are the behavioral patterns and attitudes that the teacher calls for throughout each class. **Procedures** become the *how to*, or the specific actions that are taken to support activities and circumstances within class. For example, the dance teacher considers how students will enter the studio, transition throughout the space, and be dismissed. **Behavioral goals** serve as the *hope to* within the classroom. These are generic attributes that the teacher aspires for students to embrace.[1] Let us consider these three aspects in tandem. The dance teacher expects students to respect the teacher and others. Classroom procedures require students to remain quiet and attentive. Aspirational goals within the class may ask students to try their hardest and be positive. As students strive to try their hardest, they will adhere to the classroom procedure of remaining quiet during class, and thus will demonstrate respect when the teacher is speaking.

Students' apprehension about the classroom and subsequent learning interactions can be calmed when expectations, procedures, and goals are clearly identified disseminated. A handbook or document of guidelines and policies for the studio/school and classroom informs students and guardians of established protocols and the behavioral expectations for students. Areas in such handbooks often include classroom etiquette, classroom procedures, dance attire, and attendance policy, along with tuition and payment information and the curriculum. The dance teacher may also have similar or additional rules for their individual classrooms, which may clarify their additional expectations and distinct classroom procedures. Developed guidelines and policies support the teaching philosophy and goals of the dance teacher and align with the program setting. Creating such guidelines and procedures enables the dance teacher to pause and reflect on how they want their class to be conducted and prepares them to communicate these expectations. The absence of policies can encourage miscommunication and misbehavior among participants and lead to further conflict and complications within the learning environment.

Classroom Etiquette

Etiquette includes the respectful behaviors associated with a group, culture, or activity. These behaviors are considered normal and either expected of a group or prescribed by authority. **Classroom etiquette** refers to the manner in which the instructor prefers and expects students to conduct themselves while in class. If you have participated in or observed dance classes of various genres and in a range of settings, you most likely noted that there is not one set of behavioral standards for all dance students. However, dance students are typically taught to regard the dance studio and their training with respect. This deference is instilled through the behavioral expectations and procedures established and modelled by the teacher and taught to students.

There are aspects of dance class etiquette that tend to remain consistent among the many distinct dance genres and classroom settings. Dance students are often expected to demonstrate the following examples of etiquette:

- Arrive on time.
- Be attentive.
- Limit talking.
- Stay for the entire class. Ask before leaving when class is in session.
- Practice outside of class. Come to class prepared.
- Practice spatial awareness.
- Retain instructor-guided feedback.
- Be courteous and respectful to others.
- Refrain from wearing dangling jewelry.
- Be mindful of body language. (E.G., avoid standing with arms crossed or on the hips, do not yawn, avoid checking your watch, etc.).

- Silence or turn off cell phones and keep them stored in the dance bag.
- Bow/curtsey, clap, and/or verbally thank the teacher at the conclusion of the class.
- Do not
  - chew gum or bring food and drinks into the studio;
  - wear street shoes on the dance floor;
  - lean against the mirror or sit during class unless invited to by the teacher;
  - hang on ballet *barres*;
  - take photos or videos during class without permission by the instructor;
  - obstruct the view of the teacher during demonstrations; or
  - block the sight line between teacher and accompanist.

Specific dance genres may incorporate additional expectations, such as turning toward the *barre* between ballet exercises or keeping feet still and tap shoes quiet when the tap dance teacher is speaking. Additionally, the purpose for the class, the students' age, and even the teacher's personal philosophy can shape the classroom etiquette. A dance class designed for pre-professional or professional students may differ, in some regards, from that of a class for recreational-based students. A university professor may require from dance majors the behaviors of a professional dancer, while a studio teacher of elementary students may expect basic behaviors of respect and politeness. When considering students' age, it may be logical for a teacher to expect teenagers to remain attentive throughout class and automatically physically mark through the movement as they learn. In contrast, one would anticipate preschoolers to be more energetic and chaotic due to shorter attention spans, although focus and attention may be a learning goal of the class. Finally, the teacher's individual beliefs, values, and experiences often influence the etiquette they establish within their classroom. For example, an individual that values authority may expect complete control of the classroom, whereas an individual that regards individualism and collaboration may encourage conversation within their dance class.

Once determinations regarding classroom etiquette have been established, the dance teacher should inform the class of the behavior that they expect. By explaining expectations in the class and then modeling that behavior, teachers can foster those behaviors among students. Students who see the teacher or other students execute expected behaviors will likely also replicate those same behaviors. Informing students of how they should conduct themselves at the beginning of the term can decrease or eliminate behavioral problems, confusion, and nervousness. The teacher may provide a written agreement or verbally describe the expectations for classroom etiquette. The dance teacher should help students understand that etiquette is a form of respect for the dance, others in the space, and oneself, and it is also a means for safety.

Classroom Procedures

Classroom procedures are the routine actions that the teacher and students follow to ensure an effective learning environment. Desired behavior can be encouraged, and nerves or fears can be calmed by establishing a procedure for students to follow and one in which they learn to anticipate. Consistently applied classroom procedures help students to understand how to participate in the class and recognize the behavior they should present. This familiarity can relax apprehensive students and facilitate a smooth learning process. Appropriate etiquette is then practiced within the framework of the classroom procedures.

A dance class consists of certain procedures appropriate to the genre, purpose for the class, students' age, and even the physical layout of the building and classroom. For example, consider the students' entrance into the dance studio. Perhaps students are to place their dance bags in a cubby along the wall and sit down on a colorful dot on the floor where they remain quiet and begin stretching. In another class, students may be encouraged to line up at the *barre* and are permitted to chat quietly. Yet in a different class, students may be asked to sit on the floor near the teacher and engage in conversation until class begins. During class, students may be expected to raise their hand if they have a question, maintain appropriate space between dancers, or transition quietly between activities or areas of the classroom. At the conclusion of class, the teacher may have students form a line in which reward stickers for the students or letters for guardians are passed out as they exit the studio. Established procedures may extend beyond the classroom and include expectations for student drop-off, pickup, or behavior outside of the classroom but within the dance building. The teacher may include these in the handbook and/or discuss them with students and guardians.

Classroom Attire

Students have many attire options when taking a dance class. Some students may wear a leotard and tights. Other students may wear basic exercise apparel consisting of t-shirts, tank tops, sports bras, leggings, joggers, fitness shorts, etc. Some classes may require traditional clothing specific to the dance form, such as a saree in a Bharatanatyam class. Attire is typically dictated by the genre of dance being practiced and the preference of the teacher. Thus, a classical ballet teacher may require flesh-colored tights and a solid-colored leotard for those identifying as female. A jazz dance teacher may permit students to wear anything from leotard and tights to shorts and a sports bra for the female-identifying students, whereas a hip-hop teacher may allow students to wear baggy pedestrian-inspired attire. Some teachers permit students to wear ballet skirts or various warm-up coverings and layers. Footwear for the dance is clarified as part of the dance class attire.

The teacher considers the goals and needs of the class when prescribing attire. How might expectations of dress differ for students who are participating in professional preparation or recreational enhancement? Are there financial restraints that may affect classroom attire? Additionally, a program may have modesty, inclusivity, or uniform requirements that must be considered. Some schools require a color code for dress depending on the students' technical level or age. Here, value in uniformity within the classroom is desired. A benefit of this approach may be that students feel equal within the classroom. In contrast, a uniform approach may diminish self-expression. When students are able to choose their own attire, they develop agency in self-expression.

When considering the attire that you desire, determine what will facilitate the learning objectives of the class. It is also important to be mindful of the affordability needs of students. It may be helpful or necessary for the dance studio or teacher to have supplies on hand for students to purchase at a discounted rate or to simply loan to students as appropriate. The dance teacher should inform students and guardians of the dress code. It can be beneficial for the dance teacher to model the dress code. Yet, even if the teacher does not adhere specifically to the assigned dress code, they should present themselves professionally and in a way that enables students to clearly see the movement of the body.

When the dance teacher sets the example they desire from students, the students will be more likely to follow.

Attendance Policy

Dance training in schools and private studios typically follows the schedule of an academic year, broken into fall, spring, and possibly summer terms. This allows for an average range of 8 to 16 weeks of classes per term. Skill acquisition and technical development require consistent practice, which means students should be at every scheduled class to both maintain and improve their dance abilities. An attendance policy emphasizes this essential aspect of training. The dance teacher/studio determines an appropriate policy and informs students at enrollment. Consequences for excessive absences should be considered and expressed, and the teacher should be prepared to commit to the established attendance policy.

> ### Box 12.3 Balancing Art and Business
>
> A recurring issue among private dance studios in the United States is the conflict of running an arts-based training center that is also a business. Studio owners must make a profit in order to stay open. This often requires a balancing act between following the owner's values as they relate to dance education while also maintaining an atmosphere that inspires student retention. Many dance studios within the private sector focus on preschool- through high school-aged students with varying expectations. A single class could include a range of students from those who have little desire to dance to those who have decided to pursue a career in the field. Classes may be conducted in a way that instills utmost professionalism and etiquette with a focus on serious technical training, or they may focus on the joy of movement, relaxing the professional expectations placed upon students. A business owner typically wants to engage all students in the hopes of retaining their dance students from year to year and thus maintaining enrollment income. Yet, this may sometimes prove challenging. For example, parents may place pressure on a teacher to promote a student before the student is ready to advance in level. Or, a teacher may require students to enroll in multiple genres, yet this may deter some students from attending the studio. The dance studio must find their niche and market accordingly. Students may desire to engage in dance competitions or commercial dance forms, whereas the owner prefers to focus on classical approaches to dance. In order to secure students, the owner may then need to offer additional classes or create a competitive team.

A dance teacher's philosophy of training contributes to the policies they establish for their classroom. Attendance guidelines, expectations for attire or etiquette, procedures within the class, and strategies used to control the classroom are all areas influenced by the teacher's personal values and considerations in regard to learning. Inevitably, students or guardians may challenge the policies set forth by the dance teacher. The dance teacher should consider how they can balance the art of dance with support given to their personal teaching philosophy.

FIGURE 12.1 Image depicts an informal recreational dance class taught as a K–12 enrichment activity.
Source: Courtesy of Potter Gray Elementary/Warren County Public Schools.

CULTIVATING THE LEARNING ENVIRONMENT

The goal of classroom management is to cultivate a safe space for learning and provide an environment in which dance students can develop as individuals and artists in positive ways. The best learning environments are those in which participants feel safe and confident, and the way in which the dance teacher manages the class directly contributes to this secure setting. Classroom management extends beyond discipline and includes the overall atmosphere that the teacher creates within the studio. This is accomplished as the dance teacher greets students, initiates the lesson, communicates with students, and ends the class.

Preparing the Studio Space

First impressions are important, whether they are attached to a person, a group of people, an activity, or an environment. As a student walks into the dance studio, assumptions are formed, ideas are generated, and an energy is automatically felt. Children are especially perceptive, often in ways in which adults do not realize. Students, particularly young children, will notice the teacher, the studio space, and other students.[2] It is during the students' entrance into the dance studio that the tone for the class is often set.

As the teacher prepares the studio space, they are mindful of how the physical components of the room are organized. Is the classroom cluttered and messy? Visual presentation tends to create the first impression; therefore, the dance studio should be clean and tidy. It can be difficult to work or learn in a mess. Additionally, students may discern that organization is not a value of the teacher when the dance studio is full of clutter. Extra equipment and items can become a distraction for younger students or obstacles within the movement space. Unnecessary items should be removed from the space or be well-contained within the room. Perhaps an area needs to be designated for the placement of dance bags and water bottles. The lighting within the room can also be considered. Is it adequate for instruction? Do window coverings need to be opened or closed? Some students may have sensitivities to light that need to be considered. Is there ambient noise that needs to be quieted prior to the start of the class? Again, unnecessary noise can distract the focus and attention of students.

As the teacher pre-sets the lesson, they should make necessary equipment and music easily accessible. This saves time during the class. In a ballet class, where might portable *barres* be placed? In other genres, will the mirror be considered the front? Will students travel side to side or diagonally across the room, and which side of the movement will be performed first? Where are the controls for the sound system located? Recognizing in advance how space will be used will reduce potential confusion of students and eliminate the time spent making choices while one is actively teaching. It is wise to establish a "front of the room" that will be close to the sound controls. Time spent walking from the front of the room over to sound equipment will take away from learning and allow students to lose focus or misbehave. Also, consider the areas of the room where students may and may not go. A teacher may place circular mats or stickers on the floor to designate where children should sit or stand.

It is also important for the dance teacher to take a moment to prepare themselves mentally and physically for the class. An effective teacher avoids bringing personal problems into the classroom. The students expect the teacher to have a positive energy and be ready to focus on and engage with them. Students will feed off any worry or irritability that the teacher presents, which can then disrupt the learning process. The teacher wants to ensure a positive social and emotional environment for students. Taking a moment to reset their own thoughts, emotions, and attitudes can enable the teacher to provide the best atmosphere for student learning.

Welcoming Students

The invitation into the classroom provides an important impression on the students. The teacher can create a welcoming atmosphere with actions as simple as addressing students by name, making direct eye contact, and being present as students enter the room rather than off doing something else. Children tend to gravitate toward social behavior if left unsupervised. The teacher should consider where students should go and what they should do upon entering the dance studio. Addressing students as they enter the classroom and giving them instruction to follow can curb misbehavior.[3]

Beginning the Class

Beginning each class in a similar and expected manner lets students know that class is starting and helps them transition their focus to learning. This could include a simple question posed by the teacher, a breathing activity, or a movement exploration. A teacher

Classroom Management **219**

may invite young children to quickly share something from their day. Children are often eager to talk, and this can allow them to get their thoughts out at the beginning of the class rather than the middle (hopefully). Asking older students how they are feeling that day can help a teacher gauge the energy, physical health, or mentality of the students for the day. Activities that involve communication between student and teacher generate a feeling of connection and belonging and can be valuable moments for both students and teachers.

It can also be helpful to introduce the lesson plan or theme for the class to help students prepare for what is to come. Identifying class and/or individual goals lets students know what is expected of them that day and what the focus of the class will include. Knowing this information at the start of class can help students get in the right mindset for the class.

Communication and Interaction

How teachers communicate and interact with students can generate a positive or negative atmosphere, affect student motivation, and lead to ranging student behaviors. Chapter 4 elaborated on the fact that individuals perceive information through their senses, which is then processed in their brains. Students visually and aurally gather cues from the teacher and even the dance space and then formulate perceptions of the teacher. When teachers are positive in their engagement with students, students tend to respond constructively and are receptive to the learning process. Respect and trust are then developed between teacher and student. Conversely, negative interactions deter student learning, and can incite distrust, fear, indignance, and undesirable behaviors. It is important for the teacher to remember "that perception is reality to the person perceiving."[4] The teacher should pause and reflect when a student has a negative perception of them. They can then work to understand why the student feels a certain way and determine any actions that can be taken to help the student better understand their intentions. The dance teacher should strive to treat all students fairly and to demonstrate their genuine care and support for students as individuals and dancers.

Students are consistently aware of the teacher's verbal and non-verbal communication, and these perceptions often influence the students' behavior choices. The teacher should be mindful of the words they use, the way they speak, and their facial expressions and body language. The teacher's communication choices may be dictated by the students' ages and levels of maturity. The vocabulary the teacher employs as well as the pitch and tone of voice can engage or deter students during class. Adults may find themselves speaking slower, in a higher pitch, and with a more animated tone when talking to young children than with older students. Young children tend to respond more favorably to this manner of speech. However, older students might be offended or annoyed. When speaking to younger students, it is often helpful for the teacher to bend down to be at the same eye level with the children so that their potentially towering stature does not become intimidating. Non-verbal communication can also have distinct impacts on students. Younger students may assume the teacher's lowered chin and intense stare mean the teacher is displeased with their performance. However, the teacher may have unconsciously tensed their body as they carefully observe the students' performance and ponder what exercise or activity to do next.

Students value their interactions with the teacher. Those who feel a connection and sense of belonging within the classroom are more likely to develop intrinsic motivation to engage in the learning process. As positive connections between teacher and students are fostered, students strive to maintain these bonds. Students may pay attention, put forth greater effort, and practice outside of class as a means of sustaining the positive connection. The teacher should be especially mindful of the following actions and behaviors:

- **Greet students as they enter the dance space.** A friendly smile and warm hello are inviting and can ease students' apprehension.
- **Make direct eye contact with students.** Looking students in the eye lets them know that they are seen and that their communication is intentional.
- **Try to use each student's name at least once during the class.** This reminds the student that the teacher knows who they are and values them as individuals.
- **Practice reflective listening with students.** Respectfully attend to and be supportive of students when they verbally or physically respond to discussion questions or movement prompts. **Reflective listening** is a strategy that involves seeking to understand what the student has said or done and offers the response back to the student for clarification. Teachers frequently employ this strategy when probing students for cognitive understanding. For example, a student may offer a response that does not fully address the question posed by the teacher. The teacher acknowledges the student's comment yet encourages them to continue their consideration of the question. Perhaps the teacher might say, "Yes! We do bend our knees as we land a jump, but what does this action allow to happen in the rest of our body?" Reflective listening entails both hearing and understanding the student, which in turn lets the student feel validated in their efforts.
- **Be consistent in communication patterns.** If a teacher speaks calmly to students after one exercise yet shouts following the next combination, students will develop distrust toward and possibly fear of the teacher. It is also important that the teacher not ask students a question unless they are prepared to follow through with their response. Consider this situation. A teacher asks their class, "Do you want to do this again?" The students respond with "No!" The teacher knows that they need more practice, yet if they do not listen to the students, then the students may feel as though their voices are not heard or respected. Similarly, "What do you want to do today?" can incite an array of unwanted answers. Furthermore, the teacher should be careful of promises made to students. For example, the teacher may tell a student that they can be the line leader next week. It is quite likely that the teacher will forget this promise. It can be helpful for the teacher to make notes or reminders of added information that is communicated to students.

The teacher gauges the students' attentiveness and energy at the beginning of and throughout the class. There are times when the mood of the class may drop. The teacher may need to shift to a new exercise, change location in the room, offer students a water or stretch break, or alter the lesson plan. Finally, it can be helpful to the teacher to remember to not take anything communicated by students personally. Children and adolescents (and even adults) will often say things in the heat of the moment or without awareness of the effect their words may have. At times, it may be necessary to let hurtful comments slide, or it may be best to address them appropriately.

Disruptions and Discipline

Behavioral disruptions during the dance class can occur for a variety of reasons. Students may act out in a negative manner when they are unaware of expectations, rules are not consistently enforced, or needs are not met. Additionally, student boredom, inappropriate challenges offered to the student, or adverse teacher-student relationships can also contribute to undesirable behavior. The effective dance teacher communicates expectations and is prepared to handle behavioral disruptions as they occur.

Familiarity and consistency are often the keys to classroom management. When students know what to expect during the class and from the teacher, they become more comfortable with the learning environment, thus conflict and misbehavior may be reduced. Consider the point in class when a transition between activities needs to occur. Rather than saying to 4-year-old students, "Let's move to the corner of the room," the teacher might tell students, "When I say go, we are going to stand up and quietly move to the corner and form a line." Now students are aware of the expectations prior to the action and can respond appropriately.

Maintaining Focus and Attentiveness

The teacher strives to keep students on task and attentive throughout the class. One will find that lulls in instruction can quickly allow students to become unfocused or inattentive. The teacher can save time at the beginning of the class by multi-tasking while recording attendance. Perhaps the students share a favorite color, etc. when the teacher calls their name. During class, some students may consistently hide in the back or push to the front of the classroom. The teacher should change students' lines and/or facings in the room to provide each student an opportunity to be in the front and feel seen. Additionally, the teacher should refrain from staying in the same location as they teach. Moving around the room allows students to see and experience learning from different perspectives. It limits the ability for a student to hide in the room and helps ensure that each student is observed by the teacher. These acts encourage students to stay focused and help develop positive teacher-student connections during the class.

Despite the teacher's thoughtful planning, disruptive behaviors or undesirable situations can arise during the dance class. The effective teacher prepares in advance to implement these actions and steers the class back to a positive learning environment. At times, the dance teacher may need to regain the attention of excessively chatty students. In these instances, it can prove helpful for the teacher to share a word, gesture, or action that they will say or do when they need students to be quiet and attentive. For example, the class may select a nonsense word such as *goldfish* to call out to capture students' attention. The teacher may clap a rhythm to which the students will respond with a pre-established clap or verbal response. Or, the teacher may choose to simply stand still and silent, which typically leads to a quiet hush among the students as they become either uncertain of the reason for the teacher's silence or aware that the teacher is not pleased. Removing musical accompaniment and dancing in silence or utilizing a low instructional voice are also effective strategies to reduce chatter among students.

Aside from idle chattiness, students can engage in other disruptive behavior or become defiant in their physical participation. In some instances, it can be helpful to give a

222 Class Content and Preparation

disruptive or challenging student a specific task, such as leading a line of students or standing up front with the teacher to demonstrate. It is important that the teacher be mindful of how this action is applied as it could appear to some students as a reward for misbehavior. Another behavior modification strategy might have the student sit down in a designated area to calm down. The disobedient student may be asked to sit and observe or leave the room altogether until they are ready to properly participate again. At times, a conversation with a guardian may be required.

Inevitably, disruptions not related to student behavior may occur during the dance class. Another teacher may enter the room to retrieve a needed item; sirens may shriek as emergency vehicles pass nearby; a large bug may fly across the room; the power might go out; a commotion may be made by socializing parents just outside the classroom. If possible, it is often best for the teacher to ignore the distraction and remain focused and continue with the task at hand. Students will then follow the lead of the teacher. Some distractions, though, simply cannot be ignored, and the teacher should have a plan for these types of situations.

Application of Behavior Modification Strategies

There is often an underlying reason for the disruptive behavior, and it is important for the teacher to consider why a student is misbehaving. Young brains, specifically the areas responsible for control and planning, are not fully formed until students are in their twenties.[5] Other needs, such as sleep, hunger, and acceptance, may be unmet, thus causing a student to act out. Conflicts or situations among family and friends can also affect one's behavior. If the teacher can determine the root cause of the behavior, they can then determine the best plan to address the behavior and help the student.

It is important for the dance teacher to address misbehavior immediately. The longer an undesirable action or behavior continues, the more difficult it will be for the teacher to gain positive control of the situation. The teacher often discovers that drawing students' attention to the behaviors that are desirable can be more effective than calling out unwanted behaviors. For example, the teacher may offer specific praise to those students that are on task and listening by narrating the desirable action. Here, the teacher may say, "I see students in their deep jazz lunge ready to go" rather than calling out for certain students to get into position. By recognizing the action that the teacher wants in a positive way, students become more inclined to produce the behavior.

Consistency and composure are key when the teacher implements behavior modification strategies. Although the method of discipline may vary depending upon the personality and maturity of the individual student, the teacher should be clear about the consequences of disobedience and disrespect and consistently apply them. Guidelines and policies help the teacher strategize classroom management; however, the dance teacher must then apply these expectations equally and equitably in order to gain the respect and trust of students. When the student recognizes the teacher's consistent behavior and actions, they are more likely to develop intrinsic motivation toward their learning and constructively participate. Students are often waiting to see how the teacher will react to other students and then will expect the same treatment or discipline. The teacher should not let students push them to negatively react. Children are often exceptionally keen on knowing what will upset or irritate an adult, and they will play into this knowledge. It is important for a teacher to maintain composure rather than yelling and shouting at students. The teacher should remain calm, in control of their emotions, and confident of themselves and their response to any misbehavior.

It can be beneficial for the dance teacher to involve students in the development and understanding of classroom procedures and expectations. They should explain or discuss why certain behaviors or actions are expected of the students. As students understand the what and why of classroom procedures, respect for others and for oneself is generated. For example, students remain quiet as the teacher is talking so that all students can hear what the teacher is staying and understand the instructions. Students pay attention when it is another dancer's turn, out of respect for the dancer and to continue learning themselves. Inviting students to help create classroom expectations offers students a sense of autonomy and connection within the class.

Ending the Class

The closure of a class is as important as the beginning of class and provides an opportunity to incorporate familiarity. Perhaps the class structure contains a cool-down which provides a cue to students that it is almost time for the class to conclude. It is often helpful for the teacher to remind students of the class's relevancy to their skill attainment and learning process or provide actions for them to take in preparation of the next class. Encouragement or inspiration can be offered as students depart the classroom. For younger students, this may be the time to provide "hard work" rewards such as high fives, star stickers, etc.

CHAPTER SUMMARY

There are many aspects of the learning environment for the dance teacher to consider as they prepare for and deliver a dance. The learning environment can motivate student engagement and participation, provide optimum opportunity for skill acquisition, and ensure safety. The effective dance teacher establishes and shares clear guidelines for aspects such as classroom etiquette, procedures, dance attire, and attendance expectations. The teacher creates the learning environment even before students enter the space. Considerations should be made for how students will be invited into the studio, what practices may occur at the beginning or end of the class, ways in which to effectively communicate with students, and how to deal with disruptions and behavior modification. Through establishing familiarity within the classroom, confidence and trust can be built among participates. As a result, the teacher has cultivated a learning environment that positively and effectively engages students in dance training.

PRACTICAL APPLICATIONS

1   Why is it important for teachers to articulate class expectations?

2   What do you believe is appropriate etiquette in a dance class? What shapes this philosophy?

3   What classroom procedures might be effective among different learners or within various dance genres? Create a list of classroom procedures that are appropriate for different age groups.

4 How can choices in dance attire affect the learning environment?

5 Reflect on your past dance teachers and various classes. What classroom management strategies stand out to you? Were these methods effective? Why or why not?

6 Consider potential disruptions that could occur during a dance class. What strategies might you employ in response to misbehavior or disruption in the classroom? Devise a list of behavior modification strategies that are appropriate for different age groups.

NOTES

1 Alene H. Harris and Justin D. Garwood, *Reclaim Your Challenging Classroom: Relationship-Based Behavior Management* (Thousand Oaks, CA: Corwin, 2021), 58.
2 Richard D. Korb, *Motivating Defiant and Disruptive Students to Learn* (New York: Corwin Press, 2012), 3.
3 Korb, *Motivating Defiant*, 11.
4 Harris and Garwood, *Reclaim Your Challenging Classroom*, 11
5 Korb, *Motivating Defiant*, 15.

BIBLIOGRAPHY

Clark, Dawn. "Classroom Management Challenges in the Dance Class." *Journal of Physical Education, Recreation & Dance* 78, no. 2 (2007): 19–24.
Foster, Rory. *Ballet Pedagogy: The Art of Teaching*. Gainesville, FL: University Press of Florida, 2010.
Harris, Alene H., and Justin D. Garwood. *Reclaim Your Challenging Classroom: Relationship-Based Behavior Management*. Thousand Oaks, CA: Corwin, 2021.
Korb, Richard D. *Motivating Defiant and Disruptive Students to Learn*. New York: Corwin Press, 2012.
Marzano, Robert J., and Jana S Marzano. "The Key to Classroom Management." *Educational Leadership*. Vol. 61. Alexandria: Association for Supervision and Curriculum Development, 2003.
"Professional Teaching Standards for Dance Arts." *National Dance Education Organization*, 2018. www.ndeo.org.
Strong, Michelle R.B., and Alexandra Pooley. "Structuring a Successful Dance Class: Strategies to Promote Effective and Enjoyable Learning." *National Dance Society Journal* (Print) 2, no. 1 (2017): 13.
Willis, Cheryl M. *Dance Education Tips from the Trenches*. Champaign, IL: Human Kinetics, 2004.

UNIT 5

Presentation

CHAPTER 13

Instructional Strategies

Box 13.1 Chapter Objectives

After reading this chapter, you will be able to:

- Distinguish between visual presentation, verbal instruction, and guided delivery as strategies within the dance class
- Discern the role of attentional focus within the dance class
- Recognize imagery as a teaching tool
- Identify effective cueing methods

Box 13.2 Chapter Vocabulary

attentional focus
auditory imagery
chunking
cueing
external focus
guided discovery
ideational imagery
imagery
instructional strategy
internal focus
kinesthetic imagery
modeling
pacing
tactile imagery
verbal instruction
visual imagery
visual presentation

DOI: 10.4324/b22952-19

A strategy is a method or systematic action that one takes to achieve a goal. Each time the dance teacher steps into the classroom, they utilize a variety of strategies to facilitate the learning process. An **instructional strategy**, also called teaching strategy, is a technique that one applies when teaching to ensure students achieve the learning objectives. These methods are designed to engage and assist learners in acquiring knowledge, comprehension, and improved movement skill. An effective teacher, in any subject, rarely presents all information in a singular and consistent method. Recall from Chapter 5 that students encompass differing learning styles. Because each student is unique, and subject matter can be varied and distinct, the teacher selects from a myriad of instructional strategies as appropriate for the class and/or students. The teacher thoughtfully guides the students' attention and learning with selective modes of presentation, choice in language, use of various cueing methods, and adjusted pacing.

In 2005, Seidel, Perencevich, and Kett, authors and research psychologists, devised a taxonomy of learning which has been adapted to the psychomotor domain and can apply to the teaching and learning of movement. (See Table 13.1.) Their research is centered in learning strategies applicable for the general educator, yet their developed goals of acquisition, automaticity, transfer-near term, and transfer-far term easily align with the learning of movement. Essentially, the dance teacher first strives to explain the basic mechanics or concept of a movement, which is then practiced repeatedly until it is integrated into the student's body and knowledge base, also known as skill acquisition. Next, the teacher provides ample opportunity for the student to experience this skill through various patterns and approaches as a means to reinforce students' learning of the movement or concept. Finally, the teacher encourages students to assimilate the skill or concept through variations of the movement, within new movement, and even within other styles and genres of dance.

TABLE 13.1 Depicting the taxonomy of learning (adapted from Susan R. Koff, "Innovative Instructional Strategies for Teaching Dance").[1]

Taxonomy of Learning Seidel, Perencevich, and Kett (2005)			Dance Application
Step One	**Acquisition**	Students learn the elements of the movement.	The teacher instructs the mechanics of a specific turn.
Step Two	**Automaticity**	Students develop integration of new principles through repeated practice.	The teacher has students practice the turn until they can consistently execute the skill.
Step Three	**Transfer-Near Term**	Students demonstrate the ability to apply newly learned principles through varied movement approaches.	The teacher has students practice the turn in varied positions and directions.
Step Four	**Transfer-Far Term**	Students discover the ability to apply the newly learned principles in other areas of dance (i.e., other dance genres, other types of movement).	The teacher uses aspects of spotting to help with quick direction changes in other movement patterns.

The dance teacher couples a learning goal with a teaching strategy. The instructional approach shifts depending on the age, level, movement, concept, etc. Perhaps the teacher needs only introduce a concept to students. Or, the teacher may want to ensure that the student can apply the concept in various movement situations. These two circumstances can require different or multiple instructional strategies to be employed by the teacher.

Teaching dance is a complex process. The dancer teacher continually weaves together the lesson plan with the presentation of material, cueing of ideas, direction of and encouragement of attentional focus, and implementation of practice opportunity. As a result, teaching becomes a craft requiring knowledge, consideration, experience, and reflection. The ideas contained within this chapter demonstrate measures taken by instructors that have proven effective in the progression of student learning. There are many variables when teaching. Every student is an individual with unique needs, backgrounds, and goals. The following topics contain strategies that may or may not prove effective with each student. The objective of this chapter is to suggest the diverse strategies the dance teacher can employ within the classroom.

PRESENTING MATERIAL

There are three distinct modes the dance teacher may utilize to convey information to dancers and aid in the practical application of ideas. These approaches include visual presentation, verbal instruction, and guided discovery. When thoughtfully employed, these presentational tools can enhance the students' learning. While the dance teacher may choose one of these methods as their primary delivery mode, these strategies seldom exist in isolation of at least one of the other approaches.

Visual Presentation

Many dance classes include substantial use of visual presentation as a delivery mode for material. **Visual presentation** is a depiction of the information using the visual sense and requires students to learn through observation. Dance teachers primarily incorporate this form of presentation through their physical demonstration of the movement or exercise. Oftentimes, dance students watch the teacher execute the specified movement first and then attempt to perform the movement themselves. This method provides students a meaningful image of the movement they are asked to execute. For novice dancers, the teacher may visually present movement in its full and complete form. With advanced dance students, the teacher may fully execute or visually mark the movement as they present steps and exercises.

Modeling, a distinct form of visual presentation, occurs when the teacher or demonstrator offers a visual display of specific movement, or an aspect of movement, and the students strive to execute it in the same way. The students look to the demonstrator, who fully performs an action or movement with intention, as a specific and accurate visual model of the desired outcome. Modeling often brings the students' focus to the details of technique, body shape, timing, or energy.

Another form of visual presentation is the "observe and join" method. Here, the teacher or leader begins by demonstrating, then repeating the movement. The teacher may dance the initial phrase or set number of counts, repeat the movement, and then continue to the next phrase, and so on. Pausing to repeat the movement allows students to learn through observation. As students feel ready, they join in the movement and continue to learn. This method encourages students to engage in both their visual sense and then kinesthetic sense, as little to no verbal instruction may be offered. In this instance, students must truly focus on the steps, sequence, and movement nuances as they translate their perception into physical embodiment. Tap dance teachers often incorporate a form of this delivery method when they employ call and response. The teacher allows appropriate time between their repeated demonstration of the movement or the next pattern to allow students to echo the movement. Additionally, some choreographers choose to deliver movement phrases to dancers via this method. With each repetition of the phrase, dancers visually notice and incorporate more detail to their movement execution.

Finally, visual presentation could also include the use of flash cards, posters, or digital cues such as images or videos. For example, the dance teacher may hold up cards with pictures of dance poses or movements or the names for terminology. The students view these visual presentations and then execute the corresponding movement. Given the technologically advanced world in which we live, it has become easier to use digital media as a tool when instructing students. A plethora of dance tutorials, choreography, and performances are readily accessible for students to view and from which they can learn. Additionally, the students' performance of a movement skill or choreography may be filmed by the dance teacher and then played back for the students to view. This enables the students to see their performance from the teacher's perspective, or in slow motion, and discern the strengths and weaknesses of their dance execution. In this instance, the visual presentation also becomes a form of feedback and a tool for assessment.

FIGURE 13.1 A ballet teacher models a *port de bras* as a student strives to replicate the movement.

Source: Photo by Clinton Lewis/Western Kentucky University.

Within visual presentations, the length of the movement may be as brief as a single step or an entire section of a dance. The effective dance teacher considers their intention and goal when utilizing visual presentation as an instructional strategy. If teaching a new skill, students can be encouraged to perceive and attempt the movement rather than over-think the body mechanics of the movement. A teacher may choose this mode of delivery to challenge students of various skill levels to quickly pick up and retain sequences. For younger students, shorter movement is best suited for visual presentation and can encourage attention among social-minded students. Older or more skilled students may appreciate the variety in delivery mode and find their learning style challenged. The dance teacher should consider the following factors when choosing to utilize visual presentation as a method of instruction:

- **Ensure the accuracy of the demonstration** – For this delivery method to be effective, the visual demonstration must be presented accurately. If the demonstration is not clear and correct, then students risk developing incorrect execution, poor technique habits, and delayed learning. For example, students may omit a step or demonstrate incorrect timing as they replicate the error that was visually presented by the dance teacher. Or, the dance teacher may overly involve the shoulders during their visual demonstration of a Graham contraction; this leads to the same error during student execution. Inaccurate demonstrations affect the students' perception and understanding of the movement or sequence and become the understanding upon which they will then base their attempts. Students learn the appropriate or desired body line, body placement, technique, movement sequence, energy, timing, etc. from the teacher's visual presentation.
- **Recognize the students' skill level** – Motor skill development and physical abilities can influence a student's motivation and/or reproduction of the desired movement; therefore, it is important for the dance teacher to consider the students' physical skill level when visually presenting movement. While an image of an elite ballerina modeling an arabesque with the extended leg well above 90 degrees may depict the desired movement skill, it may also discourage adolescent ballet students who do not have the strength and flexibility to execute the similar leg height and body line. A teacher may model a forced arch position to emphasize the degree of toe extension and plantar flexion (*demi-pointe*); however, a student who struggles with hallux rigidus (arthritis in the metatarsophalangeal joint, or MTP joint, that causes a stiff big toe and potential pain) may be unable to execute the same degree of flexion.
- **Recognize the students' cognitive level** – Students respond to visual presentation in diverse ways, and the dance teacher should be mindful of not just the students' physical level but also their cognitive level and approach. Students may not all be at the same stage in their cognitive and memory development. For example, the use of modeling may not be effective for young children as they have not yet developed full ability to organize and recall information. Additionally, young students often do not try to physicalize movement as it is modeled.[2] Another consideration for the teacher is the amount of exposure the student has had prior to the visual demonstration. Are they experienced enough to rely on this information alone, or do they need additional modes of instruction?
- **Recognize the students' perception ability** – Students will cognitively perceive movement in their own way. The movement attempts of students may vary even when

they all observe the same visual example as each student in a class may notice varying details of the movement during the teacher's physical demonstration. For example, the students' view of the teacher will be unique depending upon where they are located in the classroom, which can then affect their perception. If the teacher stands in the center of the studio to visually present a turn preparation in a parallel fourth position, the students standing to the teacher's left may not realize that the feet are intentionally placed beyond hips-width apart. Students standing directly behind the teacher may notice the hips-width placement yet not notice the degree in which the feet lie within the sagittal plane, which then allows for a deep bend of the legs.

- **Encourage and focus the students' motivation** – The student must be motivated to focus on the visual presentation and strive to accurately model the movement. The teacher may find that the use of peer models assists in student motivation and learning. When a student observes another student of their own age and ability performing the movement, their confidence and motivation will likely increase to model the movement themself.[3] Further, novice students may feel motivation or comfort upon observing another student succeed or struggle in their movement execution.

  Additionally, students may also attend to differing aspects of the movement when it is visually presented. Consider the following example. The teacher demonstrates an eight-count traveling phrase. Some students may notice only the sequence of movement, others may focus on the rhythm of the movement, while others yet may perceive the spatial direction. The aspect on which the students focused will influence their movement attempt.

- **Consider the skill level of the demonstrator** – Although there are times when it may be beneficial for the teacher to use a demonstrator with lower skill level, the demonstrator's level of skill can adversely influence the effectiveness of the visual demonstration. If the modeler is not skilled, the visual presentation will most likely exhibit some degree of technical errors. A demonstrator that has limited back flexibility may not be able to effectively demonstrate the degree to which the teacher would like to see a jazz layout performed by students. Students will then perceive that the demonstrator's execution is the desired look for the skill without realizing that they could extend their back farther in their own attempt. In turn, the technically weak physical demonstration may restrict students' assessment of their own execution and learning of the skill.

Box 13.3 Lateral Bias in Teaching

Most individuals write with a preferred hand. Likewise, individuals often find that one side of their body is dominant when learning movement. The right side may be stronger and more supportive, this leg may extend higher, and turns may flow easier in this direction. Movement may feel more natural to the individual when initiated with the right side of the body. Scientific research indicates that humans predominantly prefer the right-hand (approximately 90%) and the right-foot (approximately 80%).[4] Additionally, individuals may have asymmetrical physical developments that leave one side of the body stronger or more flexible than the other side. This information may explain why so many dance teachers, specifically in Western dance, first teach movement leading with the right side.

How one teaches affects the learning process and preference of the student. Students become accustomed to learning one side of movement first, which means more time tends to be spent on that side as opposed to the other side. As a result, the student may begin to favor movement initiated from a certain side of the body more. If the teacher prefers one side over the other, that side has a likelihood of emerging more often in center combinations and choreography. The teacher who is stronger at leaping with the left leg may tend to incorporate leaps with the left leg into choreography. The teacher that always instructs movement on the right side first may initiate all choreographic patterns to the right. The dance teacher must consider how they are helping students develop strength and coordination on both sides and in all limbs.

Being mindful of lateral bias is important for the dance teacher's benefit as well. The way in which the teacher visually demonstrates movement is often connected to lateral preferences. The teacher may find that they always demonstrate on the right side, which causes their left side to become a strong stabilizer, yet greater control and fluidity is developed in the right side. Demonstrating on the same side all the time can lead to overuse injuries. It is therefore beneficial to the dance teacher to develop the habit of varying the sides of the body in which they demonstrate movement.

Verbal Instruction

Verbal instruction, a popular mode of delivery within the dance class, is the use of words to describe the movement desired by the teacher. Rather than offering a physical demonstration of the movement, the teacher describes and explains either the sequence of actions, mechanics of a skill, or the manner in which movement should be executed. Verbal instruction assists in the introduction and reinforcement of dance terminology and teaching of movement concepts. One should be mindful of the following when utilizing verbal instruction:

- **Consider intention and goal** – Simply put, words matter. The effective dance teacher considers the intention of the exercise and then selects language that helps students progress toward goal achievement. If an exercise is designed to assist students in their understanding of head-tail connection, the teacher would not focus their verbal instruction on the articulation of the feet. Rather, they would verbally guide students toward an understanding of the relationship between the ends of the spinal column within dance movement. In another example, a teacher could not clarify spatial directions within an exercise without discussing the use of focus and facings of the body. The effective dance teacher recognizes that novice learners do not need verbal instruction for every potential nuance of the movement. Verbal guidance for the novice dancer only needs to include what the movement is and one or two aspects on which they can focus their efforts. Additional information would prove fruitless as the novice dancer may only be able to attend to one or two pieces of information at a time as they are learning.
- **Vocal tone and inflection matters** – The use of tone and vocal inflection can spark a student's interest in what the teacher is saying. It can also communicate what is important about the movement instruction. The emphasis of certain words draws

attention to their importance and incorporation. The dance teacher can utilize verbal instruction to convey and clarify the desired quality and dynamics of the movement. When articulating the movement sequence, the teacher can vary their pitch and emphasis to highlight movement components. The instructor may speak with a legato or staccato quality or accent certain terminology and wording that corresponds to desired accents in movement execution. These qualities and accents are also utilized when cueing students (discussed later in this chapter) during movement execution.

- **Clarify timing and rhythm** – Verbal instruction is most helpful to the student when delivered in a style that reflects the preferred tempo and rhythm of the movement. While the teacher may initial provide verbal instructions in a slow tempo, timing is still clarified for students. Prior to practice with music, the teacher should audibly share the precise tempo required for the movement execution. Instead of stating the movement sequence in a constant flow of words, the teacher articulates the movement sequence in a patterned rhythm that follows an established tempo. It is important for students to become aware of the rhythmical phrasing of the movement. Rather than speaking with a slow and disjointed cadence, the effective dance teacher incorporates rhythmical patterning into the flow of their verbal instruction. As the teacher includes a rhythmic structure in their verbal instruction, the phrasing of movement patterns is clarified, and rhythm is delineated. Additionally, musical accompanists are better equipped to select appropriate musical accompaniment when the dance teacher verbally provides clear tempo and rhythmical cues within their verbal instruction.

Verbal instruction is often an effective delivery mode with older, more skilled students or in conjunction with visual presentation. Novice dance students need visual presentation; verbal instruction alone will not suffice. Older and more experienced students may be able to learn adequately with verbal guidance alone. However, when verbally instructing students, the teacher should keep their instruction short, concise, and to the point. The dance teacher should avoid long-winded descriptions of movement. When verbal instruction includes a step-by-step approach or too much information, students may become cognitively overloaded and unable to attend to the intention and goal of the exercise. Finally, feedback, which is explored in detail in Chapter 15, is often delivered in the form of verbal instruction. Whether as a mode of presentation or feedback, students will cease paying attention if the verbal instruction is too lengthy.

Guided Discovery

Guided discovery is a delivery mode that may focus on or blend the modes of visual presentation or verbal instruction yet shifts the learning from teacher-centric to student-centric. In **guided discovery**, a verbal prompt from the teacher instructs students toward creatively answering a question or solving a problem. Along with providing the parameters in which to solve the problem, the teacher asks follow-up questions, provides further challenges, or offers feedback to guide the student toward the learning objective. While rooted in verbal instruction and/or visual presentation, this mode of learning is often utilized during improvisation and choreography classes. However, guided discovery can be applied in any movement-based class.

Guided discovery requires extensive planning as prompts and challenges need to be prepared thoughtfully to help drive the students toward desired discovery. Guided discovery can help students explore movement and compositional concepts such as time, use of space, body shapes, and energy. A phrase could be demonstrated visually or verbally, and then students are guided to investigate the phrase on their own. Individual skills could be practiced in pairs for peer response or discussion on the mechanics or technique of the skill. Students engage in trial-and-error, apply critical thinking skills, draw from previous knowledge, and assess past and current attempts of execution. Guided discovery is teacher-led but student-solved, providing students with more freedom and promoting individual expression in their learning.

For example, in a modern dance or composition class, students may be encouraged to find ways to transition up from the floor and back down, perhaps with a certain time parameter applied. Students, independently or in groups, explore movement options to discover appropriate level transitions. The teacher may then call the students back together for discussion or to provide an additional challenge. For instance, students could be encouraged to incorporate an inversion during the transition. In another example, the tap dance teacher may pair students together and prompt them to create two bars of movement to serve as a break for a pre-learned pattern of movement. A parameter could include certain terminology that can or cannot be utilized within the students' creation. Here, the students are learning compositional structures and how to develop a movement pattern. In a final example, students are taught a movement phrase and then told to explore their understanding and execution of the phrase. Students then develop questions about the sequence or mechanics or become self-prepared to perform and further practice the movement. Through guided discovery, students may work individually, in pairs, or in groups to explore and uncover their own optimal movement solution along with continuous response from the teacher. Essentially, the teacher becomes a facilitator who encourages students to problem-solve and creatively uncover new knowledge and develop skill.

Within guided discovery, the students are provided an opportunity to explore and discern effective movement execution or movement concepts. The dance teacher should consider the following when choosing to utilize guided discovery as a method of delivery:

- **Clarify the movement prompt** – The dance teacher should be clear in their articulation of the movement prompt or intention behind the exercise. If students do not understand the action on which they need to focus or the solution they need to discover, they will be unsuccessful in their discovery of movement execution or potential.
- **Consider the students' movement experience** – A dance teacher should be aware of their students' skill abilities when incorporating guided discovery as a delivery mode. If a student has yet to experience a movement skill or concept, their exploration will be limited to basic execution. A student more skilled in the dance movement will be better equipped to explore movement approaches, integrations, and nuances. A dance teacher would not expect a novice ballet student to explore the energy required in executing a *tour jeté*. In contrast, a jazz dance teacher might ask intermediate or advanced students to explore stylistic clarity in their movement execution of a center combination.
- **Consider the students' cognitive level** – The effective dance teacher is mindful of their students' cognitive abilities when utilizing guided discovery. If students do not yet comprehend a movement concept, how can they be expected to explore options and discern the most effective movement option or recognize emotions that the movement could convey? The dance teacher should be mindful of the manner in which students are able to perceive movement and consider and evaluate choices in execution.

TABLE 13.2 The modes of presenting material with dance-based examples.

Modes of Presentation	
Visual Presentation	• The tap dance teacher demonstrates a two-bar movement pattern for students to learn. • The dance teacher demonstrates a short locomotor phrase of movement for students to replicate.
Modeling	• The ballet teacher stands in *tendu croisé devant*. Students copy the pose, imitating the arms, incline of the head, and placement of the legs. • In a modern dance class, a student demonstrator creates an S-curve with their arms. Classmates copy the shape of the arms.
Observe and Join	• The tap dance teacher executes one bar of movement and pauses. Students attempt to reproduce the movement in tempo. This back-and-forth continues. As students learn, the teacher adds on to the movement. • In a hip-hop dance class, the demonstrator dances the beginning few movements of the combination, pauses, and then repeats the movement. After a few executions of this pattern by the demonstrator, they add on to the movement yet follow the same pattern of dance, pause, and start over. Students join in as they learn the movement. Their physical embodiment improves with each attempt.
Verbal Instruction	• The ballet teacher verbalizes the *grand battement* from the front of the classroom, speaking the names and actions of the movement in the tempo and rhythm they are to be executed. The students then execute the exercise. • The modern teacher explains to the students that they are to prance forward for six counts, turn over their right shoulder, and prance backward for six counts, repeating this pattern until they are across the floor. Students then prepare to execute the movement as stated. • Tap dance students are verbally instructed to practice a specific time step pattern.
Guided Discovery	• The jazz class learns a phrase of movement. The teacher has prepared a gap at the end of the phrase wherein movement is omitted between a leap and the final pose. The teacher prompts groups of students to discover their own way to move from the leap to the final pose in the eight counts provided. As the groups explore options, the teacher occasionally interjects, asking questions about movement clarity, transitions, and timing. • In a choreography class, the instructor prompts students to discover how the energy of a movement motif changes when the size of the movement changes. After students experiment with the motif, the teacher asks them various questions about their exploration.

DELIVERY IN PARTS

Whether presented visually or verbally, the dance teacher can break down the delivery of movement into segmented parts. Consider various dance classes that you have taken. Have you learned an entire movement combination all at once? Can you recall a time where you were taught the first few steps, then the next couple of movements, and then the final steps? Have you ever been taught just footwork and then later learned the arm movements? Delivery of movement – whether it is an individual skill, a short exercise, or an entire combination – is often divided into parts as a means of helping students learn. It would be difficult for the 5-year-old to learn a phrase of multiple movements at one time. However, it might not be unrealistic for the 10-year-old to learn a multi-movement exercise during the demonstration. Even guided discovery can be broken down into parts. Rather than focusing on the complete desired movement, students may be guided to explore separate or different components, or parts, of the movement.

The dance teacher may demonstrate or instruct an entire exercise to students. Or, the instructor may divide the movement or exercise into parts. For example, the teacher may demonstrate a turning leap as one segment. The same movement could also be broken down into the preparation turn, the actual leap, and the follow-through movement. A teacher may demonstrate an eight-count pattern of movement that requires actions of the legs and the arms. Rather than teaching the movement as a whole, the teacher may demonstrate the footwork, then the arms, then put the actions together. Whether teaching with visual presentation or verbal instruction, the instructor chooses whether to teach the exercise as a whole or break the exercise down into parts. In turn, the divisions in which movement or exercise parts are taught to students can help them make sequential and important connections in movement patterns. Students may also practice movement in parts. Chapter 14 further examines ways in which the dance teacher can deliver movement exercises and provide practice opportunities following whole and part methods to enhance student learning.

The dance teacher considers the manner in which movement or exercise components are combined as a tool that can help students recognize and retain sequences. **Chunking** is an instructional approach where independent parts are combined in a meaningful way to help improve short-term memory and transfer to long-term memory. The teacher can organize movement by groupings, or chunks. The way these chunks are structured become recognizable to students as they attempt to execute longer movement sequences. This strategy helps students process ideas within their short-term memory and retain movement patterns in their long-term memory.

Consider the approach one may take when learning choreography. Trained dancers tend to automatically group movements into chunks that make sense to them as a means of retaining longer sequences. This is a learned and often individual process. Trained dancers may chunk differently from their peers as they make connections and structure the choreography in a way that makes sense to them. The dance teacher can help novice students learn this approach by separating movement into logical sections as they teach. Often this results in grouping movement into counts of eight or delineating the end of movement phrases for students. A standard "three and a break" structure allows students to group movement into chunks. The first three sets are repeated phrases that can be grouped together when teaching, while the break is taught as a separate chunk. Ballet exercises at the *barre* (e.g., a *tendu* exercise) and in center (e.g., a *petit allegro* exercise) as well as tap dance patterns (e.g., an individual step within the Shim Sham Shimmy) often follow this structural patterning.

ATTENTIONAL FOCUS

Verbal instruction is a natural component of teaching. Teachers describe movement and explain what to do, how to do it, and when to do it. As a result, a relationship forms between movement and the language the dance teacher employs to communicate movement. This movement-language connection reinforces learning, making the words used very important. The student learns to recognize correct terminology and apply these labels to specific actions. The teacher may develop catchphrases to help students learn. Such phrases quickly remind students of an action or behavior they are to execute and the internal or external focus they should apply. The teacher carefully considers the language they use during verbal instruction and cueing to help students focus their attention. Attention can be defined as the process in which one attends to information. **Attentional focus** is the mental action of applying concentration toward a singular stimulus for a period of time.

We have learned that a student absorbs sensory information continuously; therefore, the dance teacher needs to help direct the student's attention and focus on the task at hand and in a specific manner. Attentional focus can be directed either internally or externally. **Internal focus** is when an individual directs their attention and effort toward the elements of the task or the individual components of the movement. When balancing in a Horton "T," the student focuses on engaging their core muscles and extending in opposition within their limbs. The dance student looks inward to the way they physicalize movement. An **external focus** requires an individual to direct their attention and effort to the outcome of the movement execution. A student may focus on leaping over a fence rather than pushing through their back leg and foot to soar through the air. Here, the student considers the outward appearance of or ideational approach to the movement execution.

The use of the mirror along with visual presentation of movement ideas by the teacher often leads to an external focus for the dance student. The student becomes accustomed to seeing body positions and limb movements as the teacher visually presents, and the student applies these external images as they attempt the movement. They view their image in the mirror, or the reflection of other students, and attempt to replicate the visual aspect of the movement. Verbal instruction, verbal cues, and guided discovery then become essential to help students harness an effective internal understanding of the movement.

As students learn the mechanics and sequence of movement, they may shift their attention to an inward focus of movement execution. They work to physically control the shape of their arms, the stretch through their feet, the rotation of their legs, the energy release into the floor, or perhaps the clarity of their footwork. In these instances, the student applies an internal focus in their attempt to reproduce movement in a specific way. With an internal focus, the student directs their attention to themselves and the manner in which they are moving their body parts. This use of internal focus often results in constrained movement as they consciously attempt to control the action.

FIGURE 13.2 In this image, dance students depict moving with internal and external focus. Image A represents students focusing on the internal feeling of the *plié* and *port de bras*. Image B displays a student looking outward into a mirror as she attempts to correct her pose.

Source: Photos by Clinton Lewis/Western Kentucky University.

Effective dancers have an internal awareness of the dance technique and their movement efforts within that technique yet also embrace an external focus necessary for the technical execution and aesthetic component of the movement. The dance teacher continuously balances this dual focus within dance training. As students learn, it can be beneficial to help them shift their focus to an external aspect. In this instance, the student focuses less on controlling the movement themself and instead allows the body to strive toward an outward goal. If not prompted to apply an external focus, the student often naturally shifts to an internal focus.[5] There are several approaches the teacher can incorporate that can encourage a student's external focus. Pictures or stickers on a wall provide an external attention cue for dancers as they turn across the floor. Images and metaphors, discussed later in this chapter, encourage an idea on which the student can focus and reproduce. External cues can further incite an external focus. A belt could be applied around a student's waist to help them level their hip placement. A sticker on a student's shoulder can help them point that sticker in certain directions to aid the correct spiral of the torso. When balancing, the dancer could focus on sustaining a plate on their head rather than keeping their feet still.

The effective dance teacher thoughtfully considers verbal instruction and cueing and how their language can assist students in applying an internal or external focus. Consider the following statement: "During the *grande plié*, feel the heels slide past one another and thighs rotate and open sideways as you descend and ascend." The students are cued to apply an internal focus on the feet and legs and control them in a specific way during the action. Contrast that approach with the following statement: "During the *grande plié*, imagine that the walls in front of and behind you are closing in as you descend and ascend." Here, the students are cued to apply an external focus by picturing imaginary walls around them and allowing the movement to happen between the walls. Rather than controlling the movement from within oneself, an external focus shifts attention to what the movement will look like, where it will extend in space, or how it will be executed. The teacher may offer externally focused verbal cues related to tempo, direction, or movement quality to encourage an external focus. Consider the following:

- "Match the tempo of my movement."
- "Let the headlights on your hip bones shine directly toward the mirror."
- "Glide across the floor like a leaf blowing in the wind."

This focus affects the overall outcome of the movement rather than the control of aspects of the movement execution.

TABLE 13.3 Identifying examples of internal and external focus in dance movement

Dance Movement	Internal Focus	External Focus
Frappé	Feel the foot brush through the floor, and lift the leg high into the air	Slice the leg dynamically into the air
Jazz layout	Notice that the working leg unfolds at the same time as the torso arches backward; engage the abdominals and glutes for support during execution; lengthen through the back of the leg in the air	Reach the working foot, both hands, and head toward opposing directions in space
Contraction	Engage the abdominals and allow the spine to curve	Imagine someone touches an ice cube to your belly button
Stomp	Strike the floor with the entire bottom of the shoe, immediately lifting it back up	Imagine killing a bug

FIGURE 13.3 Two images portray dancers performing movement described in Table 13.3. The dancer on the left performs a jazz layout. The dancer on the right performs a contraction. The dancers could apply internal or external focus as they execute either movement.

Source: Photos by Jeffrey Smith and Clinton Lewis/Western Kentucky University.

Novice dance students may find it useful to first focus on internal aspects when learning. It is wise to limit the aspects of movement on which novice students should focus, as they can struggle to concentrate on multiple areas at a time. An external focus is generally encouraged for more skilled students who have developed a greater level of automaticity within movement. Studies indicate that an external focus typically leads to more fluid and efficient movement execution and often has a superior influence on performance.[6] However, the use of both is important for all dance students to experience. As students shift their focus from internal to external aspects, there is less attention given to the self. Greater efficiency is noted within muscular effort as automatic processes within the body emerge.

USE OF IMAGERY

As we continue to consider the movement-language connection, the dance teacher often finds the use of mental imagery to be a beneficial tool in helping students to learn. **Imagery** is the use of descriptive language to provide a mental representation of an object, idea, or experience. Imagery directs the students' attention and focus, either internally or externally, as they dance with the goal of improving or enhancing movement execution. Consider a *penché* movement in a ballet class. The student may be asked to imagine their body as a seesaw. One side lifts as the other side lowers; the leg lifts high as the torso is lowered. Yet, the two sides remain connected and work together as they move through space. The visual image of the seesaw creates an internal focus as the dancer works to maintain connection between their body halves. The student could also be encouraged to imagine that their hand is holding on to an imaginary *barre* during the movement. As they focus on the kinesthetic feeling of pressing on the *barre* for balance, their movement execution becomes more successful. The dance teacher may use imagery within their movement instruction and cueing to help students execute movement correctly or perform in a desired way. The mental images become contextual or qualitative clues for the movement. Imagery can also help improve alignment issues, enhance artistry, inspire relaxation, or incite confidence in movement.

Imagery can be visual, kinesthetic, auditory, tactile, and ideational. Regardless of label, imagery can provide a mental picture or feeling to generate a specific movement outcome. Whether we see or feel the mental image, visualize an object, recall an experience, or imagine an idea, imagery can help us discover the correct technique or quality of movement.

- **Visual imagery** connects students' focus to a visual representation of a movement idea. Here, the teacher encourages students to imagine an image that then becomes a guide for the movement execution. For example, the teacher may ask students to visualize a big rose bush that they will leap over. As they imagine a vision of the rose bush, their leap extends higher in the air as they attempt to jump over the rose bush. The teacher might provide a flashcard with an image of a tornado barreling across a cornfield to serve as imagery during an improvisation exercise. The students focus on this picture which then influences their movement execution.
- **Kinesthetic imagery** offers the student a perception of physical movement. The teacher may ask students to execute a lunge position with the arms pressing forward. They may tell the students to press with their arms as though they are pushing a parked car. The students now have a clear focus of how the energy should move through their limbs, and their performance is clarified.

- During **auditory imagery**, the teacher provides sounds or words that then incite a mental image within the student. Auditory images often offer qualitative cues for students. For example, the teacher may reference a crisp drum cadence to help students understand the articulation needed within their footwork. The teacher may ask students to imagine the sound of popcorn popping. This provides a mental image of the energy and timing desired during a phrase of arm movements.
- **Tactile imagery** encompasses the aspects of touch and can also influence the quality of one's movement execution. For example, the teacher tells the students to imagine the smoothness of melted milk chocolate and then asks the students to dance with that same smooth quality. Or, the teacher may remind students of how it feels to be pricked by the thorn of a rose bush. Students may then perform a gesture with greater dynamics.
- Finally, **ideational imagery** utilizes metaphorical language to depict an external object or idea. Here, a student may be prompted to imagine that they are dancing like a leaf blowing in the wind.

Beginning-level dance students will need specific images from the teacher, whereas more skilled students will begin to discover their own ability for imagery. The teacher should be mindful of overusing any one image as it could lose its effect over time. Images that connect to everyday life are best suited with children. For an image to be effective, the student must be able to relate to it. It is of no use for the teacher to ask students to dance as if they are falling in love when the students are 4 years old. They have not yet experienced this feeling and therefore cannot produce that idea. Imagery is also not effective with a skill the student has yet to attempt. Imagery can help improve execution, but only after the student is familiar with the movement. Finally, some students are unable to picture images or ideas within their mind. Individuals with aphantasia, a phenomenon that prevents an individual from visualizing mental images, will find the teacher's use of imagery ineffective.

CUEING

Cueing is a means of prompting the dance student on how to execute a movement, the sequence of movement, or even where to focus their attention. Cues may relate to many aspects of action such as the mechanics and technique of a skill, the timing or spatial organization of the phrase, or performance aspects. The dance teacher can offer visual, tactile, and verbal prompts before or during the students' movement execution. When offering cues, the teacher should keep in mind the students' experience, skill level and abilities, and degree of comfort with and receptiveness to the different approaches. Cues are helpful to the beginning-level student who has a lot to consider when learning movement. More skilled students often require less cues; however, the cues used become tailored to more specific and nuanced details of the movement. Visual, tactile, and verbal cues can also be employed as feedback. This idea is further discussed in Chapter 15.

Visual Cues

A visual cue can prompt students before or during movement attempts. Most visual cues are in the form of non-verbal body language or other body actions. For example, a teacher's disapproving body stance can signal to a student that they have made an error, or a gesture of the arm can indicate to students which way the movement should travel. Modeling can be a means of presenting information to students; however, it can also be used as a visual cue. The teacher can visually model a desired execution or performance for the student as a means of teaching sequence or a basic step. The teacher may model a turn preparation to draw attention to the placement and pathway of the arms. Instead of verbalizing the cue, the teacher visually emphasizes an incorrect "wind up" of the arms, followed by a demonstration of the efficient starting position of the arms and reach of the leading arm to help initiate the turn. Students can tangibly see the movement of the teacher's arms and shoulders and then attempt to replicate it. Here, modeling has been used to both highlight the incorrect action as well as desired approach of execution. The teacher may choose to have a student visually demonstrate a step in either appropriate or ineffective approaches, which often encourages active problem-solving among students. It is important to note that the emphasis here is of modeling as a visual cue to present movement ideas.

Visual cues are only as effective as the student's perception of them. Students must have a direct sight line to the visual cue if they are to follow it. It is unbeneficial for the teacher to visually cue students when the students are facing away from the teacher. Students must understand and recognize a visual cue. For example, the teacher may mark tap steps with their hands; however, if the students do not recognize the connection between the articulation of the teacher's hands to the tap steps they are supposed to execute, the visual cues will be ineffective. Students must also recognize when visual cues are intended

FIGURE 13.4 A dance teacher visually points to their ear to remind students to listen and stay together as they dance.

Source: Photo by Jeffrey Smith/Western Kentucky University.

for them. If multiple students are dancing across the floor, how is one student to know that the teacher's visual prompt is intended for them? The dance teacher should ensure they have the student's attention prior to utilizing visual cues.

Tactile Cues

Tactile cueing involves physical touch, either by the teacher or by the students, and helps the student discover a kinesthetic sensation connected to movement. Attention is directed to a specific part of the body that needs to engage or relax differently during the action. Tactile cueing can be applied by the instructor or self-applied by students. Consider these examples. The teacher might gently push the back of a student's shoulder forward to remind them to feel the forward energy of that shoulder or press down on their arms to help them find the proper muscle engagement in an arm position. As the student executes a contraction or an over-curve, the teacher may gently press the lower spine to help the student perfect the movement and apply appropriate head-tail connection. Similarly, the teacher may ask the students to place their own hands on their hips to help them find proper hip placement. Students could be prompted to shake their hands as an example of the looseness desired in the ankle while tap dancing. Students may hold hands with partners and pull forward as their partner executes a movement to help them discern how to use more or less space. These examples of tactile cueing encourage the student to experience a specific aspect of movement prior to their execution of the skill or phrase. Physical touch should be applied thoughtfully and sparingly by the dance teacher to a student and requires consent by the student.

FIGURE 13.5 A dance teacher gently presses the dance student's lower spine to help them discover the appropriate body position.

Source: Photo by Kyra Rookard/Western Kentucky University.

Verbal Cues

Dancers constantly multitask during movement execution. As they dance, their focus shifts from movement sequence, to mechanics, to body alignment, to self-cueing or evaluation, to the movement of those around them in the dance space, to topics unrelated to dance, etc. Verbal cues help students to focus their attention in specific ways. Without these cues, students may attempt to concentrate on too many, or unnecessary, aspects of the movement and thus struggle to successfully execute or learn the material. Verbal cues extend beyond the verbal instruction of movement. They provide students with additional information about how to approach the movement or improve in their performance. When offering verbal cues, the dance teacher should consider the students' vocabulary and current understanding of dance in selecting what to cue and how to deliver the cue. The teacher is also mindful of the intention for the verbal cue and when it is offered.

Verbal cues that direct the students' attention and focus to a specific aspect of movement are most effective when offered prior to movement execution. If the teacher wants students to consider and focus on a feature of execution while they practice, the verbal cue needs to be offered prior to movement execution. For example, following the demonstration of a movement exercise, the teacher offers technical reminders for the students to consider as they dance. They are prompted to feel the sole of the foot brushing the floor throughout the exercise. The students have now been mentally prepared and will be more likely to physically execute the desired action.

The intention of the verbal cue may be to provide reminders of movement sequence. Sequential cues are typically given as students are dancing. Here, the teacher strategically times the calling of the movement sequence to aid the students' memory retention. In this instance, lead-in timing is crucial. Lead-in time refers to when the cue is given in relation to the initiation of the movement execution. Verbal cues provided too far in advance or right as the action is occurring are not helpful to the student. If offered too early, the student may become distracted by the cue or forget its intent altogether. If offered too late, the student cannot benefit from the cue. Rather, it is best to deliver these prompts during the preceding movement with the appropriate amount of time remaining for the student to react to the cue. This skill often takes practice for the novice dance teacher.

Additionally, verbal cues can direct the student to the immediacy of the movement prompt or even the quality that the teacher wants to see in the movement performance. Students might be prompted to smile, travel more, or make something sharper while they are dancing. The verbal cue may be a single word, such as "Reach!" or could be a one- to two-sentence explanation of what is wanted. "Remember to engage the abdominals as you hinge into the position." Short and concise cues can be useful to elicit immediate reactionary response, whereas longer stated cues prepare students to focus their attention on a specific aspect of the movement.

The vocal tone and pitch of a verbal cue can indicate specific meaning. The tone of the teacher's voice can carry positive or negative connotations. For example, the dance teacher may call out a phrase such as "Extend through space!" while the students are performing. If the teacher's tone is snappy and curt, the students may assume they are dancing poorly, and the teacher is frustrated with them. However, if the teacher's tone is spirited and cheerful, the students may be encouraged to dance bigger. Further, the tone and pitch of the verbal cue can provide musical cues to the student. The vocal quality and manner in which words are enunciated by the teacher can guide students to better understand timing and rhythm or qualitative nuances of the movement.

PACING

The pacing of a lesson plan affects not only the content of the class and material that is taught and learned but also the attention and focus of students. **Pacing** is the speed at which the teacher moves through the lesson plan. Progressing quickly through a lesson plan may allow the teacher to present all of the prepared content; however, students may not have sufficient time to learn the movement or concepts. Yet, spending too much time on a single exercise or aspect of the lesson plan could cause students to lose focus or fail to achieve the learning objective. If the tap teacher keeps 7-year-olds standing in the center, working on shuffle exercises for half of the class time, those students will most likely lose focus and become tired or bored. As a result, they may begin to socialize or present other disruptive behaviors.

The teacher must be aware of students' physical, mental, and emotional levels and how they are learning. How long will the students remain at the ballet *barre*? How much time will be spent allowing students to practice jazz leaps across the floor? How much time should the teacher take to explain a movement or concept? Depending upon the age of the student, attention spans can range from one to 15 minutes before focus is lost.[7] Additional consideration should be given to the number of students in the class as well as the amount of time it will take to find or start the music, confer lesson plan notes, or make general lesson plan decisions. When the teacher takes extra class time to work individually with students or groups or pauses too long to consider their next steps for the class, the attention and motivation of students can wane or be lost. While pacing may be factored into the creation of the lesson plan, the dance teacher should be cognizant of how the class is progressing in real time. They may find it necessary to apply modifications to the lesson plan to keep students engaged. Making effective decisions regarding the pacing of a dance class comes with experience.

FIGURE 13.6 A teacher kneels to communicate with young dance students.
Source: Photo by Jeffrey Smith/Western Kentucky University.

BUILDING BLOCKS OF EFFECTIVE TEACHING

Every class of dance students will be different, and there is no perfect method for teaching students. There are, however, some considerations that often prove helpful when teaching dance. The following list is not exhaustive by any means, nor will these strategies work in every situation. It is up to the dance teacher to recognize the learning needs of the class and adapt accordingly.

- **Speak clearly and with confidence.** If you, as the teacher, doubt yourself, the students definitely will!
- **Consider the sound level within the room.** Are you speaking loudly enough for all students to hear you regardless of if they are on the other side of the room, facing away from you, or upside down in a stretch? If there is music playing, can your verbal instructions and cues be heard above the music?
- **Face toward younger students when teaching.** Direct eye contact and facing will help younger minds remain engaged and focused. If facing students as you teach, you should mirror their movement; your left foot is their right foot. Be sure that you also reverse your verbal cues when mirroring students. This may take practice!
- **Make eye contact with your students.** Looking each dancer in the eye helps them know that you see them. With younger dancers, it is often helpful to bend or kneel down when speaking with them so that you are eye level with them. Conversation with you becomes less intimidating in this format. Be careful that you do not consistently talk to older students through the mirror. Turn and directly face them as you speak.
- **Create connections between classes.** Rather than diving right into the new material, quickly review material or an aspect previously learned to help students make mental connections to what they will learn that day. Make sure that students realize the material learned in one class connects to the next class. Remind students at the beginning of class what was worked on or achieved in the last class. At the end of the class, give them something to think about or work on in preparation for the next week. Remember, many students may only attend dance class once a week, and a lot can happen in their weekly lives. Help them make connections between classes.
- **Consider the learning styles of the students.** Do not rely on one modality of presentation or delivery. Visually show the movement, verbally say the names of the steps, offer the counts for the movement, and provide a way for the students to connect rhythmically and dynamically to the movement. Perhaps you scat or clap the rhythm of the phrase.
- **Have the students switch lines.** Students who are shy, disengaged, or lack confidence often remain in the back of the room. Encourage all students to have an opportunity to stand in the front and learn from a different spot in the room.
- **Be sure to practice at the appropriate tempo before adding music.** Students will struggle if they learn movement at one tempo, yet the speed changes drastically once music is added.
- **Ask students questions; probe their minds.** This helps the students learn and encourages problem-solving and critical thinking. You may be surprised to learn what they are thinking or in what ways they may be struggling.
- **Be creative!** Preschool-age students love to play. Engaging them through imagination and creative dance can help you achieve your learning objectives for the class. Create a balance between work and play. Discover games, activities, or songs that they like that can be used as incentive to accomplish the work (learning a skill or exercise).

248 Presentation

- **Have a through line within the class.** Content should not bounce randomly from one exercise to the next. Rather, each exercise should build upon each other to accomplish a goal. Chapter 9 discusses the importance of learning objectives and goals when lesson planning.
- **Do not make promises that cannot be kept.** Do not guarantee that a student can be a leader next time. You will most likely forget! Find a system to track leaders, if you use them, so that every student gets an opportunity in this role.
- **If students are developing bad habits, consider how you as the teacher could be contributing.** Bad habits often result from incomplete explanations of how to do a step, failing to see and correct student errors, or progressing students before they are ready.

CHAPTER SUMMARY

The application of instructional strategies that are appropriate to the students' age, skill level, class dynamics, and subject matter, can assist in students' learning and retention of information. Dance teachers select methods of presenting material that will best enhance student learning. Movement can be delivered through visual presentation, verbal instruction, or guided discovery. Each mode has its benefits and limitations. Visual presentation provides an image that students can reproduce and encourages the students to use their visual sense when learning movement. Demonstrators can model accurate positions and movement execution for the student to imitate. During verbal instruction, students must tune into their auditory sense. This mode reinforces the labels given to movement skills, and greater information and direction can be quickly spoken to students. Through guided discovery, the learning shifts to a student-centered approach and encourages critical thinking and problem-solving among the students. The teacher may divide the presentation of movement into chunks to better assist the student in processing and retaining movement.

The dance teacher also considers how the students are applying attentional focus throughout the class, recognizing the benefits and limitations of an internal and external focus. The use of imagery can assist in verbal instructions and cues by providing mental pictures to which the students can relate as they attempt skills and phrases. This is a helpful tool in directing the attentional focus of students.

Cueing helps the students understand how and in what manner to execute movement. Students may receive visual or tactile cues by watching the teacher's movements or gestures or through the use of physical touch. Verbal cues emphasize the language-movement connection and provide oral reminders of movement details. Finally, the effective dance teacher is mindful that there are a variety of strategies to utilize when instructing a class of students. Each individual and group of students are different. Recognizing differences and considering the task at hand can help teachers determine an appropriate strategy for effective teaching.

PRACTICAL APPLICATIONS

1 Why does the teacher incorporate various instructional strategies throughout a single class?

2 Devise a movement exercise. Practice teaching this exercise to a peer utilizing only verbal instruction. What is the effect? What challenge/s did instructing movement through only this method present?

3 Consider how the method of chunking assists you, as a dancer, when learning. What patterns emerge? How does the dance teacher determine to chunk movement when teaching students of various ages and levels?

4 Consider how you apply attentional focus within your own dance.

   a Do you tend to apply an internal or external?

   b Does this focus vary among dance genres?

   c Which attentional focus provides you with the most consistent success?

   d Why do you think that is?

5 How can the dance teacher aid students of various ages encompass an internal and external focus in movement execution?

6 Compose a learning objective and corresponding movement exercise. Practice teaching this exercise to students/peers with the use of various forms of imagery. Which forms were the most effective for your composed exercise and learning objective?

7 Compose a movement exercise and teach it to a student or peer. Provide only visual cues for the student.

   a Compose a new movement exercise for the student to learn. This time, provide only verbal cues.

   b Compose a third exercise for the student to learn. Now offer the student visual, verbal, and tactile cues.

   c Compare the outcomes. Which worked best? Why?

8 Imagine that you are teaching a 60-minute dance class. You are 40 minutes into the class and not yet halfway through your lesson plan. How will you decide what to keep and omit from your lesson plan?

NOTES

1 Susan R. Koff, "Innovative Instructional Strategies for Teaching Dance," *Dance Education in Practice* 2, no. 2 (2016): 15.
2 Debra J. Rose and Robert W. Christina, *A Multilevel Approach to the Study of Motor Control and Learning* (San Francisco, CA: Benjamin Cummings, 2008), 218.
3 Rose and Christina, *A Multilevel Approach*, 219.
4 Marliese Kimmerle, "Lateral Bias in Dance Teaching," *Journal of Physical Education, Recreation & Dance* 72, no. 5 (2001): 34.
5 Clare Guss-West and Gabriele Wulf. "Attentional Focus in Classical Ballet: A Survey of Professional Dancers," *Journal of Dance Medicine & Science* 20, no. 1 (2016): 24.
6 Guss-West and Wulf. "Attentional Focus in Classical Ballet," 23.
7 Rich Korb, *Motivating Defiant and Disruptive Students to Learn Positive Classroom Management Strategies* (Thousand Oaks: Corwin, 2012), 17–18.

BIBLIOGRAPHY

Christenson R., and Barney, D. "The Spectrum of Teaching Styles: Style F-Guided Discovery." *OAHPERD Journal* XLVI, no. 2 (2010): 14–16.

Dearborn, Karen, and Rachael Ross. "Dance Learning and the Mirror: Comparison Study of Dance Phrase Learning with and Without Mirrors." *Journal of Dance Education* 6, no. 4 (2006): 109–115.

Dryburgh, Jamieson. "Unsettling Materials: Lively Tensions in Learning through 'Set Materials' in the Dance Technique Class." *Journal of Dance & Somatic Practices* 10, no. 1 (2018): 35–50.

Ellison, Douglas W., and Amelia Mays Woods. "Deliberate Practice as a Tool for Effective Teaching in Physical Education." *Journal of Physical Education, Recreation & Dance* 87, no. 2 (2016): 15–19.

Guss-West, Clare. *Attention and Focus in Dance: Enhancing Power, Precision, and Artistry.* Champaign, IL: Human Kinetics, 2021.

Guss-West, Clare, and Gabriele Wulf. "Attentional Focus in Classical Ballet: A Survey of Professional Dancers." *Journal of Dance Medicine & Science* 20, no. 1 (2016): 23–29.

Haibach-Beach, Pamela S., Greg Reid, and Douglas Holden Collier. *Motor Learning and Development.* 2ndd ed. Champaign, IL: Human Kinetics, 2018.

Harbonnier-Topin, Nicole, and Jean-Marie Barbier. "'How Seeing Helps Doing, and Doing Allows to See More': The Process of Imitation in the Dance Class." *Research in Dance Education* 13, no. 3 (2012): 301–325.

Henley, Matthew. "Sensation, Perception, and Choice in the Dance Classroom." *Journal of Dance Education* 14, no. 3 (2014): 95–100.

Hsia, Lu-Ho, and Gwo-Jen Hwang. "From Reflective Thinking to Learning Engagement Awareness: A Reflective Thinking Promoting Approach to Improve Students' Dance Performance, Self-efficacy and Task Load in Flipped Learning." *British Journal of Educational Technology* 51, no. 6 (2020): 2461–2477.

Krasnow, Donna, and Virginia Wilmerding. *Motor Learning and Control for Dance: Principles and Practices for Performers and Teachers.* Champaign, IL: Human Kinetics, 2015.

Martens, Rainer. *Successful Coaching.* Updated 2nd ed. Champaign, IL: Human Kinetics, 1997.

Park, Jin-Hoon, Heather Wilde, and Charles H. Shea. "Part-Whole Practice of Movement Sequences." *Journal of Motor Behavior* 36, no. 1 (2004): 51–61.

Rhein, Zipi, and Eli Vakil. "Motor Sequence Learning and the Effect of Context on Transfer from Part-to-Whole and from Whole-to-Part." *Psychological Research* 82, no. 3 (2018): 448–458.

Rose, Debra J., and Robert W. Christina. *A Multilevel Approach to the Study of Motor Control and Learning.* San Francisco, CA: Benjamin Cummings, 2008.

Schmidt, Richard A., and Timothy Donald Lee. *Motor Control and Learning: A Behavioral Emphasis.* Champaign, IL: Human Kinetics, 1999.

Schupp, Karen. "Teaching Collaborative Skills through Dance: Isolating the Parts to Strengthen the Whole." *Journal of Dance Education* 15, no. 4 (2015): 152–158.

Stanton, Erica. "Doing, Re-Doing and Undoing: Practice, Repetition and Critical Evaluation as Mechanisms for Learning in a Dance Technique Class 'Laboratory.'" *Theatre, Dance and Performance Training* 2, no. 1 (2011): 86–98.

Wulf, Gabriele. *Attention and Motor Skill Learning.* Champaign, IL: Human Kinetics, 2007.

CHAPTER 14

Practice Methods

> **Box 14.1 Chapter Objectives**
>
> After reading this chapter, you will be able to:
>
> - Identify and implement effective methods of providing dance practice
> - Distinguish between whole and part practice, including segmentation, fractionization, and simplification
> - Recognize the positive and negative elements of various teaching and practice tools that can be incorporated into teaching dance

> **Box 14.2 Chapter Vocabulary**
>
> blocked practice
> fractionization
> instructional strategy
> mental practice
> overlearning
> part practice
> practice variability
> random practice
> segmentation
> simplification
> task complexity
> task organization
> whole practice

Practice is an essential element in the development of movement skill. Individuals practice to better understand, execute, apply, and retain ideas. In dance, practice is necessary for the student to both physically and cognitively learn skills and concepts. Therefore, it is important that students learn effective ways to practice and have practice time afforded to them. This chapter explores the concept of practice and strategies the effective dance teacher may implement to aid in student learning and retention.

DOI: 10.4324/b22952-20

WHOLE AND PART PRACTICE

The dance teacher may approach practice in two distinct manners, either through the whole method or the part method. Each mode can assist students' learning and progress, yet the effective teacher discerns when and how to offer each option when having students practice. Whole and part methods can be utilized as the dance teacher presents material as well.

Whole Practice

When embracing **whole practice**, the entire skill or exercise is practiced by students. Any trouble areas may be examined and broken down as needed; however, attention remains on practicing the whole movement. This process can also be referred to as the whole-part-whole method. Whole practice applies easily to a single movement skill. Rather than breaking down an *assemblé*, the entire step (whole part) will be demonstrated by the teacher, and the students will practice their execution attempts. If necessary, the teacher may then have students explore the movement by having students begin in a *dégagé fondu* so they can just practice the *sauté* and closing of the legs in the air before returning to execution of the whole movement.

Whole practice can also be used in teaching an entire exercise. In a modern dance class, the teacher may demonstrate an entire leg swing combination. The students then practice the whole exercise. Should the teacher notice a need, they could isolate a part of the exercise that may be confusing or challenging. Perhaps the second portion of the exercise requires a quick changing of the feet or a distinct timing that needs to be executed. After discussing and practicing that part, the teacher then returns attention and practice to the whole exercise.

Whole practice focuses on the exercise as an entity rather than breaking down the parts of the exercise. This mode is effective when encouraging students to quickly learn combinations, or when students demonstrate the ability to learn entire movement phrase at once. A dance teacher may often encourage advanced students to learn an entire progression of varying movement across the floor rather than working a single skill. The whole method is not feasible when teaching lengthy movement patterns or when working with students unable to retain complex movement patterns.

Part Practice

In contrast, **part practice** is a progressive approach to addressing material in which each phrase or component of the exercise is practiced before moving on to the next part. Rather than teaching the completed step or entire phrase, the movement is broken into smaller parts to begin with to facilitate learning and execution. This method is commonly used within the dance class and is easily recognized by dancers.

Some movement has natural divisions that make determining the various parts easier. For example, a basic turn on one leg has a preparation, a push to the turning position, the turn itself, and the landing or exit out of the turn. The teacher may have students practice stepping into the preparation, or pushing into position, and then maintaining a balance. A center combination may be easily divided by four or eight count patterns or sequences of movement that allow for a natural divide from the whole combination.

Generally, a division of movement can be created between preparation and action, but not necessarily between action and follow-through.[1] An example can be seen in the practice of a turning "C" leap in a jazz dance class. A series of *chaîné* turns into two steps with bent knees could be established as the preparation for the leap. This part can then be practiced, helping the student understand arm position or the level during the turns. The teacher may choose to add the brush of the leading leg to a back attitude position to allow the students to discover the body mechanics of the initial action. The leap off and lift of the second leg to a back attitude along with the natural step out of the leap are difficult to execute separately; therefore, these must be practiced as one unit. Ultimately, it is up to the teacher, or the student, to determine where parts fall within an exercise. The dance teacher must use their best judgment, knowing their students' mental capacity, learning stage, and skill level. Part practice can often help students chunk longer movement sequences to aid in memorization, practice, and recall.

The part method of teaching can be further broken down into three approaches: fractionization, segmentation, and simplification. The goal of each approach is to facilitate learning by removing an aspect of the whole. This could be teaching small movement segments at a time, reducing the complexity, or removing the use of a body part or eliminating a spatial or temporal variable so that students can focus on one part of the movement at time.

Segmentation

Segmentation is a progressive part method where one part is taught and practiced, then the next part is added, and so forth until the whole exercise is learned. This is a standard approach utilized in dance classes. Phrases, exercises, and combinations that include a sequence of components can easily be taught utilizing segmentation. The simplest example of this method is when the dance instructor teaches choreography. Students learn the choreography part by part, building to the whole movement sequence. Phrase A is taught, followed by phrase B, and then those two are practiced in sequence. Next, phrase C is taught, and all three parts are practiced in sequence. Students may then chunk movement patterns in terms of the progressing segments.

Fractionization

Fractionization is a part method wherein movement is separated between body parts and learned and practiced in isolation before combining the movement together as a whole. This approach can be used with a skill or a phrase that incorporates differing movement with the upper and lower body. This approach allows students to focus on the motor pattern of one body part at a time. An excellent example of the need for this approach can be found in a jazz dance class. Consider a basic 4-count grapevine movement of the feet. An arm pattern can then be added to the footwork: reach up, reach down, reach forward, reach side. A head isolation pattern could also be added. For the beginning student, learning the different movements for the legs, arms, and head can prove difficult and confusing to execute. However, if the teacher leads the students through the footwork and offers time to practice and embody that part of the phrase before adding the arm and head movements, the student will discover greater success at completing the whole exercise.

Simplification

The part method of simplification is just as it sounds. Here, the movement is simplified first upon teaching to the student. **Simplification** enables the student to focus on the basic mechanics or essential elements of the movement rather than all aspects at once. Once the student is able to execute the simplified movement, then the other variables can be incorporated. For example, the dance teacher may demonstrate an inversion in modern class. The students will be shown what the entire movement looks like so that they are aware of the ultimate goal. However, the inversion is then broken into parts so that students can start with a simple action and progress to the complete movement. In a separate tap dance example, the teacher may simplify a Hines riff into parts as they teach. Students learn the action of the initiating foot – a forward 3-count riff to a heel stand. Then, the coordinated backward spank of the opposite foot and landing on the ball of the foot is taught. Once students understand the individual parts of the step executed by each foot, they learn how to coordinate the timing of the five sounds, which alternate between the two feet. In other dance examples, students could remove a turn element and simply execute a balance, lower the height of the leg and focus instead on placement and technique, or execute a step flat footed rather than on *demi-pointe*. The tempo could also be slowed down.

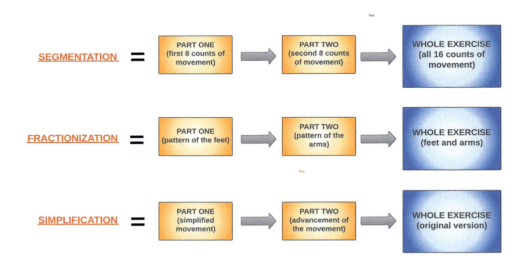

FIGURE 14.1 Diagram depicts the part methods of segmentation, fractionization, and simplification.

Whole versus Part: Which to Choose?

The dance teacher considers the individual learner and the intention behind the practice session when selecting between whole and part methods of practice. The teacher may recognize the students' focus and engagement on a particular day, which could then dictate the need of manner of part demonstration. One week, students may be prepared to mentally comprehend and attend to multiple parts. The next week, however, a single movement may provide a sufficient part during learning given the students' level of motivation and energy.

The teacher also looks at the movement itself. The complexity and organization of the movement or task may require either whole or part practice. **Task complexity** refers to the quantity of the various parts, the level challenge of the parts, and the amount of attention and focus required to execute the movement. How physically demanding is the movement for the students? Does the movement contain a lot of parts that require attention, or is it a basic movement that requires minimal mental processing? For example, a six step in hip-hop dance would be a movement of low task complexity; however, a windmill would be an example of high task complexity. Keep in mind the same movement may prove high in complexity for a beginner yet low in complexity for an advanced dancer. A standard tap time step may be high in task complexity for the novice dancer yet low in task complexity for the advanced dancer. The novice dancer may practice the time step in parts to acquire basic comprehension of and skill in execution. The advanced dancer may practice the entire time step to work speed and clarity.

Task organization refers to the manner in which components of the movement are related. An axel turn is a movement where the parts are interdependent upon one another. One could mark the pathway of the leg, but the successful execution of the axel requires the full momentum of the initial leg swing to the side coordinated with the jump and tuck of the supporting leg, the bending of the working leg close to the body, and the energy of the arms pulling into a circle or sweeping out and upward over the head. The teacher considers the following question to determine task organization. Can the parts be easily separated, or are they dependent upon each other for success of movement execution?[2] If the movement task is low in complexity yet high in organization, such as a series of *glissades* or a Lindy step in jazz dance, the whole method proves more effective. If the movement is high in complexity yet low in organization, such as a *tour jeté* in ballet or an "X" roll in modern dance, the part method should be selected. In determining whether to utilize the whole versus part method of practice, one should consider the nature of the skill being taught along with the students' capabilities.[3]

TABLE 14.1 Identifying criteria to consider when choosing the whole method or the part method.

Low task complexity	+	High task organization	=	**Whole Practice**
High task complexity	+	Low task organization	=	**Part Practice**

METHODS OF PRACTICE

The dance teacher may also use the strategies of blocked practice, random practice, and practice variability within a lesson plan. **Blocked practice** occurs when the student repeatedly works on, or drills, the same step or phrase over a length of time. In a jazz dance class, students may execute a six-step prep into a *pirouette*. This exercise is repeated multiple times across the floor as students focus on improving their turning ability. **Random practice** occurs when the student moves from one skill to another either within the same combination or throughout the class. This type of practice can include approaching a particular skill in varied ways or moving through a range of different skills and exercises. For example, the students may execute a six-step preparation into a *pirouette* followed by another phrase of separate vocabulary that continues to focus on the use of the student's spotting abilities. In contrast, students may practice leg swings, then a locomotor pattern that transitions down to and up from the floor, and then practice prances. Each exercise shifts the student's focus and practice toward a new skill.

While blocked practice may help short-term improvement of a skill, it can lead to an inaccurate sense of learning. After so many repetitions, the student may feel confident that they have achieved the skill, but they later return to the movement and realize they did not maintain their ability to successfully execute the skill. This is often the case with flash steps in tap dance. A student may drill pickups until it seems they are able to execute the step, yet when they return days later, they are unable to produce the sounds consistently. Random practice has proven to lead to better retention and generalization of a skill and improve the students' adaptability in skills and concepts.[4] The student is forced to generate a motor plan during each varied attempt of the movement, thus avoiding automaticity in execution. The structure of a traditional ballet class follows random practice, interweaving exercises that focus on slow and controlled actions with dynamic and quick movement. The dancer moves from *plié* to *tendu* to *rond de jambe*, etc., while maintaining alignment and turnout throughout the various exercises. A jazz dance class may move across the floor executing different skills – perhaps kicks, then turns, and then leaps – within each new exercise.

The dance teacher strives for students to develop the ability to generalize and transfer a skill or principle from one situation to another. Consider Fitts and Posner's third stage of learning or Gentile's second stage of learning as discussed in Chapter 5. Beginners must first understand how to do the skill, yet in the later learning stage, they vary the performance of movement allowing for deeper learning. This is accomplished through **practice variability**, which requires the practice of a skill or concept to be offered through different approaches rather than the exact same way each time. Within a class session, students can be provided both blocked and random practice opportunities. Imagine the theme of the class is the concept of spotting. Now consider two approaches the teacher could take. In scenario one, the teacher could have students work turns, in the same direction, throughout the class. Even if the position of the turn is varied, the students continue to turn the same direction, focusing on a snap or two of the head as they complete one or two revolutions. This would be an example of blocked practice. In scenario two, the teacher could have students practice a basic locomotor pattern, such as a Lindy step, and change directions during each execution. Students are encouraged to use their eyes to spot the various facings. Next, the teacher could have students drill the pattern of a six-step preparation

TABLE 14.2 Delineating blocked practice, random practice, and practice variability.

Type of Practice	Definition	Dance Application
Blocked Practice	The student repeatedly works on, or drills, the same step or phrase over a length of time.	• The last half of the dance class focuses on only *fouetté* turns. • Five-count riffs are repeatedly drilled across the floor.
Random Practice	The student moves from one skill to another either within the same combination or throughout the class.	• A traveling ballet exercise includes a collection of vocabulary and skills. • The lesson plan moves from *battements* to turns to leaps.
Practice Variability	The student practices a skill or concept through different approaches.	• Tap dance students practice drawbacks, traveling directly backward with the feet parallel, then with the feet crossing while traveling backward, then practices crossing the feet while traveling the movement sideways. • The modern dancer practices a contraction while seated; the contraction is then practiced while standing; the contraction is later incorporated into a turn.

(executed as triplets) into a jazz *pirouette*. The next exercise could have the second set of triplets become a turn, causing the student to spot one direction for the turning triplets and the opposite direction for the *pirouette*. Here, students have engaged in both random and blocked practice. Practice variability provides the student with a broad range of experiences to help them learn. The constant change in practice approach helps students to learn to apply the movement idea in different ways.

AMOUNT OF PRACTICE

Dance students work to not only learn a skill but to maintain their technique and abilities. They practice movement skills routinely either during class or on their own outside of class. **Overlearning** is continuous practice after a skill has been acquired and performance has plateaued. Overlearning allows the dance student to continue training their bodies and develop muscle memory. When a student overlearns a skill, they are striving for the consistent and successful execution of the skill that can be assimilated into various movement patterns. For example, the competitive jazz dancer may overlearn *à la seconde* turns. There are many elements of this turn that must be coordinated together, therefore repetitive practice must occur for the dancer to produce a higher success rate. The tap dancer often overlearns steps such as closed thirds or slurps, pickups, and single wings for consistent articulation of sound. The hip-hop dancer may overlearn power moves so that they can be readily executed as needed.

Overlearning can have advantages as well as disadvantages for the dance student. Energy expenditure and cognitive focus can be decreased when an individual overlearns a movement skill as muscle memory kicks in, allowing the dancer to focus on an aspect of performance other than the fundamental body mechanics of the movement execution. Movement execution is reinforced, and learning is maximized. Yet, there can come a point when overlearning can produce negative effects. During this type of practice session, the student may present frustration if improvement does not occur or if performance level deteriorates. A decrease in ability could be the result of several factors. The dancer may become bored during overlearning, fatigued, or simply lose motivation in their performance.

The craft of teaching includes determining the amount of practice time to offer students. The dance teacher must tune into their students' physical and mental capacities for the day. They must recognize the fine line between providing enough practice for learning to occur and not so much that students become bored or discouraged. It can be helpful to remind students why skills are repeatedly practiced throughout a class or term and why practice outside of class is encouraged. Teachers should explain that plateaus are a normal part of the learning process. It is during the plateau that the student can shift their focus to a different aspect of skill acquisition, such as enhanced dynamics or slow control, rather than ideal movement execution.

TEACHING AND PRACTICE TOOLS

Teachers often use equipment in the dance studio, such as the mirror or ballet *barre*, as teaching and learning tools. For example, the dance teacher often encourages students to look at themselves in the mirror as they practice so they can observe and assess their reproduction of movement shapes and lines or movement execution. Or, a teacher often has students spend a considerable amount of time at the *barre* during a traditional ballet class. Students typically hold on to the *barre* for support during approximately a third of the ballet class. The effective dance teacher is mindful of how tools, such as the mirror or *barre*, are utilized and whether they help or hinder skill acquisition.

Mirrors

The mirror is a fixture in the vast majority of dance studios. Students are encouraged to use the mirror as a learning tool for visual presentation and individual feedback. The mirror helps to provide an external cue about the outward shape or appearance. For the novice student, the mirror can be incredibly helpful when they have not yet developed accurate proprioceptive responses. Advanced students may utilize the mirror as they self-cue their movement execution.

There are also negative aspects of using the mirror. The mirror can become a distraction for students of varied ages and learning levels. For example, young students may turn their attention away from the teacher and to their own reflection in the mirror as they creatively pose or make faces. For advanced students, the mirror can distract from their kinesthetic awareness and development. Students often develop a reliance on visual cues from the mirror. This reliance is formed during the early stages of learning and can carry into their later learning stages. This visual reliance on the mirror may disrupt the ability of the advanced student to learn information kinesthetically.

It is also important to note that the feedback received from the mirror is relative to the facing and perspective of the viewer. The mirror does not provide a three-dimensional view of movement. Additionally, the use of mirrors can heighten a student's self-consciousness and body image awareness. Mirrors can increase negative competitiveness among students, whether it is in regard to self-image or skill level. On the flip side, a mirror can also improve the self-esteem of lower-level students when they see their improved movement attempts reflected in the mirror.

Ballet *Barre*

The *barre* is meant to provide support to the ballet dancer during the early portions of the class. The use of the *barre* enables the dancer to train toward correct alignment throughout the body and supports the dance during the practice of certain body positions and movements. Yet, the dance student will engage muscles slightly differently when in the center than when they are at the *barre*. This is in response to stability and control needs. A *grand plié* at the *barre* is significantly easier to execute correctly than when performed in the center without something to hold onto for balance support. When done in the center, muscles must activate more, and for some students, differently. Students tend to shift their weight onto the standing leg less when at the *barre* than when executing the same skill in the center, and the muscles of the supporting leg are not activated to the same extent as when the student is in the center of the room. Imagine the *arabesque penché* performed in the center versus at the *barre*. The dancer will find this movement more difficult to perform in the center than when holding onto the *barre*. Though *barre* work is meant to prepare the dancer for center work, muscle activation patterns differ between exercises done at the *barre* and those executed in the center. Therefore, the effective dance teacher shares these aspects within their instruction.

Miscellaneous Props

The teacher may use other miscellaneous props, such as rhythm sticks or scarves, to aid students' learning. Rhythm sticks can help students learn the musical components of tempo and rhythm in connection to movement. Scarves can help students move through space in specific ways. Pulling a scarf to the right or left as they step side and ball change can reinforce directional pathways. Students engage with these props as they practice, which can make the practice session more interesting to the student. Tangible tools within the classroom can enhance student learning, as long as the teacher makes clear, age-appropriate connections between the movement and the use of the prop.

Mental Practice

Mental practice can help dance students attain new skills or prepare for movement execution or even a dance performance. During **mental practice**, the student cognitively works through a movement or phrase rather than engaging in physical execution. As students work to acquire a skill, the combination of physical and mental practice can prove beneficial. For more skilled dance students, mental practice can also prove to be an effective learning strategy.

Mental practice allows the student to step back and connect thoughtfully with the requirements of the skill. The student may think through the actions necessary to execute each skill, imagining themselves performing each sequential step. For example, the student may visualize themself performing a challenging flash step in tap, such as repetitive shuffle grab-offs, or a spiral turn in modern class. During mental practice, the same neural pathways are activated to plan and execute movement as if physically practicing.[5] Finally, mental practice can be a helpful tool for dancers who are recovering from injuries and unable to physically participate. This form of practice allows the body to rest and reserve energy while remaining engaged in the learning process.

Somatics

Somatic-based movement exercises enable students to focus internally on the sensations and experiences perceived within the body while moving. Somatic work helps the dance student connect their mind and body. Through the application of various somatic techniques and exercises, students can discover body awareness, improve balance, and enhance their use of breath within movement. The dance teacher might consider including genre-appropriate somatic exercises in the warm-up or cool-down portion of class, or dedicating an occasional class period to somatic work. Entire books intently explore this topic and are helpful in further understanding somatic work and the specific ways to incorporate it into a genre-specific dance class.

Improvisation

The inclusion of dance improvisation can facilitate student learning. Improvisation allows students to self-select movement along with time and qualitative components. During improvisation, students experience sensory explorations and make new observations about movement or concepts. The brain must work to integrate this different sensory stimuli. Students learn to navigate spatial conflicts and balance disturbances as they spontaneously create movement and react to others moving around them. The act of improvisation may motivate some students by providing a break in the normal routine and offering an additional perspective. Concentration is broadened, and students are encouraged to take risks with their dancing. Additionally, improvisation can assist students in their expressive capabilities.

CHAPTER SUMMARY

For a student to embody movement concepts and acquire skill, practice must occur. The dance teacher may guide students through whole or part practice depending on the individual student, the purpose of the exercise, and the complexity of the movement. The student may practice entire movement patterns, or they may follow part-related approaches, such as segmentation, fractionization, or simplification. The dance teacher may incorporate opportunity for blocked and/or random practice throughout the class. The amount of time spent in practice may vary, and the teacher should help students recognize the effect of overlearning. The dance teacher delicately balances the use of learning tools – such as the mirror, ballet *barre*, mental practice, or improvisation – along with practice variability to help students improve abilities and attain learning objectives.

PRACTICAL APPLICATIONS

1   How does the dance teacher choose whether to use whole or part practice?

2   Devise a movement exercise. Determine the ways in which part practice could be offered for the exercise.

3   Identify the ways in which you, as a dancer, have engaged in blocked and random practice in a recent class.

4   How can the teacher provide practice variability in a dance class?

5   How do you identify with the concept of overlearning? What steps can the dance teacher take to help students when overlearning occurs?

6   Consider the teaching tools discussed in this chapter. In what ways do you believe the mirror and ballet *barre* help or hinder the learning process?

7   How can mental practice and improvisation help a student learn?

NOTES

1   Rainer Martens, *Successful Coaching*, Updated 2nd ed. (Champaign, IL: Human Kinetics, 1997), 81.
2   Martens, *Successful Coaching*, 80.
3   Debra J. Rose and Robert W. Christina, *A Multilevel Approach to the Study of Motor Control and Learning* (San Francisco, CA: Benjamin Cummings, 2008), 255.
4   Donna Krasnow and Virginia Wilmerding, *Motor Learning and Control for Dance: Principles and Practices for Performers and Teachers* (Champaign, IL: Human Kinetics, 2015), 225.
5   Pamela S. Haibach-Beach, Greg Reid and Douglas Holden Collier, *Motor Learning and Development*, 2nd ed. (Champaign, IL: Human Kinetics, 2018), 362.

BIBLIOGRAPHY

Berardi, Gigi. "Attention and Focus in Dance: Enhancing Power, Precision, and Artistry." *Journal of Dance Medicine & Science* 25, no. 1 (2021): 72–73.

Dearborn, Karen, and Rachael Ross. "Dance Learning and the Mirror: Comparison Study of Dance Phrase Learning With and Without Mirrors." *Journal of Dance Education* 6, no. 4 (2006): 109–115.

Foster, Rory. *Ballet Pedagogy: The Art of Teaching*. Gainesville, FL: University Press of Florida, 2010.

Guss-West, Clare, and Gabriele Wulf. "Attentional Focus in Classical Ballet: A Survey Of Professional Dancers." *Journal of Dance Medicine & Science* 20, no. 1 (2016): 23–29.

Haibach-Beach, Pamela S., Greg Reid, and Douglas Holden Collier. *Motor Learning and Development*. 2nd ed. Champaign, IL: Human Kinetics, 2018.

Harbonnier-Topin, Nicole, and Jean-Marie Barbier. "'How Seeing Helps Doing, and Doing Allows to See More': The Process of Imitation in the Dance Class." *Research in Dance Education* 13, no. 3 (2012): 301–325.

Kimmerle, Marliese. "Lateral Bias in Dance Teaching." *Journal of Physical Education, Recreation & Dance* 72, no. 5 (2001): 34–37.

Koff, Susan R. "Innovative Instructional Strategies for Teaching Dance." *Dance Education in Practice* 2, no. 2 (2016): 13–17.

Korb, Rich. *Motivating Defiant and Disruptive Students to Learn Positive Classroom Management Strategies*. Thousand Oaks: Corwin, 2012.

Krasnow, Donna, and Virginia Wilmerding. *Motor Learning and Control for Dance: Principles and Practices for Performers and Teachers*. Champaign, IL: Human Kinetics, 2015.

Martens, Rainer. *Successful Coaching*. Updated 2nd ed. Champaign, IL: Human Kinetics, 1997.

Martinell, Nicole Antonette. "Emerging Themes on the Efficacy of Ballet *Barre* Work and Its Connection to Center Work: An Investigatory Study." *Journal of Dance Education* 9, no. 4 (2009): 103–109.

Rose, Debra J., and Robert W. Christina. *A Multilevel Approach to the Study of Motor Control and Learning*. San Francisco, CA: Benjamin Cummings, 2008.

Schmidt, Richard A., and Timothy Donald Lee. *Motor Control and Learning: A Behavioral Emphasis*. Champaign, IL: Human Kinetics, 1999.

Sherman, Nestor W., and Cheryl Coker. "Teaching Approach Depends on Skill Level." *Journal of Physical Education, Recreation & Dance* 71, no. 7 (2000): 6.

Stanton, Erica. "Doing, Re-Doing and Undoing: Practice, Repetition and Critical Evaluation as Mechanisms for Learning in a Dance Technique Class 'Laboratory.'" *Theatre, Dance and Performance Training* 2, no. 1 (2011): 86–98.

Strong, Michelle R.B., and Alexandra Pooley. "Structuring a Successful Dance Class: Strategies to Promote Effective and Enjoyable Learning." *National Dance Society Journal* (Print) 2, no. 1 (2017): 13.

CHAPTER 15

Feedback and Assessment

Box 15.1 Chapter Objectives

After reading this chapter, you will be able to:

- Articulate the purpose of feedback within the learning process
- Distinguish between task-intrinsic feedback and augmented feedback
- Discuss the value of verbal, non-verbal, and guided touch feedback
- Identify ways in which the dance teacher can provide feedback to students
- Identify methods for assessing dance technique and performance

---

Box 15.2 Chapter Vocabulary

assessment
augmented feedback
extrinsic feedback
feedback
formative assessment
intrinsic feedback
knowledge of performance
knowledge of results
performance bandwidth
summative assessment

Feedback is the verbal or non-verbal response that provides information about a movement attempt. Feedback can teach, reinforce, inform, and motivate the student. Providing and receiving feedback is an important part of the teaching and learning process and could even be considered the most important aspect. The dance teacher employs feedback throughout the dance class so that students are aware of their efforts and progress – or

DOI: 10.4324/b22952-21

lack thereof – and can appropriately improve in their skill acquisition and performance. For example, any errors in execution can be noted, and a prescription for improvement can be offered. Feedback may acknowledge the manner in which the student performs, emphasizing appropriate actions. The teacher's feedback can also inform the student of an improvement or accomplishment in a skill. Finally, feedback can be used to motivate students. Here, the information provided by the teacher could demonstrate to the student that they are making progress toward a goal, thus inspiring them to continue their efforts.

There are two types of feedback that a student may receive during training: intrinsic and extrinsic feedback. **Intrinsic feedback** is the sensory information that an individual gathers while executing movement. A dance student receives visual, auditory, and proprioceptive information during execution, which they then use to assess their movement attempts or performance. The student sees in the mirror that their working leg is not extending in the correct direction. They immediately hear that tap dance sounds were missed during their execution of a riff and begins to evaluate what happened in the attempt. They notice when a knee may buckle or an ankle rolls during a movement. During a balance, the student is aware of directional leaning of the body and works to compensate for that during the movement. In contrast, **extrinsic feedback**, also called **augmented feedback**, comes from an external source and is the information that can be added to or enhance the intrinsic feedback. An external source could be the teacher, another student, or even a video recording. In these instances, the feedback provided is the external information that augments the dancer's sensory assessment of movement and is helpful when sensory feedback is lacking or insufficient.

The student dancer will improve faster when appropriate feedback is offered. The link between instructor feedback and student cannot be overemphasized. This communication allows students to continue their effort with corrective and motivational guidance provided by the instructor. Without instructor-guided feedback, students can flounder without direction to fix or improve upon an error in technique or performance. They could also lack the knowledge that they are indeed on the correct performance path. Feedback can inform the mechanics of a movement, the technical execution of a movement, and/or the performance quality. This chapter discusses the importance of feedback and the way in which it can enhance or hinder motor ability and performance.

AUGMENTED FEEDBACK

Augmented feedback provides supplemental information regarding the student's movement attempt. This form of feedback may be verbal or non-verbal and could be offered during or after the movement execution. It describes the details of the movement execution or the performance outcome and assists in the learning process. For example, the student executes a *chaîné jeté* or a calypso jump. The student intrinsically knows that they landed too loudly and that "something else" did not feel quite right. The teacher then provides information that their front foot was flexed, which resulted in a lack of articulation within the foot as they landed (thus the "thud"), and they had the wrong arm extended up (thus the "something else" that felt wrong). The teacher's augmented feedback enhanced and clarified the student's internal understanding of the movement attempt. Augmented feedback is necessary when sensory feedback alone is insufficient for improving. Yet, augmented feedback does not always need to be coupled with intrinsic feedback. There will be many times when a student is unaware of an error. This feedback then helps them better understand how the movement should be executed.

Augmented information can be categorized in two ways: knowledge of results and knowledge of performance. **Knowledge of results** (KR) is a form of verbal augmented feedback that is offered to the student after their movement attempt and is directed toward the movement outcome. This form of feedback is often necessary when task-intrinsic information does not sufficiently lead to an awareness of progress. An example might be the teacher's statement, "You didn't complete the second revolution of the turn." This statement provides the information that the execution of the goal was not successfully accomplished. The student may already be aware of this through their own intrinsic feedback. However, in some instances, the student may be oblivious. For example, the teacher may note, "The back leg was not fully extended in the *arabesque*." This knowledge often depends upon the student's proprioceptive skills and/or kinesthetic awareness. The greater self-awareness that the student has, the less the application of KR will benefit them in their execution of movement; however, it can still encourage and motivate the student, serving as a form of reinforcement.

Knowledge of performance (KP) is a form of augmented feedback that describes features or the quality of the movement attempt. KP may be verbal or non-verbal; it could be the statements made by the teacher, the teacher's use of physical touch, or viewing a video of the attempt. KP is typically the most common feedback used within the dance class. A student is often aware of a movement outcome, but the words of the teacher create the path to progress. For example, the student may recognize that they fell out of the turn; however, the teacher's feedback can provide greater clarity. The teacher may say, "You didn't complete the second revolution of the turn because you dropped your working leg and collapsed your arms." This feedback, then, can be invaluable to the student. While the student may recognize their error, they, hopefully, respect and trust their teachers to guide them toward more effective execution of movement.

Augmented feedback provides the student with awareness of what to do during movement execution, how to improve their skills, and motivation to continue. Feedback such as "Yes, you did it!" or "Your sounds are consistently improving!" can encourage a student to continue in their effort. Dance teachers should offer frequent feedback to beginners. As the stages of learning advance, the frequency of feedback should, to some degree, fade. In time, augmented feedback should lead students to task-intrinsic feedback.[1] Dance students learn to acknowledge and listen to their sensory feedback. More skilled students also learn the tools of self-evaluation and self-cueing, which help them assess their own execution.

There are instances where augmented feedback can restrict or inhibit learning. It is important that the dance teacher instructs the student in correct movement technique for the dance genre; this means both the demonstration and the feedback should be accurate. Flawed feedback can lead to errors and bad habits in movement execution. Feedback overload can also obstruct learning. Providing too much information can cognitively overload the student or discourage their effort. It is best to offer the student one or two ideas central to the task at hand and learning objectives. They can then more easily digest and apply this information. **Performance bandwidth** is the range of error that the instructor deems tolerable. The dance teacher recognizes that the beginning student has little information or experience and will most likely make a considerable number of errors. It would be fruitless for the teacher to offer feedback that addresses every error. Rather, the teacher intuitively decides which errors to temporarily ignore and what aspects of the movement execution to address. The bandwidth of the student is considered, and feedback is offered accordingly.

Forms of Augmented Feedback

The dance teacher uses augmented feedback to address various areas of movement execution. As a result, statements are typically physical, facilitating, rhythmical, and/or aesthetical in nature.[2] Some feedback may be in response to actions of the body that are incorrect. This physical feedback helps the students learn how to adjust the physicality of the movement. The teacher may tell a student that their knees are pronating instead of remaining in alignment with the ankles and feet. Feedback intended to facilitate offers insight into how movement should be done. Rather than identifying the incorrect part of the body, the teacher may tell the student to engage their inner thighs and point the knees in the same direction as the feet. Here, the student learns how to correct the pronation and facilitate proper technique.

Rhythmical-based feedback conveys direction related to the timing of the movement. Here, the teacher might tell the student that the snap of the head when spotting is too slow and needs to happen more quickly. Rhythmical-based responses could also address the relationship between movement and music. Feedback driven by aesthetics is quality based and guides the student in regard to artistic choices. The student may hear the teacher encourage them to glide, float, stretch, or lengthen. Often, the dance teacher will combine types of feedback to further clarify what needs to happen. Depending on the movement task, purpose of the feedback, and the personality and needs of the individual student, the guidance offered could be, for example, both facilitating and aesthetical. The dance teacher may offer a comment such as "the right arm needs to be lifted higher so that the line of the arms matches the line of the leg." The more specific the teacher can be with feedback, the more helpful it can become to the student.

A teacher may provide augmented feedback verbally, non-verbally, or through guided touch. As we have learned, each student is unique and learns in different ways. What works for one student may not work for another student who is demonstrating the exact same error. The dance teacher learns to deliver material in various ways and incorporate different instructional strategies as they teach. It becomes beneficial for the teacher to recognize the differences in how best to provide each mode of feedback.

FIGURE 15.1 A dance teacher offers verbal and guided touch feedback to a young student.
Source: Photo by Jeffrey Smith/Western Kentucky University.

Verbal Feedback

Verbal feedback includes the oral statements made as well as the application of any vocal inflections. The teacher must be thoughtful when determining what to say, ensuring that the statement is meaningful to the student. The student must be able to understand the verbal comment and relate its message to their movement attempts. The teacher should consider the priority of errors, starting with the bigger picture first. There is no point in zeroing in on a finite detail when the step itself was the wrong movement. Additionally, the more specific the verbal statement is, the greater success it will have in achieving the desired results.

Verbal feedback can be corrective, or pinpoint problems in execution. The teacher may provide a directive for the student to follow, correct an error by presenting a solution, or draw attention to specific problem areas. Each of these types of statements are offered to help improve the student's execution or performance. An evaluative type of feedback helps the student understand whether they are improving in their performance and specifics regarding their attempt.

Additionally, feedback may be positive or negative. Positive feedback typically is in the form of praise, pointing out or acknowledging what the student is doing correctly or their general effort. Negative verbal feedback identifies an action or attitude of the student that needs to change. This type of verbal feedback should be used very sparingly if ever. Rather than focusing on the negative, the dance teacher can cultivate a culture of trust by offering constructive feedback that is positive and provides students with a concrete point from which they can focus and work. Then, the opportunity to apply the feedback can motivate the student to continue their effort. Oftentimes, feedback may include a combination of these various types. The teacher may offer a statement of praise followed by an evaluative comment. See Table 15.1 for examples of corrective and evaluative feedback as well as positive and negative statements.

The teacher should be sensitive to the student and recognize the student's tolerance level for criticism. Teachers often have a tendency to offer too much verbal feedback to students.[3] It is important to keep in mind that individuals can only remember so much at a time, typically five to nine items in their short-term memory. Verbal feedback should be limited so that the student can quickly understand the statement and apply and retain it. Limiting this form of feedback is especially necessary for beginners so one does not overload their thought process. It can be helpful for the dance teacher to consider what the goal of the feedback is. Does the comment help the student achieve the goal? Inspire them to continue their practice toward attaining a goal? How will the dance student benefit from the feedback?

TABLE 15.1 Identifying types of verbal feedback.

Types of Verbal Feedback	Dance Examples
Corrective	• "Your leap is low to the ground. You are not sending the front leg up high enough and are not fully extending through the back leg." • "You are ending on the wrong count because your timing during the shuffle steps is incorrect. They need to be syncopated in rhythm." The teacher may demonstrate a movement two different ways and verbally explain the distinction and draw attention to the correct execution.
Evaluative	• "Your performance is moving in a nice direction. However, you need more work on phrase two." • "Your timing has improved greatly." • "You are still falling out of your turn."
Praise	• "Yes! Your movement was executed correctly!" • "Your effort has been phenomenal today!" • "That was lovely to watch!"
Negative	• "That was terrible!" • "That movement attempt was wrong in so many ways." • "You fell out of your turn, messed up the timing, and are boring to watch."

Non-Verbal Feedback

Non-verbal feedback is centered on one's body language and facial expressions. A smile, quizzical look, or throwing of the arms into the air all convey meaning to the student. This type of feedback is readily noticed by students. It can be employed by the teacher to engage and inspire a student. When the teacher acknowledges the student's effort, even with just a nod of the head, the student can become motivated to strive for continued improvement. Students are quick to recognize the positive non-verbal feedback of the teacher; however, the teacher's negative non-verbal feedback can also be quickly noticed. Standing with hands on their hips and a tight jaw could be the result of a teacher thinking about something else entirely, yet to the students in front of them, displeasure or frustration is communicated. The teacher must be aware of facial expressions and body language throughout the class. It is often best to simply maintain a neutral or pleasant expression.

Guided Touch

There are times during the dance class when verbal and non-verbal feedback may not suffice, and the teacher may choose to use guided touch to communicate the desired movement. The use of physical touch should be used sparingly, lightly, and with great care, yet it can be a valuable pedagogical tool. The teacher may physically guide the student's body into proper alignment, position, or in a particular path. Perhaps the instructor directs a student's arms into the correct position, lightly touches the back of the knee to remind students to lengthen through the leg, or helps students maintain appropriate rotation of the thigh during a *grand rond de jambe*. Physical touch can also provide information to the teacher. The teacher may tap the top of a student's shoulder. As the student reactively lowers their shoulders, the teacher learns that their observation was correct.

FIGURE 15.2 A dance teacher gently touches the back of the student's knee to remind her to fully lengthen her leg during the *arabesque*.

Source: Photo by Clinton Lewis/Western Kentucky University.

While feedback in the form of physical touch was used without much thought in previous decades, it is important that the dance teacher recognizes the valid concerns associated with touch in the classroom. Touch can cause anxiety in the student or, if delivered properly, can decrease the student's uneasiness. The teacher should be aware of the student's level of comfort with touch. A great reminder when using guided touch is to consider the acronym WAIT – Why Am I Touching.[4] The effective dance teacher is mindful of the necessity for the use of touch and how it is being applied. The teacher should always inform the student prior to the use of physical touch and explain the reason and the goal for this form of feedback. It may prove helpful to begin with distal cues as an introductory use of guided touch. The teacher might take the student's hand to bring the arm in front of the student's shoulder rather than placing their hands on the student's shoulder and arm.

The teacher should be familiar with the studio's policy regarding the use of touch and strategize a method for allowing students to provide or deny consent to be touched. This method should also make it clear that the teacher will not judge a student who does not consent to touch and will provide alternative forms of feedback. Once a student provides consent, it is important to understand that the consent may not be continual; it may not apply every week or every year that the teacher instructs the student. Therefore, it is necessary for the teacher to develop an ongoing process of consent within the classroom.

Box 15.3 Correcting Bad Habits

A teacher never wants a student to develop bad habits. However, should a student present a bad habit, the effective dance teacher should be prepared to address it. Bad habits can result from incorrect demonstrations or feedback experienced by the student. Poor movement habits could stem from a student's faulty perception during the learning process. In time, the student develops a habitual and incorrect movement pattern. Changing a habitual movement pattern requires motivation and persistence on the part of the student. For example, a student learns to successfully turn with incorrect body alignment. Because they are completing the desired turns, the student may be hesitant or unwilling to change their alignment. In instances such as this, the teacher can offer the anatomical reason for the change and/or the potential for injury that could be caused by the bad habit. The aesthetic of a movement could also be discussed wherein the teacher explains and helps the student rethink how one approach might be more aesthetically desirable than another.

The teacher may also need to remind the student that changing the poor movement habit will take physical practice. The body will not immediately adapt to a new pattern of movement. Habits are slow to change, and skill may diminish for a period of time. The student should be reminded that this is a normal part of the process and encouraged to continue in their pursuit of the new movement approach. Some students may not be capable of changing habitual movement patterns or simply not ready, in which case the teacher can reapproach the change at a later date. Finally, the student may view the feedback to change as an attack on a previous teacher. The teacher can encourage the student that there are many ways in which an individual can move and that new perspectives can lead to new discoveries.

PROVIDING FEEDBACK

The effective dance teacher will have a plan for feedback before delivering comments to students. Perhaps ideas will stem from the lesson plan, or the teacher will recall errors from a previous class. With the learning objectives of the lesson plan in mind, the teacher can anticipate reminders and feedback that will be needed for a given class. For example, after a paddle and roll combination has been demonstrated in the tap class, the teacher may cue students to clarify the ball versus the heel drop as they execute the step; this idea aligns with the articulation of the foot and clarity of sound objectives for the class. As students execute the step, the teacher may notice the students' lack of articulation and rushed timing. As a result, they will call out, "Separate your sounds!" and then vocalize accented syllables or terminology during the ball and the heel drop. This is intended to help bring the students' attention to those two parts of the step. In this instance, students were provided a verbal cue prior to their movement attempt. Feedback, along with verbal cueing, was offered during their attempt.

Feedback is most helpful when delivered as soon as possible. The more time that passes before feedback is given, the longer the student will continue the incorrect action. In the previous example, the tap dance students were reminded of the foot articulation prior to and during their movement attempt. If they continued to lack clarity of sound, the teacher could give them more specific feedback. After the movement attempt, the teacher might say, "You are rushing the timing between the ball and heel drop. Each of the four parts of the step should receive equal portions of the beat." Verbal feedback may continue with the teacher's clarification of the counts or scatting of the rhythm.

Once the feedback has been given, students must have an opportunity to apply the information and practice the movement with this added knowledge or awareness. It is

FIGURE 15.3 A tap dance teacher offers verbal and non-verbal feedback following the students' movement attempts.

Source: Photo by Clinton Lewis/Western Kentucky University.

pointless to deliver feedback to students and then immediately move on to something new. Allowing students to process the information and apply it to their movement is essential to the learning process.

The teacher should be thoughtful with the manner in which feedback is delivered. What tone of voice is appropriate? What non-verbal body language should be avoided? What words will be used, and when will the feedback be given? The sandwich method may work best with some students. Here, the teacher offers a positive or praise comment, then offers the corrective feedback, followed by another positive statement. Yet, this method may not be applicable with movement that is occurring at a fast pace. As multiple students dance across the floor, the teacher may attempt to offer various feedback as they are dancing. Here, the teacher may call out concise and specific statements, such as "Grace, stretch your feet" or "Ethan, that's better, good job!" In these instances, it is most effective if feedback is explicit and clearly addresses the receiver. The student needs time

---

Box 15.4 Positive versus Corrective Feedback

Individuals typically desire to hear positive comments, specifically about themselves. Dance students equally desire this affirmation. They want to be told that they are doing something well or correctly. They desire recognition when a skill is executed correctly or want to hear that they are a great performer. These phrases of affirmation motivate the dance student to continue in their movement attempts. The learning process for a novice student is typically motivated by affirmative feedback. Yet, there comes a point when dance students want to also hear the critical feedback. Students may become frustrated when they do not receive any feedback from the teacher, and they are not improving on their own. It is within the balance of praise and criticism that the student dancer learns and grows. One could teach by offering only praise to their students. In contrast, a teacher could offer purely constructive criticism. It is the author's belief that it is important to recognize the interplay of reinforcement and criticism in a student's training and development.

---

to process and apply the information, whether they are moving or standing still. Specific and precise feedback allows the student to comprehend and incorporate the suggestion into their movement attempt more quickly.

If the teacher's response can be delivered quickly and without explanation, then it may be called out to a student either during or immediately after their movement attempt. However, when feedback requires more detail, the teacher may pull a student aside so a deeper explanation can be offered. Should the feedback serve the entire class, the teacher may wait until all students have had an opportunity to attempt the movement or pause the students' dancing to deliver the feedback. The timing of delivering feedback can be tricky. Feedback offered during movement execution has the risk of distracting the student from task-intrinsic feedback. It can be helpful, however, if it further supports intrinsic feedback and aligns with the objective or primary feature of the movement task. Constant feedback to students may not be as useful as the teacher assumes. If consistently given, students can become reliant upon the feedback or may not retain the information because they have tuned out the continuous comments from the teacher. As the student progresses through the learning stages, the frequency of feedback will reduce. More skilled dancers are better equipped to self-cue and self-evaluate their movement execution.

The teacher should strive to earn and maintain the respect of the students as they offer feedback. As confidence builds within a student, they will be more apt to learn. The learning process will stop if a student feels pressured, humiliated, or inept. Humiliating a student can create fear or resentment within the student as well as the entire class. Therefore, the words that the teacher says matter and should be chosen carefully. Following are some final tips for the dance teacher to offer feedback in a manner that will best benefit the student:

- **Feedback should be appropriate to the student's skill level.** A beginning level jazz dancer with limited flexibility will not execute a fully extended split leap. Rather, feedback can focus on the mechanics of the leg action or the articulation of the feet.
- **Feedback should help students accept their physical abilities.** Telling a student to increase their turnout may be impossible depending on the structure of the student's hip sockets. Rather, the teacher can ask the student to fully engage their deep rotators or help them discover a specific way to still aesthetically and safely complete the movement.
- **Some feedback may be intended for an individual while other feedback may serve the entire class.** Recognize if a student is comfortable with individual feedback in front of the class or more privately delivered.
- **Feedback should benefit the student's development of skill.** The teacher should consider if the feedback will benefit the student in that moment. The dance teacher generally always has feedback that they can offer to a student, yet the teacher should consider whether the feedback is pertinent to the objective of the exercise. By thoughtfully selecting feedback offered, the teacher ensures that it can assist the student in attaining the objective of the lesson plan or improve their skill.

ASSESSMENT AND EVALUATION

Whether teaching in a private studio, K–12 classroom, pre-professional venue, or university setting, student assessment and evaluation occur in some form. **Assessment** is a method of evaluating and measuring the student's abilities as a means to determine both the student's skill level and the effectiveness of the learning process. Teachers within the private sector evaluate a student's abilities and progression as they determine the appropriate class for the student and offer evaluative feedback to the student and/or guardian. The K–12 and university dance classrooms typically require formal assessments as part of the students' academic grades. While assessments measure the students' development of skill and comprehension, the teacher can also gain valuable insight into their own teaching effectiveness.

This section focuses on the assessment of the dance students' movement, although any dance class setting could also include written or verbal assessments. Dance teachers typically engage in two types of technique and performance-based assessments: formative and summative. **Formative assessments** are the ongoing evaluations that the teacher conducts throughout a class and term to assess the students' movement execution and knowledge as learning occurs. During a class, the teacher offers feedback to students, either individually or as a group. After each class meeting, the teacher reflects on the class – what worked and what did not, the success of the students' movement attempts, etc. – and considers the next step in their learning. Formative assessments are informal and responsive. Grades are not attached to this type of assessment. Information is continually gathered by the teacher as they observe students, consider objectives, plan lessons, and offer feedback. In contrast, **summative assessments** are the assessments completed at distinct times during or at the end of a term and are intended to gather specific information as to whether the students have learned the material that has been taught and have achieved a certain skill level. This type of evaluation essentially summarizes the students' progress over a period and compares the data to specific or standardized criteria.

Assessment of dance technique and performance is ultimately subjective; however, there are methods to help incorporate objectivity into the evaluation process. Clear evaluation criteria should be developed for which information can be gathered through observation and analyzed to measure the students' abilities. This criterion will most likely stem from the devised curriculum and is considered as the teacher develops lesson plans. When criteria is determined as part of the planning process, it can then be shared with older students to help them understand what the goals are. Perhaps the dance teacher wants to ensure that the learning objectives for the year or technique level have been met by the students, or they may want to assess the students' strength and flexibility. Whether the teacher is analyzing the students' general dance alignment and movement integration or their execution of specific step, criteria must be clearly determined and clarified before evaluation can occur.

Next, the teacher should devise the method for assessing the criteria. Rubrics become extremely helpful during the assessment process. Effective rubrics are concise and clear and specifically created toward appropriately assessing student attainment of skill. Rubrics are often designed using a four- or five-point ranking scale (known as a Likert scale).[5] The point value can increase or decrease with skill level. Not every dance student can or will master each aspect of dance. Thus, the dance teacher develops ways to characterize levels of learning achievement. Following are examples of terms and descriptions that may be used in a dance assessment:

- **Novice or unsatisfactory** – The student rarely or perhaps never demonstrates the skill correctly.
- **Basic or satisfactory** – The student sometimes demonstrates correct execution of a skill.
- **Proficient or above satisfactory** – The student usually executes the skill correctly.
- **Exemplary or advanced** – The student consistently demonstrates correct execution of the skill.

Notice the use of rarely, sometimes, usually, and consistently as qualifiers for the correct display of a skill. The student may demonstrate a proficient or even advanced level in certain areas of technique and performance while scoring basic or novice in others. With a number scale following these classifications, subjective subject matter can become objective. (See the sample rubric in Table 15.2.)

Another assessment approach could be a one-point system, which lists the criteria and notes as to how the expectations were or were not being met. This approach is

Feedback and Assessment **275**

TABLE 15.2 Depicting a sample four-point assessment rubric for dance technique.

Dance Technique Assessment

Exemplary: 4 points, implies "consistent application."
Proficient: 3 points, implies "usually demonstrates."
Basic: 2 points, implies "sometimes demonstrates."
Novice: 1 point, implies "rarely demonstrates."

Criteria		Total	Comments
Movement Sequence	Demonstrates correct sequencing of movement exercises		
Placement and Alignment	Demonstrates correct placement and alignment in positions and movements		
Movement Integration	Integrates movement throughout the entire body with appropriate abdominal strength and coordination between the upper and lower torso and limbs; completes fluid transitions		
Body Positions	Demonstrates knowledge and execution of distinct body lines		
Use of Feet	Appropriately articulates through the feet		
Spatial Awareness	Demonstrates effective use of space; use of appropriate level and direction changes; moves with clear focus in space		
Rhythmic Clarity	Demonstrates rhythmic accuracy		
Use of Energy	Executes movement with appropriate force, dynamics, and quality		

similar to the example detailed in Table 15.2; however, only three columns are used and scoring is configured differently (see Table 15.3). One column lists the criteria. Another column provides room for the teacher to note that the student has accomplished the specified skill, noting any strengths. Comments regarding how the student has not yet accomplished the task appear in the final column along with additional feedback for the student.

Technique and performance can be evaluated through movement-based or written modes by the dance teacher. Self-assessments and peer assessments can be engaging ways to incorporate a student-centered approach. Surveys, video recordings, and discussions can also provide a means for assessment. Regardless of the assessment method, determinations must also be made in how to provide the evaluations to the student. In an academic-based setting, students often receive formal grades, while in private dance studios or other dance training centers, students typically do not receive grades. Feedback can be provided to the student orally or in written form. Assessment feedback is only beneficial if the student understands what the expectations were and how the assessment was conducted.

TABLE 15.3 Depicting a sample one-point assessment rubric for dance technique.

Dance Technique Assessment

Not Met (0 points)	Criteria	Met (1 point)
	Movement Sequence Demonstrates correct sequencing of movement exercises	
	Placement and Alignment Demonstrates correct placement and alignment in positions and movements	
	Movement Integration Integrates movement throughout the entire body with appropriate abdominal strength and coordination between the upper and lower torso and limbs; completes fluid transitions	
	Body Positions Demonstrates knowledge and execution of distinct body lines	
	Use of Feet Appropriately articulates through the feet	
	Spatial Awareness Demonstrates effective use of space; use of appropriate level and direction changes; moves with clear focus in space	
	Rhythmical Clarity Demonstrates rhythmic accuracy	
	Use of Energy Executes movement with appropriate force, dynamics, and quality	

Additionally, assessments can reveal information pertaining to teacher effectiveness. As the teacher completes student evaluations, they may notice that the majority of students are or are not meeting expectations. This then provides a valuable opportunity for the teacher to self-reflect on their own teaching approach as well the appropriateness of the criteria and the method of assessment. The teacher may find that a new teaching approach is necessary, additional instructional strategies are required, or a longer period of time is needed to improve or enhance the students' learning process. Conversely, the teacher may learn that expectations have been set too low and should be made more challenging.

CHAPTER SUMMARY

Feedback and assessment are critical components of the learning process. Feedback can teach, reinforce, inform, and motivate the student. Students receive feedback in two ways. The sensory information that the student gathers while executing movement is intrinsic feedback. Augmented feedback is the verbal and non-verbal information provided by the teacher. Augmented feedback could provide the student with awareness of the outcome of the movement execution (knowledge of results), or the feedback might help the student understand the features or quality of the movement attempt (knowledge of performance). Both types of augmented feedback could come in the form of verbal statements or sounds, non-verbal gestures, facial expressions, body stances, or through guided touch by the instructor. When providing feedback, timing matters. Students should be given feedback immediately following the movement attempt and provided an opportunity to process and apply the information. As the student's skill level increases, feedback may be offered less frequently as the student learns to self-evaluate.

Dance teachers continually assess and evaluate students through formative, or ongoing, assessments or through summative assessments at the conclusion of a learning cycle or term. Assessment methods should be clearly defined and made known to students. Through appropriate feedback and assessment, the teacher can enhance student learning, develop the student's acquisition of skills, and motivate the student's continued effort.

PRACTICAL APPLICATIONS

1   How do you, as a dancer, respond to intrinsic feedback and to augmented feedback?

2   Which type of augmented feedback do you find most helpful to you: verbal, non-verbal, or guided touch? Why?

3   How might the dance teacher expect students within a given class to respond to the same type of feedback?

4   Observe a dance class with specific attention to the various feedback offered by the teacher. How does the teacher deliver feedback? What type of feedback appears most helpful to the students?

5   Provide examples of KR and KP feedback relative to various learning stages.

6   Instruct a group of peers through various movement exercises. Practice providing the various types of augmented feedback as discussed in the chapter. Reflect on the experience. What did the exercise reveal regarding your approach to providing feedback?

NOTES

1   Nicola J. Hodges and A. M. Williams, *Skill Acquisition in Sport: Research, Theory and Practice* (London: Routledge, 2012), 12.
2   Joah Schlaic and Betty DuPont, *The Art of Teaching Dance Technique* (Virginia: National Dance Association, 2001), 53.
3   Hodges and Williams. *Skill Acquisition in Sport*, 5.
4   Miriam Giguere, "Dance Trends: Touch as a Teaching Tool in Dance Class: When and How to Use Tactile Feedback," *Dance Education in Practice* 5, no. 4 (2019): 31.
5   Gayle Kassing and Danielle M. Jay, *Dance Teaching Methods and Curriculum Design* (Champaign, IL: Human Kinetics, 2003), 166.

BIBLIOGRAPHY

Ambrosio, Nora. *The Excellent Instructor and the Teaching of Dance Technique*. Dubuque, IA: Kendall Hunt Publishing Company, 2018.

Barr, Sherrie. "Examining the Technique Class: Re-Examining Feedback." *Research in Dance Education* 10, no. 1 (2009): 33–45.

Chen, David D. "Trends in Augmented Feedback Research and Tips for the Practitioner." *Journal of Physical Education, Recreation & Dance* 72, no. 1 (2001): 32–36.

Chng, Lena S., and Jacalyn Lund. "Assessment for Learning in Physical Education: The What, Why and How." *Journal of Physical Education, Recreation & Dance* 89, no. 8 (2018): 29–34.

Docheff, Dennis. "Theory into Practice: Feedback: The Key to Effective Coaching." *Strategies* 23, no. 6 (2010): 34–35.

Gibbons, Elizabeth. "Teaching Tools: Feedback Strategies 101." *Dance Teacher* 26, no. 9 (2004): 107–110.

Giguere, Miriam. "Dance Trends: Touch as a Teaching Tool in Dance Class: When and How to Use Tactile Feedback." *Dance Education in Practice* 5, no. 4 (2019): 30–32.

Harding, Mary. "Assessment in the High School Technique Class: Creating Thinking Dancers." *Journal of Dance Education* 12, no. 3 (2012): 93–98.

Hodges, Nicola J., and A.M. Williams. *Skill Acquisition in Sport: Research, Theory and Practice*. London: Routledge, 2012.

Kassing, Gayle, and Danielle M. Jay. *Dance Teaching Methods and Curriculum Design*. Champaign, IL: Human Kinetics, 2003.

Krasnow, Donna, and Virginia Wilmerding. *Motor Learning and Control for Dance: Principles and Practices for Performers and Teachers*. Champaign, IL: Human Kinetics, 2015.

Moinuddin, Arsalan, Ashish Goel, and Yashendra Sethi. "The Role of Augmented Feedback on Motor Learning: A Systematic Review." *Curēus* 13, no. 11 (2021): e19695.

Rose, Debra J., and Robert W. Christina. *A Multilevel Approach to the Study of Motor Control and Learning*. San Francisco, CA: Benjamin Cummings, 2008.

Schlaich, Joah, and Betty DuPont. *The Art of Teaching Dance Technique*. Virginia: National Dance Association, 2001.

Glossary

abduction
an anatomical term that refers to movement away from the midline of the body

ability
the genetic and predetermined characteristics that influence movement performance

accessibility
the designing, building, and application of providing the means for all people of various backgrounds and abilities to engage and participate in dance

adduction
an anatomical term that refers to movement towards the centerline of the body

agonist
an anatomical term that refers to the muscle using concentric contractions to produce movement

alignment
the specific organization of the body in regard to gravity and the aesthetics of the dance movement

anatomic variation
a deviation from the accepted classic or textbook standards of human anatomy

antagonist
an anatomical term that refers to the muscle located opposite of the agonist that either relaxes and lengthens to allow the movement to happen or contracts to aid in the movement

anterior
an anatomical term that refers to the structure towards the front of the body

arousal
a physiological and psychological state that relates to the student's level of excitement

associative stage
Fitts and Posner's second stage of learning; students begin to refine their actions and focus on the how of the movement

280 Glossary

attentional focus
the mental action of applying concentration toward a singular stimulus for a period of time

auditory imagery
utilizes sounds or words incite a mental image within the student

auditory system
a part of the sensory system that is a neural network responsible for transmitting sound to the brain so that it can be identified and processed

augmented feedback
the information that comes from an external source that can be added to or enhance the intrinsic feedback

autonomous stage
Fitts and Posner's third stage of learning; students automatically produce movement and have the ability to self-cue

bar
a grouping of beats separated by a bar line within written music

behavioral goal
the generic attribute that the teacher aspires for students to embrace

bilateral transfer
the transfer of movement skills from one limb to the opposite limb

blocked practice
occurs when the student repeatedly works on, or drills, the same step or phrase over a length of time

body awareness
the ability to locate and know where the body is in space along with how to move it efficiently

BPM
identifies the precise number of beats that are played/heard within the time frame of 60 seconds

call and response
a structure wherein the leader(s) performs a musical phrase, and the group echoes the same phrase

cartilage
the connective tissue that covers the articulating surfaces of bones

central nervous system
consists of the brain and spinal cord

chrononutrition
the interaction between food and the circadian rhythm in the body

chunking
an instructional approach where independent parts are combined in a meaningful way to help improve short-term memory and transfer information to long-term memory

Glossary 281

classroom etiquette
the manner in which the instructor prefers and expects students to conduct themselves while in class

classroom expectation
the behavioral patterns and attitudes that the teacher calls for throughout each class

classroom procedure
the specific action taken to support activities and circumstances within class

classroom management
the process and strategies that the teacher employs to create a culture and environment conducive to learning

closed-loop system
neuromuscular process that relies on sensory information and external feedback to create a plan for movement

cognitive stage
Fitts and Posner's first stage of learning; students focus on understanding the basic elements of the movement

concentric contraction
movement contraction in which muscle fibers shorten to produce movement

constraint
an aspect that deters or hinders movement

crescendo
a musical term for a gradual increase in volume within the music

critical dance pedagogy
an approach to dance education that invites questioning the power structures at play that determine what is taught to whom and how the dancing body is valued

cueing
a means of prompting an individual to move in a certain way

cultural sensitivity
the awareness and acceptance of cultural differences

culturally relevant teaching
a teaching methodology in which the educator adapts their instructional strategies in consideration of the cultural affinities of the students

culture
a collection of customs shared by a group of people

curriculum
a body of knowledge and course of study divided among levels that a program follows and around which courses are planned

dance as education
dance as the vehicle, rather than subject matter itself, through which learning can occur

dance education
the information, theoretical concepts, and application of that knowledge in a broad, general sense

dance training
the acquisition of specific physical, technical, and practical skills

decrescendo
a musical term for a gradual decrease in volume within the music

degrees of freedom problem
the multiple directions in which movement could be directed within a specific body joint

depression
an anatomical term that refers to movement in which the shoulders are pressed down towards the waistline

distal
an anatomical term that refers to the structure further away from the trunk or joint in question

diversity
the spectrum of differences between people and cultures

dorsiflexion
an anatomical term that refers to the action of flexing the foot, since the top of the foot is the dorsal surface

dynamic systems approach
a theory of motor development that considers not only the individual's physical body and neuromuscular system but also factors in input from the surrounding environment and the task itself

eccentric contraction
a movement contraction in which muscle fibers shorten to work against gravity to provide a stopping action

eighth note
a type of musical note represented by a closed face note with a stem and flag; musical value equals half of a single beat

elevation
an anatomical term that refers to movement in which the shoulders are raised upwards towards the ears

equity
fair treatment and opportunity for all people, including their ability to participate, adequate representation, respectful treatment, and access to resources

eversion
an anatomical term that refers to movement in which the sole of the foot turns away from the midline of the body

Glossary 283

explicit learning
a form of learning that requires one's focus and attention

extension
an anatomical term that refers to the straightening or stretching of a joint, often causing the two bones of the joint to come into a straight line

external focus
a form of attentional focus that requires an individual to direct their attention and effort to the outcome of the movement execution

external rotation
an anatomical term that refers to movement of a part of the body outward

extrinsic motivation
a form of motivation in which one is externally driven or focused on a consequence outside of the individual

feedback
the verbal or non-verbal response that provides information about a movement attempt

flexion
an anatomical term that refers to the bending or folding of a joint that produces an angle between the two bones forming said joint

formative assessments
the ongoing evaluation that the teacher conducts to assess the students' movement execution and knowledge as learning occurs

fractionalization
a part method wherein movement is separated between body parts and learned and practiced separately before combining the movement together as a whole

general motor program
a grouping of commands stored in the memory that inform the musculature to execute a given movement or pattern of movements

goal
the broad area toward which one works, the outcome that one desires to achieve

goal orientation theory
a theory of motivation that contends that individuals are often driven by goals

guided discovery
an instructional technique that employs a verbal prompt from the teacher to instruct students toward answering a question or solving a problem

half note
a type of musical note represented by an open-faced note but with a stem; equals two beats

hidden curriculum
the assumptions a teacher makes regarding how students will behave or the skills they have acquired prior to attending their class

holistic approach
considers each student as an individual and focuses on the education of the whole student

hyperextension
allows a joint to straighten past the neutral or 180-degree range

hypermobility
stems from loose connective tissues in a joint or joints, in essence the joint is less stable because the tissues connecting the bones are weaker or abnormally loose

ideational imagery
utilizes metaphorical language to depict an external object or idea

imagery
the use of descriptive language to provide a mental representation of an object, idea, or experience

implicit bias
the automatic and often unintentional judgment, decision, or attitude embraced by an individual

implicit learning
a form of learning that occurs without the student's conscious effort

inclusion
the act of intentionally creating a dance space in which people from any background feel welcomed, supported, and valued

inferior
an anatomical term that refers to the structure below

information-processing theory
a theory of motor development that places the brain as the primary component of the processing system; information provided externally or through the senses enters the brain where it is processed, and the resulting outcome is then coordinated movement

instructional strategy
a technique that one applies within teaching to ensure students achieve the learning objective

internal focus
a form of attentional focus where an individual directs their attention and effort toward the elements of the task or the individual components of the movement

internal rotation
an anatomical term that refers to movement of part of the body inward

intrinsic feedback
the sensory information that an individual gathers while executing movement

intrinsic motivation
a form of motivation where the one is personally driven from within to engage in activity or focus their attention

Glossary 285

invariant feature
a component of a general motor program that does not change

inversion
an anatomical term that refers to movement that turns the sole of the foot towards the midline of the body

isometric contraction
a movement contraction in which muscle fibers shorten to help ligaments stabilize a structure

kinesiology
the study of human movement

kinesthetic imagery
the application of imagery that encompasses an internal idea or feeling guide movement execution

knowledge of performance
a form of augmented feedback that describes features or the quality of the movement attempt

knowledge of results
a form of augmented feedback that is offered to the learner after their movement attempt and is directed toward the movement outcome

kyphosis
a spinal curve towards the back of the body

lateral
an anatomical term that refers to the structure away from the centerline of the body

learning style
the different ways in which students approach learning

legato
a musical term for a smooth continuation of notes without any breaks

ligament
bundle of strong fibers that connects bones to other bones

long-term memory
the function of memory where information is accumulated and permanently stored

lordosis
a spinal curve towards the front of the body

mastery goal
a goal that adds to an individual's knowledge bank and/or skill ability

measure
a grouping of beats separated by a bar line within the written music

medial
an anatomical term that refers to the structure towards this centerline of the body

mental practice
a tool used within the learning process where the student cognitively works through a movement or phrase rather than engaging in physical execution

meter
the regularly recurring pattern of strong and weak beats

modeling
an instructional method where the teacher or demonstrator offers a visual presentation of an aspect of movement

motivation
an internal process that propels one to behave in a certain way or accomplish specific tasks during a determined length of time

motor behavior
an umbrella term for the various branches of study that encompass human movement, including motor control, motor development, and motor learning

motor control
the role of the nervous system in relationship to the joints and muscles producing coordinated movement

motor development
the changes in movement capacity and ability throughout the stages of one's life

motor learning
the change in skill and ability that occurs, not due to the individual's development, but through the experience of movement or engagement in practice

motor milestones
specific stages of motor development

negative transfer
when a movement experience hinders or interferes with the learning of a new movement skill

nonregulatory condition
an aspect that distracts the learner from successfully attaining the movement skill

objective
a specific and measurable action that connects to a goal

open-loop system
neuromuscular process where the brain receives input, prepares a movement plan, and sends the plan forward to the muscles so that the desired movement, or outcome, may be produced

overlearning
the continuous practice after a skill has been acquired and performance has plateaued

pacing
the speed at which the teacher moves through the lesson plan

parameter
the variations of movement execution

part practice
a progressive approach to delivering and practicing material in which each phrase or component of the exercise is taught and practiced before moving on to the next part

perception
the way in which one comprehends and interprets sensory information

performance bandwidth
the range of error that the instructor deems tolerable

performance goal
a goal that reflects the desire of a student to demonstrate their ability and competence to others and often encompasses an external assessment or judgment

periodization
the division of training into phases or cycles to stimulate physical adaptations to improve performance

personal teaching style
the manner in which one teaches that is dictated by one's personality, beliefs, and values and is manifested in one's behavior

plantar flexion
an anatomical term that refers to the action of pointing the foot, as the bottom or sole of the foot is the plantar surface

positive transfer
the transfer of movement and ideas that aids or facilitates the learning of a new movement skill

posterior
an anatomical term that refers to structure to the back side of the body

postural control
the act of achieving, maintaining, or regaining a coordinated, upright position that does not place strain on the body during movement

posture
the basic position in which the body is held when standing or in movement

practice variability
the practice of a skill or concept is offered through different approaches rather than the exact same way each time

proprioception
the ability of the one to sense their body's movement, action, and location

proximal
an anatomical term that refers to the structure closer to the trunk or joint in question

quarter note
a type of musical note represented by a filled in or black note with a stem; musical value equals one beat

rallentando
a musical term for a gradual decrease of the tempo

random practice
occurs when the student moves from one skill to another either within the same combination or throughout the class

rate limiter
a type of individual constraint that slows or hinders the emergence of a motor skill

reflective listening
a strategy that involves seeking to understand what the student has said or done and offers the response back to the student for clarification

regulatory condition
an aspect of the skill and environment that are relevant to the movement

relative energy deficiency in sport
a syndrome of impaired health and decreased performance resulting from insufficient caloric intake and/or over expenditure of energy

rhythm
the specific arrangement of musical notes by duration

schema
a set of rules

scoliosis
the unnatural curvature of the spine to the right or left, creating an 'S' shape in an x-ray when viewed anteriorly or posteriorly

segmentation
a part method wherein where one part is taught and practiced, then the next part is added, and so forth

self-determination theory
a form of motivation that suggests that individuals are motivated by a sense of agency within their learning

self-efficacy
one's belief in their competence and skill

self-esteem
the value and worth that one feels about themself; may be correlated to self-confidence

self-fulfilling prophecy
an individual takes on the characteristics of the expectations placed upon them

sequential progression
the logical advancement of dance movement

short-term memory
the memory system in which small amounts of information are stored for brief periods of time

simplification
a part method wherein focus is given to the basic mechanics or essential elements of the movement rather than all aspects at once

sixteenth note
a type of musical note represented by a closed face note with a stem and two flags; equals half of an eighth note

skill
the proficiency level one demonstrates when executing movement

somatosensory system
a part of the sensory system that is a neural network responsible for transmitting information about the perception of touch, temperature, motion, and pain

stabilizer
a muscle that contracts to hold a joint firm to allow other movement to happen

staccato
a musical term for a shortened, or punctuated note, followed by silence

stereotype
an idea or notion of how a given group will behave

stereotype threat
circumstance where one becomes so worried about demonstrating or confirming a stereotype that anxiety takes over and they end up displaying the negative behavior attached to the stereotype

summative assessment
the assessment completed at distinct times and intended to gather specific information as to whether the students have learned the material that has been taught and have achieved a certain skill level

superficial
an anatomical term that refers to the point closer to the surface of the skin

superior
an anatomical term that refers to the structure above

swung rhythm
uneven division of a beat that emphasizes the space between two sounds, producing long and short durations in rhythm

syncopation
a facet of rhythm that emphasizes the weak beats rather than the strong beats within music

synergist
a muscle that works with the other muscles to either promote or neutralize movement and can define the way the movement is executed

tactile imagery
encompasses the aspects of touch to influence the quality of one's movement execution

task complexity
refers to the quantity of the various parts, level challenge of the parts, and the amount of attention and focus required to execute the movement

task-intrinsic feedback
the sensory information that an individual gathers while executing movement

task organization
refers to the manner in which components of the movement are related

taxonomy
a systematic method of classification into a structured framework

teaching philosophy statement
a self-reflective statement that offers readers insight into the personal values and beliefs that one holds as an educator

tempo
the speed of the music

tendon
the fibrous connective tissues connecting muscle to bone

time signature
appears at the beginning of notated music identifies both the meter of the music (the top number) and which type of musical note equates to a single beat (the bottom number); appears at the beginning of notated music

transfer of learning
occurs when one experience influences an individual's ability to learn or perform a new skill

verbal instruction
an instructional strategy that entails the use of words to describe the movement desired by the teacher

visual imagery
a picture that provides a target for the movement execution

visual presentation
an instructional strategy that entails the teacher's physical demonstration of the movement or exercise

visual system
a part of the sensory system that is a neural network responsible for seeing and processing what has been seen

whole note
a type of musical note represented by an open-faced note without a stem; musical value lasts four beats

whole practice
the entire skill or exercise is demonstrated to students and practiced

working memory
an area within short-term memory where mental processing can be performed

zero transfer
occurs when a movement experience has no effect on the learning of a new movement skill

Index

Note: Page numbers in *italics* indicate a figure and page numbers in **bold** indicate a table on the corresponding page.

ability 62–63
accessibility 2, 13, *147*, 149, 153–154
Adams' closed-loop theory 94–97, 104
adolescence *see* growth spurt
American Delsarte Movement 9
anatomical structures: ankles and feet 53–55; hips 50–52; knees 52–53; shoulders, arms and wrists 55–56; torso and spine 47–50
arousal 111, 118–120, 127, 279
ASCAP 193–194
assessment 14, 117, 163, 174, 230, 232, 264, 273–277, 283, 287, 289
attire 35, 213, 215–216, 223

balance 9, 18–19, 55, 63–65, 69, 78–82, 91, **134**, 136, 163, 167–**168**, 171, 192, 241, 259–260
ballet *barre* 31, 172, 205, 214, 258–259, 261
behavior modification *see* classroom management
Bennington Experience 12
bias 115, 142–144, 232–233, 284; lateral bias 232–233
BMI 193–194

call and response 86, 187–188, 193, 230, 280
central nervous system 47, 65, *68*, 69–70, 76, 280
chunking 237, 280
classroom management 2, 132, 211–212, 217, 221–222, 281
closed-loop system 70–73, 82, 94, 281

Colby, Gertrude 10
concept of flow 118, 121, 127
constraints 76–78, 103, 139; *see also* constraints-led approach
constraints-led approach 96–97, 103
critical dance pedagogy 150, 281
cueing 93, **175**, 228–229, 234, 238–239, 241–245, 248, 271, 281; in classroom management 219, 223; in music 189; self-cueing 71, 100–101, **103**, 117, 125, 135, **164**, 167, 245, 265, 273, 281
culturally relevant teaching 147–149, 154, 281
curriculum 9–10, 16–17, 26–28, 62, 78, 86, 95, 103, 125, 161, 164–169, 175, 199, 204, 212–213, 274, 281; hidden curriculum 143, 283

dance education 7–8, 282; in ancient civilizations 10; development in the U.S. 9–13; governmental policy 14–15; *see also* critical dance pedagogy
dance training 7, 282; benefits 18–19; within higher education 12; within K-12 111; physical education 14; within private sector 28; standards 17
degrees of freedom 77, 90, 282
directions of movement 41–43
diversity 2, 13, 33, 137, *147*, 149–150, 154, 177
dynamic systems approach 74–77, 82, 96, 282

equity 2, 13–14, 33, 147, 149, 152–153, 282
etiquette 165, 190, 213–214, 216, 223, 281
Eurhythmics 9

feedback: 63, 65, 67, 70–73, 77–78, 82, 87,
    94–97, 99–101, **99**, **103**, 111–113,
    117, *120*, 122, 125–127, 133, 141,
    167, **175**, 204, 213, 230, 234, 242,
    258–259, 263, 266–273; augmented
    264, 266–270; knowledge of performance
    265; knowledge of results 265;
    see also assessment
Fitts and Posner's three-stage theory 99–102,
    104, 256, 279–281
focus: attentional 229, 238–239, 248; external
    focus 238–241, 248, 283; internal focus
    91, 238–241, 284

general motor program 73, 94–95, 283, 285
Gentile's two-stage theory 99, 102–104, 256
goal orientation theory 117–118, 123, 283
goals **20**, 33, 62, 79, 102, 110–111,
    115–120, 123–126, **134**, 143, 283,
    285, 287; and objectives 153,
    160–170, 175
growth spurt 69, 81–82, 126, 135, 139, 174
guided discovery 229, 234–238, 248, 283
guided touch *see* physical touch

H'Doubler, Margaret 10–12
holistic teacher 2, 132–133, 144, 147–148,
    150, 153, 205
hyperextension 46–47
hypermobility 46, 198

imagery 40, 67, **99**, 241–242, 248,
    284–285, 290
improvisation 8, 19, 69, 74, 96, 135, 149,
    172–*173*, 234, 241, 260–261
inclusion 2, 13, 33, 147, 149, 154
information-processing theory 74–75, 82, 283
instructional strategies 228, 283; *see also* focus,
    attentional; cueing; guided discovery;
    imagery; pacing; visual presentation; verbal
    instruction

joints 46–47; *see also* anatomical structures

lesson plans 26–28, 31, 69, 92, 111, 117,
    141, 143, 160–162, 190–192, 199, 204,
    212, 219, 229; devising 95, 99–100,
    133, 138, 141, 167, 169–171, 173–175;
    feedback 271, 273–274; IDEA 149, 153;
    practice 256–**257**; template **175**; *see also*
    curriculum; pacing; SMART planning

Maslow's Hierarchy of needs 114–115
memory 18, **20**, 67, *74*, 91–95, 231, 245;
    chunking 237, 280; general motor program
    73, 94–95, 283; long-term 74–75, 92, 285;
    muscle memory 93, 172, 257–258; short-
    term 75, 92, 268, 288; working 75, 92, 290
meter 181–182, 184, 187–188, 191, 286, 290
mirror 65–66, 200, 214, 238–239, *239*, 247,
    258–259, 261, 264
modeling 70, 87, 124, 214, 229, 231, **236**,
    243, 286
motivation 77, 87, 109–110, 121, 127, 132,
    134–136, **134**, 142, 144, 174, 188, 219,
    231–232, 246, 255, 258, 265, 270, 286;
    ARCS-V Model 121–122; arousal 119–120;
    extrinsic motivation 111–113, 212, 283;
    intrinsic motivation 110–111, *113*, 222,
    284; self-esteem and self-efficacy 118–120;
    six C's 122–127; social influences
    137–139; *see also* concept of flow; goal
    orientation theory; Maslow's hierarchy of
    needs; self-determination theory
motor behavior 2, 62, 81, 103, 286
motor control 2, 11, 18–19, 26, 30, 63, 69–70,
    80–82, 86, 94, 126, 135, 286;
    see also closed-loop system; dynamic systems
    approach; open-loop system
motor development 18, 62–63, 74, 81–82, 150,
    286; *see also* dynamic systems approach;
    information-processing theory; motor
    milestones
motor learning 2, 26, 62–64, 73, 81, 86–90,
    104, 286; *see also* Adams' closed-loop
    theory; constraints-led approach; Fitts and
    Posner's three-stage theory; Gentile's
    two-stage theory; Schmidt's schema theory

motor milestones 69, 78, 82, 286
muscular system 44–45; *see also* anatomical
    structures
music 8–10, 31, 66, **99**, 148–150, **168**, 174,
    179, 191, 234, 247, 266; beat subdivision
    182–183; games 192–193; licensing
    193–194; organization and forms 180–187

National Association of Schools of Dance 15–16
National Dance Education Organization 15–17

open-loop system 70, 73, 82, 286
overlearning 257–258, 261, 286

pacing 93, 171, 174–175, 228, 246, 286
perception 65, 75, 96, 219, 230–232, 241,
    243, 270, 287, 289
performance bandwidth 266, 287
physical touch 141, 244, 248, 265–*267*, 269–270
planes of the body 41–42
practice: blocked 96, 256–257, 280; mental
    259–261, 286; part practice 237,
    252–255, 283, 288; practice variability
    256–257, 261, 287; random 256–**257**,
    260, 288; whole practice 252, 255, 290;
    see also overlearning; task organization
proprioception 46–47, 67, 69, **101**, 287

rate limiters 77–78, 82, 288

Schmidt's schema theory 94–97, 104
self-determination theory 116, 288

self-efficacy 18, 20–21, **20**, 111, 118–120,
    127, 137, 288
self-esteem 18, 20–21, **20**, 81, 111, 118–119,
    122, 127, 135, 163, 259, 288
sensory systems 64–65, 68–69, 81–82;
    auditory 65–66, 280; somatosensory
    67, 78, 289; visual 65, 290; *see also*
    proprioception
skeletal system 46; *see also* anatomical
    structures
skill 62–63; closed and open 73
SMART planning 164–165
somatics 260
stereotype 137, 142, 144, 289

task organization 255, 290
taxonomy 160, 228; Bloom's Taxonomy 160,
    163–166
teaching philosophy 33–34
teaching style 3, 25–26, 29; definition 29, 287;
    see also teaching philosophy
tempo 66, 73, 95, 102, 179–180, 184,
    187–188, 290; in curriculum 167–169,
    167, 174; in instruction 188–191, 234,
    236, 240, 247, 254, 259

verbal instruction 65–66, 70, 86, 94, 96,
    229–230, 233–234, 236–239, **236**, 245,
    247–248, 290
visual presentation 217–218, 229–232,
    234, **236**, 238, 248, 258, 290;
    see also modeling

9781032286020